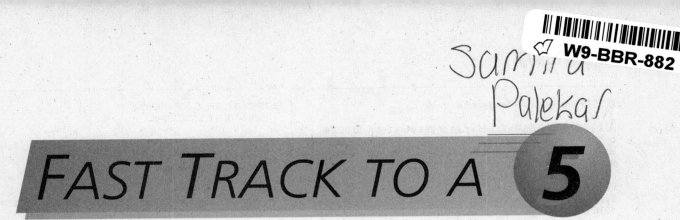

FAST TRACK TO A 5

Preparing for the AP* Environmental Science Examination

To Accompany
Living in the Environment
16th and 17th Editions
by G. Tyler Miller, Jr., and Scott E. Spoolman

David Hong
Diamond Bar High School, Diamond Bar, California

Karen Lionberger
Chattahoochee High School, Alpharetta, Georgia

BROOKS/COLE
CENGAGE Learning™

Australia • Brazil • Japan • Korea • Mexico • Singapore • Spain • United Kingdom • United States

*AP and Advanced Placement Program are registered trademarks of the College Entrance Examination Board, which was not involved in the production of, and does not endorse, this product.

ISBN-13: 978-0-538-49382-6
ISBN-10: 0-538-49382-8

Brooks/Cole
20 Davis Drive
Belmont, CA 94002-3098
USA

Cengage Learning is a leading provider of customized learning solutions with office locations around the globe, including Singapore, the United Kingdom, Australia, Mexico, Brazil, and Japan. Locate your local office at: **www.cengage.com/global**

Cengage Learning products are represented in Canada by Nelson Education, Ltd.

To learn more about Brooks/Cole, visit **www.cengage.com/brookscole**

Purchase any of our products at your local college store or at our preferred online store **www.cengagebrain.com**

Printed in the United States of America
1 2 3 4 5 6 7 14 13 12 11 10

CONTENTS

ABOUT THE AUTHORS

DAVID HONG teaches AP Environmental Science at Diamond Bar High School in Diamond Bar, California. Since 1999, he has served as an AP exam reader, table leader, and question leader. He has served on both the AP Environmental Science Development Committee and the College Board's Science Academic Advisory Committee. A College Board consultant, he has been a presenter at the AP Annual Conference and a member of the AP Annual Conference Steering Committee.

KAREN LIONBERGER has been teaching AP Environmental Science for seven years; she presently teaches at Chattahoochee High School in Alpharetta, Georgia, where she is the Science Department Chair. For four years, she has been an AP exam reader, and has helped lead AP workshops for the Georgia Department of Education. She has written portions of the Instructor's Guide for *Living in the Environment*, and has been a content editor for other AP study guides.

PREFACE

Throughout the writing of this book, we asked ourselves, "What information and what kind of practice do our own students need in order to be best prepared to take the AP Environmental Science exam?" This review guide is our answer to that question. In this *Fast Track to a Five* we have tried to create the kind of thorough and useful review guide that we have always wanted for our own students. We hope that in doing so, we have created a guide that every student can use to prepare for the AP Environmental Science exam. While this review guide was written to accompany the sixteenth and seventeenth editions of *Living in the Environment* by Miller and Spoolman, it is a resource that can accompany any textbook used in this course. We have worked diligently to provide rigorous, meaningful multiple-choice and free-response practice questions that will adequately prepare you for the types of questions you will face on the actual AP exam. Lastly, whether or not you take the AP exam, we hope that working through this guide will serve not only as an effective way to review all of the content of the AP Environmental Science course, but also as a means to providing insight into implementing environmentally sustainable practices that are critical to all of our futures.

Writing this book necessitated many late nights and long weekends of seclusion. We would like to thank our families and friends for their patience, encouragement, and understanding throughout that time. We would also like to thank our content reviewers, Thomas (Berry) Cobb and Carol Widegrin, for their valuable expertise, insight, and assistance with the content of this guide. And finally, we would like to thank our editor, Margaret Lannamann, for bringing the two of us together; for signing on Berry and Carol; for her patience with us when we missed deadlines; for understanding that our own students and everyday job responsibilities always came first; and for her guidance as we navigated through the writing, editing, and copyediting of *Fast Track to a Five: Preparing for the AP Examination in Environmental Science*.

David Hong
Karen Lionberger
February 2010

Part I

Strategies for the AP Examination

PREPARING FOR THE AP* ENVIRONMENTAL SCIENCE EXAM

Taking on the challenge and rigor of an Advanced Placement course can be an enriching experience in your academic career. Whether you are taking an AP course at your school or you are working on an AP course independently, the stage is set for an immeasurable intellectual experience. As the school year progresses, you will gain a deeper understanding of the scientific processes, concepts, and methodologies required to understand the mechanisms that drive our natural world. Environmental science is an interdisciplinary study by which you will acquire the ability to identify and analyze both natural and anthropogenic environmental problems. By the end of this course you will also be able to assess the relative risks associated with these environmental problems as well as suggest more sustainable solutions and alternatives to the current conventional methods that cause environmental damage. This course will provide an exhilarating and awakening experience for you through the study and understanding of today's global environmental problems and their solutions.

Sometime during the spring, as May approaches, the AP exam will start to feel more like a tangible obstacle you will soon face. At times, the amount of material you must master to be successful on the Advanced Placement exam may seem somewhat overwhelming or intimidating. If you are dreading the AP exam, just know that you are not the only one. However, there are some simple exam tips and review steps you can follow that will get you on the fast track to making that 5.

First and foremost, it is imperative to maintain the motivation and a positive attitude to guide your preparation. If you manage your time effectively, you will meet this one major challenge—mastery of a large amount of material in a short period of time. You should develop a review schedule to help direct your study time so that you spread out your review over the course of at least several weeks to a month prior to the exam rather than relying on just a few short days of cramming. This book is designed to put you on a fast track to success on the AP Environmental Science exam. Sticking to your review schedule and allowing enough practice time prior to the exam will help you master the course material and will also give you an invaluable amount of confidence on the day of the exam.

---

*AP and Advanced Placement Program are registered trademarks of the College Entrance Examination Board, which was not involved in the production of, and does not endorse, this product.

3

WHAT'S IN THIS BOOK

This book is keyed to *Living in the Environment,* 16th and 17th editions, by G. Tyler Miller and Scott E. Spoolman. This review guide follows the College Board Topic Outline, and is therefore compatible with all textbooks used in the course of study for AP Environmental Science. This review book is divided into three sections. Part I offers suggestions for getting yourself ready, from signing up to take the test and sharpening your pencils to organizing a free-response essay. At the end of Part I you will find a Diagnostic Test. This test has elements of the Environmental Science examination (100 multiple-choice questions and 4 free-response questions), although the multiple-choice questions are organized according to the College Board Topic Outline. (On the actual AP exam, and on the practice tests at the end of this book, the questions are not ordered according to content). After you go through the answers at the end of the Diagnostic Test, you will see how the examination is weighted for each content area; a cluster of wrong answers in one area will identify the major topics in which you may need extended review. Page references at the end of each answer indicate where you will find the discussion on that particular point in the 16th and 17th editions of *Living in the Environment.* Scoring your diagnostic exam will also be explained, so you will have some idea of how well you can do.

Part II, made up of nine chapters, is designed around the textbook *Living in the Environment* while also covering the College Board topic outline for the AP Environmental Science Exam (see below). The percentages give you an idea of how many questions out of 100 you may see on the exam from that particular content area.

I. Earth Systems and Resources (10–15%)

II. The Living World (10–15%)

III. Population (10–15%)

IV. Land and Water Use (10–15%)

V. Energy Resources and Consumption (10–15%)

VI. Pollution (25–30%)

VII. Global Change (10–15%)

These chapters are not a substitute for your textbook, class discussions, or laboratory experiences, but they do offer a review that will further help you prepare for the exam. At the end of each chapter, you will find fifteen multiple-choice questions and one practice free-response essay question based on the content of that chapter. Again, you will find page references at the end of each answer directing you to the discussion on each particular point in the 16th and 17th editions of *Living in the Environment.*

Part III is a short supplementary section listing case histories, environmental laws, and individuals important in environmental science. Part IV offers two complete AP Environmental Science examinations. At the end of each test, you will find the answers, explanations, and page references to the 16th and 17th editions of

Living in the Environment for the 100 multiple-choice and 4 free-response questions.

SETTING UP A REVIEW SCHEDULE

The best way to ensure mastery of the content for this exam is to keep up with your reading, homework, and laboratory assignments each week of the school year. Even if you have not been able to master each content unit during the year, there are some review tactics that will help you assemble a strong collective knowledge of the course material.

Begin your review by reading thoroughly through Part I of this book. This section will give insight into the format of the exam, the type of multiple-choice questions, and strategies for answering both the multiple-choice and free-response questions. Next, take the diagnostic test at the end of Part I. This will allow you to identify specific concepts you need further review on and can guide your schedule for review.

You should begin setting up a calendar of review for yourself several weeks to a month prior to the exam. This will afford you enough time to work through each of the nine review chapters in Part II of this book. Schedule extra time for the topics on which you need further review—as identified by taking the diagnostic test. Sharpen your skills at multiple choice and free response with the sample questions at the end of each content chapter. By the time you're done reviewing you will be ready for the full-length practice exams found in Part IV. These practice exams, unlike the diagnostic tests, will not have questions grouped together by topic and will give you a more realistic look into how you might perform on the actual AP Environmental Science exam.

What should you do if your time for review is limited? The first thing you should do is take the diagnostic test in Part I to see what topics you are weakest in and should therefore start with. Use the Key Terms section at the beginning of each chapter to see if you have a working knowledge of the vocabulary that will be used during the AP exam. After reviewing each chapter's vocabulary take the practice tests in Part IV.

BEFORE THE EXAMINATION

First and foremost you need to make sure you are registered to take the AP exam. Most schools have already taken care of this aspect of the exam for you, but you should check with your AP teacher or coordinator to make sure your paperwork has been submitted to College Board. If you have a documented disability and will need testing accommodations on the exam you should ensure that it has been reported by your AP coordinator to College Board. If you are studying AP independently, call AP Services at the College Board for the name of the local AP coordinator, who will help you through the registration process. You should also check your calendar for conflicts and speak to your school's AP coordinator about making arrangements to take an alternate AP exam on a later date. The

College Board will allow students with more than one AP exam at the same time on the same date to take an alternate exam on a later date. Other acceptable circumstances that warrant an alternate exam include conflicts with IB or state-mandated exams, and religious holidays. Conflicts with athletic or academic contests, and even family vacations are also acceptable; however, there is an additional charge for taking an alternate exam for those reasons.

Just like with any test, the night before the exam you should get plenty of sleep so that you have enough energy to stay focused during the entire three hours of testing. This is not the time to stay up studying all night. Instead, focus on briefly reviewing broad concepts such as common solutions to major environmental problems or frequently used vocabulary terms. You might also skim through the chapter outlines found in Part II of this book. The night before the test is a good time to get together everything you will need the next morning for the exam.

What will you need on the morning of the exam? First you need to eat a good breakfast so that you have plenty of energy for the test— being tired can actually cause you to give up too easily on a question and cost you points on the exam. For the exam you will need a sharpened No. 2 pencil to answer the multiple-choice section. Also, you will need a blue or black ink pen for your essays on the free-response portion of the exam. It is a good idea to take two or three pencils and pens so you have plenty of back-up choices if one fails to work properly. It is also a good idea to take a watch with you in case the testing room does not have a clock. It will be important to be aware of the time on both your multiple-choice section and the free response to allow you to utilize your time effectively. Make sure you take with you anything that has been requested by your AP coordinator—such as your Social Security number, photo ID, or registration ticket. Remember that calculators are NOT allowed on the AP Environmental Science exam. Cell phones are also not permitted in the exam rooms.

Finally, it is important that you are completely comfortable while taking the exam. Wear clothes and shoes that are comfortable. Some students also like to bring a jacket or sweatshirt in case the testing room is too cold and becomes uncomfortable to test in. It is also a good idea to bring a snack to eat during the break. You will have a short break between the multiple-choice portion, which is 90 minutes long, and the free-response portion, which is also 90 minutes long. Three hours of testing is a long time and you don't want to be hungry going into the essay section of your test.

TAKING THE AP ENVIRONMENTAL SCIENCE EXAMINATION

The AP Environmental Science examination consists of two sections: Section I has one hundred multiple-choice questions; Section II has four free-response questions. You will have ninety minutes for each section. There will be a short break between the two sections of the exam. You must write an essay for each of the four questions. You should monitor the time during both sections of the exam and move nimbly through both sections so you do not get bogged down on one multiple-choice question or on one essay.

STRATEGIES FOR THE MULTIPLE-CHOICE SECTION

Here are some important rules of thumb to help you work your way through the multiple-choice questions:

- **Terminology** Each question has a stem that may be in the form of a question or statement, and five options that are the possible answers to the question. Exactly one of the five options is correct.
- **There is one correct answer; however...** Sometimes, the "correct" answer is "the best" among the options given. In that case, more than one answer may actually be correct, but one is the best option.
- **Manage the time.** With 90 minutes to answer 100 questions, you have less than one minute to answer each question. Check your pace; try to answer 25 questions every 20 minutes. This will leave 10 minutes at the end of the exam to look back over your answers.
- **Cover the options.** Try reading the stem with the options covered. Answer in your mind, and then select the option that is closest to your answer.
- **Carefully and completely read the entire question.** The item writers may have intentionally included attractive options for students who are rushing through the exam.
- **Write in your multiple-choice booklet.** As you eliminate options, cross them out by drawing a line through them. On questions with a negative stem or roman numerals (see question types below) write a T or an F next to the options as you work through the question. If you skip an extremely difficult or long question, circle it and return to it after you have answered all of the easy questions. If it helps you to do so, underline key words in a question that help you to focus on what is important in the question. Use the test

booklet as scratch paper for any questions that require calculations. Calculator use is not permitted on the AP Environmental Science exam.

■ **Fill in your answer document carefully.** If you must erase, do so completely. Bring a white plastic eraser to use on your answer document. Your exam will be scored by a machine and any stray marks may be read as answers. When you skip questions, don't forget to skip the corresponding lines on your answer sheet, or you will waste time erasing and moving answers later.

■ **Answer every question.** Points are no longer deducted for incorrect answers on AP exams, so you should answer every question.

■ **Guessing advice.** If you must guess, make a random selection from the options that you did not eliminate. Avoid picking an option that you do not know is correct, if it only "sounds right" to you. Picking options that sound right could lead you into a trap set by the item writer for a student, who like you, knows a little bit, but not quite enough about the question to select the one best answer. If you must make a guess, do so by making an unbiased random selection from the options that remain after you have eliminated those you are certain are wrong.

TYPES OF MULTIPLE-CHOICE QUESTIONS

There are a few different types of multiple-choice questions on the AP Environmental Science Exam.

OPTIONS-FIRST QUESTIONS The multiple-choice section of the AP Environmental Science Exam usually begins with about twenty options-first questions. These questions require you to use the same set of options for a series of questions. You may use the same option as the answer for more than one of the questions, and some may not be used at all. A good way to think about this type of question is as a series of questions that all happen to have the same set of options. If you think about them in that way, you will never wonder if an option can be correct more than once, or if you will use all of the options. For example:

(A) Mercury
(B) Carbon monoxide
(C) Lead
(D) Ozone
(E) Sulfur dioxide

1. A secondary air pollutant that is formed in photochemical smog
2. A contaminant of coal that accumulates in the tissues of some species of fish
3. Reacts in air to form acids which can fall to the ground as acid rain

ANSWERS:

1–D. Ozone is the only secondary pollutant among the five options.

2–A. Mercury is a contaminant in coal that vaporizes when the coal is burned. After falling back to earth, the mercury is washed into aquatic ecosystems where it may be assimilated in the tissues of fish.

3–E. Sulfur dioxide reacts with other substances in the air to form acids that can fall to the ground as acid rain.

TRADITIONAL QUESTIONS

Nearly all of the multiple-choice questions will be traditional multiple-choice questions. These questions will be straightforward questions with five options and one correct answer. These questions simply require you to read the question and select the most correct answer. For example:

1. Which of the following is an asphyxiant produced during incomplete combustion reactions?
   (A) Mercury
   (B) Carbon monoxide
   (C) Lead
   (D) Ozone
   (E) Sulfur dioxide

ANSWER: B. Carbon monoxide is produced during incomplete combustion and it is an asphyxiant.

NEGATIVE STEM QUESTIONS

You should expect to encounter few of this type of question, but be prepared for them. They may be the hardest questions on the exam. If the answer is not immediately obvious to you, you may want to circle this type of question and return to it later. In negative-stem questions, all of the options are correct except for one. These questions usually begin with a statement like, "All of the following are correct EXCEPT..." or "Which of the following is NOT...". In either case, there will be four options that are in the correct context, and one that is not—that is the correct answer. One way to approach these questions is as a series of true/false questions. There is only one false answer, and that is the correct answer. It will help you to keep track of which options are true and false if you mark them with a T or an F as you read. For example:

1. Which of the following is NOT one of the criteria air pollutants monitored by the U.S.-EPA?
   (A) Mercury
   (B) Carbon monoxide
   (C) Lead
   (D) Ozone
   (E) Sulfur dioxide

ANSWER: A. Mercury is not one of the criteria air pollutants monitored by the U.S.-EPA. The criteria air pollutants are carbon monoxide, lead, ozone, sulfur dioxide, nitrogen oxides, and particulate matter. If you marked the options with a T or F, answer A should be the only option with an F next to it.

ROMAN NUMERAL QUESTIONS

You should also expect to encounter relatively few Roman numeral questions. These questions are not as difficult as the negative stem questions because you are looking for correct answers. In Roman numeral questions, there are usually three or four answers labeled with Roman numerals. One or more of the answers could be correct. You are then provided with a series of options from which you select the correct Roman numeral or set of Roman numerals. The option with the Roman numerals followed by the correct answers is correct. For example:

1. Which of the following are toxic heavy metals?
    (I) Mercury
    (II) Carbon monoxide
    (III) Lead
    (A) I only
    (B) II only
    (C) III only
    (D) I and II only
    (E) I and III only

ANSWER: **E.** Mercury and lead are toxic heavy metals, and carbon monoxide is not a toxic heavy metal, which makes Roman numerals I and III the only two correct answers.

LEAST AND MOST LIKELY QUESTIONS

This type of question may have two or more options that are correct, but only one that is the least or most likely. When answering these questions, don't answer until you have read through all of the options, and if more than one is correct, rank the likeliness of each correct option by placing a number next to the option.

1. If released or formed in the atmosphere, which of the following will least likely result in long-term environmental damage to an ecosystem?
    (A) Mercury
    (B) Carbon monoxide
    (C) Lead
    (D) Ozone
    (E) Sulfur dioxide

ANSWER: **B.** Carbon monoxide is not persistent, nor does it bioaccumulate. Unlike ozone or sulfur dioxide, carbon monoxide does not produce long-term ecological damage.

DATA INTERPRETATION AND ANALYSIS QUESTIONS

In this type of question, there is a data set, graph, or chart for you to review and interpret. These questions may require that you do some calculations to determine the answer. Often there is more than one question that makes use of the data set, graph, or chart. You should do all scratch work in the test booklet. Calculators are not permitted on the AP Environmental Science exam.

U.S. Airborne Lead Air Quality 1980–2005

Year	Lead Concentration (µg/m3)
1980	1.25
1985	0.67
1990	0.29
1995	0.11
2000	0.09
2005	0.09

1. The percent change in the airborne lead concentration between 1980 and 2000 was closest to which of the following?
   (A) 10%
   (B) 17%
   (C) 81%
   (D) 87%
   (E) 93%

ANSWER: E. To determine the percent change: take the difference between the two values, divide that difference by the original value, and multiply by 100. In this case 1.25 – 0.09 = 1.16 divided by 1.25 equals 0.928 multiplied by 100 equals 92.8%, which is closest to 93%. You should be prepared to do arithmetic like this on your AP Environmental Science exam. Remember, no calculators, so practice your math!

2. Which of the following best explains the trend in the data of U.S. airborne lead concentrations?
   (A) The inclusion of lead in the EPA's list of Criteria Air Pollutants
   (B) The phaseout of the use of lead-based paints
   (C) The widespread use of catalytic converters
   (D) The elimination of lead additives in gasoline
   (E) The use of wet scrubbers on coal-fired power plants

ANSWER: D. The plummet in airborne lead concentrations during the 1980s and 1990s is due to the phaseout of the use of tetraethyl lead as an additive in gasoline. Note that more than one of the options are reasonable reasons why lead emissions were reduced; this question illustrates the second bullet in the strategies above: **"There is one correct answer; however... Sometimes, the 'correct' answer is 'the best' among the options given."**

FREE-RESPONSE QUESTIONS

The free-response portion of the AP Environmental Science exam is 90 minutes long. During this time you must answer four questions. This allows you approximately 22 minutes for each essay. It is very important that you watch your time on each essay and not to get wrapped up in just one. Remember that these essays account for 40% of your exam score and therefore each essay is worth 10% of your overall grade.

While individual free-response questions may have several sub-parts, keep in mind that the total of all parts is worth 10 points. Typically, each sub-part of a free-response question will be worth 2 to 4 points, depending on complexity and number of parts of the question. It is possible for the points available to total more than ten, but the maximum score for any free-response question is ten. Different parts of a free-response question often are not of equal difficulty, but usually one or two parts will be simpler than others. Answer the easiest part of the question first and do not omit an entire question just because some parts seem difficult. Partial credit is always available on such questions, but only if an answer is given and knowledge about the question being asked is demonstrated.

Each question in the free-response section will be broken down into separate parts such as: a), b), c), etc. Even individual parts to a question can be further broken down, for example:

a) Calculate the following by using statistics given in the table.
    i.   How many gallons of water did the family use in one month?
    ii. What is the annual cost of electricity for operating their dishwasher?

TYPES OF FREE-RESPONSE QUESTIONS

DATA-SET QUESTIONS

You will have at least one question that is a data-set question, often referred to as the math question, and it will center around a graph, diagram, table/chart, or statistics given in the introductory paragraph. Approximately 50% of your points on this type of question will be earned by doing arithmetical calculations. Even though this is considered the math question, these questions typically have one to two parts you can earn points on that do not deal directly with any calculations or graphing but rather with the environmental issue or concept the question refers to. So, if you don't feel you can do the math part of the question **don't give up!** Read the remaining sections of the free-response and answer the portions that are conceptual and not mathematical. Remember to always **show your work** (only in the pink answer booklet) for any calculation and give the appropriate units with each number written.

REMINDER: Calculators are not permitted on the AP Environmental Science exam so you will need to be comfortable using basic algebra such as multiplying and dividing exponents and scientific notation.

DOCUMENT-BASED QUESTION (DBQ)

You will have one question that is prompted with some type of document that will pertain to the questions being asked. It is important to remember these prompts are primarily used to introduce the questions. Although you may need to use some numbers or information provided in the document to help answer a question, do not expect to pull all of your answers directly from the passage given. A common mistake that students make is to simply repeat information given in the document as their answer. As mentioned, the purpose of the document is to introduce the question or questions. Students are expected to demonstrate comprehension by adding information learned from readings or class.

SYNTHESIS AND EVALUATION

There are two synthesis/evaluation questions on the free-response section of the AP Environmental Science exam. It may be easiest to understand what a synthesis/evaluation question is by understanding what it is not. That is, if you determine that a question is not a math question, and it is not a DBQ, then it is a synthesis/evaluation question. A synthesis/evaluation question will require you to write an essay in which you demonstrate your knowledge about one of the numerous topics of study in the AP Environmental Science course. Your ability to earn points in these essays will be determined by your knowledge of the subject matter. In rare cases, you may be required to perform a simple calculation in a synthesis/evaluation question; however the calculation will likely be worth only one or two points. These questions will usually have a small paragraph to introduce a topic and then 4–5 questions or prompts pertaining to that topic. As with all free-response questions you may be required to identify, describe, explain, discuss, etc. Be sure to identify the verbs used to ask the question (identify, describe, discuss, etc) and follow the free-response tips listed below when writing your essay. An example of what these types of questions may look like:

1. The harvesting of wood for fuelwood, and charcoal made from fuelwood, is increasing at an alarming rate. This is causing the deforestation of many areas, particularly in developing countries. Many of these countries are now cutting down trees at a rate 10–20% faster than they are being replanted.
    (a) Identify TWO uses of fuelwood in developing countries.
    (b) Describe how deforestation impacts the global carbon cycle.
    (c) Identify and describe one environmental problem and one economic benefit which result from clear-cutting forests.
    (d) Discuss TWO sustainable forestry practices that could be implemented in these countries.
    (e) Write an argument in support of the practice of sustainably harvesting fuelwood.

VOCABULARY USED IN FREE-RESPONSE QUESTIONS

You can earn a maximum of 10 points on each of the four free-response questions. You should pay close attention to the word choice used in each part of the free response. Keying in on what type of verb is being used in the question can help you maximize both your time and points on your essay section.

IDENTIFY OR LIST: This term is asking you to give a specific object, advantage, disadvantage, cause, solution, etc. It is important to always write in prose on every question. Even if it may seem like you can answer this type of question in one word—don't. You must write the answer in a complete sentence to get any credit.

For example, the question above states, "Identify two uses of fuelwood in developing countries." The answer can be as short as, "Two uses of fuelwood in developing countries are for home heating and cooking." However, you would earn no points for simply writing "heating and cooking."

DESCRIBE OR EXPLAIN: These terms are asking you to further illustrate your answer by using details beyond just identifying an object or solution. Often you will see these terms used with the exact number of solutions or objects you are to describe. A good description will usually take more than one sentence.

For example, the question may state "Describe TWO benefits of using fuelwood." A good response to this prompt is, "Two benefits of the use of fuelwood are the ability for people to heat their homes and to cook their food without the need of fossil fuels. Unlike our conventional fuel sources, if managed sustainably, fuelwood can be a renewable resource."

Or

For example, the question above states, "Describe how deforestation impacts the global carbon cycle." A good response to this prompt is, "Deforestation removes trees that function as carbon reservoirs by absorbing carbon dioxide during photosynthesis. This will increase carbon dioxide levels in the atmosphere."

Note: It is also possible to have a combination of two verb choices in one question. They may ask you to either "Identify and describe...." or "Identify and explain...". You should simply follow the rules of both verbs as given in examples above.

DISCUSS: Here you need to really elaborate on your answer to the question. Often, you will receive 2–3 points for this type of question; therefore, it is important to write additional detail and go beyond a simple description or explanation in your answer. A good discussion will usually take several sentences or an entire paragraph.

For example, the question asks, "Discuss a benefit to using fuelwood over current conventional fossil fuels." A good response to this prompt is, "A benefit of using fuelwood over fossil fuels is the reduction in sulfur dioxide emissions associated with coal burning practices. By decreasing sulfur dioxide emissions we also reduce acid deposition problems that cause tissue damage to trees in terrestrial ecosystems and cause fish kills due to lowered pH in aquatic systems." Remember, your discussion questions require you to not only identify and define concepts but to further elaborate on the issue at hand.

Or

For example, the question above states, "Discuss TWO sustainable forestry practices that could be implemented in these countries." A good response to this prompt is, "One practice is the use of tree plantations, which can grow fast-growing tree species and be managed so that the rate of tree harvesting is equal to the rate of replenishment. This will reduce the need to cut native forests. A second practice is selective cutting, which will remove some, but not all of the trees from forests. Trees can then be replanted in the areas from which they were removed and the forest allowed to recover before being cut again. This will minimize the area of tree cover being lost in native forests."

WRITE AN ARGUMENT: An argument is a series of statements all in support of a stated position on an issue. This is the only time that students may be rewarded for writing a lengthy list. An argument is the most *extensive* and detailed response that you could be called upon to write and it will likely be at least one paragraph in length.

For example, the question above states, "Write an argument in support of the practice of sustainably harvesting fuelwood." A good response to this prompt is, "Harvesting fuelwood sustainably avoids using practices like clear-cutting forests. Clear-cutting causes soil erosion, and runoff into waterways causing sedimentation, which decreases primary productivity, increases fish kills due to suffocation, and results in poor water quality for people who depend on the waterways for their domestic water use. Furthermore, when the rate of tree harvesting exceeds the rate of replanting, tracts of forest that function as carbon dioxide reservoirs are no longer available, which will increase carbon dioxide levels in the atmosphere and further global climate change."

FREE-RESPONSE TIPS

- **Don't go green on the APES free-response section.** For your free-response portion of the exam, you will be given a green booklet with the questions in it and a pink answer booklet with the questions and the space in which you will write your answers. The green insert stays at your local school and will never be seen by an AP exam grader. So, make sure all of your calculations, scratch work, and answers are written in your pink answer booklet— especially for any mathematical calculations.
- **Collect your thoughts.** Read each question carefully, thinking about the verb types being used. Take a few minutes to organize your answer in your mind before you begin.
- **Write in prose.** Always answer in complete sentences. Make sure you are writing clearly and large enough for your reader to read your answer easily. Outline forms or bulleted lists are not acceptable and will not be graded.

- **Be careful about creativity.** Shy away from using examples or solutions that are specific to your local region or are uniquely your own ideas. Remember, answers on the rubric for the free-response section must be able to be applied to every single student across the country and around the world that takes this exam. Therefore you should only use commonly known examples or solutions. Avoid fabricating information as well. It is a waste of time and will not earn any points.

- **Be time-conscious.** You only have approximately 22 minutes per essay. If you work on the essays you feel most comfortable with first, it can increase the amount of time you have for the ones you don't know as well. Do not get bogged down working on "one hard one."

- **Strike out to save time.** If you make a mistake, don't waste valuable time and lose your momentum on a question by attempting to completely obliterate or erase your work; cross or strike out your original answer with a single line or an "X" and keep moving forward.

- **Read the verbs in the question carefully.** Note any verbs such as *identify, describe, explain, and discuss.* Make sure once you are done answering that you ACTUALLY answered **all** the parts to the question.

- **Read the question carefully.** You may be prompted to describe an environmental problem in one part of a question, an economic problem in another, and an environmental benefit in a third. Underline or circle the key terms "environmental" and "economic," and be certain to provide an appropriate response. Note: a good rule of thumb is to read "environmental" as "ecological" and to write about how the topic being addressed in the question affects the abundance, diversity, or distribution of life.

- **Label your answers** so there is no doubt where your answer is. All questions have very specific parts such as a, b, c, or i, ii, iii. This will also help you ensure that you have finished answering the question and can move on or come back as needed.

- **Do not restate the question** in your answer—it is a waste of time. You also do not need to have any introduction or conclusion parts to your essay. Remember— you cannot win over your reader. He or she is simply looking for correct statements that demonstrate knowledge of the concept.

- **Follow through with your thoughts or examples** by defining or explaining any key terms you use. Many students fail to get points because they didn't finish their thoughts. An easy way to accomplish this is to define any key terms you use in the essay and provide examples to illustrate what you mean.

- **Do not write long lists as your answer!** If the question says "Identify TWO" then identify only two items. The graders are instructed to grade only the first two items even if a student writes a longer list. Thus, if two items are requested, and a student lists six items of which the first two are incorrect, no points will be given even if the last four of the six answers were correct.

- **Do not use clichés** for answers (for example, "there is no away in pollution" or "not in my backyard"). Instead you should scientifically explain your answer to get the points.

- **Be concise**—do not tell the reader everything you know on the topic. Make sure you are only answering what they ask for so you do not waste valuable time that could be used on other essays.

- **Answer the question that you were asked**...not just any question to which you happen to know the answer. Sometimes, in an effort to fill space, students will launch into a dissertation that is not relevant to the question that was asked. Don't waste valuable time writing about all the things you know on another topic that is not related to the question.

- **A picture is worth 1000 words only if they ask for it.** Draw a picture or diagram only if it is specifically asked for in the question.

- **Neatness counts.** Messy or illegible writing is very difficult to grade. You do not want to make it hard on your AP reader to award you points on your essay. It is **always best** if they can easily find and read your answers for each essay question. If they cannot decipher your handwriting then awarding points is more difficult.

- **Math-based free-response questions.** When asked to do calculations **show your work**. You normally need to show your work and **label units** to receive credit on math questions. Also, if you have no idea how to do the calculations portion of the free response, **keep reading!** A math-based free-response question almost always contains a part of the question you could answer without the calculations being done. Make sure all of your work and answers are in your **pink** answer booklet!

- **Practice your math!** Every AP Environmental Science student should be comfortable working with metric prefixes, decimals, percentages, fractions, algebra, exponents, and scientific notations.

A DIAGNOSTIC TEST

The purpose of this diagnostic test is to give you some indication of how prepared you are for the actual AP Environmental Science Exam. Although this test is representative of the types of questions you may see on the exam, it is impossible to predict how you would do on the actual AP exam since each test is unique. The first section of the exam consists of 100 multiple-choice questions and counts for 60% of your grade. You have 90 minutes to complete this portion of the exam. Calculators may not be used on any portion of the AP Environmental Science Exam. Remember to follow the test-taking tips included in Part I of this book.

ENVIRONMENTAL SCIENCE
Section I: Multiple-Choice Questions
Time: 1 Hour and 30 Minutes
Number of Questions: 100

Part A

Directions: Each set of choices below, labeled A through E, will refer to a question or statement directly following the lettered choices. The questions or statements may also refer to a diagram or graph. Each lettered answer may be used more than once, only once, or not at all. Choose the one lettered choice you feel best answers the question or statement above.

Questions 1–3 refer to the following aquatic zones:

(A) bathyl
(B) euphotic
(C) littoral
(D) limnetic
(E) abyssal

1. photosynthetic zone in a lake ecosystem dominated by phytoplankton

2. marine zone that is low in dissolved oxygen but supports life due to high nutrient levels

3. shallow water lake zone that supports an abundance of emergent and submergent vegetation

Questions 4–6 refer to the following processes:

(A) chemosynthesis
(B) fermentation
(C) photosynthesis
(D) aerobic respiration
(E) transpiration

4. This is a process whose end products can vary from methane gas to ethyl alcohol.

5. This process converts compounds like carbon dioxide or methane into carbohydrates using an energy source such as hydrogen sulfide.

6. The rate of this process depends on atmospheric conditions such as wind, temperature, and relative humidity.

Questions 7–10 refer to the following soil and rock components:

(A) minerals
(B) loam
(C) igneous
(D) sedimentary
(E) metamorphic

7. a mixture of soil that forms from the mixture of clay, silt, and sand

8. often formed from the remains of dead organisms compacted over millions of years (for example, coal)

9. an element or inorganic compound that typically has a solid crystalline internal structure

10. forms below or on the earth's surface from molten rock material welling up from the upper mantle

Refer to the graph for questions 11–12.

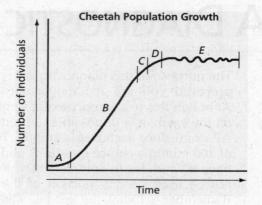

Cheetah Population Growth

11. location of biotic potential for the population

12. location of stable growth around population-carrying capacity

Part B

Directions: Five answer choices, lettered A through E, will follow each one of the following questions or incomplete statements below. The questions or statements may refer to a graph, diagram, or table. Choose the one answer that best fits each question or completes the statement.

13. The world's supply of recoverable uranium ore is approximately 4.8 million metric tons. If the global consumption rate for uranium is 200 metric tons per day, about how many years will the uranium supply last?
(A) 150 years
(B) 125 years
(C) 90 years
(D) 70 years
(E) 20 years

14. Waterlogging is a result of
I. over-irrigation by farmers to leach salts deeper into the soil
II. water accumulating underground and gradually raising the water table
III. over-irrigation of crops that leave salt residue in the topsoil layers

(A) I only
(B) II only
(C) III only
(D) I and II only
(E) I, II, and III

15. A country in Stage III (Industrial) of demographic transition would be characterized by
(A) high birth rates and low death rates
(B) rapidly growing population
(C) low birth rates and high death rates
(D) low birth rates and low death rates
(E) negative population growth

16. Which of the following would be used in a secondary sewage treatment process?
    (A) Bar-screen removal of solid waste
    (B) Grit tank to remove large floating objects
    (C) Use of chlorine or ozone to disinfect water
    (D) Specialized filters to remove nitrates or phosphates
    (E) Aerobic bacteria used to biodegrade organic wastes

17. It is common for gold mines to have large storage ponds on site that typically contain which of the following toxins?
    (A) Mercury
    (B) Cyanide
    (C) PCBs
    (D) Dioxins
    (E) Formaldehyde

18. General class of pollution that characterizes urban area with frequent, high intensity sunshine and mobile air emissions due to heavy transportation is
    (A) photochemical smog
    (B) carbon monoxide
    (C) industrial smog
    (D) chlorofluorocarbons
    (E) asbestos

19. Eight days after a $20.0 g/m^3$ sample of radon gas (with a half-life of about four days) is emitted into a sealed room, how much of the gas remains?
    (A) $5 g/m^3$
    (B) $2.5 g/m^3$
    (C) 1/6 of the original sample
    (D) 1/12 of the original sample
    (E) 1/8 of the original sample

20. A preventative method to reduce the effects of cattle on rangeland is
    (A) selective cutting
    (B) no-till agriculture
    (C) subsidies for the meat industry
    (D) rotational grazing
    (E) contour plowing

21. The rough-skinned newt is one of the most toxic organisms in North America. The only predator that has adapted resistance to the newt is the garter snake. Over time this predator-prey interaction exerts pressure between the two species and has increased the newts' toxicity as well as the snakes' resistance. This is an example of
    (A) resource partitioning
    (B) speciation
    (C) coevolution
    (D) divergent evolution
    (E) allopatric speciation

22. Which of the following is NOT a distillation product of crude oil?
    (A) Peat
    (B) Greases
    (C) Pesticides
    (D) Plastics
    (E) Gasoline

Questions 23 and 24 refer to the following graph:

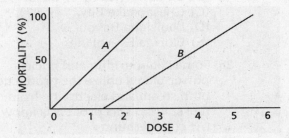

23. Which dose would most likely represent the LD50 for toxin A?
    (A) Dose 1
    (B) Dose 2
    (C) Dose 3
    (D) Dose 4
    (E) Dose 5

24. Where is the threshold level for toxin B?
    (A) There is no threshold level for toxin B
    (B) Between doses 1 and 2
    (C) At dose 3
    (D) Between doses 3 and 4
    (E) At dose 6

GO ON TO NEXT PAGE

25. Which of the following is an example of a large-scale water transfer project that has caused much environmental damage?
    (A) Love Canal, New York
    (B) Yangtze River, China
    (C) Three Mile Island, Philadelphia
    (D) Aral Sea, former USSR
    (E) Minamata, Japan

26. What type of commercial fishing practice causes devastating damage to coral reefs and sea mounts due to the use of weighted nets that drag along the ocean bottom?
    (A) Long-line fishing
    (B) Aquaculture farming
    (C) Drift-net fishing
    (D) Purse-seine fishing
    (E) Trawling fishing

27. The largest estuary in the United States, declared a "dead zone," for which the federal government paid $250 million to farmers to leave the area around the estuary unplanted, is
    (A) The Great Lakes system
    (B) St. Lawrence River Basin
    (C) Chesapeake Bay
    (D) Louisiana Bayou
    (E) Florida Everglades

28. Some coal-burning and nuclear power plants utilize the production of both steam and electricity from one fuel source. This process is known as
    (A) cogeneration
    (B) internal combustion
    (C) electric resistance heating
    (D) fuel cells
    (E) green architecture

29. Which of the following is mined to make inorganic fertilizers and some detergents?
    (A) Halite (salt ore)
    (B) Sand resources
    (C) Phosphate salts
    (D) Limestone ($CaCO_3$)
    (E) Cobalt

Question 30 refers to the climatograph.

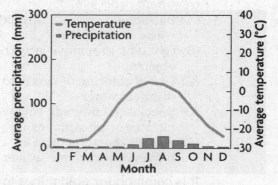

Source: **National Oceanic and Atmospheric Administration**

30. This climatograph could represent which of the following?
    (A) Antarctica
    (B) Alaska
    (C) Kenya
    (D) Australia
    (E) Brazil

31. Excessive inputs of nitrogen have been known to cause explosive growth of toxic microscopic algae that can poison fish and marine mammals. This outbreak is also known as
    (A) oxygen demanding waste
    (B) sedimentation
    (C) a red tide
    (D) biomagnification
    (E) a dead zone

32. Recently, scientists reported finding mercury in over 2,700 fish sampled from 12 different U.S. states. All of the following are solutions to reducing mercury levels that organisms are exposed to EXCEPT
    (A) increasing waste incineration practices to reduce landfill use
    (B) removal of Hg from coal prior to burning in electrical power plants
    (C) conversion of coal to liquid or gaseous fuel sources
    (D) utilizing more renewable energy sources such as wind and solar for electrical needs
    (E) recycling mercury-containing batteries and CFLs

33. Which of the following respiratory diseases was a rapidly spreading epidemic in China before it was successfully contained by 2003?
(A) West Nile
(B) Malaria
(C) Swine Flu
(D) SARS
(E) HIV

34. If limiting nutrients, such as phosphates or nitrates, are added to a lake ecosystem it is LEAST likely to result in
(A) depletion of oxygen in the water
(B) stimulated algae growth
(C) fish kills
(D) decrease in biodiversity
(E) decrease in gross primary productivity by algae

35. All of the following are options to reduce some of the air pollutants caused by coal combustion EXCEPT
(A) increase in the use of bituminous coal supplies and decrease in the use of anthracite coal for home heating

(B) injection of calcium carbonate (limestone) into the gases during combustion
(C) physical or chemical cleaning of coal prior to combustion
(D) conversion of coal into synthetic natural gas to be used for energy
(E) use of electrostatic precipitators

36. Characteristic(s) of an organism that increase its risk of becoming endangered include which of the following?
(I) Narrow distribution
(II) Fixed migratory patterns
(III) Feed on low trophic levels

(A) I only
(B) II only
(C) III only
(D) both I and II
(E) I, II, and III

37. Which of the following is still being used in the United States to control pest populations?
(A) Dieldrin
(B) DDT
(C) Atrazine
(D) Chlordane
(E) Aldrin

Question 38 refers to the graph below where levels of oxygen and carbon dioxide were observed in a pond over a 24-hour period.

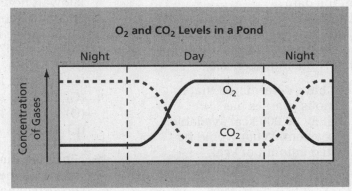

O_2 and CO_2 Levels in a Pond

38. What most likely caused the decrease in oxygen concentrations during the night?
(A) A sudden input of thermoelectric water from a power plant
(B) Decreased photosynthesis by phytoplankton and aquatic plants

(C) Increased evaporation from the surface of the pond
(D) Increased aerobic respiration by fish
(E) Runoff of fertilizers from local agricultural fields

GO ON TO NEXT PAGE

39. Recently scientists have found increasing cases of malaria in geographic areas that have not previous shown any cases of the disease. This is most likely due to
    (A) the mosquitoes' moving to new locations as their habitat has been destroyed
    (B) an increase in global temperature, making new areas suitable for the mosquito that carries the disease to live in
    (C) a dramatic decline in available vaccines for the disease
    (D) the introduction by shipping practices into new environments of the mosquito that carries the disease
    (E) an increase in the mosquito population since the ban on DDT began in developed nations

40. Which of the following is NOT a problem associated with electrical production from hydroelectric dams?
    (A) Flooding of terrestrial lands that destroy or fragments wildlife habitat
    (B) Displacement of people along overpopulated waterway areas
    (C) Reduction of silt downstream from the dam
    (D) Interruption of migratory pattern of some fish species
    (E) Large output of thermal pollution from producing electricity

41. Ecologists have determined that a field of various grasses has approximately 20,000 kcal available for the ecosystem. What would be the estimated amount of kcal available to secondary consumers in the food chain of this ecosystem?
    (A) 2.0×10^2 kcal
    (B) 2.0×10^3 kcal
    (C) 2.0×10^4 kcal
    (D) 2.0×10^5 kcal
    (E) 2.0×10^6 kcal

42. The area noteworthy for its frequent earthquakes and volcanic activity, also known as "The Ring of Fire," is found in the
    (A) southern Atlantic Ocean
    (B) basin of the Pacific Ocean
    (C) Antarctic seas
    (D) Dead Sea
    (E) northern Indian Ocean

43. Scientists commonly measure concentration of water pollutants in terms of ppm or ppb. One ppm is also equivalent to one mg of a toxin per liter of water. Therefore, one ppb would be equivalent to
    (A) g/L
    (B) mg/L
    (C) µg/L
    (D) ng/L
    (E) kg/L

44. All of the following are ways that biogas (methane) is produced in the environment EXCEPT
    (A) swamps and bogs
    (B) landfills
    (C) rice production
    (D) cattle ranching
    (E) solar production

45. How much energy is saved, in kilowatt hours, if a family that uses a 100-watt light bulb for an hour a day for 30 days switches to a 60-watt bulb instead?
    (A) 1.2 kWh
    (B) 1.2×10^1 kWh
    (C) 1.2×10^2 kWh
    (D) 1.2×10^3 kWh
    (E) 1.2×10^4 kWh

46. Nitrogen, the most abundant gas in the atmosphere, cycles through the ecosystem and is primarily controlled by
    (A) evaporation and precipitation
    (B) the activity of microscopic bacteria
    (C) chemical exchange with the oceans
    (D) uptake of nitrates by plants
    (E) erosion of rocks by wind and rain

47. Instead of using chlorine in the disinfecting stage of a municipal wastewater treatment plant, they could also use
   (A) UV light
   (B) alcohol
   (C) ammonia
   (D) nitrates
   (E) chloroform

48. Over 50% of natural background radiation exposure for humans comes from
   (A) gamma ray exposure from cosmic sources
   (B) ultraviolet radiation from the sun
   (C) consumer products such as TVs, cell phones, and computers
   (D) release from nuclear power plants producing electricity
   (E) terrestrial radiation from radon in bedrock material

49. The project started by Wangari Maathai in Kenya to re-plant native trees to decrease soil erosion and improve the quality of lives by providing renewable fuelwood sources is known as the
   (A) Kyoto Treaty
   (B) Greenbelt Movement
   (C) Healthy Forestry Initiative
   (D) Reclamation and Recovery Movement
   (E) Rangeland Improvement Act

Question 50 refers to the graph below.

Monthly fluctuations in carbon dioxide levels compared to annual average of carbon dioxide level.

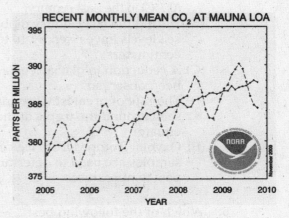

Source: National Oceanic and Atmospheric Administration

50. The cyclical peaks in atmospheric carbon dioxide concentration would correspond to
   (A) the increase in burning of coal during winter months
   (B) slash and burn agriculture occurring in the tropics
   (C) winter months in the Northern Hemisphere
   (D) release of carbon dioxide during waste incineration
   (E) increased volcanic activity around the Hawaiian Islands

51. Some countries are increasing their use of a desalination process that uses high pressure to force saltwater through a membrane filter with pores small enough to remove the salt. This process is known as
   (A) reverse osmosis
   (B) water-logging
   (C) distillation
   (D) salinization
   (E) drip filtration

GO ON TO NEXT PAGE

52. Which of the following is an <u>incorrect</u> statement concerning global climate change?
    (A) Our global mean temperature has increased approximately 1.3°F (0.7°C) in the past century.
    (B) During the last century global sea levels have risen by 10 to 20 centimeters.
    (C) A reduction in glacial ice has been observed.
    (D) The rate of greatest warming is seen around the tropic at the equator.
    (E) Oxygen isotopes from ice core samples are used to determine past temperatures.

53. Which of the following best exemplifies global collaboration for protecting biodiversity?
    (A) Endangered Species Act
    (B) CERCLA
    (C) CITES
    (D) NEPA
    (E) The Kyoto Treaty

54. During a growing season, a farmer grows a crop that returns nitrogen to the soil in the same field with a plant that requires a lot of nitrogen. This would be an example of
    (A) polyvarietal cultivation
    (B) agroforestry
    (C) intercropping
    (D) crop rotation
    (E) monoculture

55. Which of the following is NOT a characteristic associated with estuaries and wetland ecosystems?
    (A) Are economically valuable for commercial and recreational fishing
    (B) Serve as groundwater recharge systems
    (C) Provide natural nursery areas for many aquatic organisms
    (D) Are breeding grounds for many different species of waterfowl
    (E) Increase impacts of flooding during rainy seasons in countries along the equator

56. Which of the following rocks is formed from compacted shells and skeletons?
    (A) Coal
    (B) Limestone
    (C) Rock salt
    (D) Marble
    (E) Granite

Questions 57 and 58 refer to the age-structure below.

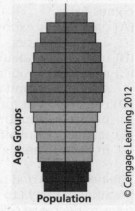

57. This age structure best represents a country that is most likely
    (A) experiencing high infant mortality and rapid population growth
    (B) experiencing higher birth rates and decreasing death rates
    (C) experiencing decreasing life expectancy and an increase in birth rates
    (D) entering pre-industrial demographic transition
    (E) experiencing zero to negative population growth

58. The age structure above would best illustrate the growth of which country?
    (A) Germany
    (B) Nigeria
    (C) Kenya
    (D) Saudi Arabia
    (E) Bangladesh

59. Coal-burning power plants and light-water nuclear reactors have which of the following in common?
    (A) Sulfur dioxide emissions that combine readily to form sulfuric acid
    (B) Fly ash released into the atmosphere
    (C) Input of thermal pollution into local rivers and streams
    (D) Mercury released into aquatic waters from atmospheric deposition
    (E) Carbon dioxide emissions

60. Typically, large urban cities are a few degrees warmer than their surrounding suburbs. This is an example of
    (A) a minor biome
    (B) a warm front
    (C) weather
    (D) a microclimate
    (E) a temperature inversion

61. If a population of 100,000 experiences 2,000 births, 1,600 deaths, 200 immigrants, and 100 emigrants in the course of one year, what is its net annual percentage growth rate?
    (A) 0.3%
    (B) 0.003%
    (C) 0.5%
    (D) 0.005%
    (E) 1.0%

62. Based on the theory of island biogeography, you would predict that large islands near the mainland would have relatively
    (A) high immigration and low extinction rates
    (B) high immigration and high extinction rates
    (C) low immigration and low extinction rates
    (D) low immigration and high extinction rates
    (E) relatively the same immigration and extinction rates

63. The waste material remaining once the desired metallic ore is removed is known as
    (A) minerals
    (B) gangue
    (C) soot
    (D) ore
    (E) spoils

64. Kudzu was brought to Georgia in the 1930s from Japan in order to control soil erosion, and since then it has outcompeted native species for resources making it an example of
    (A) a specialist species
    (B) habitat fragmentation
    (C) an invasive species
    (D) an indicator species
    (E) a keystone species

65. The layer that constitutes most of the earth's volume is the
    (A) lithosphere
    (B) mantle
    (C) oceanic crust
    (D) core
    (E) magnetosphere

66. Which of the following would cause the disappearance of the lichen communities in a particular area?
    (A) Ozone loss
    (B) Nutrient loading into the ecosystem
    (C) High rates of soil erosion
    (D) Air pollution
    (E) Increased UV radiation

67. Which of the following is a gas that contributes significantly to the greenhouse effect and is a byproduct of bacterial metabolism?
    (A) Nitrous oxide
    (B) Sulfur dioxide
    (C) Ozone
    (D) Nitrogen dioxide
    (E) Hydrogen sulfide

GO ON TO NEXT PAGE

68. Which statement best illustrates why replacement-level fertility in developing countries is 2.5 and in developed countries it is 2.1?
    (A) Developing nations are still in transitional demographic growth where total fertility levels are high.
    (B) Developed nations are in stage three of demographic growth where fertility level is stable.
    (C) Fertility in developing nations is higher due to the lack of education and contraceptive devices.
    (D) Developing nations will have more children die before reaching reproductive age.
    (E) Developing nations have a higher population and therefore will have a higher replacement-level fertility.

69. Overgrazing of riparian land near stream banks by livestock can lead to
    (A) changes in local climate from increasing transpiration rates
    (B) decreases in water temperature in the streams
    (C) reduction in gross productivity by phytoplankton from decreased water clarity
    (D) increasing dissolved oxygen content
    (E) large amounts of nitrates and phosphates being removed prior to entering streams

70. Which of the following is likely to enter local waterways as a result of rainwater seeping through a mine or mine waste pile?
    (A) Nitrates and phosphates
    (B) Arsenic and mercury
    (C) Thermal pollution
    (D) Vinyl chloride
    (E) PCBs and dioxins

71. What type of mining is commonly used to remove valuable coal resources from hilly or mountainous terrain?
    (A) Open-pit mining
    (B) Area strip mining
    (C) Sub-surface mining
    (D) Mine drainage
    (E) Contour strip mining

72. If the annual growth rate of the U.S. population is 1.0% and it continues to grow at this rate for one year, approximately how many people would be added?
    (A) 3×10^3
    (B) 3×10^4
    (C) 3×10^6
    (D) 3×10^8
    (E) 3×10^9

73. Biomass can be
    I. solar energy converted to chemical energy
    II. derived from living or recently living organisms
    III. energy available for trophic levels

    (A) I only
    (B) II only
    (C) III only
    (D) I and II only
    (E) I, II, and III

74. As a pond goes from an early successional stage to late succession, it acquires all of the following characteristics EXCEPT:
    (A) Water in the pond becomes richer in nutrients.
    (B) The water quality decreases in organic matter.
    (C) Water in the pond experiences eutrophication.
    (D) The pond becomes less oligotrophic.
    (E) Sediments increase and clarity of water decreases.

Questions 75 and 76 refer to the graph below.

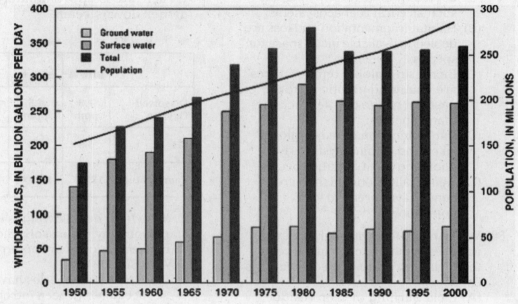

Source: USGS water use statistics site

75. What is the % increase in total water usage per day from 1950 to 1980?
    (A) 20%
    (B) 25%
    (C) 50%
    (D) 75%
    (E) over 100%

76. Which of the following statements best illustrates the increasing use of surface and ground water supplies in the United States?
    (A) As population increases so does the demand for irrigation water to produce food and coolant water to produce electricity.
    (B) The increasing population uses more municipal water for drinking supplies.
    (C) Water use continues to rise as the population becomes more affluent in the United States.
    (D) As population increases there is more need for residential water use.
    (E) Increasing surface water is being utilized for hydroelectric power.

77. What type of plate boundary could have produced the Aleutian Trench?
    (A) Oceanic plate boundary
    (B) Divergent plate boundary
    (C) Convergent plate boundary
    (D) Transform fault boundary
    (E) Continental plate boundary

78. Producing staple crops, such as corn or rice, in hilly regions suffering from topsoil loss due to erosion would benefit most from using which of the following agricultural practices?
    (A) Plantation cropping
    (B) Intensive subsistence farming
    (C) Industrial monoculture
    (D) Terracing
    (E) Slash and burn agriculture

GO ON TO NEXT PAGE

79. Which statement best illustrates why most species are currently becoming endangered due to human activities?
    (A) Acidification of ocean waters is depleting biodiversity hotspots such as coral reef ecosystems.
    (B) Habitat fragmentation and loss are depleting available niche space for species.
    (C) Increasing global temperatures are changing abiotic factors past the range of tolerance for many species.
    (D) Eutrophication in major global lakes and estuary systems is depleting most aquatic species.
    (E) Genetically modified food crops' genes have spread to wild populations.

80. Which of the following agricultural activities in the United States accounts for the largest share of greenhouse gas emissions?
    (A) Field burning of crop residue releases carbon monoxide gases.
    (B) Heavy uses of phosphate-based fertilizers evaporate from crop fields.
    (C) Cattle being farmed for meat production release large amounts of methane gas.
    (D) Fossil fuels used in farm machinery yields high amounts of hydrocarbons.
    (E) Waste lagoons on feedlots release nitrogen dioxide.

81. Which country is responsible for the majority of the globally produced farmed fish from aquaculture practices?
    (A) Germany
    (B) United States
    (C) Australia
    (D) Japan
    (E) China

Questions 82–83 refer to the table below, which depicts water quality sample results taken at four different sites along a river. Starting with Site A, each site is approximately 2 miles further downstream.

	Site A	Site B	Site C	Site D
Dissolved Oxygen	7.3 ppm	4.5 ppm	3.2 ppm	3.1 ppm
pH	6.3	6.5	6.1	6.4
Temperature	17.8°C	17.5°C	17.6°C	17.4°C

82. Which of the following is a likely reason why the dissolved oxygen concentration is dropping from Site A to Site D?
    (A) Non-native species have accidentally been introduced into the river system.
    (B) The temperature drop in the river is causing the drop in dissolved oxygen.
    (C) Runoff of a local feedlot's waste lagoon water has entered the river.
    (D) The river becomes more diverse downstream and therefore has more aerobic organisms utilizing the oxygen.
    (E) A local power plant is inputting large amounts of thermal pollution.

83. What is a chemical water quality test that should be performed to provide more answers as to why the dissolved oxygen content is dropping?
    (A) Secchi disk test
    (B) Imhoff cone test
    (C) Nitrate test
    (D) River flow rate
    (E) Fecal coliform test

84. Which statement best illustrates a drawback to using genetically modified organisms (GMOs) for food?
(A) GMOs can grow in slightly salty soils.
(B) They spread pest resistance to local weed populations.
(C) GMOs give a higher yield than ancestral crop varieties.
(D) They tolerate high levels of herbicides.
(E) The GMOs require less water than ancestral crop varieties.

85. The over-withdrawal of groundwater from an aquifer may lead to land collapsing and can damage roadways, sewer lines, and building foundations. This is known as
(A) land subsidence
(B) tectonic collapse
(C) land subduction
(D) aquifer depletion
(E) infiltration

86. There are some recent movements to convert hazardous industrial sites into usable urban development such as housing, office or retail space. These abandoned industrial sites are known as
(A) brownfields
(B) conservation easements
(C) ecoindustrial parks
(D) resource exchange sites
(E) reclamation sites

87. Increasing in use in developing countries are large, reflective, parabolic dishes that are used to heat food and water. These solar cookers are an example of
(A) active solar heating
(B) solar cell energy
(C) passive solar heating
(D) photovoltaic cells
(E) heliostats

88. An earthquake measuring 7.0 on the Richter scale is how many more times greater in magnitude than an earthquake measuring 5.0 on the Richter scale?
(A) 10 times greater
(B) 100 times greater
(C) 1000 times greater
(D) 10,000 times greater
(E) 100,000 times greater

89. Natural gas extracted from the earth is a mixture of gases that contains a 50–90% concentration of this gas.
(A) butane (C_4H_{10})
(B) propane (C_3H_8)
(C) ethane (C_2H_6)
(D) methane (CH_4)
(E) hydrogen sulfide (H_2S)

90. A switch in dependency from coal burning, used to generate electricity, to wind and solar energy would help alleviate all of the following environmental concerns EXCEPT
(A) carbon dioxide emissions
(B) mercury entering aquatic ecosystems
(C) industrial-based smog
(D) acid rain
(E) loss of stratospheric ozone

GO ON TO NEXT PAGE

Questions 91–93 refer to the global map below.

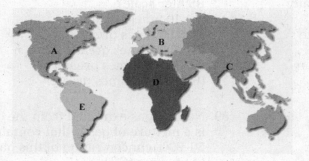

91. area of the world experiencing the highest total fertility rate

92. area of the world with the largest percentage of global population

93. area of the world that consumes a large amount of global resources per capita

94. Some plants, such as poplars, can absorb toxic organic chemicals and break them down into less harmful compounds. This is known as
(A) chemical remediation
(B) phytodegradation
(C) natural decomposition
(D) phytostabilization
(E) toxin sequestration

95. The secondary pollutants in photochemical smog are
(A) nitric acid and carbon dioxide
(B) ozone and nitric acid
(C) sulfuric acid and carbon dioxide
(D) sulfur dioxide and hydrocarbons
(E) benzene and carbon monoxide

96. A farmer is struggling with a low plant yield. A soil test reveals his soil has a pH of 4.5. In order to increase crop yield the pH needs to be around 6.5. Which soil amendment should be added to the field?
(A) Lime
(B) Water-insoluble compounds
(C) Phosphates
(D) Compost
(E) Humus

97. Which of the following best illustrates a food chain found in a tundra ecosystem?
(A) Lichen → lemmings → foxes → wolves
(B) Aspen → deer → black bear → lynx
(C) Trees → zebras → cheetahs → scavengers
(D) Cacti → insects → lizards → hawks
(E) Grasses → kangaroo rats → snakes → hawks

98. A health impact associated with increasing ozone loss is
(A) asthma
(B) neurological disorders
(C) chronic bronchitis
(D) cataracts
(E) lung cancer

99. Habitat fragmentation is reducing the number of larger vertebrates who depend on large contiguous tracts of habitat space in order to sustain the population size. A possible solution for these larger vertebrates is to provide
(A) breeding grounds
(B) national parks
(C) watershed monitoring
(D) habitat corridors
(E) hunting restrictions

100. In developing countries the indoor air pollutants that pose the greatest threats are from open fires and inefficient stoves. In developed nations the most common indoor air pollutants that pose a threat are from
(A) radon gas
(B) pet dander
(C) volatile organic compounds
(D) second-hand cigarette smoke
(E) asbestos

Section II: Free-Response Questions
Time: 1 Hour and 30 Minutes
Number of Questions: 4

Section II of the AP Environmental Science Exam counts for 40% of the total test grade. You will have four essay questions, each involving several parts. Calculators may not be used on the free-response section.

1. With approximately 300 million people, the United States produces over 200 million tons of waste each year. There has been an overall trend in recycling products in the last three decades. The table below gives the total amount generated, recycled, and discarded for several products generated in the municipal waste stream.

Products Generated in the Municipal Waste Stream
(in thousands of US tons)

Product	Generated	Recovered (Recycled)	Discarded
Paper	39,120	17,860	21,260
Cardboard	38,290	25,080	13,210
Plastic (containers and packaging)	13,010	1,730	11,280

(a) i. According to the estimates given, how many pounds of trash in one year does the average U.S. citizen produce? (1 U.S. ton = 2,000 lbs)
   ii. How many pounds of trash does a U.S. citizen produce each day?
   iii. If 140 million tons of waste end up in the landfill and the rest is recycled, what percent of our products are being recovered?

(b) Discuss which product has the lowest percentage of recovery and what benefits would be gained from increasing recycling rates of this product.

(c) Describe a method of waste disposal for products that enter the municipal waste stream but are NOT recovered (recycled).

(d) From the method of waste disposal you choose in part (c), explain TWO environmental consequences associated with that method.

2. Scientists estimate that at least half of the world's known species of terrestrial plants and animals live in tropical rain forests. However, these forests are being deforested at an alarming rate.

(a) Other than providing habitat to a wide range of biodiversity, identify and describe TWO ecosystem services that forests provide.

(b) About half of the wood harvested in tropical regions is utilized as fuel. Explain why this is a necessary resource in these developing countries.

(c) Other than fuelwood resources, discuss why tropical forests are being deforested at such a rapid rate in developing countries.

(d) Discuss another method of energy production that could be utilized in tropical regions and why it is a better option over using fuelwood.

(e) Describe TWO ways consumers in developed nations can help discourage deforestation of tropical forests.

3.

> Coral reefs occupy only 0.2% of the ocean floor. These ecosystems provide vital ecological and economic services. Corals are massive colonies of tiny polyp animals that build their calcium carbonate skeleton around their soft tissue. Corals grow extremely slowly. On average corals grow between 0.3 cm to 10 cm per year. Almost all corals have symbiotic algae, *zooxanthellae*, growing inside their tissues. Corals are sensitive to many abiotic conditions such as water temperature and clarity. A 2005 report by the World Conservation Union found that 15% of coral reefs have been destroyed and another 20% severely damaged. Since corals are sensitive to environmental change many have suffered due to human activities..

(a) Scientists have found that colonies of brain coral can grow as large as 1.8 m in size. What is the minimum and maximum amount of years it could have taken this coral to grow?
(b) Explain the relationship between the coral polyp and the *zooxanthellae* algae.
(c) Identify and describe TWO ecosystem services that coral reefs provide.
(d) Human activities are contributing to the destruction of coral reefs. Discuss a human activity that will further the loss of coral reef ecosystems.
(e) Identify and describe ONE economic or societal benefit that coral reefs provide.

4. Diarrheal diseases, which kill around 2 million people globally each year, mostly impact children in developing countries. Although the use of water for hygiene is important, more important is the access to clean drinking water resources.
(a) Identify and describe a type of disease contracted through contaminated drinking water.
(b) Blue-baby syndrome is a disease contracted through contaminated groundwater resources. Explain what pollutant is responsible for the disease and how it enters the groundwater system.
(c) Discuss TWO other sources of groundwater contamination that can lead to infectious disease.
(d) Describe a water quality test that can be performed to determine the disease potential.
(e) Identify a federal law aimed at protecting drinking water quality and discuss its goals.

ANSWERS FOR MULTIPLE-CHOICE QUESTIONS

Using the table below, score your test.

Determine how many questions you answered correctly and how many you answered incorrectly. You will find explanations of the answers on the following pages.

1. D	21. C	41. A	61. C	81. E
2. E	22. A	42. B	62. A	82. C
3. C	23. A	43. C	63. B	83. C
4. B	24. B	44. E	64. C	84. B
5. A	25. D	45. A	65. B	85. A
6. E	26. E	46. B	66. D	86. A
7. B	27. C	47. A	67. A	87. C
8. D	28. A	48. E	68. D	88. B
9. A	29. C	49. B	69. C	89. D
10. C	30. B	50. C	70. B	90. E
11. B	31. C	51. A	71. E	91. D
12. E	32. A	52. D	72. C	92. C
13. D	33. D	53. C	73. E	93. A
14. D	34. E	54. C	74. B	94. B
15. D	35. A	55. E	75. E	95. B
16. E	36. D	56. B	76. A	96. A
17. B	37. C	57. E	77. C	97. A
18. A	38. B	58. A	78. D	98. D
19. A	39. B	59. C	79. B	99. D
20. D	40. E	60. D	80. C	100. C

1.　　**ANSWER: D.**　The limnetic zone is the upper zone found in deep lake ecosystems. This is the open surface area away from shore that receives an abundant amount of sunlight to support photosynthesis by phytoplankton. The high concentration of phytoplankton and zooplankton constitutes the base of the food chain in this ecosystem (*Living in the Environment,* 16th ed., pages 174–175 / 17th ed., page 181).

2. **ANSWER: E.** The abyssal zone is the deepest zone in the oceanic ecosystem. This zone receives no sunlight and is very cold. However, decaying organic matter drifts down to the bottom (marine snow) from upper levels, providing plenty of nutrients to support life (*Living in the Environment*, 16th ed., pages 170–171 / 17th ed., page 173).

3. **ANSWER: C.** The littoral zone is the area closest to shore in deep lake systems. This area is teeming with life and has a myriad of submergent (below water) and emergent (rooted in water but stand above water-line) plant species. This area also has a large input of nutrient runoff from land (*Living in the Environment*, 16th ed., pages 174–175 / 17th ed., page 181).

4. **ANSWER: B.** Fermentation is an anaerobic respiration process (occurs in the absence of oxygen). Microbes such as yeast and bacteria commonly use fermentation since they typically live in environments with little to no oxygen present. One type of by-product of fermentation for these microbes is commonly ethyl alcohol (*Living in the Environment*, 16th ed., page 59 / 17th ed., page 61).

5. **ANSWER: A.** Hydrothermal vent systems exist on the deep ocean floor in the absence of sunlight. These ecosystems rely on chemosynthetic bacteria that produce chemical energy in the form of carbohydrates from the release of hydrogen sulfide from the vent. They represent the base of the food chain, as they are primary producers for this ecosystem (*Living in the Environment*, 16th ed., page 59 / 17th ed., pages 59–60).

6. **ANSWER: E.** Transpiration is the loss of water from the surface of leaves in plants. Transpiration rates depend on the temperature, relative humidity (water vapor in the air), and the velocity of the wind (*Living in the Environment*, 16th ed., pages 65–66 / 17th ed., page 67).

7. **ANSWER: B.** Loams are soils that contain a mixture of clay, silt, and humus and are good for growing most crops (*Living in the Environment*, 16th ed., page 281 / 17th ed., page 284).

8. **ANSWER: D.** Sedimentary rock is made from the sediments of dead plant and animal remains that erode over time and through deposition and pressure become rock formations such as sandstone, shale, and limestone (*Living in the Environment*, 16th ed., page 353 / 17th ed., page 354).

9. **ANSWER: A.** A mineral is an element or inorganic compound that occurs naturally in the earth's crust as a solid with a regular internal crystalline structure. Some consist of only one element (gold, silver, diamonds) while others exist as inorganic compounds, such as salt and quartzite (*Living in

the Environment, 16th ed., page 353 / 17th ed., pages 353–354).

10. **ANSWER: C.** Igneous rock is rock formed when molten rock or magma wells up from the earth's interior, cools, and solidifies into rock masses, such as granite and lava (*Living in the Environment*, 16th ed., page 353 / 17th ed., page 354).

11. **ANSWER: B.** The biotic potential is the capacity for population growth under ideal conditions. Most species grow exponentially ("J" shaped curve) when conditions are ideal (*Living in the Environment*, 16th ed., page 109 / 17th ed., pages 114–115).

12. **ANSWER: E.** Together the biotic potential of a species and the environmental resistance (competition) determine the carrying capacity. Typically, the population of any given species will stabilize around carrying capacity as resources such as food, space, and water become limited (*Living in the Environment*, 16th ed., page 110 / 17th ed., pages 114–115).

13. **ANSWER: D.**

$$4.8 \times 10^6 \text{ metric tons} \times \frac{1\,\text{day}}{2.0 \times 10^2 \text{ metric tons}} = 2.4 \times 10^4 \text{ days}$$

$$2.4 \times 10^4 \text{ days} \times \frac{1\,\text{year}}{365\,\text{days}} = 66\,\text{years}$$

(*Living in the Environment*, 16th ed., page 369 / 17th ed., page 369).

14. **ANSWER: D.** Waterlogging is when irrigation water accumulates underground which gradually raises the water table. Farmers often do this to leach damaging salts in the soil into deeper layers. However, since it raises the water table, saline water envelops the root tissue of the plant, decreasing yield and often causing death (*Living in the Environment*, 16th ed., page 289 / 17th ed., page 292).

15. **ANSWER: D.** A country in the Industrial stage of demographic transition is experiencing low birth rates and low death rates (*Living in the Environment*, 16th ed., pages 132–134 / 17th ed., pages 139–140).

16. **ANSWER: E.** Secondary sewage treatment processes involve a biological process. They utilize aerobic bacteria to naturally break down any oxygen-demanding organic wastes (*Living in the Environment*, 16th ed., page 554 / 17th ed., page 551).

17. **ANSWER: B.** Many countries use a type of gold extraction known as cyanide heap leaching. They spray large amounts of cyanide salts onto open-air piles of crushed rock to extract the gold. The cyanide solution then drains into large

storage lagoons that can leach into groundwater supplies or run off into local waterways during heavy rains (*Living in the Environment,* 16th ed., page 344 / 17th ed., page 346).

18. ANSWER: **A.** Photochemical smog is a mixture of primary and secondary pollutants formed under the influence of UV radiation. This typically forms in urban areas with frequent emissions from car exhaust that provide the primary pollutants such as nitric oxide (NO) and hydrocarbons (*Living in the Environment,* 16th ed., pages 476–477 / 17th ed., pages 474–475).

19. ANSWER: **A.** The half-life for radon gas is approximately four days. Therefore, every four days only ½ of the original isotope remains. After eight days, ½ × ½ = ¼ of the original isotope remains, or 5 g/m³. After 4 days (or one half-life) 50% of the original isotope would remain, or 10g/m³. After another 4 days (eight days total), only 50% of that remaining isotope would be left (10 g/m³ × 0.5 = 5 g/m³) (*Living in the Environment,* 16th ed., page 40 / 17th ed., not included).

20. ANSWER: **D.** To prevent overgrazing of rangeland and a reduction in yield, ranchers can practice rotational grazing. In rotational grazing cattle are confined by portable fencing to one area for a short time and then moved to a new location. This gives the grassland time to rebound from the feeding cattle (*Living in the Environment,* 16th ed., pages 231–232 / 17th ed., page 235).

21. ANSWER: **C.** This is a classic example of coevolution. Coevolution is when populations of two different species interact in a way over such a long period of time that changes in the gene pool of one species can lead to changes in the gene pool of the other species (*Living in the Environment,* 16th ed., page 104 / 17th ed., page 109).

22. ANSWER: **A.** Peat is not a product from the distillation of crude oil. It is decayed plant matter found in swamps and bogs and is the beginning stage of possible coal formation (*Living in the Environment,* 16th ed., pages 375, 383 / 17th ed., page 382).

23. ANSWER: **A.** Line A is an example of a non-threshold response, where the harm of the toxin increases along with the dose. The LD50 for this toxin is the dose that causes 50% of the test population to die. This would be closest to dose 1 (*Living in the Environment,* 16th ed., pages 455–456 / 17th ed., pages 453–454).

24. ANSWER: **B.** Line B is an example of a threshold response curve. A threshold is the lowest dose for which mortality is observed for at least one member of the target population. For line B the threshold for this test organism is between

doses 1 and 2 (*Living in the Environment*, 16th ed., pages 455–456 / 17th ed., pages 453–454).

25. ANSWER: **D.** The former Soviet Union withdrew large amounts of water from the Aral Sea for irrigation of cotton and rice fields. Due to excessive removal of water the Aral Sea has lost almost 90% of volume, and salinity has risen sevenfold, which has caused the extinction of many of the local aquatic, bird, and mammal species (*Living in the Environment*, 16th ed., pages 329–331 / 17th ed., pages 332–333).

26. ANSWER: **E.** Trawling fishing practices use weighted funnel-shaped nets that drag along the bottom of the ocean to catch bottom-dwellers such as shrimp, cod, flounder, and scallops (*Living in the Environment*, 16th ed., page 251 / 17th ed., pages 258–259).

27. ANSWER: **C.** The Chesapeake was declared a dead zone by the U.S. government due to the low levels of dissolved oxygen and the depletion of biodiversity. This was sparked by cultural eutrophication stemming from an input of fertilizers from local agricultural areas (*Living in the Environment*, 16th ed., pages 172–173 / 17th ed., pages 179–180).

28. ANSWER: **A.** Cogeneration systems, also called combined heat and power systems, utilize the steam produced during electrical generation to heat the building instead of releasing it as a waste product. This practice increases the overall net gain of energy and therefore increases efficiency (*Living in the Environment*, 16th ed., pages 402–403 / 17th ed., pages 419–420).

29. ANSWER: **C.** Phosphate salts are another example of a non-metallic mineral that is mined in the United States. Other common examples include salt, sand (silicon dioxide), and limestone (calcium carbonate) (*Living in the Environment*, 16th ed., page 355 / 17th ed., page 355).

30. ANSWER: **B.** Based on the information in the graph, this biome's average temperature, even in the warmest months, doesn't get much above freezing. Therefore this is most likely representative of the tundra biome. Although Antarctica is a tundra ecosystem, it is in the southern hemisphere and the warmest months would not be June to September. The best answer would be Alaska (*Living in the Environment*, 16th ed., page 151 / 17th ed., page 154).

31. ANSWER: **C.** Red tides are outbreaks of microscopic, single-celled algae (dinoflagellates) and can be toxic to many aquatic species including mammals. Nutrient-loading into oceanic systems is one trigger of these types of events

(*Living in the Environment*, 16th ed., page 549 / 17th ed., page 545).

32. ANSWER: A. Incineration of waste is actually a source for elemental Hg to enter the atmosphere. Once in the atmosphere it is oxidized into inorganic Hg and converted by bacteria to the toxic, organic methyl mercury that can accumulate in living organisms. Therefore, increasing incineration practices will not decrease exposure in organisms (*Living in the Environment*, 16th ed., pages 450–451 / 17th ed., page 449).

33. ANSWER: D. The severe acute respiratory syndrome (SARS) first appeared in China in 2002. The World Health Organization helped to contain this highly contagious disease by July of 2003 (*Living in the Environment*, 16th ed., page 444 / 17th ed., not included).

34. ANSWER: E. Since nitrates and phosphates are limiting nutrients, when they are present in abundance they will promote excess growth in phytoplankton (microscopic algae). An algal bloom is often the beginning of cultural eutrophication (*Living in the Environment*, 16th ed., pages 539–541 / 17th ed., pages 175, 536–537).

35. ANSWER: A. Bituminous coal has a higher concentration of sulfur than anthracite coal. Also, since anthracite has more Btus per pound, coal consumption could be reduced. Increasing the use of bituminous coal would produce more sulfur dioxide and therefore sulfuric acid (acid rain) in the atmosphere (*Living in the Environment*, 16th ed., pages 382–383, 491 / 17th ed., pages 381–382, 487).

36. ANSWER: D. Some characteristics of organisms make them vulnerable to becoming endangered or extinct. These characteristics include having a narrow distribution, a fixed migratory pattern, feed at high trophic levels, are commercially valuable, rare, and require large territories (*Living in the Environment*, 16th ed., page 188 / 17th ed., page 194).

37. ANSWER: C. Atrazine is one of our most prolifically used pesticides. It is an herbicide used primarily in the Midwest to control competing weed species. The other pesticides in the question are part of the "dirty dozen" identified and banned by most countries including the United States. DDT, however, is still being used in many developing countries to combat malaria (*Living in the Environment*, 16th ed., page 459 / 17th ed., page 456).

38. ANSWER: B. Phytoplankton and aquatic plants are photosynthetic autotrophs. They will use carbon dioxide being produced by consumers during photosynthesis when

sunlight is present (during the day) and release oxygen as a byproduct of producing chemical energy. At night, photosynthesis in plants declines as sunlight is not plentiful; therefore carbon dioxide is not being utilized as often (*Living in the Environment*, 16th ed., pages 57–60 / 17th ed., pages 58–61).

39. ANSWER: **B**. The *Anopheles* mosquito that carries the *Plasmodium* parasite is typically only found in tropical climates around the equator. However, due to increasing climate change these mosquitoes are able to expand their distribution (*Living in the Environment*, 16th ed., pages 445–446 / 17th ed., pages 443–445).

40. ANSWER: **E**. Hydroelectric dams use the potential energy stored in water and convert mechanical energy in moving water to generate electricity. They do not use coolant water and therefore do not release thermal pollution into local waterways, as coal burning and nuclear power plants do (*Living in the Environment*, 16th ed., pages 418–419 / 17th ed., pages 415–416).

41. ANSWER: **A**. The ecological efficiency in an ecosystem refers to the usable chemical energy that transfers from one trophic level to the next as biomass. Much of the energy is lost as heat as it moves through the food chain (second law of thermodynamics). As a general rule, only 10% of the energy is available at the next trophic level. Therefore if 20,000 kcal are available from plants, then only 2,000 kcal are available to herbivores and only 200 kcal are available to secondary consumers. 200 kcal = 2.0×10^2 kcal (*Living in the Environment*, 16th ed., page 62 / 17th ed., pages 63–64).

42. ANSWER: **B**. One hotspot of tectonic activity, such as volcanoes and earthquakes, occurs in the Pacific Ocean basin. This area is home to almost 75% of the earth's active and dormant volcanoes (*Living in the Environment*, 16th ed., pages 350–351 / 17th ed., pages 349–353).

43. ANSWER: **C**. One part per million (ppm) is equivalent to one milligram per liter (mg/L), or 10^{-3} g/L. Since one part per billion (ppb) is 1,000 times smaller than one ppm, this is equivalent to 10^{-6} g/L or a microgram/liter (μg/L) (*Living in the Environment*, 16th ed., not included / 17th ed., not included).

44. ANSWER: **E**. Methane is released by enteric fermentation by bacteria in the digestive tracts of cows. Methane is also released as a by-product of anaerobic bacteria metabolism commonly occurring in landfills, swamps, and bogs. Rice paddies that simulate swamps and bogs also release methane (*Living in the Environment*, 16th ed., pages 497–500 / 17th ed., pages 493–497).

45. **ANSWER: A.** The family initially uses 100W×30 hours (in a 30 day period) = 3,000 watts per hour or 3 kilowatt hour. If they switch to a 60-watt bulb they will use 60W × 30 hours = 1800 watts per hour or 1.8 kilowatt hour. Therefore 3 kWh – 1.8 kWh = 1.2 kWh (*Living in the Environment*, 16th ed., pages 400–402 / 17th ed., pages 398–400).

46. **ANSWER: B.** The nitrogen cycle is predominately controlled by bacterial activity. Nitrogen is the dominant gas in the atmosphere (N_2) and is converted by bacteria to ammonia and nitrates that are taken up by plants. Bacteria also convert ammonia back into atmospheric nitrogen gases such as N_2, N_2O, and NO_2 (*Living in the Environment*, 16th ed., pages 68–70 / 17th ed., pages 71–72).

47. **ANSWER: A.** Some studies have shown that chlorine can combine with other organic compounds to form chlorinated hydrocarbons. Chlorinated hydrocarbons have been shown to cause cancer, nervous system damage, and possible endocrine disruption. Therefore, alternatives to chlorine are increasing in use, such as ozone and ultraviolet light (*Living in the Environment*, 16th ed., page 554 / 17th ed., page 551).

48. **ANSWER: E.** The average human is exposed to a small amount of background radiation every day from a variety of sources such as food, space, and terrestrial sources. An individual in the United States receives about 300 millirem of radiation from natural sources each year. Radon accounts for more than half of this exposure to radiation [Source: The U.S. Nuclear Regulatory Commission, December, 2004] (*Living in the Environment*, 16th ed., pages 484–486 / 17th ed., page 483).

49. **ANSWER: B.** Wangari Maathai started the Greenbelt Movement in her village in Kenya. It has spread to over 6,000 villages and they have planted over 30 million trees. This has decreased soil erosion and is breaking the cycle of poverty by providing valuable fuelwood resources as well as building material and food (*Living in the Environment*, 16th ed., page 230 / 17th ed., page 217).

50. **ANSWER: C.** Atmospheric levels of carbon dioxide fluctuate yearly with seasonal changes in uptake of carbon dioxide by plants. This fluctuation occurs with the northern hemisphere's seasons since the largest concentration of forests are there (*Living in the Environment*, 16th ed., pages 498–500 / 17th ed., pages 495–497).

51. **ANSWER: A.** The process described is reverse osmosis. Some countries, especially in arid regions such as Saudi Arabia, are increasing their use of this process. This can supply fresh drinking water to areas that are limited in supply (*Living in the Environment*, 16th ed., page 332 / 17th ed., page 333).

52. **ANSWER: D.** As the atmosphere warms, it causes convection that transfers heat from the equator to the arctic regions. Therefore, the polar regions seem to be experiencing a more rapid rate of climate change (*Living in the Environment*, 16th ed., pages 508–509 / 17th ed., pages 505–507).

53. **ANSWER: C.** The Convention on International Trade in Endangered Species (CITES) was signed by almost 170 countries and prohibits commercially traded species that are endangered or are at risk of becoming endangered (*Living in the Environment*, 16th ed., pages 206–207 / 17th ed., page 209).

54. **ANSWER: C.** Intercropping (a type of polyculture) involves growing two or more different crops at the same time on the same plot. To reduce the need for fertilizers farmers can grow nitrogen-fixing plants (legumes) with crops that require a lot of nitrogen, such as corn (*Living in the Environment*, 16th ed., pages 279–281 / 17th ed., page 283).

55. **ANSWER: E.** Wetland and estuary ecosystems provide many ecosystem and economic services. They are areas that reduce the impact of flooding, especially during rainy seasons. Coastal estuaries also reduce the impact of storm surges from hurricanes (*Living in the Environment*, 16th ed., pages 166–167 / 17th ed., pages 173–175).

56. **ANSWER: B.** Limestone (calcium carbonate) is an example of sedimentary rock that is formed from the remains of dead plant and animals. Limestone is specifically formed from compacted shells, skeletons, and other remains of dead organisms (*Living in the Environment*, 16th ed., pages 353–354 / 17th ed., pages 353–355).

57. **ANSWER: E.** This country has few individuals in the pre-reproductive and reproductive age groups. This country would be experiencing a zero to negative population growth (*Living in the Environment*, 16th ed., pages 131–132 / 17th ed., pages 135–137).

58. **ANSWER: A.** Due to a high total fertility rate, Nigeria, Kenya, Saudi Arabia, and Bangladesh would be experiencing rapid population growth. However, Germany is actually declining in population (*Living in the Environment*, 16th ed., pages 131–132 / 17th ed., pages 135–137).

59. **ANSWER: C.** Like coal, nuclear power plants rely on large amounts of coolant water that is taken in from local waterways. Typically, this water cycles back to the local

waterway and is extremely hot. This can lower the dissolved oxygen in that area and make species vulnerable to disease (*Living in the Environment*, 16th ed., pages 387, 534 / 17th ed., pages 387, 532).

60. ANSWER: **D.** A microclimate is a local region that differs in climate from the surrounding area. Cities have large amounts of asphalt, concrete, and other building materials that absorb and hold heat. These urban areas tend to be warmer than surrounding areas (*Living in the Environment*, 16th ed., page 145 / 17th ed., page 151).

61. ANSWER: **C.** Population change = (2,000 births + 200 immigrants) − (1,600 deaths + 100 emigrants). 500 new individuals are added to the population. 500/100,000 = 0.005 (100) = 0.5% growth rate (*Living in the Environment*, 16th ed., page 109 / 17th ed., page 130).

62. ANSWER: **A.** According to the theory of island biogeography, species diversity on islands is determined by the rate of immigration and the rate of extinction. Large islands have more resources and therefore less extinction. Since this island is close to the mainland it would also have a higher rate of immigration (*Living in the Environment*, 16th ed., page 90 / 17th ed., page 94).

63. ANSWER: **B.** Ore extracted from the earth has two components—the ore mineral (such as copper, aluminum) and waste material known as gangue (*Living in the Environment*, 16th ed., page 359 / 17th ed., page 360).

64. ANSWER: **C.** Invasive species are non-native organisms accidentally or intentionally introduced to an ecosystem. They can become invasive when there are no natural predators to keep populations in check. Typically, they outcompete local native species for resources and cause biodiversity loss (*Living in the Environment*, 16th ed., pages 197–201 / 17th ed., pages 198–203).

65. ANSWER: **B.** The earth's mantle makes up over 80% of the earth's volume. This highly viscous layer exists between the earth's core and crust (*Living in the Environment*, 16th ed., pages 346–347 / 17th ed., pages 347–348).

66. ANSWER: **D.** Lichen communities are indicator species for air pollution. Some lichen species are sensitive to specific air pollutants such as sulfur dioxide from coal burning power plants (*Living in the Environment*, 16th ed., page 475 / 17th ed., page 473).

67. ANSWER: **A.** Nitrous oxide is naturally produced by bacterial denitrification processes in soils. Nitrous oxide is a greenhouse gas and is increasing in abundance as bacteria

convert excess nutrients from fertilizers in the soil into this gas in the atmosphere (*Living in the Environment*, 16th ed., page 69 / 17th ed., page 72).

68. **ANSWER: D.** The replacement-level fertility is the average number of children a couple must have in order to replace themselves. Since more children in a developing nation will die prior to reaching reproductive age than will in a developed nation, their replacement-level fertility average is slightly higher (*Living in the Environment*, 16th ed., pages 126–127 / 17th ed., page 130).

69. **ANSWER: C.** Livestock often like to graze on vegetation along stream banks (riparian land). This will increase soil erosion and sedimentation into local streams, therefore decreasing water clarity and photosynthesis (*Living in the Environment*, 16th ed., pages 231–232 / 17th ed., page 340).

70. **ANSWER: B.** Mercury and arsenic are common pollutants that leach out of mines and mine waste piles as water from precipitation percolates through. These pollutants can enter local waterways and cause damage to aquatic organisms (*Living in the Environment*, 16th ed., page 359 / 17th ed., page 358).

71. **ANSWER: E.** Contour strip mining is used on hilly or mountainous terrain. It utilizes large power shovels to cut a series of terraces into the side of the hill so that the coal can be extracted (*Living in the Environment*, 16th ed., page 357 / 17th ed., page 357).

72. **ANSWER: C.** The current U.S. population is approximately 307 million. If it grows by 1%, then approximately 3 million, or 3×10^6, people will be added to the population in one year ($3 \times 10^8 \times 0.01 = 3 \times 10^6$) (*Living in the Environment*, 16th ed., page 126 / 17th ed., page 127).

73. **ANSWER: E.** Biomass is the dry weight of all organic matter found in organisms in the ecosystem. This can be stored chemical energy from photosynthesis (solar energy converted to chemical energy) or respiration. This stored energy is what is available to be utilized by organisms in each trophic level. It can also be burned to create energy, as is the case with fuelwood (*Living in the Environment*, 16th ed., page 62 / 17th ed., page 63).

74. **ANSWER: B.** The pond ecosystem will move from an oligotrophic ecosystem (early successional) to a eutrophic ecosystem (late successional). This will *increase* organic matter in the water. The water will also become more diverse and the clarity will decrease as sediments increase (*Living in the Environment*, 16th ed., pages 174–175 / 17th ed., pages 181–183).

75. **ANSWER: E.** In 1950 the total water withdrawal was approximately 175 billion gallons per day. In 1980 the total water withdrawal was 375 billion gallons per day. This is an increase of 200 billion gallons per day / 175 billion gallons per day = 114% increase in water usage. [Statistics and graph taken from the USGS] (*Living in the Environment,* 16th ed., pages 321–322 / 17th ed., pages 324–326).

76. **ANSWER: A.** The largest use of water in the United States is to irrigate croplands and to provide coolant water for electrical power plants. [Statistics and graph taken from the USGS] (*Living in the Environment,* 16th ed., pages 321–322 / 17th ed., page 320).

77. **ANSWER: C.** There are three main types of plate boundaries: convergent, divergent, and transform faults. Convergent plate boundaries create subduction zones as one oceanic plate rises up over another, pushing the other plate into the mantle. Trenches normally form at the boundary of two converging plates (*Living in the Environment,* 16th ed., page 347 / 17th ed., page 349).

78. **ANSWER: D.** Terracing is an effective agricultural practice that is used to grow food in regions with steep slopes and hills. Terracing converts the land into a series of broad, nearly level terraces that run across the land's contours (*Living in the Environment,* 16th ed., page 302 / 17th ed., pages 304–305).

79. **ANSWER: B.** The two primary reasons for biodiversity loss is habitat destruction (fragmentation) and the introduction of invasive species that outcompete native species (*Living in the Environment,* 16th ed., pages 193–199 / 17th ed., pages 197–203).

80. **ANSWER: C.** A large percentage of greenhouse gases emitted from agricultural activities is from livestock that emit methane gas due to enteric fermentation of bacteria in their intestines (*Living in the Environment,* 16th ed., pages 292–293 / 17th ed., page 293).

81. **ANSWER: E.** China produces 70% of the world's farmed fish. They mostly utilize inland ponds and rice fields to harvest herbivorous species such as carp. The carp feed off phytoplankton populations that are maintained in these fields by providing fertilizers from agricultural wastes such as manure (*Living in the Environment,* 16th ed., page 285 / 17th ed., pages 287–288).

82. **ANSWER: C.** If local feedlot waste (oxygen-demanding waste) has entered the waterway it would cause the dissolved oxygen to drop as aerobic bacteria break down the organic material (*Living in the Environment,* 16th ed., pages 535–536 / 17th ed., pages 533–534).

83. **ANSWER: C.** Although the fecal coliform test is a good indicator of animal waste contamination, it is a biological test, not chemical. The best choice for this question should be a nitrate test to determine if any nutrient loading is occurring (*Living in the Environment*, 16th ed., pages 535–536 / 17th ed., pages 533–534).

84. **ANSWER: B.** Many genetically modified crops have been engineered to increase pest resistance. However, these genes easily spread to local weed populations through pollen distribution. This is a drawback because if weed populations become naturally pest-resistant we will need to increase herbicide use to control them (*Living in the Environment*, 16th ed., page 291 / 17th ed., pages 293–294).

85. **ANSWER: A.** The continuous withdrawal from an aquifer without allowing enough time for natural recharge can cause the sand and rock in the aquifer to collapse. A type of land subsidence is a sinkhole, which can appear suddenly (*Living in the Environment*, 16th ed., page 323 / 17th ed., pages 326–327).

86. **ANSWER: A.** Brownfields are abandoned industrial sites that often have toxic soil and buried waste that must be removed before any new construction can begin. These sites are common in urban areas where former industrial cites are converted into downtown living, working, and shopping spaces (*Living in the Environment*, 16th ed., page 583 / 17th ed., page 579).

87. **ANSWER: C.** These simple solar cookers directly utilize the sun's energy without the use of fans or pumps to distribute the heat and are therefore a good example of passive solar heating (*Living in the Environment*, 16th ed., pages 411–413 / 17th ed., pages 409–413).

88. **ANSWER: B.** The Richter scale used by scientists to record the magnitude of earthquakes increases by a factor of ten for each unit. Therefore a 7.0 earthquake is 10 times the magnitude of a 6.0 earthquake and 100 times the magnitude of a 5.0 ($10 \times 10 = 100$) (*Living in the Environment*, 16th ed., page 350 / 17th ed., page 352).

89. **ANSWER: D.** Natural gas is a mix of all of the gases listed as choices in the question. However, methane typically makes up more than half of the mixture (*Living in the Environment*, 16th ed., page 381 / 17th ed., page 380).

90. **ANSWER: E.** Reducing the amount of coal being burned would help alleviate all of those environmental concerns except for the loss of ozone found in the stratosphere. This

destruction of ozone in the stratosphere is caused primarily by chlorine molecules from CFCs (*Living in the Environment*, 16th ed., pages 382–385 / 17th ed., pages 381–385).

91. ANSWER: D. Africa is currently experiencing the highest total fertility rates. Total fertility rate is the average number of children being born to a woman during her reproductive years. In developed countries the average TFR is around 2.1. The TFR in Africa ranges from 3.0 to as high as 7.0 (*Living in the Environment*, 16th ed., page 126 / 17th ed., page 140).

92. ANSWER: C. China, although it has rapidly slowed its population growth due to its "One Child Policy," represents almost 25% of the world's population with its 1.3 billion inhabitants (*Living in the Environment*, 16th ed., pages 135–136 / 17th ed., page 125).

93. ANSWER: A. The United States only makes up roughly 5% of the global population. However, due to its affluence, the U.S. utilizes a large amount of resources (coal, oil) per capita (*Living in the Environment*, 16th ed., pages 127–128 / 17th ed., pages 131–132).

94. ANSWER: B. Using plants to remediate toxins in the environment is becoming more common (phytoremediation). One type of phytoremediation involves the plant actually breaking down the organic toxin into a nontoxic organic form is known as phytodegradation (*Living in the Environment*, 16th ed., page 579 / 17th ed., pages 574–575).

95. ANSWER: B. The most common secondary pollutants in photochemical smog are ozone, nitric acid, aldehydes, and peroxyacyl nitrates (PANs) (*Living in the Environment*, 16th ed., page 477 / 17th ed., page 474).

96. ANSWER: A. Soil amendments are often added to soils to increase water retention or increase or decrease pH. Adding lime (or dolimitic limestone) will increase the pH of the soil (increase alkalinity) (*Living in the Environment*, 16th ed., page 281 / 17th ed., page 284).

97. ANSWER: A. The key hint here for choosing a food web is identifying the right primary producer first. The tundra ecosystem's dominant primary producers are lichen and moss (*Living in the Environment*, 16th ed., page 150 / 17th ed., pages 158–159).

98. **ANSWER: D.** The major health impacts associated with an increasing ozone loss (increased UV exposure) are cataracts, skin cancers, sunburns, and possible immune system suppression (*Living in the Environment*, 16th ed., page 524 / 17th ed., page 522).

99. **ANSWER: D.** Some scientists suggest the use of habitat corridors to protect larger vertebrates who utilize large tracts of land. Corridors permit migration of individuals or populations from isolated locations that are created by habitat fragmentation (*Living in the Environment*, 16th ed., page 237 / 17th ed., pages 140–141).

100. **ANSWER: C.** The most common indoor air pollutants in a developed nation come from volatile organic compounds released from common household items. This can include things like formaldehyde from insulation and fabrics, chloroform from chlorine-treated hot water in showers, and methylene chloride from paint thinners (*Living in the Environment*, 16th ed., pages 483–484 / 17th ed., pages 481–483).

SCORING GUIDELINES FOR FREE-RESPONSE QUESTIONS

1. (a) i. According to the estimates given, how many pounds of trash in one year does the average United States citizen produce? (1 metric ton = 2,200 lbs)

   2 points can be earned—1 point for correct set-up with units and 1 point for correct answer

   $$\frac{200 \times 10^6 \text{ tons/yr}}{300 \times 10^6 \text{ people}} = 0.667 \frac{\text{tons}}{\text{person}} \rightarrow 0.667 \frac{\text{tons}}{\text{yr}} \times 2,000 \frac{\text{lbs}}{\text{ton}} = 1,334 \frac{\text{lbs}}{\text{year}}$$

   Or $\dfrac{2.0 \times 10^8 \text{ tons of trash}}{3.0 \times 10^8 \text{ people}} = 2/3 \text{ tons/yr} \rightarrow \dfrac{2 \text{ ton}}{3 \text{ year}} \Big| \dfrac{2,000 \text{ lbs}}{\text{ton}} = 1,334 \text{ lbs/year}$

   (acceptable range for answer is 1320–1350 lbs/year)

   (a) ii. How many pounds of trash does a United States citizen produce each day?

   1 point can be earned for the correct set-up with answer

   $\dfrac{21,334 \text{ tons/yr}}{365 \text{ days/yr}} = 3.65 \text{ lbs/day*}$ (acceptable range is 3.5–4.0 based on answer from part i)

   *Students must use answer in part i. However, if they got part i wrong, but used that answer correctly in part ii they may still earn a point.

(a) iii. If 140 million tons of waste end up in the landfill and the rest is recycled, what percent of our products is being recovered?

1 point can be earned for the correct set-up with answer

200 million − 140 million = 60 million tons recycled

60 million / 200 million = 0.3 or 30% recycled.

(b) Discuss which product has the lowest percentage of recovery and what benefits would be gained from increasing recycling rates of this product.

2 points can be earned—1 point for ID of product and 1 point for correct benefit of recycling

ID OF PRODUCT

According to the table, plastics are being recycled the least (do not need to give %)

BENEFITS OF RECYCLING

- Reduces air and water pollution
- Saves energy
- Reduces demand for mineral resources
- Reduces greenhouse gas emissions
- Reduces solid waste disposal space (landfill space)
- Creates jobs and money

(c) Describe a method of waste disposal for products that enter the municipal waste stream but are not recovered (recycled).

2 points can be earned—1 point for correct waste disposal method and 1 point for description of method

Method	**Description**
Landfill	open dumps: fields or holes in the ground where garbage is deposited; sanitary landfill: wastes are spread out into thin layers, compacted and covered frequently with clay or plastic foams
Incineration	waste is burned in large incinerators—can be used to create energy

(d) From the method of waste disposal you choose in part (c), explain TWO environmental consequences associated with that method.

2 points can be earned—1 point for each correct environmental consequence of method from part (c)

Method	Environmental Consequence
Landfill	air pollution from toxic gases and trucks used to transport and on site
	releases greenhouse gases such as methane and carbon dioxide that contribute to climate change
	toxic waste can enter groundwater supply
Incineration	releases air pollutants such as dioxins
	releases carbon dioxide gas which contributes to climate change
	can produce large amounts of fly ash—even if removed the ash must be landfilled
	can release heavy metals like mercury into the air

2. (a) Other than providing habitat to a wide range of biodiversity, identify and describe TWO ecosystem services that forest provide.

2 points can be earned—1 point for each correctly identified ecosystem service with description

ECOSYSTEM SERVICES

- Support energy flow and the cycling of nutrients (chemical cycles)
- Source of oxygen through photosynthesis
- Help regulate the hydrologic cycle by absorbing and releasing water
- Purification of water (absorbs toxins from soil)
- Stores atmospheric carbon dioxide
- Moderates local and regional climates
- Reduces soil erosion with large root systems and leaf litter protection for topsoil

(b) About half of the wood harvested in tropical regions is utilized as fuel. Explain why this is a necessary resource in these developing countries.

1 point can be earned for a correct explanation of use for fuelwood or charcoal

Fuelwood or charcoal made from wood is utilized in many developing nations as their source of energy to heat their homes and cook their food.

(c) Other than fuelwood resources, discuss why tropical forests are being deforested at such a rapid rate in developing countries.

2 points can be earned—1 point for identifying describing causes of deforestation and 1 point for description

CAUSES OF DEFORESTATION

Cattle ranching – land is cleared to provide space for cattle for increasing meat demands

Roads – roadways are increasing to access the interior of forest resources (logging roads)

Cash crops – increase lands available to produce crops such as sugar cane, cocoa, soybeans

Logging – clearing of trees to sell for building materials

Settler farming – increased population demands more space for people to live and farm

(d) Discuss another method of energy production that could be utilized in tropical regions and why it is a better option over using fuelwood.

3 points can be earned—1 point for identifying another viable energy source, 1 point for describing use and 1 point for advantage over fuelwood

ENERGY SOURCE

Natural gas – can be utilized in stoves for heating and cooking

Solar energy – parabolic dishes and solar ovens can be used for cooking or heating water

Biomass – remains from crops can be used as biofuels

Methane – the natural gas generated from crop and animal waste

Wind energy – wind turbines used to create energy for electric hotplates for cooking food

ADVANTAGES

- Renewable resources that can meet growing population demands without depleting habitat space
- Causes less indoor air pollution than current fuelwood stoves

(e) Describe TWO ways consumers in developed nations can help discourage deforestation of tropical forests.

2 points can be earned—1 point earned for each method described

REDUCING WOOD PRODUCT NEEDS BY

- Recycling paper goods (including cardboard, newspapers)
- Reducing use of paper or lumber products
- Buying and using recycled paper products and goods (paper, napkins, pencils, etc)
- Switching to wood alternatives such as bamboo flooring instead of hardwood flooring
- Utilizing alternative packaging materials such as recycled plastic products
- Only buy lumber from certified sustainable logging companies

3. (a) Scientists have found that colonies of brain coral can grow as large as 1.8 m in size. What is the minimum and maximum amount of years it could have taken this coral to grow?

2 points can be earned—1 point for correct set-up and 1 point for correct answer with units

$$\frac{1.8 \text{ m} \mid 100 \text{ cm}}{1 \text{ m}} = 180 \text{ cm} \quad \frac{180 \text{ cm}}{10 \text{ cm/yr}} = 18 \text{ yrs} \quad \frac{180 \text{ cm}}{0.3 \text{ cm/yr}} = 600 \text{ yrs} = 180 \text{cm}$$

$$= 18 \text{ years to } 600 \text{ years}$$

(b) Explain the relationship between the coral polyp and the zooxanthellae algae.

2 points can be earned—1 point for identifying a mutualistic relationship (or describing that both organisms benefit) and 1 point for describing how each organism benefits

Algae provide coral polyps with chemical energy (food, glycerol, glucose, amino acids) and oxygen from photosynthesis so they can make carbohydrates and proteins. Corals provide the algae with a protected environment and the compounds needed for photosynthesis.

Human Activity	Description	Elaboration
Use of Fossil Fuels	climate change is warming ocean waters carbon dioxide absorption in ocean waters is cause acidification (decreasing pH) rising sea levels	increased temperatures can destroy the symbiotic algae causing coral bleaching rising sea levels kills algae as it reduces sunlight intensity increasing pH dissolves the calcium carbonate test of the corals
Coastal Development	sedimentation into ocean water is decreasing clarity	as clarity of the water decreases so does the sunlight intensity that the symbiotic algae depend on
Fishing practices	trawling vessels scrap nets along ocean bottom	this physically destroys coral reefs which take a long time to grow
Recreation/Tourism	people damage corals when diving	this physically destroys coral reefs which take a long time to grow
CFCs/Ozone loss	increased UV light	increased UV exposure can kill the symbiotic algae in the coral polyps

(c) Identify and describe TWO ecosystem services that coral reefs provide.

2 points can be earned—1 point for each correct ecosystem service with description

Ecosystem Services

- Provide habitat space to a variety of organisms
- Moderate atmospheric temperatures by removing carbon dioxide from the water
- Act as natural barriers against storm damage along coastline
- Reduce erosion caused by waves and storms
- Provide habitat for algae that give off oxygen

(d) Human activities are contributing to the destruction of coral reefs. Discuss a human activity that will further the loss of coral reef ecosystems.

3 points can be earned—1 point for identifying a human activity, 1 point for describing the activity and 1 point for elaborating on how that activity negatively impacts coral reefs

(e) Identify and describe ONE economic or societal benefit that coral reefs provide.

1 point can be earned for identifying a correct economic or societal service and describing the benefit. *Cannot be an environmental benefit.*

Societal/Economic Benefits

- Provides food for fish populations
- Source of potential medicines
- Tourism industry provides jobs
- Fishing industry provides jobs
- Areas of recreation for humans
- Source of building materials in developing countries

4.(a) Identify and describe a type of disease contracted through contaminated drinking water.

2 points can be earned—1 point for correct ID of disease and 1 point for correct description of symptoms

Disease	Description
Typhoid Fever	Diarrhea, severe vomiting, enlarged spleen, inflamed intestine, often fatal if not treated
Cholera	Diarrhea, severe vomiting, dehydration, often fatal if not treated
Bacterial dysentery	Diarrhea; rarely fatal except in infants without proper treatment

Disease	Description
Enteritis	Severe stomach pain; nausea, vomiting; rarely fatal
Hepatitis B	Fever, severe headaches, loss of appetite, abdominal pain, jaundice, enlarged liver, rarely fatal
Amoebic dysentery	Severe diarrhea, headache, abdominal pain, chills, fevers, can lead to death if not treated
Giardiasis	Diarrhea, abdominal cramps, belching, fatigue
Cryptosporidium	Severe diarrhea, and possible death for people with weakened immune systems
Schistosomiasis	Abdominal pain, skin rash, anemia, chronic fatigue, and chronic general ill health

(b) Blue-baby syndrome is a disease contracted through contaminated groundwater resources. Explain what pollutant is responsible for the disease and how it enters the groundwater system.

2 points can be earned—1 for identifying the correct pollutant and **1** point for description of source

Correct pollutant

Blue baby syndrome is caused by high nitrate concentrations in groundwater supplies used as drinking water.

Description of source

Nitrates most commonly enter groundwater supplies by leaching of nitrogen-based fertilizers into soil layers through percolation of water (either from heavy rains or irrigation).

(c) Discuss TWO other sources of groundwater contamination that can lead to infectious disease.

2 points can be earned—1 point for each correct source with description

Sources

- Leaks or runoff from waste lagoons on animal feed lots
- Leaks in buried septic tank systems
- Overflow or discharge of municipal sewage from sewer lines

(d) Describe a water quality test that can be performed to determine the disease potential.

2 points can be earned—1 point for correct water test and 1 point for correct description of test

Water Quality Test

- Fecal coliform test – used to indicate the potential for fecal contamination in water
- Nitrates – tests for excessive levels of nitrates in water from excess fertilizers or animal waste
- Dissolved oxygen – can indicate presence of animal waste which is oxygen demanding

(e) Identify a federal law aimed at protecting drinking water quality and discuss its goals.

2 points can be earned—1 point for correct identification of the law and 1 point for description

Safe Drinking Water Act (1974) – established national drinking water standards, called maximum containment levels, for pollutants that have adverse effects on human health.

Clean Water Act (1972) – established regulations for pollutants entering surface waters including municipal wastewater effluent.

CALCULATING YOUR SCORE

This scoring worksheet is based on the 2008 AP Environmental Science released exam. While the AP grade conversion chart is NOT the same for each testing year, it gives you an approximate breakdown.

SECTION 1: MULTIPLE CHOICE

$$\underline{\hspace{4cm}} \times 0.90 = \underline{\hspace{4cm}}$$

Number Correct (out of 100)   Weighted Section I Score

SECTION II: FREE RESPONSE

Document-Based Question $\dfrac{\underline{\hspace{2cm}}}{\text{Score}} \times 1.50 = \dfrac{\underline{\hspace{2cm}}}{(Do\ not\ round)}$
(out of 10)

Data-Set Question $\dfrac{\underline{\hspace{2cm}}}{\text{Score}} \times 1.50 = \dfrac{\underline{\hspace{2cm}}}{(Do\ not\ round)}$
(out of 10)

Synthesis & Evaluation Question $\dfrac{\underline{\hspace{2cm}}}{\text{Score}} \times 1.50 = \dfrac{\underline{\hspace{2cm}}}{(Do\ not\ round)}$
(out of 10)

Synthesis & Evaluation Question $\dfrac{\underline{\hspace{2cm}}}{\text{Score}} \times 1.50 = \dfrac{\underline{\hspace{2cm}}}{(Do\ not\ round)}$
(out of 10)

$$\text{Sum} = \dfrac{\underline{\hspace{2cm}}}{\substack{\text{Weighted} \\ \text{Section II} \\ \text{Score}}}$$

COMPOSITE SCORE

$$\dfrac{\underline{\hspace{2cm}}}{\substack{\text{Weighted} \\ \text{Section I} \\ \text{Score}}} + \dfrac{\underline{\hspace{2cm}}}{\substack{\text{Weighted} \\ \text{Section II} \\ \text{Score}}} = \dfrac{\underline{\hspace{2cm}}}{\substack{\text{Composite} \\ \text{Score}}}$$

AP GRADE CONVERSION CHART

Composite Score Range	AP Grade
107–150	5
87–106	4
75–86	3
62–74	2
0–61	1

Part II

A Review of AP Environmental Science

1

FUNDAMENTALS OF ENVIRONMENTAL SCIENCE

KEY CONCEPTS

- Resource consumption and sustainability are influenced by poverty and affluence.
- An ecological footprint may be used to compare the sustainability of different lifestyles.
- There are many types of pollution and categories of pollutants.
- Appropriate experimental design is essential for conducting sound scientific investigation.
- The chemistry of several key elements is central to the study of the environment.
- Energy flow, conversions, and degradation are governed by the laws of thermodynamics.
- Environmental systems and feedback can be used to simplify and model complex relationships.

Fundamentals of environmental science are discussed in depth in *Living in the Environment*, 16th ed., Chapters 1 and 2 / 17th ed., Chapters 1 and 2.

KEY VOCABULARY

affluence

Aldo Leopold

anthropogenic

closed system

controlled experiment

dependent variable

developed nations

developing nations

ecological footprint

ecosystem services

61

environmental ethics	output
first law of thermodynamics	per capita
gross domestic product (GDP)	pH
half-life	point source
heat	positive feedback loop
independent variable	poverty
input	power
isolated system	renewable resource
negative feedback loop	second law of thermodynamics
nonpoint source	sustainability
nonrenewable resource	tragedy of the commons
open system	

FUNDAMENTAL PRINCIPLES

This chapter highlights some of the fundamental principles of environmental science that a well-prepared APES student should know. These principles include concepts that usually are introduced early in an APES course, and then are repeated and are expanded upon throughout the course. As such, they are likely to appear more than once on the AP exam.

If you have completed or nearly completed an APES course, you should be familiar with most of the concepts presented in this chapter. If that is not the case, you may find it necessary to refer to your text or the latter chapters of this review guide to obtain some more information.

NATURAL RESOURCES

Anything we use from earth ie coal oil

Anything that humans obtain from nature that is useful or economically valuable is considered a natural resource.

Renewable Resources: Resources that are replenished in a period of time that will allow them to be replenished for human consumption (up to about 100 years). Examples include solar energy, wind energy, timber, water, fertile soil, and fisheries.

We want to switch to renewable sources because non renewable sources will not be sustainable for much longer

Nonrenewable Resources: Resources for which a fixed quantity is available for human use; they are not renewed in a viable period of time for human reuse. Examples include, coal, crude oil, copper, iron, and gold.

SUSTAINABILITY

Sustainability refers to the practice of using a resource at a rate that is less than or equal to the rate at which it is naturally replenished. For example, if the grass in a pasture grows at an average rate of one inch per day and cattle eat the grass at an average rate of less than one inch per day, the pasture is being used sustainably. However, if cattle are eating an average of two inches of grass from the pasture each day, the pasture is being used unsustainably and it will eventually be depleted of grass. Renewable resources can be used sustainably; however, in many cases it takes a conscious effort to do so. Examples of renewable resources that are often depleted due to unsustainable use are timber, fertile soil, and fisheries.

Nonrenewable resources by definition, when used, are always used unsustainably; however, in the case of some metallic mineral resources (e.g., copper, iron, and aluminum), through reuse and recycling practices, they can be depleted at a rate that is slow enough to allow their reserves to last for hundreds of years. In some cases, reuse and recycling of nonrenewable resources is either insufficient or impossible and as a result the resource may be depleted at a rapid rate. Such is the case with crude oil, coal, and uranium.

we have to be careful because even renewable sources take time to be renewed

TRAGEDY OF THE COMMONS

A resource that is free and available to everyone in a population is considered a "common." Examples include publicly owned forests, rangelands, fisheries, open ocean, air, rivers, and aquifers. Commons are vulnerable to depletion or degradation by individuals if they acquire or use more than their share; this occurs when each individual reasons that if he or she doesn't use the resource someone else will, and that that small exploitation is insignificant in comparison to the size of the commons. The result is a degradation of the resource and therein is the "tragedy" of the commons. It is not necessary for individuals to behave immorally or irrationally to degrade a commons. Rather, individuals are behaving rationally and in their own personal best interest when they exploit a common.

remember the fish experiment and think of public places

There are strategies to avoid a tragedy of the commons. Regulations or restrictions placed on the use of the resource can be effective measures for protection. A quota system, as derived for example through fishing licenses or pollution credits, also can be effective when strictly enforced. Another strategy is to privatize a commons, by dividing it up among the population. The rationale is that it is unlikely that individuals will deplete or degrade a resource that they own since they would then bear the entire cost of its overuse.

we must conciously see commons and ensure that we dont degrade them

POVERTY AND AFFLUENCE

Poverty is a significant obstacle to sustainability and environmental protection. Without the means to provide for their daily needs, people living in poverty cannot choose environmental protection over their survival and that of their families.

Affluence is a more significant obstacle to sustainability than poverty. **Affluence** refers to the rapid unsustainable consumption of resources that is associated with the lifestyles of citizens in developed countries. As additional people enter the growing middle classes of developing countries like China and India, the environmental costs of affluence increase.

we are an affluent nation ... we are the problem

DEVELOPED AND DEVELOPING COUNTRIES

Relatively affluent countries that have a high **per capita** (or per person) **gross domestic product (GDP)** are considered to be developed countries. The countries that are considered developed include the United States, Canada, Japan, Australia, and most of Europe. Less affluent countries with lower per capita GDPs are considered developing countries. The countries that are classified as developing include China, India, the countries in Africa, and Southeast Asia. The least developed countries of the world are found in sub-Saharan Africa: countries like Nigeria, Ethiopia, Somalia, and Sudan. Many countries are moderately developed, including China, India, and Brazil.

We create the affluence problem

ECOLOGICAL FOOTPRINT

We did this and found that if everyone lived like us we would need 3 earths to sustain us

An ecological footprint is the amount of biologically productive land and water that is required to provide all of the resources to support the lifestyle of the owner of the footprint, as well as to absorb all of the pollution produced by the processing, manufacturing, use, and disposal of those resources. An ecological footprint can be determined for an individual, a city, a state, or a country, and the per capita ecological footprint of a population is one way to measure a country's affluence. A good way to gain an understanding of the concept of an ecological footprint is to calculate your own ecological footprint at the website, www.myfootprint.org/.

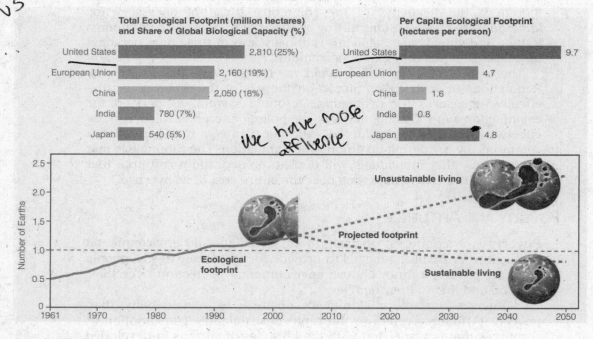

we have more affluence

ECOSYSTEM SERVICES

Nature provides humans with numerous economically valuable services that can be classified as ecosystem services. One example of an ecosystem service is pollination; bees, butterflies, and other insects pollinate agricultural crops. Without pollinators, it would cost farmers billions of dollars to hire the workforce necessary to hand-pollinate their crops, and those costs would be passed along to consumers. Thus, pollination is an ecosystem service, and as a result, any proposed human activity that could be detrimental to the survival of insect pollinators should have the value of their service factored into the decision-making process. Other ecosystem services include water purification and storage, climate regulation, flood control, protection from ultraviolet (UV) radiation, protection from storms, pest control, lumber production, pharmaceutical production, food production, soil formation, nitrogen fixation, and recreational opportunities. The value of all the ecosystem services provided to humanity by nature is estimated to be as high as $30 trillion. When arguing in favor of environmental protection, it is important to consider the economic value of ecosystem services.

ENVIRONMENTAL ETHICS

Aldo Leopold is known for the land ethic, stating that humans are only one member of a complex community and should not abuse nature as if it belongs to them. This is related to the moral argument that all life has a right to exist and no single species can deny that right to another. Some places can be deemed aesthetically, culturally, or spiritually valuable and are protected for those reasons alone. Ecologically, besides the ecosystem services provided for humans, it can be argued that ecosystems have too many complex species interactions to be fully understood and that they should be preserved because no one knows how eliminating one seemingly insignificant piece of nature will affect the entirety of life on earth.

AP Tip

Environmental Science is a topic that is frequently in the news. Students who keep up to date on current events, and who are familiar with the most significant environmental events in recent history, will find that knowledge useful. Using examples from recent events may be appropriate, helpful, and, more important, point-worthy on the APES exam. The AP exam writers also keep up with current events, and often use news stories as a basis for questions. Recent examples include questions about biofuels, methane digesters, electric cars, infectious diseases, and genetically modified crops.

POLLUTION

Pollution refers to the contamination of a resource that decreases its purity and renders it unsafe for human health. There are many different sources and types of pollution. Whenever you are writing an answer to a free-response question regarding pollution, always be specific. On the APES exam there may be many questions for which an understanding of pollution is required. Do not simply write that something "causes pollution"; state that it "causes *air* pollution" or "results in *water* pollution" and whenever possible be even more specific by identifying an actual pollutant; for example, "carbon monoxide is released into the air" or "nitrates run off into local waterways."

be specific

Point source: A source of pollution that introduces pollutants into the environment from a single point or source. Point sources are relatively easy to identify, regulate, and control. Examples include smokestacks, drainpipes, and sewage discharge pipes. A few examples of facilities commonly associated with point sources of pollution are factories, power plants, refineries, and sewage treatment plants.

You can directly point out what caused it

Nonpoint source: A pollution source that introduces pollutants into the environment over a large area rather than at a single point. In comparison to point sources of pollution, nonpoint sources are more challenging to regulate and control. Examples include pesticide and fertilizer runoff from agricultural lands and golf courses; oil runoff from roads and parking lots; sediment pollution and dust from construction sites and strip mining operations; and wind-blown topsoil from agricultural lands.

very hard to say who caused these

EXPERIMENTAL DESIGN

Expect the APES exam to include experimental design and data analysis questions. In order to be prepared for such questions, study the way scientists set up experiments. The most common type of experiment that you will need to analyze or design is the **controlled experiment**. Here are a few tips:

- Don't forget the control! ✓
- Write a testable scientific hypothesis. ✓   *hypothesis*
  - Identify the dependent and the independent variables and predict the relationship.
    - Isolate one variable to measure and one variable to manipulate.
    - The **independent variable** is manipulated during the experiment.
    - The **dependent variable** is measured during the experiment.   *depends on what changed*
    - For example, if you want to design an experiment to determine how soil pollution affects elderberry bushes, first select two variables—one that you can manipulate and one that you can measure. You can manipulate the concentration of a pollutant in the soil; so pick one—for example, salt. Now pick something that you can measure,

dependent V / independent V

like the number of elderberries that are produced by each bush.

- Your hypothesis might then be: Increased salt concentrations in soil result in a decrease in the number of berries produced by elderberry bushes. Or, if you prefer a question: Will increased salt concentrations in soil result in a decrease in the number of berries produced by elderberry bushes?

[handwritten: example experiment setup]

- The hypothesis should include a prediction for both variables. Here are a few bad hypotheses for comparison:
  - Salt affects elderberry bushes. (This is a bad hypothesis because it fails to predict whether an increase or decrease in salt will affect the bushes, and it <u>fails to identify the expected effect</u> on the bushes.)
  - Does soil pollution cause fewer berries on elderberry bushes? (This is a bad hypothesis because it does not identify a specific pollutant.) *[handwritten: lack specifity]*
  - Increased salt concentration in soil affects the berries of elderberry bushes. (This is a bad hypothesis because it does not identify the expected effect on the berries.)

[handwritten: bad hypothesis ∅ do not use]

- <u>Don't forget the control!</u> The control is an exact duplicate of the experiment with no manipulation of the independent variable. In this example, the control could be an elderberry bush grown without the addition of salt.

[handwritten: control]

- Collect and analyze data.
  - Identify the data that must be collected.
  - Be thoughtful about how to graphically present data.
  - It is common practice to plot the dependent variable on the y-axis and the independent variable on the x-axis and then perhaps to sketch in a best-fit line to show the relationship between the two variables.

[handwritten: use graphs]

- Draw conclusions.
  - Use the data to draw conclusions.
  - Determine if the hypothesis is supported by data.
  - Do not draw conclusions that are not supported by data.

[handwritten: make sure data supports conclusions]

- Publicize the results—science is an open process that is carried out in public, and the findings of scientists are available for inspection and scrutiny from both the public and the scientific community.
- <u>Don't forget the control!</u>

CHEMISTRY

The successful completion of a course in which some basic chemistry is taught is recommended as a prerequisite for APES. During the time spent reviewing for the APES exam, it is important to note the important chemistry that is involved in the cycling of nutrients, resource use, and pollution. It is also important to remember that some of the chemicals in our environment are naturally occurring, and some, like chlorofluorocarbons, are **anthropogenic**, or manmade.

[handwritten: anthropomorphic = man like]

[handwritten: Antho = Man]

Review the important chemistry required to understand the concepts in environmental science. The chemistry of carbon, nitrogen, oxygen, phosphorus, and sulfur is most likely to be tested. It is important to know the difference between an element, a compound, an atom, an isotope, and an ion. It is also important also know some chemical nomenclature. Time spent reviewing chemistry will help to avoid confusing nitrogen dioxide (NO_2) with nitrous oxide (N_2O), nitrate (NO_3), nitrite (NO_2), or nitric oxide (NO).

[handwritten: Nomenclature?]
[handwritten: 3]   *[handwritten: 2]*

AP Tip

One way to lose a point in a free-response essay on the APES exam is by contradicting yourself. In an essay, if you need to identify a chemical compound and if you are certain that you know either the formula or the name of a chemical, but not both, write only that of which you are certain. If you write a correct formula with an incorrect name, or vice versa, you risk earning, and then losing a point for contradicting yourself.

[handwritten: do not add info you dont know]

Carbon: The backbone of all organic compounds, which includes all of the important molecules found in living organisms. Fossil fuel use shifts the equilibrium of the global carbon cycle. Carbon dioxide is an important greenhouse gas.

[handwritten: CO2]

Nitrogen: The most abundant element in the earth's atmosphere at 78%. Found in the amino group of every amino acid, the building blocks of proteins, also components of nucleic acids. Nitrogen runoff from agricultural land is an important contributor to nutrient pollution in waterways. Nitrous oxide is an important greenhouse gas.

[handwritten: 1st Abundant and in every amino group]
[handwritten: building blocks of protein]
[handwritten: causes pollution]

Oxygen: The second most abundant element in the atmosphere at 21% and the most abundant element in the earth's crust. Oxygen was not a significant component of the atmosphere when it was formed, but was added later through photosynthesis by green plants, especially cyanobacteria. Oxygen is necessary for cellular respiration.

[handwritten: 2nd]

Phosphorus: A component of nucleic acids and phospholipids. In many ecosystems, phosphorus is the limiting factor for primary production (plant growth). Phosphorus runoff from agricultural land is an important contributor to nutrient pollution in waterways. Phosphorus does not have a significant presence in the earth's atmosphere.

[handwritten: Pollutes waterways]

Sulfur: A component of some amino acids and proteins. Sulfur is a major constituent of volcanic eruptions and a contaminant of coal that contributes to acid rain.

[handwritten: Contributes to acid rain and volcanoes]

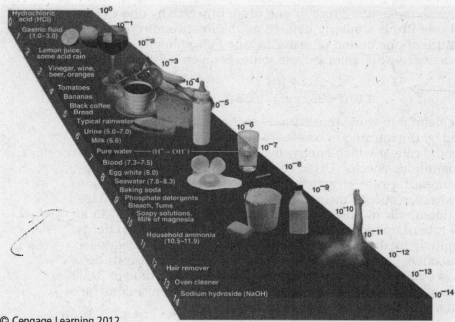

© Cengage Learning 2012

pH

pH is a logarithmic scale covering a range of 0–14 that is used to differentiate between acidic and basic environments. Neutral environments have a pH of approximately 7. A basic solution will have a high pH; for example, household ammonia may have a pH of 10–11. An acidic solution will have a low pH; for example, vinegar may have a pH of 3 and acid rain may have a pH of 4–5. Rainwater naturally has a slightly acidic pH of 5.5–6.0 due to dissolved carbon dioxide from the atmosphere that forms a dilute solution of carbonic acid in raindrops.

RADIOACTIVITY

Radioactive elements decay at a characteristic rate that is typically measured by the **half-life** of a sample. The half-life is the time it takes for one-half of a sample to decay. Half-lives vary from a fraction of a second to billions of years.

ENERGY AND POWER

Energy can take many forms, including mechanical, electrical, chemical, nuclear, solar, thermal, and heat. Physicists refer to energy as "the ability to do work," giving the idea that all energy can somehow be used to move objects or perform mechanical labor. Accordingly, work and energy are measured by the same units. In the metric system, the unit of energy is the joule (J).

Heat is a special form of energy that initially was not recognized as such. The history of heat has left us with different names for its units of measure, namely calories and Btus (British thermal units), but heat is just another form of energy. One calorie is defined as the heat

Neutral = 7
basic = high pH
acidic = low ph

calculated using the half life formula
Ex =

Energy is the ability to do work

required to raise the temperature of one gram of water by one Celsius degree, and one Btu is similarly defined as the heat required to raise the temperature of one pound of water by one Fahrenheit degree. The connection between Btus, calories, and joules is given by:

$$1 \text{ cal} = 4.184 \text{ J}$$
$$1 \text{ Btu} = 252 \text{ cal} = 1055 \text{ J}$$

It may be helpful to know that 1 Btu is approximately the amount of heat released by the burning of one large kitchen match.

Power is the rate at which energy is used, so it is related to but not the same quantity as energy. Using the fueling of a car as an analogy, power measures the rate at which gasoline (energy) is pumped into your tank, whereas energy measures the amount of fuel in your tank. The international unit of power is the watt, which is equivalent to an energy flow rate of one joule per second. To convert power to energy, one must multiply by the time of use. For example, 1 joule = 1 watt-sec. For electrical energy, the commonly accepted unit is the kilowatt-hour (kWh). This is equivalent to 1,000 joules/sec flowing for a time of 3,600 seconds, or a total of 3.6 million joules. Other conversions are illustrated in the practice examples given below.

The first law of thermodynamics, also known as the law of the conservation of energy, establishes that energy cannot be created or destroyed, only converted from one form to another. **The second law of thermodynamics** states that in all energy conversions, some low-quality heat (waste heat) must always be produced. This prevents the reversal of an energy transformation and the construction of any device with 100% efficiency.

Converting from one unit to another requires the correct use of conversion factors. Any conversion factors required on the APES exam will be provided. Common metric prefixes (micro-, milli-, centi-, kilo-, mega-, and giga-) are deemed common knowledge.

micro-	10^{-6} or 1/1,000,000	kilo-	10^{3} or 1,000
milli-	10^{-3} or 1/1,000	mega-	10^{6} or 1,000,000
centi-	10^{-2} or 1/100	giga-	10^{9} or 1/1,000,000,000

PRACTICE

Besides providing some practice with unit conversions, the following problems illustrate some of the possible math skills required on the APES exam. **Calculators are not allowed on the APES exam**, and you must show all of your work, with units, to ensure that you will receive full credit. Accordingly, you should practice working problems including units and get in the habit of showing how the units cancel during the computation. By carrying units along with your work, you often can see whether numbers should be multiplied or divided. Thus, you can save yourself a lot of grief and be sure to get full points on a problem. Moreover, if a problem is properly set up, including units, but the numbers are incorrect, you are more likely to get partial credit than if the reverse is true.

Conversion factors:

1 kilowatt-hour (kWh) = 3400 British thermal units (Btu)
1 kilowatt-hour = 8.6 3 10^5 calories
1 calorie = 4.184 joules
1 barrel = 159 liters = 42 gallons

[handwritten: VI know these]

1. A city that uses ten billion Btus of energy each month is using how many kilowatt-hours of energy?

   Answer:

   [handwritten: $1 \times 10^{10} \times \frac{1}{3.4 \times 10^2} =$]

   $$1 \times 10^{10} \text{ Btu} \times \frac{1 \text{ kWh}}{3.4 \times 10^2 \text{ Btu}} = 2.9 \times 10^6 \text{ kWh}$$

2. One barrel of crude oil provides about six million Btus of energy.

   a. Assuming that all of the energy in the crude oil could be converted to electricity with 100% efficiency, how many kilowatt-hours of energy will one liter of crude oil provide? *[handwritten: How?]*

   b. With the same assumption, how many calories of energy will one gallon of crude oil provide?

   Answer:

   a. $$\frac{6 \times 10^{10} \text{ Btu}}{1 \text{ barrel}} \times \frac{1 \text{ kWh}}{3.4 \times 10^2 \text{ Btu}} \times \frac{1 \text{ barrel}}{1.59 \times 10^2 \text{ Btu}} = 3.75 \times 10^4 \frac{\text{kWh}}{\text{liter}}$$

   b. $$\frac{6 \times 10^{10} \text{ Btu}}{1 \text{ barrel}} \times \frac{8.6 \times 10^6 \text{ calories}}{3.4 \times 10^2 \text{ Btu}} \times \frac{1 \text{ barrel}}{42 \text{ gallons}} = 1.8 \times 10^7 \frac{\text{calories}}{\text{gallon}}$$

   [handwritten: understand conversions and how to get rid of C factors]

3. If one barrel of crude oil provides six million Btus of energy and releases 150 pounds of CO_2 per million Btus of energy, how much CO_2 is produced by each barrel of crude oil?

   Answer:

   $$\frac{6 \text{ million Btu}}{1 \text{ barrel}} \times \frac{150 \text{ lbs CO}_2}{1 \text{ million Btu}} = 900 \frac{\text{lbs CO}_2}{\text{barrel}}$$

SYSTEMS AND FEEDBACK

One approach to environmental science is to consider the earth to be made up of a collection of environmental systems. Each system in turn is a collection of components that all work together to perform a function or a set of functions. Systems may be small or large, from a tiny pool of water to the Mississippi River watershed to the global water cycle, and they can overlap one another. By considering each system individually, the task of evaluating how human activities affect the environment may be simplified. Systems have boundaries and whether materials are exchanged across the boundaries determines the type of system.

[handwritten: digestive respiratory Etc.]

Open System: Systems that exchange both energy and matter across their boundaries. Most environmental systems are open systems.

[handwritten: O = Exchange of E and M]

[handwritten: EX= global water system]

[handwritten: C= Exchange of E but Not M]

[handwritten: No examples]

[handwritten: I = No exchange]

Closed System: Systems that exchange energy but not matter across their boundaries. The global water cycle is one example of a closed system since no matter (water) enters or leaves the system.

Isolated System: Systems that exchange neither energy nor matter across their boundaries. There are no examples of isolated environmental systems.

Since most environmental systems are open, they have both energy and matter crossing their boundaries. The energy and matter that enters a system is **input** while that which leaves the system is **output**. Energy and matter may also be stored and flow within the system.

FEEDBACK LOOPS

[handwritten: Entry = input   exit = output]

[handwritten: 1 C → leads to other e]

When one component of a system is changed it can trigger a series of changes to the system that, in turn, results in further change to that component. When this occurs in a system it is called a feedback loop. There are two types of feedback loops.

Positive feedback loop: When the initial change to a component of the system is amplified by the series of changes within the feedback loop. This amplification may either result in a further increase or decrease in the initial change to the system. This type of feedback destabilizes a system and results in the proverbial "vicious cycle."

[handwritten: a further increase in the direction of the initial change]

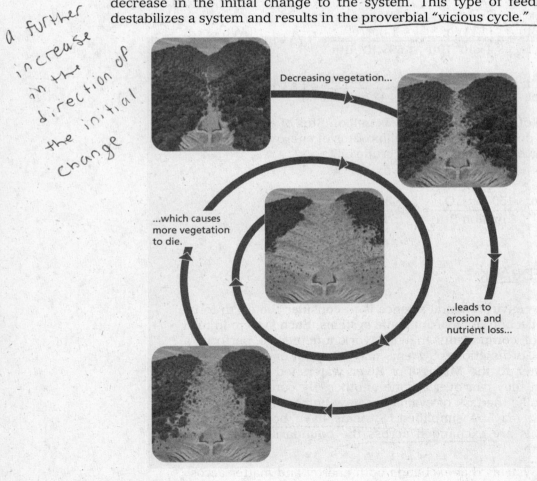

Decreasing vegetation…

…which causes more vegetation to die.

…leads to erosion and nutrient loss…

© Cengage Learning 2012

Negative feedback loop: When the initial change to a component of the system is undone by the series of changes within the feedback loop. The reversal may be an increase in a component of the system followed by a decrease, or vice versa. This type of feedback stabilizes a system and is common in environmental systems.

is always going back towards equilibrium

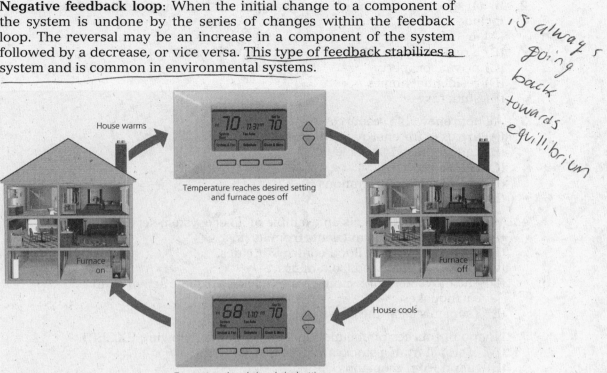

House warms

Temperature reaches desired setting
and furnace goes off

Furnace
on

Furnace
off

House cools

Temperature drops below desired setting
and furnace goes on

© Cengage Learning 2012

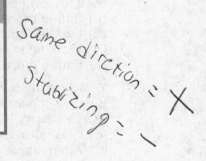

Same direction = X
Stabilizing = ✓

AP Tip

When determining whether a feedback loop is positive or negative, focus on the initial and final states of the system. If the system change is in the same direction as the input it is a positive feedback loop. If the system change is in the opposite direction, it is a negative feedback loop. Don't get hung up in the details.

MULTIPLE-CHOICE QUESTIONS

1. Which of the following data regarding a renewable resource is the most important in determining if the resource is being used sustainably?
    (A) The rate at which the resource is naturally replenished
    (B) The difference between the rate of replenishment and the rate of consumption of the resource
    (C) The demand for the resource by human populations
    (D) The total amount of the resource that is available
    (E) The difference between the total amount of the resource that is available and the demand for the resource.

2. In a tragedy of the commons an example of a "common" could include
   (A) an ocean fishery
   (B) a golf course
   (C) private property
   (D) residential homes
   (E) students

3. All nonrenewable resources
   (A) are used for energy production
   (B) can be reused
   (C) can be recycled
   (D) are considered commons
   (E) are exhaustible

4. Which of the following is an example of an ecosystem service?
   (A) A parasite attains nutrients from its host.
   (B) Wetlands provide flood control for cities.
   (C) Copper is extracted from mines.
   (D) The movement of tectonic plates causes volcanic activity and earthquakes.
   (E) Tsunamis clear the coastland of debris.

5. Nonpoint sources of pollution include all of the following EXCEPT
   (A) overspill from a stockyard
   (B) runoff from croplands
   (C) a smokestack from a power plant
   (D) fertilizer overflow from lawns
   (E) urban runoff from streets

6. Which of the following would decrease one's ecological footprint?
   (A) Traveling by airplane rather than driving
   (B) Eating more meat
   (C) Purchasing a larger home
   (D) Walking to school rather than driving
   (E) Eating more processed and packaged food

7. Which of the following is NOT a basic necessity that a significant number of people living in poverty lack?
   (A) Electricity
   (B) Clean drinking water
   (C) Adequate health care
   (D) Television
   (E) Adequate sanitation

8. One million watts is a _____ watt.
   (A) micro-
   (B) milli-
   (C) kilo-
   (D) mega-
   (E) giga-

9. One millionth of a gram is a _____ gram.
   (A) micro-
   (B) milli-
   (C) kilo-
   (D) mega-
   (E) giga-

10. The "land ethic" is associated with which of the following people?
    (A) Rachel Carson
    (B) Gifford Pinchot
    (C) John Muir
    (D) Aldo Leopold
    (E) Theodore Roosevelt

11. Energy is always conserved. This principle is stated in the
    (A) second law of thermodynamics
    (B) second law of enthalpy
    (C) first law of entropy
    (D) first law of thermodynamics
    (E) third law of thermodynamics

12. Consider the following scenario: The temperature of your skin increases, which leads to an increase in perspiration. Perspiration evaporates from the surface of your skin. The temperature of your skin decreases. This is an example of
    (A) a positive feedback loop
    (B) a negative feedback loop
    (C) synergy
    (D) a closed system
    (E) an open system

13. In any energy transformation, some energy is always degraded to low quality energy. This principle is stated in the
    (A) second law of thermodynamics
    (B) second law of enthalpy
    (C) first law of entropy
    (D) first law of thermodynamics
    (E) third law of thermodynamics

14. The atomic number of oxygen is 8. A neutral oxygen-18 atom is composed of which of the following:
    (A) 8 protons, 10 neutrons, and 10 electrons
    (B) 10 protons, 8 neutrons, and 8 electrons
    (C) 8 protons, 8 neutrons, and 8 electrons
    (D) 8 protons, 10 neutrons, and 8 electrons
    (E) 8 protons, 5 neutrons, and 5 electrons

15. Which of the following is NOT a form of electromagnetic radiation?
    (A) Microwaves
    (B) Ultraviolet light
    (C) Infrared light
    (D) Radio waves
    (E) Sound waves

FREE-RESPONSE QUESTION

[handwritten top right: A. People do not understand the clams use in the ecosystem and they selfishly take whatever they want because no one cares about what happens without clams]

[handwritten left margin: b. They could create a max number of clams that can be taken. They can make clam hunting only legal during some seasons.

i. DDT being dumped into the ocean is creating a decrease in the crab population]

For hundreds of years, clams have been dug up along Fremont Beach for food, first by Native Americans, and these days, by tourists. Today, the clam population is at an all-time low, and many scientists agree that clams will inevitably become extinct in Fremont. Dr. Hwang, a marine biologist, believes that in addition to overharvesting, DDT that was dumped into the ocean during the 1950s and 1960s near Fremont Beach could be another factor in the dramatic decrease in the clam population.

a) Write an argument to explain why the decline in the clam population due to overharvesting could be considered an example of a tragedy of the commons.

b) Discuss two actions that the government could take to prevent further decline of the clam population due to the tragedy of the commons.

[handwritten right margin: Collect ocean samples and test the ddt amounts]

c) Design a controlled experiment to support or refute the claim by Dr. Hwang that DDT played a role in the clam's demise. Include a detailed description of the experiment including:

   i.   a hypothesis

   ii.   the identity of the dependent and independent variables

   iii.   a description of the data to be collected and a description of how controls are to be used in the analysis

ANSWERS

MULTIPLE-CHOICE QUESTIONS

1. **ANSWER: B.** In order to be used sustainably, the difference between the rate of replenishment and the rate of consumption of the resource must be determined. If the rate of replenishment is higher, the resource is being used sustainably; if it is lower, then it is being used unsustainably (*Living in the Environment*, 16th ed., page 12 / 17th ed., page 11).

2. **ANSWER: A.** A common is a resource owned by all. An ocean fishery is an example of such a resource (*Living in the Environment*, 16th ed., pages 12–13 / 17th ed., page 15).

3. **ANSWER: E.** Nonrenewable resources are exhaustible (*Living in the Environment*, 16th ed., pages 13–14 / 17th ed., page 11).

4. **ANSWER: B.** Ecosystem services are economically valuable services provided to humans by nature. Of the five, only "B" meets the criteria of an ecosystem service (*Living in the Environment*, 16th ed., various pages / 17th ed., pages 8–9).

5. **ANSWER: C.** A smokestack from a power plant is a point source of pollution (*Living in the Environment*, 16th ed., page 16 / 17th ed., page 14).

6. **ANSWER: D.** Walking to replace driving will reduce one's consumption of fossil fuels and, as a result, decrease one's ecological footprint (*Living in the Environment*, 16th ed., pages 14–16 / 17th ed., pages 15–16).

7. **ANSWER: D.** Television is not required to meet one's basic needs (*Living in the Environment*, 16th ed., page 18 / 17th ed., page 22).

8. **ANSWER: D.** A megawatt is 106 or 1,000,000 or one million watts (*Living in the Environment*, 16th ed., page S2 / 17th ed., page S2).

9. **ANSWER: A.** A microgram is 1026 or 1/1,000,000 or one millionth of a gram (*Living in the Environment*, 16th ed., page S2 / 17th ed., page S2).

10. **ANSWER: D.** Aldo Leopold, the author of *A Sand County Almanac*, is associated with the land ethic (*Living in the Environment*, 16th ed., page 22 / 17th ed., not included).

11. **ANSWER: D.** This is a statement of the first law of thermodynamics (*Living in the Environment*, 16th ed., page 42 / 17th ed., pages 46–47).

12. **ANSWER: B.** The initial change is a temperature increase and the final change is a temperature decrease. This feedback loop meets the criteria of a negative feedback loop (*Living in the Environment*, 16th ed., pages 44–45 / 17th ed., page 50).

13. **ANSWER: A.** This is a statement of the second law of thermodynamics (*Living in the Environment*, 16th ed., page 43 / 17th ed., page 47).

14. **ANSWER: D.** Because the atomic number is the number of protons, oxygen must have 8 protons. The mass number is given as 18 in the isotopic notation, and since the mass number is the number of protons and neutrons, there must be 10 neutrons. A neutral atom will have an equal number of electrons and protons—8 (*Living in the Environment*, 16th ed., pages 35–36 / 17th ed., page 39).

15. **ANSWER: E.** Sound is a form of kinetic energy associated with the movement of air molecules. It is not a form of electromagnetic radiation (*Living in the Environment*, 16th ed., page 42 / 17th ed., page 44).

FREE-RESPONSE SCORING GUIDELINES

a) Write an argument to explain why the decline in the clam population due to overharvesting could be considered an example of a tragedy of the commons.

3 points can be earned—1 point for each correct statement in support of the premise that the decline in the clam population is the result of a tragedy of the commons.

- The clams are a common natural resource (owned by everyone).
- The small harvest by Native Americans was sustainable.
- Each individual is compelled by human nature to take more than their fair share.
- Individuals do not need to act irrationally or immorally to exploit the resource.
- More people taking more and more clams depletes the clam population faster than it is naturally replenished.
- The clam population will eventually be exhausted.

b) Discuss two actions that the government could take to prevent further decline of the clam population due to the tragedy of the commons.

4 points can be earned—1 point for each correct strategy and 1 point for a correct description.

Strategy	Description
Quotas	Quotas can be established to limit the number of clams that can be harvested.
Fines/Penalties	Laws can mandate fines or penalties that deter individuals from illegally harvesting clams.
Privatization	The beach can be converted to private ownership to provide incentives for the protection of clams by owners who are more likely to maintain healthy clam populations since they alone will bear the financial burden for loss of the clam population.
Create a reserve/national park	By protecting the beach and making it illegal to harvest the clams, the population can be protected.
List the clams on the U.S. endangered species list	The U.S. Endangered Species Act makes it illegal to harm a listed species.

c) Design a controlled experiment to support or refute the claim by Dr. Hwang that DDT has played a role in the clam's demise. Include a detailed description of the experiment including:

   i.   a hypothesis

   ii. the identity of the dependent and independent variables

   iii. a description of the data to be collected and an explanation of how controls are to be used in the analysis

4 points can be earned—1 point for a correct hypothesis, 1 point for correct identification of the independent variable, 1 point for correct identification of the dependent variable, and 1 point for a correct description of the data to be collected and its analysis.

Hypothesis (examples of acceptable hypotheses are listed below)
- An increase in DDT concentrations in ocean water increases clam mortality (the death rate of clams).
- An increase in DDT concentrations in ocean water decreases the size of the clam population.

Note: An acceptable hypothesis lists two variables and the anticipated cause and effect relationship between the two variables (e.g. "an increase/decrease in variable A causes an increase/decrease in variable B"). Vague hypotheses such as "DDT affects clams" or "DDT kills clams" are not acceptable.

Independent Variable – The DDT concentration is the independent variable.

Dependent Variable – The clam mortality, death rate of the clams, or the size of the clam population is the dependent variable.

Data collected – The number of clams that survive or die per unit time (hour, day, week, month, year, etc.).

Controls – A baseline mortality or survivorship rate determined from data collected on clams in a control sample that have not been treated with DDT. These rates are to be compared with those from treated samples.

2

INTRODUCTION TO THE LIVING WORLD

KEY CONCEPTS

- Life is supported by the flow of energy and the cycling of nutrients through the ecosystem.
- Energy flowing through an ecosystem is converted to a less usable form (heat) as it is transferred from one trophic level to the next.
- Populations evolve over time due to genetic variability and natural selection.
- The earth's geologic and climatic activity changes environmental conditions and therefore impacts biodiversity and natural selection.
- Species have evolved to fill specific niches and have developed unique interactions with one another.
- Populations and communities reflect changing environmental conditions.

An introduction to the living world is discussed in depth in *Living in the Environment*, 16th ed., Chapters 3, 4, and 5 / 17th ed., Chapters 3, 4, and 5.

[handwritten margin notes: ∘ life cycles ∘ trophic levels ∘ evolution ∘ climate change]

KEY VOCABULARY

abiotic	chemosynthesis
adaptation	commensalism
assimilation	community
biodiversity	consumers
biomass	decomposers
biotic	detritivore

81

exponential growth

generalist species

geographic isolation

greenhouse effect

indicator species

invasive species

K-selected species

keystone species

logistical growth

mutualism

natural selection

population

primary productivity

primary succession

producers

r-selected species

scavengers

secondary succession

specialist species

transpiration

trophic level

INTRODUCTION TO ECOLOGY

Ecology =
Interdependance
+ interaction
of
organisms

One fascinating aspect of environmental science is understanding the complex relationships and the interdependence of all organisms on the planet. **Ecology** is the study of living organisms and how they interact with one another as well as with the nonliving world. The part of the earth where these organisms interact with one another and the **abiotic** factors (air, water, and soil) in the environment is known as the **biosphere**. All living things are composed of cells which are the basic unit of life. These microscopic compartments, covered with a thin membrane, contain the machinery to support all of life's processes. Organisms can be either single-celled (such as bacteria and most protists) or multicellular (such as fungi, plants, and animals). All cells share some common characteristics such as a cell membranes and DNA. Based on their cellular structure, organisms are classified as either prokaryotes, which have no distinct nucleus or membrane bound organelles, or eukaryotes, which contain both. Bacteria, the oldest known cells, are the single-celled prokaryotes. The remaining kingdoms of life (classification of organisms) all consist of eukaryotic cells that can be either unicellular or multicellular in size. Ecologists work with a hierarchy of life consisting of:

All things have
cells

Pro= No
distinct
organelles,
less complex

Eukarotes =
more complex

Population: a group of individuals of the same species that live in the same place at the same time. *POP = live Same place Same time*

Community: all the populations of different species that live in one place at one time. *Com = all of pop*

Ecosystem: a community interacting with one another and the abiotic factors in their environment. *All = total*

EARTH'S LIFE-SUPPORT SYSTEMS

It is no surprise that living organisms require certain fundamental processes in order to sustain life. What are these processes? There are three basic processes that make it possible for life not only to exist, but to flourish here on earth. These processes are:

A one-way flow of energy from the sun: Energy from the sun arrives at the earth in the form of solar radiation, which is required for life on earth. Approximately half of solar radiation is in the form of visible light. Another 40% arrives as infrared radiation that is largely responsible for planetary heating. Less than 10% is in the form of ultraviolet radiation that promotes molecular reactions in the atmosphere and on earth. Only about 0.1% of all solar energy is captured by primary producers to start the food web. The rest of this energy helps to warm the earth's surface, which in turn generates wind circulation patterns, and also causes the evaporation of water. As solar radiation is utilized, low-quality heat is released into the environment (first and second laws of thermodynamics).

Cycling of nutrients: For the most part, the earth acts as a closed system for matter. Therefore, there is a fixed supply of nutrients on the planet that must continually be recycled to support life.

A consistent force of gravity: Gravity holds our atmosphere close to earth and facilitates the flow of nutrients and water, which are vital to the growth and reproduction of organisms.

The earth has four major systems that regulate and support life in the biosphere—the atmosphere, hydrosphere, geosphere, and biosphere. Examine the figure below.

Handwritten margin notes:
1/2 = V Light
40% = Ired radiation
10% = UV radiation
.1% is captured by primary producers
fixed supply of nutrients that are recycled

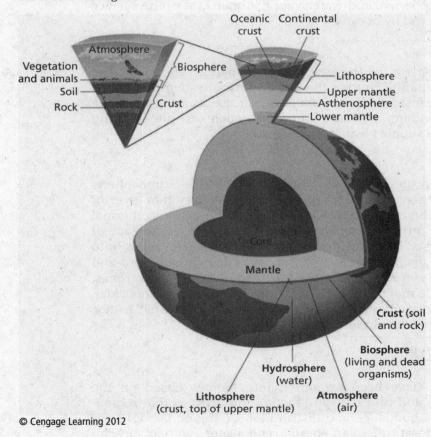

ATMOSPHERE

[handwritten margin note: Nitrogen, oxygen and argon make up the troposphere]

The majority of the atmospheric mass exists within the first two layers extending up from the earth's surface. The **troposphere**, the bottom layer where weather occurs, extends anywhere from 0–17 km above the earth's surface, depending on your location. The troposphere is 78% nitrogen and 21% oxygen. The remaining 1% includes mostly argon gas. However, it also includes our greenhouse gases that are responsible for warming the surface of the earth. These naturally emitted gases include water vapor, carbon dioxide, and methane. These gases absorb the radiation emitted by earth's surface as long wavelength infrared radiation. As those molecules gain kinetic energy and vibrate they release even longer wavelength infrared radiation, which warms the surface of the earth and is known as the **greenhouse effect**. The next layer, the stratosphere, contains our **ozone** (O_3) layer that is responsible for filtering out approximately 95% of the harmful incoming ultraviolet light. The warming and protection these atmospheric layers provide make it possible for life to exist on land and at the surface of the ocean.

[handwritten margin note: Contains protective ozone]

HYDROSPHERE *[handwritten: water]*

[handwritten margin note: 71% of earth is hydrosphere]

Water is a powerful force that is continuously shaping our earth through erosive forces. The hydrosphere consists of all of the water available on the planet. Water is found in many various forms on the planet including liquid (surface and underground), ice (polar ice, permafrost, and icebergs), and water vapor. About 71% of the surface of the earth is covered by oceans.

GEOSPHERE *[handwritten: inner earth]*

[handwritten margin note: inner parts of earth]

The geosphere consists of the earth's crust, mantle, and core. The earth's crust and mantle contain the soil and rock system that house the nonrenewable fossil fuels and minerals we use as natural capital. The soil also contains valuable nutrients, such as nitrates and phosphates, which support living organisms.

BIOSPHERE *[handwritten: life]*

[handwritten margin note: All layers of atmosphere we live in biosphere]

The biosphere includes all of the layers of the atmosphere, hydrosphere, and geosphere where life exists. This very thin layer of life extends from the depths of the oceanic floor where hydrothermal vent communities thrive to approximately 9 km above the surface of the earth. Scientists have divided major terrestrial life zones into **biomes** that have distinct climates that dictate their unique flora and fauna. Aquatic life zones have also been divided into two major zones. These zones include **marine zones**, salt water areas, such as intertidal, coral reefs, open-ocean, and estuarine areas, and **freshwater zones**, such as lakes, rivers, and streams.

ECOSYSTEM STRUCTURE

Earth's life zones have been organized into biomes based on the **abiotic** (nonliving) and **biotic** (living) factors that exist in that region. By examining the abundance and distribution of abiotic factors such as nutrients, temperature, solar energy, and water, we can predict what type of flora and fauna will be successful in that area. This is because each organism can live only within a specific **range of tolerance** for the physical and chemical variations that exist within their environment. The range of tolerance for an organism may vary slightly within the population due to the genetic variability of that species. Most species will have an **optimum range** at which their growth will be maximized. Certain abiotic factors such as water temperature, dissolved oxygen, or salinity for aquatic organisms and solar energy (sunlight), water, and nutrients for plants will influence what the optimum range will be for any given species. Often abiotic factors will limit a population's ability for growth and reproduction. For example, nitrates and phosphates, necessary nutrients for plant growth and development, are often in limited supply in the soil and therefore are **limiting factors** for plant growth in the ecosystem.

ENERGY FLOW IN ECOSYSTEMS

Organisms in the ecosystem are organized into a hierarchy of feeding orders or **trophic levels**. Trophic levels are assigned based on the organism's method for acquiring energy and nutrients from the ecosystem. Simply put, energy passes from one trophic level to the next and organisms are either producing energy for the ecosystem or consuming energy from it.

Producers: These organisms are self-feeders, or often referred to as **primary producers** or **autotrophs**, because they acquire nutrients by converting compounds or energy from their environment. Producers represent the first trophic level in the ecosystem and provide organisms who are consumers with a source of energy. Most of the producers acquire nutrients through the process of **photosynthesis** that converts solar energy into energy-rich carbohydrates for consumers.

$$\text{Photosynthesis: Solar energy} + 6H_2O + 6CO_2 \rightarrow$$
$$C_6H_{12}O_6 \text{ (glucose)} + 6O_2$$

So what types of organisms are involved in photosynthesis? On land the dominant producers are green plants. Since the earth's surface is 71% ocean, phytoplankton (single-celled algae) that float on the surface of the ocean are an important global primary producer. Green plants and algae are also the producers in freshwater ecosystems and along marine coastlines. Believe it or not, there are communities that thrive without the input of the sun's energy. **Hydrothermal vent** communities, found deep on the oceanic floor where no sunlight can penetrate, rely on specialized bacteria as producers. These bacteria convert sulfur compounds, such as hydrogen sulfide, escaping from the vents into organic compounds for consumers through a process known as **chemosynthesis**. The following is reaction is just one basic example of bacterial chemosynthesis.

$$\text{Chemosynthesis:}$$
$$\text{Heat} + 3H_2S + 6CO_2 + 6H_2O \rightarrow C_6H_{12}O_6 \text{ (glucose)} + 3H_2SO_4$$

Handwritten margin notes:
- this has to do with adaptability
- know optimum range
- less energy is given as you get higher less organisms at the top
- mostly plants
- know this well
- No sunlight needed

we are consumers

Consumers: These organisms in the ecosystem cannot produce their own energy and therefore rely on the production from producers. Consumers also referred to as **heterotrophs** ("other-feeders"), obtain their energy by feeding on organisms or their remains. Most consumers rely on the process of **aerobic respiration** to breakdown glucose consumed from other organisms. This process requires oxygen and releases the carbon dioxide that producers depend on. Notice that the reactants in aerobic respiration for consumers are the products from photosynthesis by producers.

$$\text{Aerobic Respiration: } C_6H_{12}O_6 + 6O_2 \rightarrow 6CO_2 + 6H_2O + energy$$

However, many **decomposers** (bacteria and fungi) can breakdown these organic compounds without the use of oxygen in a process known as **anaerobic respiration** or **fermentation**. For example, yeast (single-celled fungi) can produce energy through alcohol fermentation and are currently being used in the biofuels industry.

$$\text{Ethanol Fermentation: } C_6H_{12}O_6 \,(glucose) \rightarrow 2C_2H_5OH \,(ethanol) + 2CO_2$$

They get most energy

Types of consumers are:
- Primary consumers (herbivores): These consumers eat only primary producers. Examples would be rabbits, deer, some insects, and zooplankton in aquatic ecosystems.
- Secondary consumers (carnivores and omnivores): These consumers feed on other consumers for energy. Some rely only on feeding on other heterotrophs and are referred to as carnivores, or meat eaters. Some feed on both consumers and plants and are referred to as omnivores. Examples of carnivores are some birds, frogs, spiders, and fish. Examples of some omnivores are foxes, pigs, and humans.

Tert = top

- Tertiary consumers: These consumers are predators at the top of the food chain and are typically carnivores. They usually have very few natural predators in the ecosystem. Examples would be hawks, killer whales, and wolves.

feed on detritus materials

- Detritivores: These consumers feed on detritus material. Detritus is composed of parts of dead organisms and fragments of waste of living organisms. Examples include earthworms, mites, and some beetles. Larger organisms that feed on carrion, rotting carcasses, are known as **scavengers** and would include organisms like vultures.

break down

D = dead material

- Decomposers: These are bacteria and fungi in the ecosystem that recycle organic material from dead organisms into inorganic nutrients that support the growth and development of primary producers. They speed up decomposition rates by secreting enzymes that help break down the body tissue of organisms.

A Food Chain

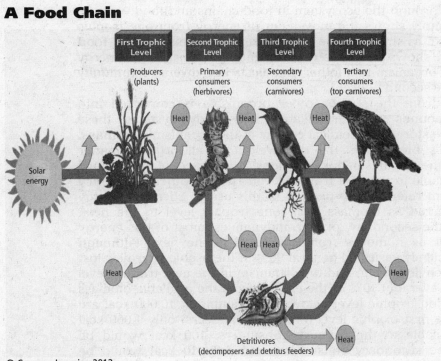

© Cengage Learning 2012

goes in one line

An Oceanic Food Web

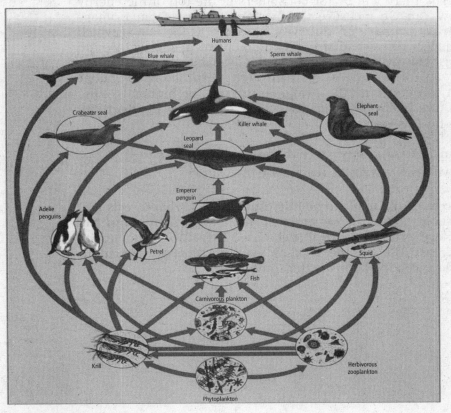

© Cengage Learning 2012

this is interconnected more complex

know the difference

Energy flows through the ecosystem in food chains and food webs. A **food chain** simply shows the movement of energy from one trophic level to the next, as shown in the first figure on the next page. A **food web**, however, shows the more complex interrelationships of energy flow from one organism to another that exists in a diverse community as shown in the second figure.

As energy from the sun or other organisms is converted into organic compounds and assimilated into body systems these compounds are stored as chemical energy in the organism's **biomass.** The organism's biomass is the dry weight of all organic matter contained in the organism and provides a measure of how much energy is available to the next trophic level. The **ecological efficiency** in an ecosystem refers to the percent of this usable chemical energy that is transferred as biomass from one trophic level to the next. According to the second law of thermodynamics, most of this energy is lost as heat as it moves from one level to the next. Although ecological efficiency varies, in general 90% of the usable energy is lost as heat to the environment, and the organism in the next trophic level only gains (on average) 10% of the energy from the available biomass in the supporting trophic level below. For example, if 10,000 kcal are available at the first trophic level (primary producers) only 1,000 kcal would be available to the primary consumers, 100 kcal would be available to the secondary consumers, and only 10 kcal would be available to the tertiary consumers. The rest of the energy is lost to the environment as low-quality heat.

EE = Bio Mass Level to level

Obviously the more energy available at the base of the food chain, the more energy there will be for consumers at the top of the energy pyramid. How can we measure the available energy from primary producers? **Gross primary productivity** is defined as the rate at which primary producers convert solar energy into chemical energy through photosynthesis. However, since some of the available chemical energy available to an organism is lost through respiration, a better measurement to determine the available energy for higher trophic levels in the ecosystem is to measure the **net primary productivity** that accounts for this loss.

Know

> *Net Primary Productivity = Gross Primary Productivity (photosynthesis) – aerobic respiration (by plants)*

Primary productivity tends to be highest in tropical rain forests and in estuarine ecosystems. In general, as you move away from the equator, primary productivity will decrease. Therefore, biodiversity will also decrease due to the lack of available energy needed to support the various populations in the community.

AP Tip

For the AP exam, it will be important that you have a clear understanding of the different roles microbes play in the ecosystem. Much of the earth's diversity we can't even see! These organisms, collectively known as microbes or microorganisms, include bacteria, single-celled protists, and fungi. They provide invaluable ecological services such as decomposing organic waste (fungi and bacteria) to producing much of our atmospheric oxygen (phytoplankton). Although we typically associate bacteria with disease, we actually couldn't survive without them! Millions of bacteria live in and on your body keeping harmful fungal populations in check and regulating your digestive and immune systems. So, let's hear it for the little guys!

LoL

BIOGEOCHEMICAL CYCLES: CYCLING OF MATTER IN THE ECOSYSTEM

CHONPS

Six major elements, carbon, hydrogen, oxygen, nitrogen, phosphorus, and sulfur (C.H.O.N.P.S.), make up the majority of biomass in living organisms. It is important to remember that these elements will continuously cycle through living systems in different forms as biomass is consumed and assimilated, decomposed, or combusted (fossil fuels). For example, the carbon stored in the biomass of a tree can either be consumed and stored as organic compounds in herbivores, recycled by bacteria and fungi, or released as carbon dioxide, carbon monoxide, and hydrocarbons as we burn it for energy (fuelwood).

These vital elements, mostly in molecule or compound form, are persistently cycled through our air, water, soil, and biomass of living organisms by both biological and physical forces. The continuous renewal cycles of these various nutrients for living organisms are known as **biogeochemical cycles.** The major cycles include the carbon cycle, hydrologic cycle, nitrogen cycle, phosphorus cycle, and sulfur cycle. As these nutrients move through the ecosystem they may accumulate in specific locations for longer periods of time. The locations where nutrients collect are known as the **reservoirs** for that particular nutrient and commonly include the atmosphere, water, or soil and rock. Unfortunately, human activities have also altered these natural cycles and these alterations will therefore impact population growth of organisms in communities.

Understand the continuous cycle

HYDROLOGIC CYCLE (WATER)

Water is a critical component to all living things. The water cycle helps to distribute and purify earth's vital quantity of this necessary compound. The dominant reservoirs of water exist as surface water (oceans, lakes, rivers), ground water, atmospheric gas, and polar ice caps and glaciers. The movement of water across the earth's surface has helped to shape and form the topography of the land we see today through erosion. The hydrologic cycle is powered by the energy of the sun, which triggers major processes of **evaporation**, **precipitation**, and **transpiration**. Evaporation changes liquid water into water vapor in the atmosphere. Most of the water vapor in the air from evaporation comes directly from the oceans. The majority of the water that evaporates from terrestrial areas comes from transpiration. Transpiration is a process by which water that is absorbed by plants, usually through the roots, evaporates into the atmosphere from the plant surface. Precipitation of water primarily becomes surface runoff that flows into lakes, rivers, and streams and eventually makes its way back to the oceans. Some surface runoff infiltrates past soil layers into areas of porous rock, sand, or gravel, known as an **aquifers**, where it becomes part of the **groundwater system**.

HUMAN IMPACTS ON THE HYDROLOGIC CYCLE

Withdrawal: We remove large amounts of water for societal and industrial uses, often times faster than natural recharge can replace the water resource.

Increased chance of flooding: By removing large areas of wetlands or creating new non-porous tracts of land (parking lots, roads, buildings) we decrease the earth's natural absorptive abilities and increase erosion and the chance for flooding.

Deforestation: Clearing large amounts of vegetation for urban growth, agriculture, mining, etc., decreases transpiration rates, which can decrease precipitation in some areas as well as reduce infiltration of water into soils. This also increases the chance of flooding as well.

CARBON CYCLE

Carbon is the backbone of the living world as it forms the organic monomers (chemical building blocks) that make up our larger organic macromolecules (polymers). This includes cellular components such as DNA, carbohydrates, proteins, lipids, and other important compounds that sustain life. In the biosphere, carbon is primarily exchanged as a carbon dioxide gas in a cycle between **producers** and **consumers**. Primary producers intake carbon dioxide during photosynthesis in order to produce complex carbohydrates such as glucose, cellulose, and starch. Aerobic respiration by consumers and decomposers then breakdown these carbohydrates and release carbon dioxide back into the atmosphere or aquatic system. Much of our carbon is stored in marine sediments. Carbon is also stored in **fossil fuels** that formed from the deposition of organisms' remains that were exposed to intense heat and pressure over millions of years. Carbon stored in fossil fuels is not released and cycled as carbon dioxide in the atmosphere until it is extracted and burned for energy purposes. The major reservoirs of carbon include:

■ **Oceans:** Oceanic sediments are the largest reservoir of earth's carbon. Like oxygen, carbon dioxide is also dissolved in aquatic ecosystems to support life's processes. Much dissolved carbon dioxide is converted to bicarbonate and carbonate ions. These ions typically combine with calcium to form calcium carbonate, which makes shells of marine organisms and sediments that over time form limestone rock.

■ **Biosphere:** This reservoir includes carbon stored in freshwater systems, soil, and the biomass of living organisms.

■ **Atmosphere:** Carbon dioxide gas makes up only a small portion of the troposphere (0.038%). However, this greenhouse gas acts as a natural thermostat for earth's surface temperature. Terrestrial producers and consumers will regulate the concentration of atmospheric carbon dioxide through photosynthesis and respiration.

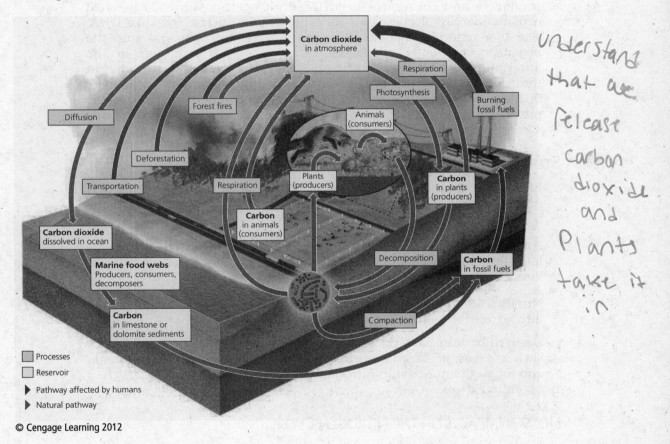

© Cengage Learning 2012

HUMAN IMPACTS ON THE CARBON CYCLE

The major impact we have on the carbon cycle is increasing the carbon dioxide concentration in the atmosphere. This increase in this greenhouse gas is associated with **global climate change**. We mainly increase concentration of CO_2 in two ways:

■ **Burning of fossil fuels:** The burning of coal, oil, and natural gas for electrical, heating, and transportation purposes releases large amounts of carbon in the form of CO_2, that would otherwise be sequestered in the rock layers of the earth.

■ **Clear-cutting:** Removing large tracts of forest, especially in tropical regions, faster than they can grow back decreases the amount of carbon dioxide that is naturally stored in plants through photosynthesis.

NITROGEN CYCLE

LF=
Limits
amounts of
growth
due to
quantity

The nitrogen cycle is one of the most important nutrient cycles in ecosystems, as it is often a limiting factor for primary productivity. The largest reservoir for nitrogen is found in our atmosphere where nitrogen gas (N_2) makes up 78% of the troposphere. Although nitrogen seems plentiful for primary producers, only two forms of nitrogen serve as nutrients, ammonium (NH_4^+) and nitrates (NO_3^-). Primary producers and consumers need these nitrogen compounds to build organic macromolecules such as proteins and nucleic acid, like DNA. The two natural processes that can convert nitrogen gas into the organic compounds producers can use are 1) lightning in the atmosphere and 2) nitrogen-fixing bacteria in the soil, water, and in the roots of some plants. The process by which primary producers take in inorganic nitrogen compounds and consumers take in organic nitrogen compounds and transform them into a part of their own body systems is known as **assimilation**.

?

STEPS OF THE NITROGEN CYCLE

Know
this
cycle

Nitrogen fixation: conversion, by bacteria in the soil and cyanobacteria in aquatic systems, of nitrogen gas (N_2) in the atmosphere into ammonia and ammonium.

$N_2 \longrightarrow A \longrightarrow NO_3^-$

Ammonification: decomposers convert organic remains of organisms into detritus and eventually into inorganic ammonia and ammonium ions.

Nitrification: bacteria convert ammonia or ammonium ions in the soil into nitrate ions (NO_3^-) for plants to uptake.

Denitrification: bacteria primarily in the sediments of aquatic zones such as lakes, oceans, swamps, estuaries, and bogs, convert ammonia and ammonium ions into nitrogen gas (N_2) and nitrous oxide (N_2O), a greenhouse gas.

HUMAN IMPACTS ON THE NITROGEN CYCLE

Cause
cultural
eutrophication

Excess nitrates: nitrates from animal feedlot waste and municipal sewage discharge runs off into nearby waterways. These extra nutrients create anoxic, low dissolved oxygen, conditions in waterways which deplete the aquatic diversity (known as eutrophication).

Burning of fossil fuels: burning of these fuels releases nitric oxide (NO) into the atmosphere where it is converted to nitrogen dioxide (NO_2), a raw material for photochemical smog, and nitric acid (HNO_3), a contributor to acid rain.

Using inorganic fertilizers: by adding large amounts of nitrogen-based inorganic fertilizer to agricultural systems, we increase denitrification by anaerobic bacteria. Through this process the bacteria release the greenhouse gas nitrous oxide (N_2O) into the atmosphere which further exacerbates global climate change.

PHOSPHORUS CYCLE

Unlike other nutrient cycles we have discussed, the phosphorus cycle does not move through the atmosphere. This is because phosphorus does not exist in a gaseous phase on earth. Therefore, the largest reservoir of phosphorus is in oceanic sediments and terrestrial rock layers. Since this cycle depends on the erosion of sediments and rocks to release valuable phosphates (PO_4^{3-}) for producers, phosphate is considered a limiting factor for primary productivity. Phosphate is an important component of DNA, ATP (cellular energy), and the bones and teeth of vertebrates.

[handwritten margin note: Phosphorus is Not in gaseous state in Atm. Ph=LF]

HUMAN IMPACTS ON THE PHOSPHORUS CYCLE

Phosphate run-off: Excess phosphate runs off into nearby waterways from sewage, mining waste, and fertilizers. Like nitrates, these excess phosphates can promote algal growth in aquatic systems, which eventually leads to low levels of oxygen and therefore depletes aquatic diversity (eutrophication).

[handwritten margin note: Causes Eutrophication]

SULFUR CYCLE

[handwritten note: like phosphorus]

The largest reservoir for sulfur exists in oceanic sediments, rock and mineral layers of the earth. Sulfur is emitted into the atmosphere in several ways—volcanic activity releases sulfur dioxide (SO_2), anaerobic bacteria release hydrogen sulfide (H_2S), and oceanic sea spray and forest fires emit particles of ammonium sulfate. Also, certain marine algae release volatile dimethyl sulfide that act as condensation nuclei in the atmosphere and can affect cloud cover, thereby impacting climate.

HUMAN IMPACTS ON THE SULFUR CYCLE

Release of Sulfur Dioxide: SO_2 is added to the atmosphere in several ways. Sulfur is an impurity in coal and petroleum. Therefore, the burning of coal and oil as well as the refinement of petroleum into gasoline are all processes that release the gas into the atmosphere. Once in the atmosphere, sulfur dioxide can form sulfuric acid (H_2SO_4) that contributes to the majority of our acid deposition problems. Sulfur dioxide can be removed before, during, or after the combustion process. This is not true of carbon dioxide gas created during combustion since it is formed from the carbon fuel itself.

ECOSYSTEM DIVERSITY

Now that you understand the basic components of ecosystems and the processes that sustain them, let's explore how the wide diversity of life that exists on earth came to be. Currently, scientists have named approximately 1.8 million different species. **Biodiversity** refers to the variety of species, the genes they contain, and the ecosystems they live in. In general, species diversity is most concentrated around the equator and declines as we move either north or south toward the poles. Why is biodiversity important? Research suggests that ecosystems that are highly diverse are typically more stable and able to withstand environmental change. The variety of life on our planet serves in essential ecological roles as well as provides **natural capital** for humans. The biodiversity of organisms supplies us with food sources, fuelwood, energy, and medicines. Their activity in the ecosystem also provides us with water and air purification services and restores vital nutrients to our soil systems.

How can we measure biodiversity? The **species diversity** of any given area is the number of different species in one area at one time (**species richness**) combined with the relative abundance of individuals within each of those species (**species evenness**).

BIOLOGICAL EVOLUTION BY NATURAL SELECTION

Over the last 3.7 billion years, the dynamic processes on earth have led to a myriad of species that we see today equipped with unique, complex adaptations for survival. Most people are familiar with the idea that mutations, random changes in the DNA of a cell, can occur at any time. Although rare, these small changes have provided the means for the **genetic variability** we see not only between populations in a community but even among individual organisms within a population. The question still remains, how have these small changes in a single organism's DNA led to the abundant amount of biodiversity that exists today? This question was answered by Charles Darwin in his detailed descriptions and published evidence of the concept he termed **natural selection**.

NATURAL SELECTION

According to Charles Darwin and Alfred Wallace, natural selection is a biological mechanism for **evolution**. Some organisms have particular traits, or genes, that give them an increased chance for survival in their environment. Therefore, they will most likely reproduce more often than other organisms lacking these genes and will increase the percent of the population who express this successful trait. For example, any organism that is better suited than others to escape predation or compete for resources such as nutrients is more likely to survive and pass on these successful traits. The genetically inheritable traits that make an organism more likely to survive and reproduce are known as **adaptations**. The ability for these organisms to leave more offspring than other individuals in the population is known as differential reproduction. The change in the genetic make-up of a population over time is referred to as **evolution** (or **biological evolution**).

Typically, natural selection produces small changes in the genetic make-up of a population over time. However, in some cases, these selective forces can lead to an entirely new species (known as **speciation**).

Remember, it is populations that evolve over time by becoming genetically different—not individuals!

How Can Geologic and Climatic Events Impact Natural Selection?

It is important to remember that an organism's traits are only relatively successful. This means, the traits that lead to differential reproduction for that particular organism, may not continue to do so anymore due to environmental changes.

- **Geologic Events**
  - Tectonic activity: Tectonic plates are various portions of the earth's lithosphere that move over time with the flowing mantle that lies underneath. Tectonic activity impacts life in numerous ways.
  - Movement of continents due to plates shifting has either brought populations into new areas in which they can disperse or it has separated populations from one another and they must adapt to their new conditions.
  - Earthquakes and volcanoes have long had an impact on the diversity of life on the planet. These types of geologic activity typically occur along plate boundaries and can separate populations or even eradicate populations as their habitats are destroyed.
- **Climatic Events**
  - Just as the earth's tectonic activity over the last 4.6 billion years has been a dynamic force for life's diversity, so too has climate change. Periods of warming and cooling (ice ages) have shaped earth's ecosystems as long-term climatic events have historically changed sea levels, caused glaciers to form or recede, and shifted locations of biomes. Organisms unable to adapt to changing conditions have become extinct and replaced with organisms better suited for the new environment.

think of rock pocket mice from bio

Pangea "diversity spread"

How do new species arrive from these types of environmental changes? Often geologic and climatic events can physically separate populations for long periods of time. This is known as **geographic isolation**. Since these populations will now be exposed to different environmental pressures, the traits that make one population successful will not necessarily make the other population successful. Over time, these new traits that lead to differential reproduction in each population will become more prevalent (natural selection). Their inability to pass these new traits between the separated populations, or restricted gene flow, is referred to as **reproductive isolation**. Over long periods of time, hundreds to millions of years, these types of

[margin note: Think of the finches on galapogos island]

isolation events can lead to one species evolving into two distinct species and is therefore known as a **speciation** event.

EXTINCTION AND BIODIVERSITY

As these geologic and climatic changes take place, some organisms may not survive through the changing conditions. When an entire species disappears from the earth it is known as **extinction**. Although scientists estimate a generally low level of extinction for much of earth's history, known as **background extinction**, there have been five **mass extinction** events. In a mass extinction large groups of species are wiped out over millions of years. The extinction rate during a mass extinction can vary anywhere between 25–95% of the species on earth being eliminated. It would seem at first that mass extinctions would have a lasting, devastating impact on earth's biodiversity. However, these extinctions open ecological roles, or **niches**, for organisms that were previously filled. A niche is an organism's way of life including everything that would effect its survival and reproduction (such as availability of nutrients and energy, space, temperatures, etc.).

Generalist species have broad niches since they have a variety of food sources and demonstrate a wide range of tolerance for environmental conditions.

[margin note: Specialists specialize and need special specific things]

Specialist species have narrow niches and typically feed on only one food source and most likely tolerate only a narrow range of environmental conditions.

Nonnative organisms can also be a driving force in the extinction of **native species**, or organisms that typically live and flourish in that particular environment. When nonnative species are introduced either intentionally or accidentally to a new environment, they typically do not face as much natural predation or disease and therefore out-compete native species. These types of nonnative species are known as **invasive species** and can have devastating impacts on biological diversity in ecosystems.

[margin note: base species very needed]

Keystone species: Although all species play an integral role in maintaining the integrity of their ecological community, some organisms play a vital role in sustaining the community's habitat and biodiversity. The disappearance of a keystone species has a much larger impact on the community than scientists would predict based on their size and population density. These species can fill a variety of roles in different ecosystems, such as pollinators (bees, bats) or predators (American alligator, sea otter). If a decline or removal of a keystone species occurs, their community will suffer extinctions or major population crashes.

Indicator Species: These species can provide an early warning that damage to a community or an ecosystem is occurring. Indicator species are typically sensitive to change in certain abiotic factors in the environment.

[margin note: Show change / indicate]

Case Study: Where are all the amphibians?

Since amphibians spend part of their life cycle in both water and on land they are often referred to as **indicator species**. Indicator species can serve as an early warning sign to possible damage occurring in the ecosystem. Human activities such as causing habitat loss and increase pollution from pesticides have resulted in a rapid decline in amphibian species (frogs, toads, and salamanders). In a recent assessment, scientists discovered that over 33% of all known amphibians are currently threatened with extinction.

COMMUNITY INTERACTIONS

Remember we discussed earlier how organisms fill a variety of niches in an ecological community. It would make sense that in biologically diverse areas, it is not uncommon for the niches of two species to overlap. The overlap increases competition and can affect the availability of resources, such as food or nutrients, for each species and can therefore limit population growth. This produces five main types of interactions among species: **interspecific competition**, **predation**, **parasitism**, **mutualism**, and **commensalism**. These types of community interactions will impact how successful an organism in a population will be at surviving and reproducing. Therefore the following interactions are also driving forces behind natural selection.

- **Interspecific competition:** The competition between two or more species for the same limited resources in the environment such as food, nutrients, space, sunlight. For example, a thrush and a bluebird both fighting over insects in a tree would be an example of interspecific competition.

  different animals fighting for resource

- **Predation:** When a predator feeds on all or part of another organism known as its prey. Both predators and prey alike have developed unique strategies for survival.
  - **Pursuit and ambush:** Some predators, such as the cheetah, catch their prey through the advantage of speed.
  - **Mimicry:** Some nontoxic prey have gained protection by looking similar to other toxic organisms (e.g., viceroy mimics the toxic monarch butterfly).
  - **Camouflage:** Both predator and prey utilize the added advantage of "blending in." Predators may use this strategy to ambush organisms, where prey may use it to stay out of plain sight.
  - **Chemical warfare:** Many prey species use common strategies of poisons, tasting awful, smelling foul, or irritation (such as a stinging or itching reaction).

  Poisons

Predator and prey interactions can exert strong natural selective forces on one another. The predators will survive based on traits that have made them more successful at catching their prey. In a similar manner, prey will survive based on traits that made them least likely to get eaten. When two species interact in this manner over a long period of time and thereby influence changes in the gene pool of each population, due to natural selection, it is known as **co-evolution**.

■ **Parasitism**: One organism (parasite) gains energy by living on or inside a host organism. Examples of these types of interactions include ticks on mammals or hookworms inside of mammals. Unlike typical predation, parasites are usually much smaller than their hosts and rarely kill them.

only 1 benefits and 1 is hurt

■ **Mutualism**: Two organisms interact in a manner that is a beneficial to both in some way.

both benefit

■ *nutritional mutualism* – birds removing ticks and parasites from the backs of rhinos.

■ *gut inhabitant mutualism* – microorganisms such as bacteria or protozoa that live in the intestines of cows, humans, termites, etc., and secrete enzymes that aid with digestion.

■ **Commensalism**: This interaction benefits one species but has little to no impact on the other. An example would be the Brazilian epiphytic bromeliad. This plant takes root on the trunk of tropical trees in the rainforest. The plant does no harm to the tree but gains a greater access to water, sunlight, and nutrients. Since the tree suffers *no adverse effects* from the presence of the bromeliad, this is an example of commensalism rather than parasitism.

1 benefits No one is hurt

Competition

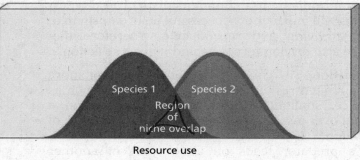

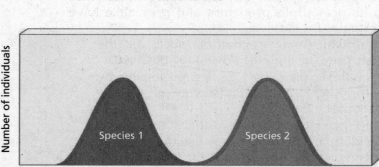

No comp

In the top diagram, species will compete due to nich overlap. However, in the bottom diagram, species niches have narrowed by natural selection and now they no longer compete.

© Cengage Learning 2012

Resource Partitioning: Five species of insect-feeding warblers in Maine spend part of the time feeding only in a distinct portion of the spruce trees.

© Cengage Learning 2012

The concept of the **competitive exclusion principal** states that two species whose niches significantly overlap will both suffer from the limitation of resources. If one species is more successful at acquiring resources, the other species must migrate to a new area, alter niche requirements through adaptation by natural selection, or face a major population decline and possibly extinction. Some organisms alter their niche requirements by utilizing limited resources in different ways, at different times, or in different places. This "sharing" of resources among organisms to reduce competition is known as **resource partitioning**.

ECOLOGICAL SUCCESSION

We know that the physical environment itself is a constantly changing factor for any community or ecosystem. Communities are exposed to unpredictable and sporadic events such as fires, volcanic lava flows, climate change, or habitat loss due to human activities. The gradual change in species abundance and diversity after such events is known as **ecological succession**. There are two types of ecological succession that take place after environmental disturbances. **Primary succession** is the establishment of a biotic community from a previously life-less terrain (or bare rock). Examples of this type of succession would include events such as lava flows that solidify to form new rock or receding glaciers that expose barren rock. A much more common type of succession is **secondary succession** where a disturbance in the ecosystem has damaged or removed part of the established community but leaves in place soil or sediments. Examples of this type of succession would include forest fires, major storms or natural disasters, and human activities such as the clear-cutting of forests.

[handwritten margin notes: Worse one has to leave; Partitioning is sharing; After events; P = from Lifeless]

Primary

Exposed rocks

Lichens and mosses

Small herbs and shrubs

Heath mat

Jack pine, black spruce, and aspen

Balsam fir, paper birch, and white spruce forest community

Time

Secondary

Annual weeds

Perennial weeds and grasses

Shrubs and pine seedings

Young pine forest with developing understory of oak and hickory trees

Mature oak-hickory forest

Time

© Cengage Learning 2012

Obviously Pioneer = first

In both cases, **pioneer species** are the first to move into the ecosystem and begin the colonization process. However, pioneer species will differ in succession events since there is no soil or sediment during primary succession. Over time, pioneer species will be replaced and a series of new species will come about in the ecosystem as it changes from early succession to mid-succession to late succession. The diagrams above give you some idea of what type of organisms would be present in each stage: the first figure shows primary succession; the second figure shows secondary succession.

POPULATION DYNAMICS: WHAT AFFECTS POPULATION GROWTH?

Just like communities, individual populations will also change in response to changing biotic and abiotic conditions in their environment. Populations in communities can change in **size, density** (number of organisms in a given area), **distribution**, or **age structure**. Already in this chapter you've learned the importance of many of the factors that will regulate population size and distribution of species in the ecosystem. These factors will include the availability of nutrients (nitrogen, phosphorus, water, sunlight), abundance of predators or competing species, or human activities.

CHANGING POPULATIONS

Distribution: Populations have various distribution or dispersion patterns within the ecosystem. The three general patterns are **random**, **clumped**, and **uniform**. For most communities, you will find populations living together in clumps or patches. This pattern typically arises as organisms gather around nutrients or resources that may also be in one area or as organisms group together for protection, cooperative hunting, or possible collaborative care of their young. Some organisms may demonstrate a uniform or random distribution pattern but this is rare in most communities.

Clumped is most common due to food in one area

Size: It is easy to determine a population's changing size by simply measuring all the new organisms added to the population, either through birth or immigration, and subtract those organisms that leave the population, either through death or emigration.

> *Change in Population Size:*
> *(N) = (birth + immigration) – (death + emigration)*

Know the equation

Ecologists can also predict whether a population will be growing in size over the next few years by examining the **age structure** of a population. If a majority of individuals within the population are in the **pre-reproductive** or **reproductive** years, the population most likely will increase. In contrast, if a majority of the individuals are in the **post-reproductive** years, than one could predict the population's size will not increase and could potentially decline.

Growth: Populations typically show two types of growth patterns. When populations can grow at their intrinsic rate of increase (r) they will experience **exponential (geometric) growth** since they are not limited by resources and can therefore increase by a fixed rate each year. Or, populations will grow **logistically** whereby after the initial rapid growth the population size will level off due to declining resources or increasing competition. This upper limit for logistic growth is known as the **carrying capacity (K)** for the population and past this point the population will die back. Organisms that are capable of rapid **exponential growth** are typically referred to as **r-selected** species and organisms that are limited by resources and competition are referred to as **K-selected** species.

Eg = only in no limit factors

K = Limited

$$r = Eg$$
$$RTg$$

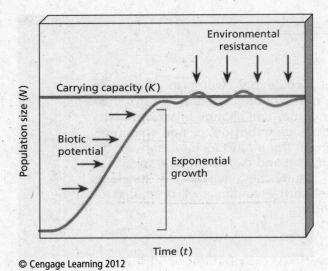

© Cengage Learning 2012

CHARACTERISTICS OF R-SELECTED VERSUS K-SELECTED SPECIES

r-selected species	K-selected species
▪ pioneer species (early successional)	▪ late successional species
▪ have many small offspring	▪ have fewer, larger offspring
▪ come to maturity to reproduce early	▪ later reproductive age
▪ capable of withstanding environmental changing conditions	▪ not capable of withstanding environmental changing conditions
▪ fluctuate wildly above and below carrying capacity	▪ population will stabilize near carrying capacity
▪ adults are typically small in size	▪ adults are typically larger in size
▪ little to no parental care for their offspring	▪ give some type of parental care for offspring
▪ generalists	▪ high ability to compete
▪ low ability to compete	

Know this table

very helpful table

MULTIPLE-CHOICE QUESTIONS

Refer to the following terms for questions 1–3.
(A) Nitrification
(B) Denitrification
(C) Nitrogen fixation
(D) Assimilation
(E) Ammonification

1. Also known as mineralization, this process is carried out by decomposers and returns nutrients in organic matter back to the soil.

2. The process that can release nitrous oxide, a greenhouse gas, into the atmosphere.

3. Plants converting inorganic nitrogen compounds into organic compounds such as amino acids.

4. Coyotes are opportunistic predators that are found throughout most of North America. They typically feed on small mammals, insects, and fruits and vegetables. They are known for their dietary adaptability. The best description of their role in the food web would be
(A) an herbivore that is a generalist
(B) a carnivore that is a tertiary consumer
(C) an omnivore that is a specialist
(D) a primary producer that supports the base of the food chain
(E) an omnivore that is a generalist

5. Which of the following is correct concerning r-selected species characteristics?
    I. Short life spans
    II. Little to no parental care
    III. Produce fewer, larger offspring

    (A) I only
    (B) II only
    (C) III only
    (D) I and II only
    (E) I, II, and III

6. The 10% rule of energy transfer in food chains is due to
(A) first law of conservation of matter
(B) second law of thermodynamics
(C) law of gravity
(D) second law of conservation of matter
(E) competitive exclusion principle

7. Much of the current tropical forest biomes are experiencing a rapid rate of decreasing forest cover due to logging and conversion of forests to agricultural lands. Scientists estimate, if this trend continues, that the loss of forested land would
   (A) increase the concentration of water vapor in the air due to increased transpiration
   (B) cause a decrease in soil erosion in those areas being forested
   (C) increase the amount of biodiversity in that area
   (D) increase the amount of total carbon dioxide in the atmosphere
   (E) decrease the available nitrogen since decomposition rates are greatest in the tropics

8. All of the following gases make a significant contribution to the natural greenhouse effect EXCEPT
   (A) methane
   (B) sulfur dioxide
   (C) water vapor
   (D) carbon dioxide
   (E) nitrous oxide

Questions 9 and 10 refer to the following graph.

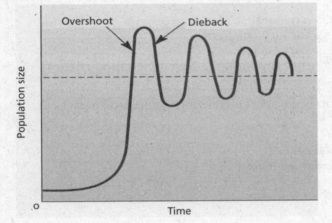

9. The upper growth limit represented by the dashed line in the graph above is known as
   (A) biotic potential
   (B) intrinsic rate of increase
   (C) age structure
   (D) density variable
   (E) carrying capacity

10. The graph above represents the population growth of an herbivore over several generations. Which of the following is most likely a reason for the continuous overshoot and dieback experienced by the population?
   (A) Habitat fragmentation by clear-cutting forests
   (B) Density of population causes vegetation to become limited
   (C) Weather related events that start forest fires
   (D) Hunting by humans during particular seasons
   (E) A change in the climate of the forest ecosystem

11. Many legume plants have specialized fungi, known as mycorrhizae, living in their roots providing inorganic nutrients such as phosphates and nitrates. The fungus gains valuable nutrients from the roots of the plants. This relationship is an example of
    (A) mutualism
    (B) commensalism
    (C) parasitism
    (D) predation
    (E) competition

12. Around hot-water vents deep in the ocean live specialized communities. Bacteria turn hydrogen sulfide into reduced carbon compounds through chemosynthesis. The bacteria then provide food to other life forms. Compared to terrestrial food chains, the bacteria fill the same role as
    (A) heterotrophic, primary consumers
    (B) anaerobic decomposers
    (C) heterotrophic, tertiary consumers
    (D) autotrophic, primary producers
    (E) heterotrophic, secondary consumers

13. The building of a new highway in a heavily forested area separates individuals of a beetle population living in this area. Over time, the population can no longer reproduce with one another and may become two distinct species. The mechanism for speciation in this event is
    (A) mutation
    (B) geographic isolation
    (C) genetic drift
    (D) selective breeding
    (E) gene flow by migration

14. As our global climate becomes warmer, many mountain glaciers are melting. When these ice sheets recede they expose new surface area to become inhabited by organism. Which of the following best represents the organisms' succession on the new rock?
    (A) Lichens → grasses → shrubs → trees
    (B) Mosses → grasses → lichens → trees
    (C) Grasses → trees → mosses → lichens
    (D) Shrubs → grasses → trees → lichens
    (E) Trees → shrubs → grasses → moss

15. On land, water that reaches the atmosphere from the surface of leaves does so through a process known as
    (A) condensation
    (B) evaporation
    (C) precipitation
    (D) sublimation
    (E) transpiration

FREE-RESPONSE QUESTION

Yellowstone Park's Grey Wolf

Over the last few decades, scientists have come to realize the importance of top-down control of the ecosystem by tertiary predators. An example of this was seen with the removal of the grey wolves from Yellowstone National Park. Many local ranchers encouraged this removal of the predator, as they were starting to feed on their livestock. After the wolves were removed in the 1920s, many organisms in the Yellowstone ecosystem started to suffer. Naturally, wolves feed on the local elk population. Elk typically feed on the aspen trees that were abundant in Yellowstone prior to the wolves being removed. Other organisms also benefit from the wolves, such as ravens and coyotes that often get the wolves' "leftovers" from an elk kill. Wolves were reintroduced to the park in 1995. In 2008, the grey wolf was removed from the endangered species list.

(a) Diagram a natural food web that could exist in Yellowstone Park based on information provided in the article.

(b) Describe TWO environmental problems that could be associated with the removal of grey wolves from Yellowstone National Park.

(c) Discuss a possible societal or economic concern that could arise from reintroducing wolves back into the area.

(d) Besides human interaction, describe TWO other environmental factors that could regulate the wolf population in the park.

(e) Identify and describe one law or treaty currently in place to protect endangered terrestrial organisms

ANSWERS

MULTIPLE-CHOICE QUESTIONS

1. ANSWER: E. Ammonification occurs when decomposing bacteria, and sometimes fungi, convert detritus material into simpler, inorganic nitrogen compounds such as ammonia (NH_3) and ammonium ions (NH_4^+) that plants can absorb (*Living in the Environment*, 16th ed., pages 68–69 / 17th ed., pages 71–72).

2. ANSWER: B. Through the process of denitrification, bacteria in water-logged sediments (lakes, estuaries, bogs, wetlands) convert ammonia and ammonium ions into nitrogen gas (N_2) and nitrous oxide (N_2O) (*Living in the Environment*, 16th ed., pages 68–69 / 17th ed., pages 71–72).

3. ANSWER: D. In assimilation, plants take up inorganic nitrogen compounds, such as nitrates and ammonium ions, and convert

them to organic compounds such as amino acids (*Living in the Environment*, 16th ed., pages 68–69 / 17th ed., pages 71–72).

4. **Answer: E.** Since the coyote eats both meat and vegetation he is considered a consumer that is an omnivore (*Living in the Environment*, 16th ed., page 59). However, since his niche includes a wide variety of food sources he is considered to be a generalist (*Living in the Environment*, 16th ed., page 59 / 17th ed., page 60).

5. **Answer: D.** r–selected species would be organisms such as weeds or cockroaches. These organisms typically exhibit exponential growth, are smaller in size, have short life spans, and give little to no parental care to their offspring (*Living in the Environment*, 16th ed., page 168 / 17th ed., pages 88, 117).

6. **Answer: B.** Only 10% of the energy stored in an organism moves on to the next trophic level because 90% of the energy is lost as heat. This is due to the second law of thermodynamics that states that as energy is converted to useful work much of the energy is lost to the environment as low quality energy (heat) (*Living in the Environment*, 16th ed., page 62 / 17th ed., pages 63–64).

7. **Answer: D.** Since trees are primary producers, they take in large quantities of carbon dioxide so that they can photosynthesize. If large tracts of trees are being removed, through clear-cutting or deforestation, then more carbon dioxide will be in the atmosphere due to reduced photosynthesis rates (*Living in the Environment*, 16th ed., page 67 / 17th ed., pages 70–71).

8. **Answer: B.** Although sulfur dioxide is an infrared active molecule, it is not generally considered to be a significant contributor to the greenhouse effect because of its short lifetime in the atmosphere. SO_2 converts quickly to SO_3 and then to H_2SO_4, which contributes to acid rain but not to climate change (*Living in the Environment*, 16th ed., page 144 / 17th ed., page 151).

9. **Answer: E.** The upper limit of a population is referred to as carrying capacity (K). This is the maximum population of a particular species that a given habitat can support over a given period of time (*Living in the Environment*, 16th ed., pages 110, 113 / 17th ed., page 114).

10. **Answer: B.** Organisms that exhibit logistic growth will most likely be limited by density-dependent factors in their environment. One such factor would be a lack of food sources as the population density gets too high. Other factors could include an increase in disease or competition for resources as population density increases over time (*Living in the Environment*, 16th ed., pages 110, 113 / 17th ed., page 117).

Understand explanations

know the why

11. ANSWER: A. Mutualism is a relationship where both organisms benefit in some way. In this example the fungus feeds off of sugars produced by the plant and the plant gains valuable inorganic nutrients, such as nitrates or phosphates, from the fungus (*Living in the Environment*, 16th ed., pages 101, 106 / 17th ed., page 110).

12. ANSWER: D. Hydrothermal vent systems exist so deep in the ocean that no sunlight can reach them. Therefore they rely on the chemosynthetic bacteria to begin the food chain by converting sulfur compounds into reduced carbon compounds to serve as nutrients to other organisms in this ecosystem. In terrestrial ecosystems, plants begin the food chain by converting sunlight into reduced carbon compounds (sugars) that serve as nutrients to other organisms (*Living in the Environment*, 16th ed., page 59 / 17th ed., pages 59–60).

13. ANSWER: B. The road serves as a barrier to the divided beetle population. Reproductive isolation will occur due to the inability for gene flow between the two groups. This type of geographic isolation can lead to a speciation event over time as the populations will be exposed to different pressures in their environments (*Living in the Environment*, 16th ed., page 86 / 17th ed., page 91).

14. ANSWER: A. Glaciers receding and exposing new rock is an example of primary succession since no prior ecosystem has inhabited this area. The first organisms to colonize an area in primary succession are pioneer species such as lichen or moss. They are followed by mid-successional species such as grasses and shrubs and eventually followed by trees in late succession (*Living in the Environment*, 16th ed., pages 116–117 / 17th ed., page 119).

15. ANSWER: E. Transpiration is the process by which plants lose water to the surrounding environment from openings in their leaves known as stomata (*Living in the Environment*, 16th ed., page 65 / 17th ed., page 67).

FREE-RESPONSE SCORING GUIDELINES

(a) Diagram a natural food web that could exist in Yellowstone Park based on information provided in the article.

2 points can be earned – 1 point is earned for correctly identifying all 5 organisms—grey wolf, elk, aspen, ravens, and coyote and 1 point is earned for correctly linking organism in a food web (with arrows in correct direction of flow of energy)

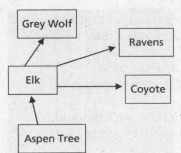

(b) Describe TWO environmental problems that could be associated with the removal of grey wolves from Yellowstone National Park.

2 points can be earned – 1 point for each correctly explained environmental issue
- overgrazing by an abundant elk population not being kept in check by wolves
- loss of aspen trees due to overgrazing could deplete food supply for other herbivores and insect species
- loss of vegetation by overgrazing elk could further erosion in the area
- decline in scavenger population who depend on wolf kills, such as ravens and coyotes
- removal of aspens, which are more fire resistant, may allow the growth of other smaller nonresistant trees that will spread forest fires more easily

(c) Discuss a possible societal or economic concern that could arise from reintroducing wolves back into the area.

2 points can be earned – 1 point for correctly identifying a societal or economic concern and 1 point for elaborating on the concern
- possible loss of income for ranchers due to wolves preying on livestock (sheep)
- potential human injury risk as the wolf population rises
- increase in spending by state or federal government to track and monitor wolf populations (example DNR or Park Service)
- loss of human food sources if wolves are feeding on livestock
- possible loss of property value in areas located near the park

(d) Besides human interaction, describe TWO other environmental factors that could regulate the wolf population in the park.

2 points can be earned – 1 point for each correct description of a population control
- weather-related events such as violent storms sparking forest fires

100% ever

- as wolf population density increases, competition for prey will also increase; therefore food source may be a limiting factor
- possible spread of disease through the wolf pack
- natural competition for resources with other species in the area, such as bears
- drought could limit the aspen population, which could reduce the elk population and therefore prey supply for the wolf

(e) Identify and describe one law or treaty currently in place to protect endangered terrestrial organisms.

2 points can be earned – 1 point for correctly identifying the law or treaty and 1 point for a correct description of the law

Endangered Species Act – Designed to identify and protect endangered species in the United States by making it illegal to hunt, kill, collect, or injure any endangered species. It also prohibits federal funds for projects that will damage the habitat of an endangered species.

CITES (Convention on International Trade in Endangered Species) – This international treaty bans the hunting, capturing, selling, or collecting of any threatened or endangered species.

good use of laws

BIODIVERSITY AND CONSERVATION

KEY CONCEPTS

- Factors such as the earth's rotation, atmospheric and ocean movements, and topographic features influence climate and global distribution of biomes.
- Abiotic factors such as dissolved oxygen, sunlight, salinity, and nutrients needed for photosynthesis, as well as temperature, regulate biodiversity in aquatic ecosystems.
- Terrestrial ecosystems provide vital ecological services such as providing oxygen, storing atmospheric carbon dioxide, filtering water, reducing soil erosion, influencing climate, absorbing and releasing water, and providing habitat space for numerous organisms.
- Coastal zones provide vital ecosystem services including nutrient cycling, moderate climate, absorbing carbon dioxide, providing habitats and nursery areas for many organisms, and reducing the impacts of storm surges.
- Both terrestrial and aquatic ecosystems provide humans with vital economic resources such as food resources, energy resources, medicines, building materials, and areas for recreation.
- The increasing human population is stressing our global ecosystems and depleting biodiversity by creating habitat loss, habitat fragmentation, introducing invasive species, pollution, and causing climate change.
- Current practices that sustain human activities need to be modified so that biodiversity in both terrestrial and aquatic ecosystems can be preserved.

Biodiversity and conservation are discussed in depth in *Living in the Environment,* Chapters 7–11, in both the 16th and 17th editions.

Key Vocabulary

def'nd through chapter

abyssal	mass extinction
background extinction	nekton
bathyl	old-growth forests
benthos	oligotrophic
clear-cutting	pastures
climate	permafrost
Coriolis effect	plankton
cultural eutrophication	prevailing winds
currents	rain shadow effect
dissolved oxygen	rangelands
El Niño	riparian zones
endangered species	runoff
estuaries	second growth forests
euphotic	selective cutting
eutrophic	source zone
greenhouse effect	strip cutting
habitat fragmentation	thermocline
inland wetlands	threatened species
intertidal zone	transition zone
La Niña	turbidity
limnetic	upwelling
littoral	watershed
marine vs. freshwater biomes	weather

WEATHER AND CLIMATE: AN INTRODUCTION

Understanding the factors that influence climate is an integral piece in gaining insight into what dictates terrestrial biodiversity. It is not random or haphazard placement that has led to the global distribution of biomes. Rather it is differences in climatic patterns such as temperature and precipitation that led to the formation of these terrestrial ecosystems such as deserts, grasslands, and forests.

FACTORS THAT INFLUENCE CLIMATE

What is the difference between weather and climate? The **climate of** an ecosystem is that area's general pattern of atmospheric or weather conditions over long periods of time (decades to thousands of years). In contrast, **weather** is the local area's short-term temperature, precipitation, humidity, and other physical conditions of the troposphere measured over hours or days. Terrestrial climates vary across the earth due to patterns in global air circulation and ocean currents that unevenly distribute heat and precipitation. Three main factors affect how heat and moisture from the equator (tropics) are distributed by air circulation patterns to other parts of the earth's surface.

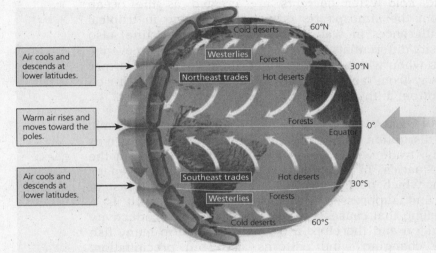

© Cengage Learning 2012

1. **Properties of air, water, and land**: Solar energy creates continuous evaporation from ocean water, especially at the equator, thereby transferring heat from the oceans to the atmosphere. This creates cyclical convection cells that circulate air, heat, and moisture across the surface of the earth.

2. **Uneven heating of the earth's surface**: Since the shape of the earth is a sphere, solar radiation is not equally distributed across its surface. Sunlight is much more concentrated at the equator where the radiation is more direct, unlike the poles where the radiation enters at an angle and spreads out over a greater surface area. This helps explain why tropical regions along the equator are hot and arctic regions at the poles are cold. The differences in heating from the equator to the poles help create our global wind patterns.

3. **Rotation of the earth on its axis**: As the earth rotates on its axis, heated air masses begin rising above the equator and are deflected to the west or east over different parts of the planet's surface. As you can see in the diagram below, large regions of convection **cells** are created as warm, moist air rises and cools, and the resulting cooler, drier air begins to sink. This helps create our global

[handwritten margin notes:] Climate = long; weather = short; think: when talking do u ask how or weather; you ask weather because it is daily and short term

prevailing wind patterns that distribute heat and moisture in the atmosphere. Due to the **Coriolis effect**, the earth's rotation causes winds to be deflected to the right (clockwise) in the northern hemisphere and to the left (counterclockwise) in the southern hemisphere.

ATMOSPHERE AND OCEAN: INTERACTIONS THAT INFLUENCE CLIMATE

The atmosphere and the ocean are strongly linked as they impact one another. The heat from the ocean impacts atmospheric circulation just as atmospheric winds affect ocean currents. Prevailing winds and the rotation of the earth produce the earth's major oceanic **currents**. Warm-water and cold-water currents are created as the ocean absorbs heat from the atmosphere, primarily occurring in tropical waters. These differences in water temperature (**thermocline**) also create water density differentials that can fuel ocean **upwelling** events. Upwelling occurs when winds blowing along the coast push warmer surface water away from land and draw up deep cold, nutrient-rich water from the bottom to the top.

EL NIÑO – SOUTHERN OSCILLATION (ENSO) Every few years in the Pacific Ocean, there is a disruption of the ocean-atmosphere system known as El Niño. Typically, trade winds push warmer water away from the coast of South America. In El Niño years, trade winds weaken or reverse direction, which pushes warmer water toward the coast of South America and suppresses the thermocline. The result is a decrease in upwelling that causes a reduction in primary productivity by the phytoplankton and therefore a dramatic decline in many fish populations. The changing wind patterns also shift precipitation, causing flooding in some areas, such as Peru, and bringing drought to other areas, such as Brazil and parts of Indonesia. La Niña, which typically follows an El Niño, cools coastal surface water and restores upwelling events. La Niña, in general, has the opposite effects on the ocean-atmosphere system than El Niño. However, it can mean more Atlantic coast hurricanes as well as colder winters in the northeastern United States but warmer, drier winters in the southeastern United States.

RAIN SHADOW EFFECT Large bodies of water can create land and sea breezes because water absorbs and releases heat more slowly than land. Large topographic features also have major impacts on climate as well. As prevailing winds pick up moisture from the ocean and move across land, the moving air mass is forced upward over mountains. As this air mass rises it will cool and release much of its moisture as rain and snow on the windward side of the mountain. On the leeward side the descending air is therefore drier. As this air descends, it warms and picks up moisture from the landscape below, thereby leading to arid and semi-arid conditions on this side of the mountain. This is known as the **rain shadow effect**.

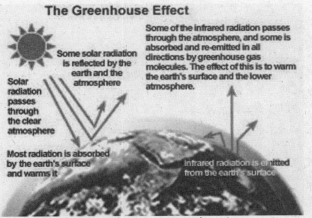

The Greenhouse Effect

Some solar radiation is reflected by the earth and the atmosphere

Solar radiation passes through the clear atmosphere

Most radiation is absorbed by the earth's surface and warms it

Some of the infrared radiation passes through the atmosphere, and some is absorbed and re-emitted in all directions by greenhouse gas molecules. The effect of this is to warm the earth's surface and the lower atmosphere.

Infrared radiation is emitted from the earth's surface

http://www.epa.gov/climatechange/images/greenhouse.jpg

THE GREENHOUSE EFFECT   The earth's climate has greatly fluctuated over the last 5 billion years from ice age events to long periods of warming. However, our climate has been relatively stable over the last 2,000 years. According to the EPA, our current global average temperature is approximately 15°C (59°F), but without an atmosphere the average temperature would be only –18°C (0°F). The difference between the natural atmospheric temperature and the temperature we actually experience is accounted for by the warming properties of the earth's atmosphere known as the **greenhouse effect.** Primarily only four naturally produced gases—water vapor, methane, carbon dioxide, and nitrous oxide—help influence the earth's average temperature by significantly contributing to the greenhouse effect. These gases allow incoming, shorter-wavelength UV radiation through the atmosphere but trap outgoing longer-wavelength infrared radiation (heat) being emitted from the earth's surface. They emit even longer infrared radiation (heat) back into the troposphere thereby warming the lower atmosphere. Without these greenhouse gases our planet would be too cold for most living organisms to survive.

[handwritten margin notes: we cause the gh effect; water vapor, nitrous oxide, methane, CD; heat is added]

EARTH'S BIOMES: TERRESTRIAL DIVERSITY

Biomes are large terrestrial regions characterized by similar climate, soil, plants, and animals regardless of their global locations. Differences in average annual rainfall (precipitation) and temperature help us predict what type of desert, grassland, or forest biome we would see in a given geographical region.

Types of Forest Biomes: Our three main types of forest biomes, tropical, temperate, and taiga, are all dominated by trees. Forests, when compared to other biomes, are areas of high productivity and biodiversity.

[handwritten margin notes: 3 types; high pp + biod]

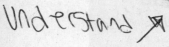

© Cengage Learning 2012

Understand the structure well (handwritten)

More moist (handwritten)

Major Types of Grasslands: Grasslands exists in areas where there is too much moisture for desert biomes and too little moisture for forest biomes. Grassland ecosystems are regulated by seasonal drought, occasional fires, and the grazing of herbivores. Typically grasslands are found in the interior of continents. Low average precipitation and various average temperatures produce tropical, temperate, and cold grasslands.

Major Types of Deserts: Desert ecosystems occur in continental interiors where little precipitation is often distributed unevenly throughout the year. This also occurs on the leeward side of large mountain ranges (rain shadow effect). These biomes experience intense heat and evaporation during the day and cooler nights due to rapid heat loss from the little vegetation available to help radiate the heat more slowly.

Ch = CA (handwritten)

The Chaparral (Temperate Shrubland): The chaparral biome, also known as a temperate shrubland, is found along the coastal areas of southern California, parts of the Mediterranean, and central Chile. This area is characterized by low-growing evergreen shrubs and occasional small trees. Like grassland ecosystems, plants here are adapted to occasional fires, which encourage seed production in many plant species. Fires can also increase nutrient availability in the soils depending on intensity and duration of the burn.

Type of Forest	Locations	Characteristics
Tropical Rain Forests	Typically found along the equator but also found from the equator to 30°N and 30°S Brazil, Central America, Indonesia, Central Africa	■ year-round consistently warm temperatures, high humidity, and heavy rainfall ■ dominated by broadleaf evergreen plants ■ high primary productivity and biodiversity ■ distinct strata (zones) such as canopy, emergent, sapling, and ground, provide habitat space for the abundance of life ■ poor soil quality due to low concentrations of stored nutrients
Temperate Deciduous Forests	Found between 30° and 60° north and south latitudes Eastern United States, most of Europe	■ moderate temperatures that fluctuate with seasons ■ dominated by a few species of broadleaf deciduous trees such as maple, beech, oak, and hickory ■ trees go dormant in winter by dropping their leaves in the fall ■ slow rate of decomposition of leaves provides abundant leaf litter and nutrients stored in the soil
Taigas (Boreal Forests)	Found just south of the arctic tundra in northern regions of North America (Canada), Asia, and Europe	■ winters are long, dry, and extremely cold ■ dominated by a few species of conifers such as pine, hemlock, cedar, and spruce ■ trees have small, waxy, needleshaped leaves to survive the cold winters ■ plant diversity is low ■ slow decomposition of needles; nutrient poor, acidic soils

Ecological Roles of Mountains: Although mountain ranges are not classified as one of our major biomes, they have dramatic impacts on our ecosystems by

■ often providing habitat for many endemic species that are found no where else in the world
■ helping to regulate earth's climate due to snow and ice reflecting solar radiation back into space
■ melting mountain-top snowpack each spring and summer, providing surface water in streams for use by animals

[handwritten margin note: All warm dry]

[handwritten margin note: Know all biomes what lives there]

Type of Grassland	Locations	Characteristics
Tropical Grassland (Savannas)	Largely found in Eastern Africa and also parts of South America and Australia	▪ warm temperatures and alternating warm and dry seasons (will experience several months of little/no rainfall) ▪ large grazing herbivores such as gazelles, zebras, wildebeests ▪ plants have deep roots to utilize groundwater supplies
Temperate Grasslands (tall-grass and short-grass prairies)	Found in Midwestern and western United States and Canada; also found in parts of South America and Russia	▪ rainfall determines whether it is a tall-grass or a short-grass prairie (tall-grass prairies receive almost three times as much rain as short-grass) ▪ winters are cold, summers are hot and dry ▪ as grasses die and decompose annually, large amounts of organic matter accumulates in the soil, making this area highly productive for crops ▪ high winds and rapid evaporation promote fires in the summer and fall that eliminate other competing species
Cold Grasslands (arctic tundra)	Found just south of the arctic tundra in northern regions of North America (Canada), Asia, and Europe	▪ frigid, treeless plains that are covered with snow and ice much of the year ▪ extreme cold forms **permafrost**—underground soil in which captured water stays frozen for more than two consecutive years ▪ vegetation is limited to low-growing grasses, moss, and lichen ▪ animals, such as arctic foxes and wolves, have adaptations such as thick coats of fur to survive the harsh climate

Type of Desert	Locations	Characteristics
Tropical Deserts	Cover much of northern Africa (the Sahara), and parts of the middle east (Saudi Arabia)	▪ surface areas have little vegetation and are dominated by rocks and sand that are often blown about by frequent windstorms ▪ extremely high daytime temperatures
Temperate Deserts	Found in the southwestern United States (Mojave and Sonoran deserts)	▪ receive more precipitation than tropical deserts ▪ characterized by patchy drought-resistant shrubs, cacti, and other succulents ▪ have high daytime and low nighttime temperatures
Cold Deserts	Areas of the United States known as the Great Basin (Idaho, Utah); Gobi desert in northern China and southern Mongolia	▪ vegetation is very sparse ▪ winters are extremely cold

AQUATIC LIFE ZONES

Approximately 71% of the earth's surface is covered with saltwater. We divide the saltwater realm into four areas known as the Atlantic, Pacific, Indian, and Arctic oceans. Some basic abiotic factors help influence the presence of life in aquatic systems. These factors include sunlight, dissolved oxygen, and how clear the water is. **Turbidity** is the measure of how cloudy the water is due to suspended sediments or solids and greatly reduces sunlight from reaching photosynthetic organisms. **Salinity**, the concentration of dissolved salts in a given volume of water, also regulates aquatic life. Aquatic ecosystems are therefore divided into two life zones—freshwater and marine.

OCEANS AS NATURAL CAPITAL

The ocean provides us with many vital ecological benefits. We also harvest and utilize the vast resources present in the ocean, providing humans with numerous economic benefits.

ECOLOGICAL BENEFITS
▪ provides habitats and nursery areas
▪ moderates climate
▪ absorbs CO_2
▪ reduces storm impact (estuaries, mangroves)

ECONOMIC BENEFITS
- food resources
- oil, natural gas, and mineral resources
- transportation routes
- provides areas for recreation

MARINE (SALTWATER) LIFE ZONES

Marine (saltwater) life zones include not only open oceanic waters but also shorelines, estuaries, coral reefs, and mangroves. The term **plankton**, a Greek word meaning "drifter," is used to describe the bottom trophic levels in the ocean. The dominant primary producers in the marine ecosystem are **phytoplankton**. Phytoplankton are free-floating single-celled algae such as diatoms. Phytoplankton populations are limited by available sunlight and are therefore found in the **euphotic zone**, or upper layer of the ocean. **Zooplankton** are drifting herbivores that make up the primary consumers in our marine ecosystems. The zooplankton group includes a variety of organisms from single-celled protozoa to a diversity of crustaceans, such as krill and copepods. Stronger-swimming organisms like fish are referred to as **nekton**. Bottom-welling organisms are known as **benthos** and live on or in the marine sediments found on the oceanic floor. For instance, oysters attach themselves to the bottom whereas clams and worms actually burrow into the sand. Other benthos organisms, such as crabs and lobsters, simply live on the ocean floor. These organisms are good scavengers, feeding on the detritus material that settles down to the bottom. These different types of consumers in aquatic systems are limited by **dissolved oxygen** concentrations, temperature, and food resources. Bacteria in marine zones, just as in terrestrial ecosystems, are decomposers that break down organic waste into the nutrients required by aquatic primary producers. Life in the oceans exists in three major zones: coastal, open sea, and ocean bottom. The greatest biodiversity in the marine ecosystem occurs in coral reefs, estuaries, and the deep-ocean floor. These ecosystems provide the necessary habitat space and nutrients to support an abundance of life.

COASTAL ZONES   This area of the ocean is from the high tide mark to the edge of the continental shelf. The water in this area is warm and rich in nutrients. Since these ecosystems receive ample amounts of sunlight they are also areas of high net primary productivity. The coastal zone contains approximately 90% of all marine species.

ESTUARIES   These coastal zones form where freshwater rivers meet the salty waters of the ocean. In temperate zones these areas include bays, inlets, sounds, and salt marshes; in tropical zones they include mangrove forests. Estuaries are highly productive due to large inputs of nutrients from the river and ample sunlight that supports only a few dominant primary producers. Typically, only a few plant species do well with the variations in temperature and salinity that occur daily and seasonally with changing tides and river inputs. Estuaries provide many vital ecological services. The large amount of vegetation in this ecosystem acts as a natural filter to prevent toxins, excess nutrients, and sediments from entering the waterways. They also provide large habitat space for many species and serve as breeding grounds for not only aquatic organisms but waterfowl as well. Since estuaries lie right

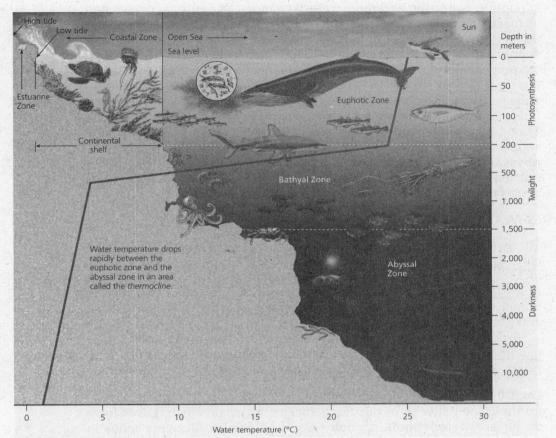

High tide
Low tide
Coastal Zone
Open Sea
Sea level
Sun
Depth in meters
0
50
Photosynthesis
Estuarine Zone
Euphotic Zone
100
Continental shelf
200
500
Bathyal Zone
Twilight
1,000
1,500
Water temperature drops rapidly between the euphotic zone and the abyssal zone in an area called the *thermocline*.
Abyssal Zone
2,000
3,000
4,000
Darkness
5,000
10,000

0   5   10   15   20   25   30
Water temperature (°C)

© Cengage Learning 2012

on the coastline, they also provide a natural buffer from storm surges created by hurricanes or tsunamis.

INTERTIDAL   The diversity of life that exists in this zone is influenced by the stress of the rising and falling tides that occur about every six hours due to the gravitational pull of the moon and sun. Some intertidal zones have gently sloping, sandy shores while others have rocky shorelines where tidal pools form in deep rock crevices from the crashing and retreating waves. Most organisms in the intertidal zone have some adaptation to withstand wave activity, whether it is by burrowing in sediments, attaching to rocks, or retreating into their shells.

CORAL REEFS   These slow-growing, highly diverse ecosystems occur primarily along the equator in warm tropical waters. They are sensitive to any type of salinity or temperature change. They also require clear water so sunlight can reach the mutualistic, photosynthetic algae (zooxanthellae) that provide nutrients to coral polyps. Although coral reefs cover less than 1% of the earth's surface, they provide millions of people with food and jobs.

OPEN OCEAN AND SEA FLOOR   The open sea is a great expanse of the ocean that extends off the continental shelf. This region is defined by

[handwritten margin notes: "inter tidal", "where wave activity occurs", "great barrier reef"]

sunlight penetration and temperature changes as depth increases and is therefore classified into vertical zones. The **euphotic zone** is the upper layer of the open ocean and receives plenty of sunlight to support an abundance of phytoplankton. This layer is rich in dissolved oxygen and supports many larger predatory fish. This area is naturally low in nutrients except in areas where upwelling occurs. The **bathyl zone**, or the middle layer of the vertical oceanic column, receives very little sunlight and consequently contains no photosynthetic organisms. The dominant organisms in this zone, such as smaller fish and zooplankton, migrate to the euphotic zone at night to feed. The **abyssal zone** receives no sunlight. However, there are plenty of nutrients to support life here as most organic waste from upper zones settles to the bottom—this is known as **marine snow**.

FRESHWATER LIFE ZONES

There are limited supplies of freshwater on earth since 97% of the earth's water is saline (oceans). Almost 2% of our water supplies are locked up as frozen freshwater in icecaps and glaciers. Therefore there is less than 1% of remaining freshwater that is readily accessible to humans or organisms as groundwater or surface water (lakes, wetlands, and rivers).

Freshwater life zones can be separated into two main types: **lentic** (standing) bodies of water such as lakes, inland wetlands, bogs, and ponds, and **lotic** (moving) bodies of water such as rivers and streams.

LAKES (LENTIC ZONES)   As you can see in the diagram above, lakes make up the large majority of our fresh surface water on earth. Lakes form as surface water runoff, groundwater, and rainfall fill depressions in the earth's surface that have been created through tectonic, glacial, volcanic, and human activity (reservoirs for dams). Lakes vary greatly in surface area, depth, and nutrient concentrations. Deep lakes have distinct zones that are defined by their depth and distance from shore.

Littoral zone: This shallow zone is closest to shore and receives plenty of sunlight and nutrients and therefore supports a wide variety of life. There are many species of **submergent** (underwater) and **emergent** (rooted in water yet penetrates air/water boundary) plants in this zone.

Limnetic zone: This upper layer of the lake, away from shore, receives a large amount of sunlight that supports abundant growth of phytoplankton. These primary producers make up the base of the food chain in the lake and supply the majority of the dissolved oxygen for aerobic consumers.

Profundal zone: This mid-level lake zone receives little sunlight and is low in nutrients and dissolved oxygen. Organisms living in this zone must be adapted to colder water and pressure.

Benthic zone: This bottom lake zone contains mostly decomposers who feed on the organic waste that trickles down from the upper zones.

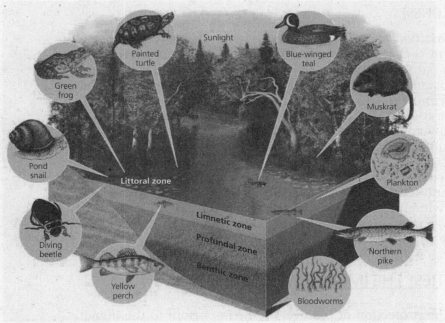

© Cengage Learning 2012

NUTRIENT ENRICHMENT IN LAKE SYSTEM Lakes are classified by concentration of nutrients and primary productivity rates. Clear, deep lakes that have low nutrient levels and therefore limited primary productivity are referred to by ecologists as **oligotrophic**. These lakes are typically colder and support a wide variety of fish species due to the high levels of dissolved oxygen. Over time, lakes will naturally start to increase in nutrient concentration and decrease in depth. This is due to the runoff of sediment and organic material, increasing the level of organic nutrients in the lake. These added nutrients will also promote the growth of primary producers over time. Once lakes have accumulated a high concentration of nutrients that support high levels of net primary productivity by producers they are known as **eutrophic**. These lakes are often more shallow and murky than oligotrophic systems. This same process can occur as large amounts of nutrients are added to lake systems due to human activities, such as runoff of fertilizers; this is known as **cultural eutrophication**.

[handwritten margin note: Oligotrophic= has less PP   Eutropic has more PP]

INLAND WETLANDS (LENTIC ZONES) This freshwater life zone includes swamps (dominated with trees), marshes (dominated by grasses), flood plains, and bogs. These ecosystems are away from coastlines and are covered with freshwater either all or part of the time. Similar to marine estuaries, these areas have an abundance of biodiversity, high levels of net primary productivity, and provide numerous ecosystem services. These services include:

- natural recharge to groundwater system
- habitat space to many organisms (for example, beavers, fish, migratory waterfowl, otters)
- acting as a nursery for many aquatic species and spawning ground for many fish
- filtering toxins and excess nutrients from waterways
- reducing flooding and erosion

RIVERS (LOTIC ZONES)

Rivers are classified as moving water systems that receive most of their input and recharge from **runoff** of precipitation or snow melt. This moving surface water also carries with it sediments and dissolved substances it picks up along the way. The land area that delivers this runoff to the river or its tributaries (small streams that feed into rivers) is known as the drainage basin or **watershed**. The downward movement of water as the river flows to the ocean creates three basic zones. The **source zone** contains rivers and streams that are directly fed by mountain snowmelt. They are fast moving, shallow, and cold, and low in nutrients. The **transition zone** typically has streams and rivers with more turbid water due to the increase in sediments flowing into them. They are typically deeper, wider, slower moving, and contain less dissolved oxygen than the rivers and streams in the source zone.

HUMAN ACTIVITIES: THE IMPACT ON BIODIVERSITY

Why should the protection of biodiversity be important to the human population? Not only do organisms provide vital ecological services such as providing oxygen, recycling nutrients, and keeping natural populations in check, they also serve numerous economic roles as well. Some of these economic services provided by organisms include food products (crops and livestock), lumber, paper, fuelwood, and medicines. However, human population has experienced a rapid rate of increase over the last two hundred years. This growth has elicited a continuous increase in the destruction of natural habitat space of wild species in order to make room for societal expansion (cities, farms, houses). Increasing population growth also fuels the demands for harvesting earth's natural resources that also depletes wild species not only through habitat destruction but also through pollution, overfishing, and climate change. The major cause of biodiversity depletion is habitat loss, habitat fragmentation, and introduction of invasive species.

Habitat Loss: Scientists have discovered that the largest impact on species diversity is habitat loss. Large areas of forested areas (deforestation), wetlands, and grasslands have been destroyed to create room for urbanization or agricultural fields. Many tropical rainforests are currently being subjected to slash-and-burn agricultural practices. This is devastating to biodiversity as the tropics have the largest concentration of different species. Coastal ecosystems such as coral reefs, mangroves, and estuaries are also being destroyed by fishing practices and removal for purposes of urban development.

Habitat Fragmentation: Fragmentation of a habitat occurs when large adjacent ecosystems are divided into smaller, more isolated areas by the addition of housing developments, urban areas (cities), roadways, removal of trees (logging practices), or creating agricultural fields. Since habitat space is being reduced, this can increase population density and therefore increase competition for resources. Organisms will therefore be more susceptible to disease, predators, and natural disasters such as fires.

Invasive Species: Many nonnative species have been introduced into new ecosystems either intentionally or accidently. We have deliberately introduced some species into new ecosystems for new food crops, medicines, or soil erosion control. However, many species are accidently introduced to new ecosystems as they "hitchhike" their way across the globe through transportation practices. For example, many insects have entered new areas through shipping crates made from wood in their native habitat. If these new species out-compete native species for resources and do not have any known predators in their new environment, they can become invasive species. Most invasive species have a high reproductive rate (r-selected) and are generalists. Invasive species typically experience uncontrolled population growth in their new environment and deplete the native species population. Examples of intentionally introduced species include Japanese beetles, Nile Perch, African honeybees, Kudzu, and the European wild boar. Examples of accidently introduced invasive species include the Zebra mussel, Gypsy moth larvae, Formosan termites, and Argentina fire ant.

EXTINCTION

As you learned in Chapter 2, for most of the long history that life has existed on earth there have been very slow, continuous, low levels of **background extinction**. In general, biodiversity on earth has continued to increase over time except for five **mass extinctions** that eliminated 50–95% of species on the planet. **Biological extinctions** occur when a species is no longer found in any ecosystem on earth. Although this type of extinction can occur naturally, some species are becoming prematurely extinct at a rapid rate due to human activities. Examples include, but are not limited to, the Golden Toad, Dodo bird, and Passenger Pigeon. Some species are at risk for biological extinction. Scientists have two categories to describe organisms at risk. **Endangered species** are organisms whose population size has decreased to such a low level that they are at extreme risk of becoming extinct over most or all of their natural habitats. Organisms whose populations are declining due to human activity and could potentially become endangered in the near future are referred to as **threatened species.** Some species have characteristics that make them particularly vulnerable to possible extinction. These characteristics include low reproductive rates (K-selected), need for large territories, feeding at top of food chain (tertiary consumers), specialized niche, and narrow distribution. Also, organisms that are of value commercially, such as elephants for their tusks, are at a higher risk than others.

LEGISLATION AND TREATIES TO PROTECT ENDANGERED SPECIES

U.S. Endangered Species Act of 1973: This law is intended to identify and provide protection for organisms that are at risk for extinction (endangered). This act prohibits any federal agencies (except the Defense Department) from following through with projects that would change or destroy the habitat of any identified endangered species. This law also allows for fines to be imposed on private lands that have modified or disrupted the habitat of an endangered species.

Convention on International Trade in Endangered Species (CITES): This 1975 treaty to place bans on the selling, hunting, or capturing of threatened or endangered species has now been signed by 172 countries. However, the strength of this treaty varies on how well it is actually enforced in the different countries.

[handwritten: Stopped trade of animals]

SUSTAINING TERRESTRIAL DIVERSITY

FOREST ECOSYSTEMS

Ecologists classify forests as either old-growth forests or secondary-growth forests. An **old-growth forest** has not been modified by human activities or natural disasters in 200 years or more. **Secondary-growth forests** form from secondary succession once land has been cleared due to human activity (deforestation) or some type of natural disaster (fires, volcanoes, hurricanes). Scientists estimate that forested areas provide habitat for two-thirds of the earth's terrestrial species, and tropical rain forests are home to more than 50% of the world's species. Not only are forests areas of high biodiversity but they provide crucial ecosystem services such as releasing oxygen, storing carbon dioxide, reducing soil erosion, promoting nutrient cycling, and influencing local and regional climate. Forests afford many economic benefits to humans as well by providing recreational areas, medicines, fuelwood, and jobs in lumber and paper industries.

[handwritten: Need to know all the forest types we are doing this]

THREATS TO FOREST ECOSYSTEMS Although forests provide numerous economic and ecological services, they are currently under a rapid rate of removal due to deforestation practices. **Deforestation** either temporarily or permanently removes large tracts of forested land for fuelwood, agriculture, or urban development. In areas like South America, Africa, and Indonesia, large tracts of tropical forests are being removed to provide space for cash cropping, raising livestock, or harvesting timber resources. According to the United Nations, Indonesia has already removed approximately 78% of its original intact forested land. This type of habitat loss and fragmentation greatly depletes the wealth of biodiversity found in tropical forests.

LOGGING PRACTICES In order to begin harvesting a forested area, logging roads are established first. These roads fragment the habitat and increase soil erosion into local rivers and streams. There are three main types of logging practices: clear-cutting, selective cutting, and strip cutting.

Clear-cutting: Clear cutting removes all of the trees in one area at one time. Although this is the most efficient method for loggers, it causes the most damage to the forest ecosystem. Clear-cutting of forests ecosystems results in the heavy loss of soil nutrients, increased sediment loading into rivers and streams, and biodiversity loss. **Tree plantations** (tree farms) are areas that are commercially maintained for timber resources. They typically have one to two genetically uniform tree species that will be clear-cut and replanted at regular intervals. Theses areas are not biologically diverse and, over time, this practice depletes the nutrients in the soil.

More sustainable methods of logging would include:

Selective cutting: In selective cutting, either mature or intermediate-age trees are selectively removed from forested areas that have an uneven-age tree community.

Strip cutting: Strip cutting involves removing an entire strip of trees along the contour of the land in a narrow corridor that allows for quick regeneration of the trees. Once the strip begins to grow back the loggers will clear-cut another strip of trees next to the first.

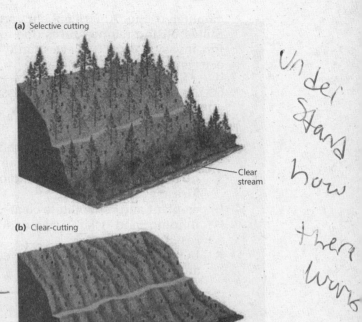
(a) Selective cutting — Clear stream

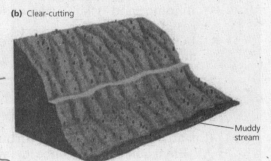
(b) Clear-cutting — Muddy stream

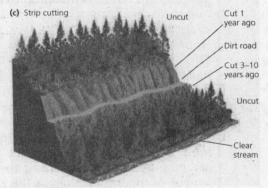
(c) Strip cutting — Uncut, Cut 1 year ago, Dirt road, Cut 3–10 years ago, Uncut, Clear stream

© Cengage Learning 2012

FOREST FIRES Surface fires, fires that only burn leaf litter on the forest floor, can be beneficial to forests by stimulating germination in some trees and freeing up vital mineral nutrients. Since surface fires remove large amounts of flammable ground material they also help prevent more serious fires. If surface fires do not occur for several decades, then the forest ecosystem is a risk for a crown fire. Crown fires burn tops of trees and spread easily from one treetop to the next. These large forests fires are difficult to control and kill not only the trees but local wildlife. These fires also increase soil erosion into local waterways and can cause destruction to human urban developments and housing. In many tropical regions large tracts of forested land are being cleared through burning practices. These fires will greatly reduce wildlife populations, increase local air pollution, and increases atmospheric carbon dioxide. A strategy for reducing harm caused by forest fires is to set small prescribed fires in high-risk areas to remove large areas of overgrown underbrush. In 2003, the Healthy Forests Restoration Act was passed allowing timber companies to remove medium-size commercially valuable trees in an attempt to thin forests at risk for fires. However, many critics of this act say that removing these trees actually promotes the growth of smaller, more flammable trees, putting forests at even greater risk for forest fires.

INSECTS AND CLIMATE CHANGE Forest ecosystems have also fallen victim to invasive insect species and disease introduced into the United States. Diseases such as Dutch elm and chestnut blight have almost eliminated the American elm and chestnut trees from the United States. Rising temperatures due to climate change make it even easier for invasive insect species and diseases to do well in our forest ecosystems.

SOLUTIONS FOR SUSTAINING FOREST ECOSYSTEMS

■ practice strip cutting and selective cutting rather than clear-cutting logging methods
■ protect remaining old-growth forests
■ certify timber grown by sustainable methods
■ governments in tropical regions provide subsidies to sustainable forestry practices
■ re-plant and rehabilitate clear-cut forests
■ funding and visitor regulations in national parks and wildlife reserves
■ build habitat corridors between fragmented forests to encourage animal migration

[handwritten margin note: look these ove]

[handwritten margin note: Know Current Stuff]

AP Tip

It is a good idea as you go through your course of study in AP Environmental Science to make note of the important people who have contributed to this field. You may be asked to recall their importance on the AP Exam. For example, Wangari Maathai is a Kenyan woman who won the 2004 Nobel Peace Prize for starting the Green Belt Movement. This movement began as a humble tree nursery in her backyard and has now grown to over 50,000 members in over 6,000 different villages in Africa. Today, this project has planted over two billion trees in 55 different countries. While reducing soil erosion, these trees also provide sustainable supplies of fuelwood, building materials, and food. Such projects also reduce poverty for women as they are employed in maintaining the nurseries and have a new source of income by selling the products from the trees that are harvested. For a full list of important people to know for the AP Environmental Science Exam, see the list in the Supplement section in Part 3.

GRASSLAND ECOSYSTEMS

Much like forests, grasslands provide many ecological services such as promoting nutrient cycling, encouraging soil formation, controlling erosion, and storing carbon dioxide. Historically, these ecosystems have been valuable to humans as cropland due to their fertile soils and the abundant grasses that provide food for grazing livestock. Grasslands are utilized for livestock grazing in two ways: rangelands and pastures. **Rangelands** are wide-open, non-restricted areas for grazing by grass-eating and shrub-eating livestock (cattle, sheep, goats). **Pastures** are fenced areas that are maintained by ranchers through planting of domesticated grasses or shrubs.

Overgrazing: Overgrazing occurs when the number of livestock animals exceed the carrying capacity for that particular rangeland, thereby depleting the grass cover. This exposes valuable topsoil to erosion by wind and water, and it also compacts soil, decreasing its water retention properties.

SUSTAINING GRASSLAND ECOSYSTEMS Grassland ecosystems are naturally maintained by periodic fires. Fires can eliminate other plants competing with grasses' space and resources and it may promote the availability of valuable soil nutrients. Recently, ecologists have been conducting controlled burns in these ecosystems to try and promote native grasses to damaged regions.

Grasses grow from the base of the blade, not the tip, so if grazing livestock is done in a sustainable manner then grasslands serve as a renewable resource. An alternative method for grazing livestock is known as rotational grazing. In **rotational grazing** cattle or livestock are contained in fenced-off spaces where they are rotated from one field to another over the course of the year. This way, ranchers can control the amount of grazing that occurs to their fields and can prevent overgrazing of any one area.

[handwritten margin note: have them rotate so is less overgrazed]

SUSTAINING AQUATIC ECOSYSTEMS

THREATS TO MARINE ECOSYSTEMS

Much like forests, the major threat to marine ecosystems is habitat destruction. Much of our coral reefs, mangroves, and estuary systems have suffered major damage at the hands of human activities. Many coastal estuaries have been drained and mangroves removed to provide urban development space. Other human activities that put these areas at risks are unsustainable fishing practices, climate change, and pollution.

Overharvesting: Current fishing practices are not only depleting biodiversity by causing damage to ocean habitats, they are also causing a rapid decline in our commercially important fish populations. Although most commercial fishing vessels target only a small group of valuable fish species, many non-target species are also killed in the miles and miles of netting and baited hooks used by the fishing industry. These species are referred to as **bycatch**. Bycatch from fishing practices depletes numerous non-commercial fish species, turtles, marine mammals (seals, dolphins), and sharks.

[handwritten margin note: great barrier reef is dying]

Pollution: It is predicted that by 2020 almost 80% of the world's population will live on or near the coast in urban areas. Most of the pollution that makes its way to the ocean comes from land-based activities along the coast. This coastal pollution includes runoff of sediments from building and agricultural activities, fertilizers, pesticides, industrial solvents and waste, plastics, and excess nutrients from animal feed lots or municipal sewage that leads to eutrophication.

this is all very bad and mostly our fault

know

Climate Change: The rising global temperature is causing severe impacts to oceanic systems. The average sea level has risen by 10–20 cm over the last 100 years. Rising sea levels can cause habitat destruction to many coral reef and mangrove ecosystems. The Arctic region is currently warming twice as fast as the rest of the world, which means a reduction in floating sea ice. This ice is extremely important to polar bears as they utilize this surface area for hunting seals. The United States listed the polar bear as a threatened species under the Endangered Species Act in 2008.

Invasive Species: Species from all over the world are being transported to new ecosystems through ballast water in cargo ships. Almost two-thirds of the introduced nonnative marine species have occurred by ship, ballast water being most common (EPA statistics). These invasive species are depleting biodiversity in marine ecosystems by outcompeting and thereby eliminating local native species.

SOLUTIONS FOR SUSTAINING MARINE BIODIVERSITY

- practice sustainable commercial fishing that reduces bycatch
- set catch limits for commercial fish species below sustainable maximum yield
- filter organisms from ship ballast water to reduce invasive species
- establish no-fishing zones and marine sanctuaries
- reduce carbon dioxide emissions to reduce impacts of climate change
- use integrated coastal management techniques

Marine Mammal Protection Act of 1972: This act prohibits, with certain exceptions, any United States citizen from harassing, hunting, or killing any marine mammals. This act was amended in 1994 to include:

- a program to monitor incidental taking of marine mammals during commercial fishing practice (bycatch regulations)
- preparation of stock assessments for all marine mammals in waters under United States jurisdiction

THREATS TO FRESHWATER ECOSYSTEMS

Many freshwater systems have been damaged by human activities. Rivers and lakes have suffered a 50% loss in fish species due to human interaction. River species have been depleted due to the building of dams along our major rivers limiting the flow of water and nutrient-rich silt downstream. Lakes are being impacted by the overharvesting of water resources for agricultural irrigation practices and municipal use in homes and industries.

Pollution: Our freshwater systems have a constant influx of toxins from human activities. These toxins include, but are not limited to, pesticides, industrial solvents, oils, sediments, and excess nutrients from fertilizers and animal wastes. These excess nutrients deplete biodiversity by causing **cultural eutrophication** in many of our lakes and inland wetlands.

Destruction of riparian zones: Riparian zones are strips of vegetation that surround streams and rivers. Vegetation in these zones acts as a natural buffer by controlling floods and by filtering and removing many of the toxins and excess nutrients before they reach our waterways. Construction in these zones, or their actual removal through stream channelization, can destroy a natural stream ecosystem.

riparian = buffer zone

Invasive Species: An increasing problem in our lake ecosystems is invasive species. The Zebra mussel has had devastating impacts on our Great Lakes while the sea lamprey is killing native fish species throughout the United States and Canada. The Nile Perch was introduced to Lake Victoria (Africa) in the 1950s as a food source. Since that time it has caused the extinction or near depletion of many of the native fish species, particularly cichlids. Scientists estimate the annual cost of aquatic invasive species in the United States to be approximately $9 billion a year (www.nbii.gov—a division of the USGS).

Sustaining Freshwater Biodiversity: In 1968, the United States passed the National Wild and Scenic Rivers Act. Under this legislation, rivers were classified as wild rivers accessible only by trail, or scenic; and those free from dams and accessible by only a few roadways. These rivers are protected from damming, widening, dredging, or filling. Other methods for protecting freshwater ecosystems include:

know the acts!! all of them

- reuse treated wastewater for irrigation to reduce reservoir use
- protect and increase riparian buffer zones
- reduce fertilizer use in agricultural fields and urban homes and golf courses
- reduce use of pesticides on agricultural fields

MULTIPLE-CHOICE QUESTIONS

1. Which of the following biomes is maintained through occasional fires?
   (A) Tundra
   (B) Tropical forest
   (C) Grassland
   (D) Mountain ranges
   (E) Taiga

2. Characteristics that would lead to a nonnative organism's becoming invasive in a new environment would include which of the following characteristics?
   I.   High reproductive rate
   II. Short-lived
   III. Generalists

   (A) I only
   (B) II only
   (C) III only
   (D) I and III only
   (E) I, II, and III

3. Which of the following non-point pollution types is most likely to cause cultural eutrophication in lake ecosystems?
   (A) Oil from parking lots
   (B) Fertilizer from agricultural fields
   (C) Heavy metals from mining practices
   (D) Sediments from erosion of agricultural fields
   (E) Pesticides from agricultural fields

4. Photosynthetic organisms such as phytoplankton would be most abundant in which oceanic zone?
   (A) Bathyl
   (B) Benthos
   (C) Littoral
   (D) Limnetic
   (E) Euphotic

5. All of the following are associated with an El Niño event EXCEPT
   (A) decreased upwelling events
   (B) suppressed thermocline in the Pacific Ocean
   (C) increased Atlantic coast hurricanes
   (D) torrential rain and flooding in Peru
   (E) drought in Indonesia

6. Which country would have the largest percentage of boreal forests?
   (A) Russia
   (B) United States
   (C) Australia
   (D) Brazil
   (E) Nepal

7. The land area that delivers recharge to smaller tributary streams that flow into larger rivers is known as
   (A) watershed
   (B) source zone
   (C) flood plain
   (D) delta
   (E) estuary

8. Oceanic currents act as a conveyor belt system creating a connected loop of deep and shallow ocean currents that transfers warm and cold water between the tropics and the poles. The strongest influence on this system of ocean currents is due to
   (A) upwelling events that bring cold nutrient-rich water from the bottom to the top
   (B) the rotation of the earth on its axis
   (C) differences in water density due to temperature and salinity concentrations
   (D) atmospheric convection causing large inputs of freshwater into the ocean by precipitation
   (E) location of continents that help determine direction and flow of ocean currents

9. The most biologically diverse areas of the ocean include coral reefs and estuaries. All of the following characteristics are reasons why these ecosystems can support such a high level of diversity EXCEPT:
(A) They are areas of high primary productivity.
(B) Both ecosystems have abundant nutrient flow that supports phytoplankton populations.
(C) Coral reefs and estuaries receive an abundant amount of sunlight.
(D) Both ecosystems provide plenty of habitat space for organisms.
(E) These ecosystems do not have commercially important species; therefore human impact on biodiversity is limited.

10. Deep lakes that are characterized by steep banks and have a relatively small supply of plant nutrients are known as
(A) autotrophic
(B) euphotic
(C) mesotrophic
(D) oligotrophic
(E) eutrophic

11. Marine biologists have found that increasing atmospheric carbon dioxide levels are lowering ocean pH, a condition known as ocean acidification. This also causes a decrease in the concentration of calcium carbonate ions. If this rise were to continue it would have a devastating impact on coral ecosystems because
(A) it would cause a decline in the endosymbiotic algae the coral depend on
(B) it would decrease the ability of the corals to form their exoskeleton
(C) it would increase the amount of dissolved oxygen beyond the tolerance of the coral
(D) it would increase the turbidity of the water beyond the corals' range of tolerance
(E) it would decrease the number of crustaceans that act as keystone species in the coral reef ecosystem

12. The direction of the rotation of large cyclones—winds around the center of a cyclone rotate clockwise in the northern hemisphere and counterclockwise in the southern hemisphere—is due to the
(A) earth's rotation
(B) temperature differences in oceanic currents
(C) Coriolis effect
(D) tropical vortex effect
(E) uneven heating of the earth by the sun

13. This ecosystem is characterized by long, hot summers and moderate, moist winters. It supports many small mammals, and most vegetation germinates after a period exposed to fire. It is mostly found along coastal areas such as the Pacific coast of North America, southern Texas and Mexico, and the coastal hills of Chile and the Mediterranean.
   (A) tundra
   (B) desert
   (C) grassland
   (D) chaparral
   (E) taiga forest

14. The Amazon Basin, in South America, is the world's largest tropical rainforest. Forest cover in the "Arc of Deforestation" in the southern region of the basin is rapidly decreasing due to logging and conversion of forests to agricultural lands. Scientists estimate that if this trend continues it will reduce the forest coverage to only 20% of its original size by the year 2016. The loss of forested land would most likely
   (A) increase the concentration of water vapor in the air due to increased transpiration rates
   (B) decrease the local regional flooding that occurs
   (C) increase available supplies for plant-derived medicines
   (D) decrease the amount of total atmospheric nitrogen
   (E) increase the amount of total atmospheric carbon dioxide

15. All of the following are threats to biodiversity in river systems EXCEPT
   (A) increasing of riparian zones along stream banks
   (B) pesticides entering local rivers from agricultural runoff
   (C) habitat fragmentation by dams
   (D) runoff of animal wastes from feedlots
   (E) dredging river bottoms to increase ability for transportation

FREE-RESPONSE QUESTION

The Chesapeake Bay is the largest estuary in the United States. It has had a long history of water pollution problems due to human activities in the states surrounding the bay that makes up the watershed. The Chesapeake has nine major tributary rivers that feed into the estuary. Scientists are monitoring the concentrations of nitrates and phosphates that are entering the estuary each year. Load is the mass of nutrient transported by streamflow over time, and is estimated as the product of nutrient concentration and streamflow (reported here in pounds per year, or lbs/yr). The three rivers that have the highest flow—the Susquehanna, the Potomac, and the James Rivers—contribute the largest nutrient loads to the tidal part of the Chesapeake Bay Basin. Yield is the load per unit area of each basin (reported in pounds per year per square mile, or lbs/yr/mi²), and is computed by dividing load by basin area. Although the larger rivers typically have more nutrient yield, scientists are also concerned with the nutrient contributions from some of the smaller rivers. Scientists are currently examining nutrient concentrations from the Mattaponi River in Virginia that has 600mi² of upstream surface area land.

(a) The Mattaponi River contributes a load of 60 million pounds of nitrates every four months into the Chesapeake Bay estuary. Calculate the yearly load of nitrates into the Chesapeake from this tributary river.

(b) Calculate the nutrient yield that this tributary river contributes each year into the Chesapeake Bay.

(c) Identify and describe TWO ecological services provided by estuary systems.

(d) Discuss how the increase in nutrient levels in this estuary can impact the aquatic diversity.

ANSWERS

MULTIPLE-CHOICE QUESTIONS

1. **ANSWER: C.** Grassland ecosystems are maintained by occasional fires that eliminate competing plant species as well as increase availability of nutrients in the soil (*Living in the Environment*, 16th ed., page 232 / 17th ed., pages 156–158).

2. **ANSWER: D.** Characteristics that make a nonnative species a successful invasive species include the ability to reproduce quickly, their long life, ability to feed on many different things, and a wide range of tolerance (generalists) (*Living in the Environment*, 16th ed., page 201 / 17th ed., page 198).

3. **ANSWER: B.** Cultural eutrophication occurs from high levels of limiting nutrients, such as nitrates and phosphates, entering waterways. These nutrients often come from runoff of agricultural areas in the form of fertilizers or animal waste. They can also come from runoff of urban lawns and golf courses that have been treated with fertilizers (*Living in the Environment*, 16th ed., pages 174–176 / 17th ed., pages 182–183).

4. **ANSWER: E.** Since phytoplankton, such as diatoms and dinofla-gelletes, are primary producers and require sunlight for photosynthesis, they will be most abundant in the euphotic zone, as it is the top layer of the ocean and receives the most sunlight (*Living in the Environment*, 16th ed., pages 164–166 / 17th ed., pages 172–173).

5. **ANSWER: C.** During an El Niño the increased wind shear over the Atlantic Ocean is responsible for less hurricane activity. Wind shear is defined as the amount of change in the wind's direction or speed as altitude increases. This means the tropical storms that develop have latent heat spread over a greater surface area, decreasing the chance of organizing into

a hurricane (*Living in the Environment*, 16th ed., pages 143, S48–S49 / 17th ed., pages S26–S27).

6. **ANSWER: A.** The taiga biome (also known as the boreal forest or coniferous forest) is largely found in Russia and also Canada (*Living in the Environment*, 16th ed., page 146 / 17th ed., page 153).

7. **ANSWER: A.** The watershed, also known as a drainage basin, is the land area that delivers runoff, sediment, and dissolved substances to a stream (*Living in the Environment*, 16th ed., page 176 / 17th ed., page 183).

8. **ANSWER: C.** Oceanic currents develop from differences in density of water due to temperature and salinity. Less dense, warmer water with a lower salinity will rise as dense, cold, salty water will sink. This process, aided by prevailing wind patterns, creates shallow- and deep-water currents that form a conveyor belt system around the earth (*Living in the Environment*, 16th ed., pages 142–143 / 17th ed., pages 150–151).

9. **ANSWER: E.** Both coral reef ecosystems and estuaries are in the coastal zone and can be easily accessed by humans. They do support an abundance of biodiversity and many species in these ecosystems are commercially important to humans (*Living in the Environment*, 16th ed., pages 166–170, 254 / 17th ed., pages 168, 177–179).

10. **ANSWER: D.** Lakes are typically classified by nutrient content levels. Oligotrophic lakes have very low nutrient levels and are typically very deep with steep banks and clear water (*Living in the Environment*, 16th ed., pages 174–175 / 17th ed., pages 181–182).

11. **ANSWER: B.** This would impact the coral's ability to create its exoskeleton since it is largely composed of calcium carbonate (*Living in the Environment*, 16th ed., pages 166–170, 254 / 17th ed., pages 168, 177–179).

12. **ANSWER: C.** The Coriolis effect is caused by the rotation of the earth. Large-scale wind patterns are deflected to the right (clockwise) in the northern hemisphere and to the left (counterclockwise) in the southern hemisphere (*Living in the Environment*, 16th ed., page 143 / 17th ed., pages 148–150).

13. **ANSWER: D.** The chaparral ecosystem is found in limited distribution on the earth. It is also known as the temperate scrubland and borders many desert ecosystems (*Living in the Environment*, 16th ed., page 152 / 17th ed., page 159).

14. **ANSWER: E.** Trees are primary producers and during the process of photosynthesis they take in carbon dioxide and store it in their tissue as biomass and release oxygen. Removing large amounts of forested land from the earth

would increase total atmospheric levels of carbon dioxide through a reduction in the terrestrial stores of carbon (*Living in the Environment,* 16th ed., pages 222–226 / 17th ed., pages 224–227).

15. **ANSWER: A.** Riparian zones are vegetation areas that border stream banks. They aid the stream by filtering out toxins and excess nutrients before they reach the streams. They also keep soil intact and prevent erosion and sedimentation into the waterway. Therefore, increasing riparian buffers would help protect river biodiversity—not deplete it (*Living in the Environment,* 16th ed., page 232 / 17th ed., page 235).

FREE-RESPONSE SCORING GUIDELINES

(a) The Mattaponi River contributes a load of 60 million pounds of nitrates every four months into the Chesapeake Bay estuary. Calculate the yearly load of nitrates into the Chesapeake from this tributary river.

2 points can be earned—1 point for correct setup and 1 point for correct answer with units

$$\frac{60 \times 10^6 \text{ lbs. nitrates}}{4 \text{ months}} \left| \frac{12 \text{ months}}{1 \text{ yr}} \right.$$

= 180 million lbs/yr of nitrates

(you may also simply multiply 60 million lbs. by 3 as your setup)

(b) Calculate the nutrient yield that this tributary river contributes each year into the Chesapeake Bay.

2 points can be earned—1 point for correct setup and 1 point for correct answer with units

$$\frac{180 \times 106 \text{ lbs/yr}}{600 \text{ mi}^2} = 300{,}000 \text{ lbs/yr/mi}^2$$

(c) Identify and describe TWO ecological services provided by estuary systems.

4 points can be earned—2 points for each correctly identified ecological service with correct description
- ▪ storm buffers—estuaries are buffer zones against storm surge and protect inland areas from erosion
- ▪ water filtration—estuaries naturally remove toxins from the water
- ▪ habitat—estuary systems are highly diverse and provide space for many organisms

answer page

■ breeding ground—many aquatic organisms come here to breed as well as many waterfowl

■ productivity—estuaries are areas of high primary productivity which supports large amounts of diversity

(d) Discuss how the increase in nutrient levels in this estuary can impact the aquatic diversity.

2 points can be earned—1 point for describing how nutrient loading increases algal growth and 1 point for a negative impact to biodiversity due to algal growth

Negative impacts due to algal growth
■ decreased penetration of sunlight reduces submergent vegetation and photosynthesis
■ bacteria from rapidly decomposing algal blooms consume available oxygen and lower dissolved oxygen in ecosystem thereby causing fish, oysters, and crustaceans to die off
■ nutrient loading can provide conditions for invasive nonnative species to succeed and outcompete native populations

answer pg.

4

HUMAN POPULATION, FOOD, AND AGRICULTURE

KEY CONCEPTS

- The rule of 70 is a useful shortcut that can be used to make estimations involving exponential population growth.
- Age-structure diagrams can be used to predict likely future population changes for a country.
- The demographic transition model is a helpful tool for understanding the population dynamics of both developing and developed nations.
- The green revolution allowed food production to keep pace with growing populations in the second half of the 20th century.
- Soils are delicate and complex mixtures of organic and inorganic material combined with living soil organisms.
- Current food production methods for growing crops, livestock production, and aquaculture place a burden on the environment.
- Genetically modified crops have desirable characteristics; however, all of the possible environmental costs associated with them may not be clearly understood.
- Modern harvesting methods have decimated the world's fisheries, thereby requiring stringent fishery management.

Human population, food, and agriculture are discussed in depth in *Living in the Environment*, 16th ed., Chapters 6 and 12 / 17th ed., Chapters 6 and 12.

KEY VOCABULARY

A horizon	kwashiorkor
age structure diagram	long-line fishing
anemia	malnutrition
B horizon	marasmus
baby boom	monoculture
biological control	no-till agriculture
bycatch	O horizon
C horizon	organophosphate
chlorinated hydrocarbon	pesticide
contour plowing	pesticide treadmill
crop rotation	plantation agriculture
crude birth rate	population momentum
crude death rate	purse seine fishing
DDT	Rachel Carson
deforestation	replacement-level fertility
demographic transition	rule of 70
desertification	slash-and-burn agriculture
doubling time	soil erosion
emigration	soil horizon
factory farm	soil salinization
genetically modified organism GMO	soil triangle
goiter	subsistence agriculture
green revolution	terracing
immigration	total fertility rate
industrialized agriculture	traditional agriculture
infant mortality rate	trawler fishing
inorganic fertilizer	waterlogging
integrated pest management	

HUMAN POPULATION

The world's population is approaching seven billion and continues to grow. About one-third of the human population lives in its two most populated countries, China and India, with over one billion people each. The United States is the third most populous nation on Earth with over 300 million people. Historically, human population grew slowly before the advent of agriculture, approximately 10,000 years ago. About 200 years ago, growth accelerated rapidly following the industrial revolution. The population had an infamous decline in the 14th century due to the bubonic plague. Today, over one-half of the world's population lives within 50 miles of a coastline.

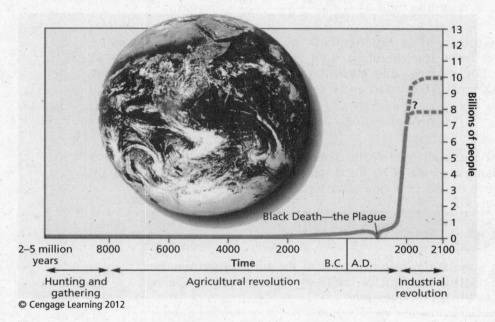

© Cengage Learning 2012

DEMOGRAPHICS

Some of the quantities that demographers (population experts) use to understand the population of a country or a region are listed below.

Total fertility rate: The average number of children born to a woman during her lifetime.

Replacement-level fertility: The average number of children a couple must bear to replace themselves in the population. The average is slightly higher than two children per couple because some children die before reaching reproductive age.

Infant mortality rate: The number of babies out of every 1000 births who die before reaching their first birthday.

Crude birth rate: The number of births per 1000 people in a population.

Crude death rate: The number of deaths per 1000 people in a population.

Immigration: The migration of people into a population.

Emigration: The migration of people out of a population.

THE RULE OF 70

The rule of 70 is a useful tool for estimating the **doubling time** of a population that grows exponentially. To use the rule divide 70 by the annual growth rate of the population expressed as a percent. The result will be the time (in years) required for the population to double. For example, the doubling time of a population growing at 2% each year is 70 divided by 2, or 35 years.

$$\text{doubling time} = \frac{70}{\%\ \text{growth rate}} = \frac{70}{2} = 35 \text{ years}$$

The growth rate of an exponentially growing population may also be estimated from the doubling time by using the same formula in reverse. For example, the growth rate of a population that doubles every 14 years is 70 divided by 14, or 5%.

$$\%\ \text{growth rate} = \frac{70}{\text{doubling time}} = \frac{70}{14} = 5\%$$

Note that crude birth or death rates must be converted to percentages before using the rule of 70. To do this, simply divide the crude rate by 10 (or move the decimal one place to the left).

AP Tip

Human population growth is one of the topics that may be used to provide the data for the free-response question, also known as the "math question."

EXAMPLE 1   In 2010, the population of Upper Fremont is 200,000 and growing at a rate of 2% each year.

(A) If the rate of population growth remains constant, calculate the population in 2045.

(B) If the rate of population growth remains constant, calculate the population in 2080.

ANSWERS: 400,000. Determine the doubling time of the population by dividing 70 by 2 to get 35 years. Since one 35-year period passes between 2010 and 2045, the population will have doubled once from 200,000 to 400,000.

800,000. In another 35 years, it will be 2080 and the population will have doubled again from 400,000 to 800,000.

EXAMPLE 2   The population of Lower Fremont was 20,000 in 1968. In 2010 the population is 160,000. Assuming that the growth is exponential, calculate the average annual percentage rate of population growth in Lower Fremont since 1968.

ANSWER: 5%. To solve this problem you must first determine the number of years that elapsed between 1968 and 2010 (42 years), and the number of times the population doubled. Beginning with the initial number, we see that the population experienced three doublings in the 42 years between 1968 and 2010. Now, the doubling time can be determined by dividing 42 by 3 to get 14 years. The average annual growth rate is equal to 70 divided by 14 or 5%.

EXAMPLE 3 In 2010, the crude birth rate in East Fremont was 25 and the crude death rate was 11. Calculate the percentage growth rate of East Fremont in 2010. If the population was 15,000 in 2010, and the population growth rate remains constant, when will the population reach 30,000?

ANSWER: 1.4%; 2060. To solve this problem begin by determining the growth rate of the population. The crude growth rate is equal to the crude birth rate minus the crude death rate, i.e., 25 − 11 = 14 per 1000. Expressed as a percent, the growth rate is then 1.4%. Since we are looking for the year in which the population will have doubled once, use the rule of 70 to determine the doubling time of the population (70 / 1.4 = 50 years). Add 50 years to 2010 to get the answer, 2060.

AGE-STRUCTURE

The age-structure of a population is the distribution of males and females in different age groups. **Age-structure diagrams** are useful in determining the future growth or decline of a population. A crucial factor for determining future growth is the number of females in the reproductive and pre-reproductive age groups because the total fertility rate of these women will determine the number of births in the population. Age-structure diagrams are unique graphical representations of the population for a country or region. By comparing the age-structure diagrams for one country over many years, it is possible to infer social changes that occurred in the country, and predict future changes to the population growth rate of the country. By comparing the age-structure diagrams of different countries to one another, it is possible to infer differences in the social conditions within the countries and the relative population growth rates of those countries. For example, the broad base of the age-structure diagram for developing countries indicates high **population momentum** and could be indicative of a population with a high infant mortality rate, poor health care, a cultural preference for large families, or a lack of opportunities for women, while the narrow base of a developed country indicates low population momentum and could indicate an aging population that is growing slowly, or undergoing negative population growth. The United States has a bulge that has been moving through its age-structure diagrams since the late 1940s due to the **baby boom** that occurred following World War II.

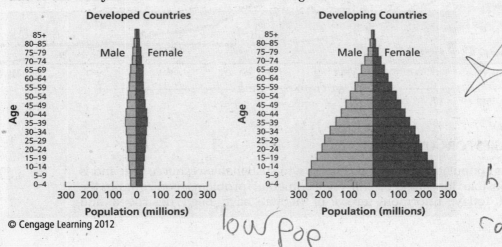

© Cengage Learning 2012

DEMOGRAPHIC TRANSITION

The demographic transition model is a feature of the population growth pattern for countries as they change from primarily agricultural economies to industrialized nations. Prior to beginning industrialization, countries typically exhibit relatively high birth and death rates, which cancel each other out, resulting in a population growth rate close to zero and a stable population size. As the transition to industrialization begins, the first thing to occur is that death rates fall, in part due to improvements in medical care and sanitation, while birth rates remain high. During this time the population growth rate of the country increases because death rates are lower than the birth rates. After the population adjusts to the new way of life in a more industrialized nation, birth rates begin to fall as death rates also continue to fall. The population growth rate remains high during this period of time, which, along with the first step could last anywhere from a few decades to hundreds of years. Eventually, the death rate stabilizes and the birth rate falls to approximately the same level. This results in a growth rate close to zero and a stable population size. Thus, a country with a relatively small, stable population enters a demographic transition, and after many decades or centuries of rapid population growth, its population stabilizes at a significantly higher level. Eventually, after the country is industrialized, the birth rate may drop below the death rate, which will lead to negative population growth.

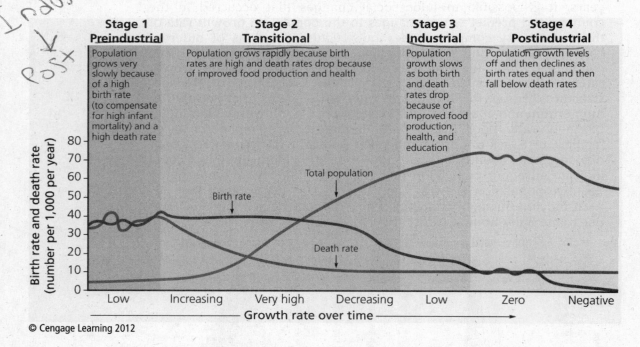

© Cengage Learning 2012

STRATEGIES FOR SUSTAINABILITY

Human population growth is a barrier to sustainable resource use, and is responsible for most of the environmental problems confronting the world today. Enormous areas of habitat have been destroyed and polluted to provide for the food, energy, and shelter needs of the growing population.

For both the moral imperative and its effectiveness, the empowerment of women is an important strategy for slowing the rapid population growth in much of the developing world. Providing educational and employment opportunities for women, along with equivalent rights to those of men, will increase the average age at which women have their first child and result in women bearing fewer children during their reproductive years—lowering the total fertility rate of the population.

The one-child policy implemented in China during the 1970s decreased the country's total fertility rate by more than one-third, from nearly six, to less than two children per woman in approximately 35 years. However, there are concerns over human rights violations associated with the penalties and treatment of those who violate the policy. The policy of China and other countries that attempt to slow population growth by limiting the number of children per couple also may result in male-dominant populations due to cultural preferences for male children. This has social implications when there are far more men than women reaching reproductive age.

IMPACTS OF POPULATION GROWTH

Infectious diseases are spread more quickly in densely populated areas. The modern city is an ideal environment for the spread of old (influenza, cholera, and the common cold) and newly emergent (SARS, HIV/AIDS, and West Nile fever) diseases. The growth of international travel has allowed diseases that once would have been isolated to local populations to spread around the world.

With slower population growth, and an increased GNP, the per capita wealth in China has grown, adding hundreds of millions of new middle class citizens to the world. With increased industrialization, participation in the high-tech industry and a population over one billion, India also is adding tens of millions of people annually to the middle class. These more affluent individuals place an added burden on the environment as their lifestyles require more resources in order to maintain or keep pace with their social status.

In contrast to China, the population growth of India has not slowed significantly and the number of people living in poverty continues to grow. Along with the rest of the developing world, the rapid growth of a population living in poverty comes with many environmental costs, including the degradation of forests, fisheries, soils, and waterways as a result of desperate attempts to survive.

SOILS

There are thousands of different types of soils in the world. Soils vary due to differences in geography, parent material, climate, age, and the presence of soil organisms. Soils are composed of a complex mixture of weathered rocks, partially decomposed organic material, and organisms. Soils can take thousands of years to form. The parent material that is broken down to form soil is often transported great distances by water and wind, and may not be related to the bedrock on which the soil forms. The particle size of the broken-down parent material influences the texture and porosity of the soil. Particle sizes arranged in order from large to small are sand, silt, and clay.

Soils are usually formed into horizontal layers called **soil horizons**. Looking at a cross section of a soil reveals its profile. For most soils, its profile reveals that nearly all of the living organisms are found close to the surface. At the surface of soil is the **O horizon**, which is composed of partially decomposed organic material and/or leaf litter. Beneath the O horizon is the **A horizon**, or topsoil, which is composed of mineral-containing weathered parent material and organic matter (humus). Plants spread most of their roots to absorb water and minerals in the A horizon. Beneath the A horizon is the **B horizon**, or subsoil, which contains a lower concentration of organic material than the first two layers and a higher concentration of mineral particles. Beneath the B horizon is the **C horizon**, which is composed of weathered parent material sitting on top of bedrock.

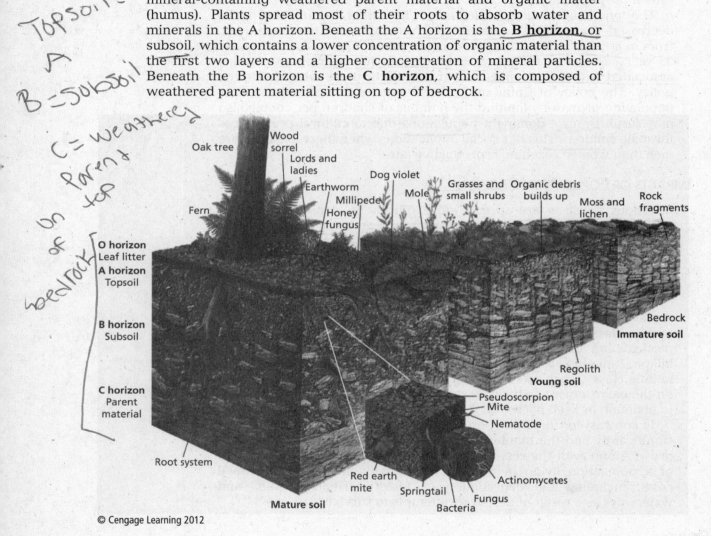

© Cengage Learning 2012

SOIL TRIANGLE

The soil triangle is used to determine textural classes of soil from the percentages of sand, silt, and clay in the soil.

To determine soil texture using the soil triangle, the lines from each side must be extended in the correct direction. Proceed as follows:

- Clay side first. Extend a line horizontally from the percent clay (the line should be parallel to the side labeled "percent sand").

- Silt side second. Extend a line diagonally downward from the percent silt (the line should be parallel with side labeled "percent clay").
- Sand side last. Extend a line diagonally upward and to the left from the percent sand (this line should be parallel with side labeled "percent silt").

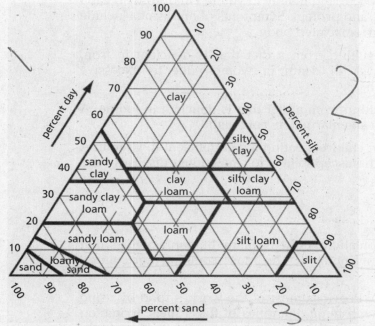

http://soils.usda.gov/technical/manual/print_version/chapter3.html

For example, if a soil is 30% clay, 30% silt, and 40% sand, the texture is clay loam.

AGRICULTURE

On average, people must consume approximately 2,200 calories (kcal) of food per day to live an active and healthy life. Currently, there is more than enough food being produced to meet the basic nutritional needs of every person on earth; however, the areas of food production are unevenly distributed amongst the population. Wheat, rice, and corn are the three crops that humans most depend on for calories and nutrients. In recent years, the use of grain (especially corn) as an energy source has contributed to rising food prices and may be a contributing factor to hunger.

FEEDING A GROWING POPULATION

A lack of sufficient protein, carbohydrates, fats, vitamins, or minerals leads to **malnutrition** and hunger.

Undernutrition: A problem most associated with the populations of developing countries; however, it is also a problem among those living in poverty in developed countries.

Overnutrition: A problem that leads to obesity is most associated with developed countries; however, it is also a problem in developing countries where a Western diet has been widely adopted.

Kwashiorkor: A condition occurring mainly in young children who eat a diet that is severely deficient in protein. Symptoms of kwashiorkor include a bloated, distended belly and puffy skin.

Marasmus: A condition occurring mainly in young children who eat a diet that is low in calories and protein. Symptoms of marasmus include stunted growth and a thin, emaciated body.

Anemia: A condition resulting from a diet that is deficient in iron. Anemia increases the risk of death in women due to excessive bleeding during childbirth.

Goiter: A condition resulting from a diet that is deficient in iodine. A swollen neck results from an enlarged thyroid gland.

Vitamin A Deficiency: In children, eating a diet deficient in vitamin A can result in increased susceptibility to infectious diseases and blindness.

TYPES OF AGRICULTURE

Feeding the growing population is one of many human activities that place a strain on the environment. The most common agricultural practices are listed below.

Industrialized agriculture: Provides most of the world's food by using heavy equipment along with huge quantities of fossil fuels, irrigation water, **inorganic chemical fertilizers**, and pesticides to farm high-yielding **monocultures**.

Plantation agriculture: Commonly used in developing countries to grow cash crops such as coffee, sugar cane, bananas, and cacao. Plantations require large inputs of chemical fertilizers and pesticides, and they are often located on land from which tropical forests were cleared.

Traditional or subsistence agriculture: The practice of farming to provide for one family's food needs with enough remaining to sell or trade for additional necessities. Traditional agriculture relies heavily on the hard work of humans and draft animals with low inputs of commercial agricultural products.

Slash-and-burn agriculture: The practice of cutting down and burning tropical forests to clear the land for planting crops and raising livestock. After a few years of farming in the nutrient-poor tropical soils, farmers must slash and burn another section of forest to continue producing crops. Plantation and traditional agriculture both rely on the slash-and-burn method for clearing land.

THE GREEN REVOLUTION

The green revolution is the name given to a set of technologically advanced agricultural practices that dramatically increased crop yields after World War II. The key advancements included the development of high-yielding monoculture crops; the use of large inputs of **inorganic fertilizer**; heavy use of pesticides; intensive irrigation; and the development of strategies that allowed for growing multiple crops on the same plot of land during the year.

GENETIC ENGINEERING AND CROP PRODUCTION

In recent years, **genetically modified organisms (GMOs)** have become more and more a part of modern industrialized agriculture. Scientists have successfully transplanted genes from unrelated organisms into crops that resist frost, repel pests, and fix nitrogen. However, there is concern that the practice of mixing genes in ways that they could never have mixed in nature could have unforeseen effects on biodiversity, increase the pesticide resistance of pest species, lower the nutritional value of food, or create new food allergens.

They are unnatural and not good

ENVIRONMENTAL PROBLEMS ASSOCIATED WITH AGRICULTURE

SOIL EROSION: After plowing or harvesting, soil that is exposed to the elements is susceptible to being blown away by winds or washed away by water. Excessive irrigation may cause soil erosion while crops are being grown even if the land is not exposed. Although soil is considered a renewable resource, the rate of formation of new soil is slow and most soils that are under cultivation are currently being used unsustainably. A few soil conservation strategies for reducing soil erosion are listed below.

- **No-till agriculture** refers to farming without plowing the land, which avoids exposing the soil to direct sun, wind and water.
- **Terracing** involves converting a hilly slope to flat terraces that follow the contours of the slope. This makes it possible to farm heavily sloped hillsides, and is common in many rice-growing areas in Asia.
- **Contour plowing** is the practice of plowing across the slope of a hill rather than up and down the slope. This reduces erosion by slowing runoff and preventing water from gaining momentum as it flows unimpeded down a slope, which increases erosion.
- **Windbreaks** are rows of shrubs or trees that are planted next to or around fields to slow down the winds that could blow topsoil off of the land.

Deforestation: Results from clearing land for agriculture. The removal of trees destroys habitat for plants and animals that live in the understory of the trees; reduces cover, which dries out soil; increases soil erosion by eliminating the root infrastructure that held the soil in place; and eliminates a carbon reservoir, which increases atmospheric carbon (as carbon dioxide).

Fertilizer runoff: Leads to nutrient pollution, which results in cultural eutrophication and hypoxia in waterways.

AP Tip

Terminology: When answering a free-response question, avoid dropping terms without demonstrating an understanding of what they mean. A term like "eutrophication" may not earn a point unless the answer includes some indication of a basic understanding of the term's meaning.

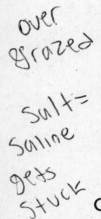

Desertification: Occurs when marginal lands on the outskirts of deserts are overgrazed by livestock or farmed. The removal of native vegetation causes the soil to dry out and the area is slowly incorporated into the expanding desert.

Soil salinization: Occurs on heavily irrigated land in arid climates when irrigation water evaporates regularly, leaving behind trace amounts of dissolved salts that accumulate until the salt concentration in the soil reaches levels that prevent growing viable crops.

Waterlogging: Occurs when irrigation water accumulates and raises the water table to a level where it interferes with the growth of crops by submerging their roots.

CONTROLLING PESTS

Any living thing that competes with humans for food is considered to be a pest. To control most pests, specialized chemicals have been developed that kill or control the pest population.

Herbicides: Used to control weeds.

Fungicides: Used to control fungus.

Rodenticides: Used to control rodents (mostly rats and mice).

Insecticides: Used to control insects.

Broad spectrum pesticides are pesticides that kill many different (a broad spectrum of) species, which is an environmental problem when "good" species like bees, spiders, and ladybugs are killed along with the target species. **Chlorinated hydrocarbons** (such as **DDT** and dieldrin) and **Organophosphates** (such as malathion and parathion) are broad spectrum pesticides.

   Narrow spectrum pesticides are selected to kill only the target (a narrow spectrum of) species, which is the preference.

THE PESTICIDE TREADMILL

Following the application of a pesticide, it is unlikely that every individual of the targeted pest population will be killed. The survivors will be individuals with some resistance to the pesticide. Those survivors reproduce and pass their genes for pesticide resistance on to their offspring. After a few generations have reproduced, the farmer may decide that another application of pesticides is necessary. If the farmer applies the same amount of the pesticide, the descendents of the survivors of the first application will not be killed at the same rate, and the farmer may decide to increase the strength of the pesticide by increasing the amount used or the concentration. Again, the application of the pesticide, even at increased strength, is unlikely to kill every individual of the targeted pest population. And, again, the survivors will be individuals with resistance to the pesticide who will reproduce and pass their genes for even greater pesticide resistance on to their offspring. This example of a positive feedback loop is called the pesticide treadmill.

COSTS AND BENEFITS OF PESTICIDE USE

The way decisions are made about pesticide use is an example of the role economics plays in the decision-making processes that affect the environment. The price of food is determined by the economic forces of supply and demand. The current price influences the decision of every farmer who must decide whether the cost of applying a pesticide to his or her crops is worth the additional yield that will result. The farmer does not need to consider external costs that will be borne by society, such as the ecological effects of pesticide runoff into waterways, or the health effects to anyone who is exposed to the pesticides, including the workers who spray the fields, residents who live nearby, anyone exposed to contaminated water or soil that results from the application of the pesticides, and consumers exposed to pesticide residues on food. If these external costs were borne by the farmer, it would influence their decision and consequently could result in many different outcomes including increasing the cost of food, decreasing pesticide use, improving the health of the population, and even lowering taxes.

INTEGRATED PEST MANAGEMENT (IPM)

The goal of IPM is not to completely eradicate pests, only to reduce their numbers to economically tolerable levels. This is accomplished through the combination of complementary pest management strategies. IPM makes use of the natural enemies of the pest species, **crop rotation**, the use of pheromones or introduction of sterile males into the population to interfere with reproduction, and limited use of carefully applied narrow spectrum or natural pesticides.

this reduces the numbers

CIRCLE OF POISON

There are numerous pesticides that have been banned in one country, while still being legally used in others. Some pesticides that are banned in the United States, for example, are still produced and exported to other countries where they can be legally applied to crops. The crops are then harvested and exported to the United States for consumption. This practice, which continues to expose United States residents to a banned pesticide, is known as the "circle of poison."

RACHEL CARSON

The author of the book *Silent Spring*, published in 1962, raised public awareness about the environmental consequences of DDT use, and played a pivotal role in raising public awareness about environmental issues at the beginning of the modern environmental movement in the United States.

MEAT PRODUCTION

Meat consumption is growing as the level of personal income rises in developing countries, and as more people enter the middle class around the world. The production of meat increases the burden that agriculture places on the environment. It takes 5–10 pounds of grain to produce one pound of meat. In addition to multiplying the environmental problems associated with grain production (habitat destruction, fertilizer and pesticide use) by a factor of 5–10, meat production often occurs, in part, on **factory farms** or feedlots. A factory farm is a large-scale animal confinement operation that can house hundreds of thousands or even millions of animals in a single location where they can be fattened quickly for meat production. Environmental concerns about factory farming include the substantial use of antibiotics and growth hormones, massive water consumption, air and water pollution resulting from the disposal of animal wastes, and an increase in emergent infectious diseases and deadly bacteria (such as mad cow disease, avian flu, H1N1 and *E. coli* 0157-H7).

Aquaculture is the practice of farming aquatic organisms. In freshwater, examples of farmed species of fish include carp, tilapia, catfish, and trout. In saltwater, examples of farmed species include seaweed, mollusks (such as oysters, clams, and mussels), crustaceans (such as shrimp) and fish (such as salmon and yellowtail). Environmental concerns about aquaculture include nutrient pollution due to excess food and biological wastes, excessive antibiotic use, changes to genetic diversity as a result of farmed escapees cross-breeding with native species, and degradation of aquatic ecosystems.

FISH HARVESTING

A variety of fishing techniques are used to harvest wild marine species. Modern fish harvesting methods use satellites, sonar, and refrigerated ships to decimate fisheries around the world. Modern fish harvesting and the environmental problems associated with them include:

Long-line fishing: Up to 80 miles of fishing line is strung out in the water with thousands of baited hooks attached to it, then hauled in to catch swordfish, tuna, and shark. Species that are inadvertently caught and killed (also known as **bycatch**) includes sea turtles, dolphins, and sea birds.

Purse seine fishing: A net is used to surround a large school of fish such as tuna, herring or mackerel. The net is then closed at the surface like a purse and hauled aboard the ship. Bycatch includes any fish that is in the area, but commonly includes dolphins that were feeding on the school of fish that was caught.

Drift-net fishing: A net is set to hang in the water from the surface to as far as 50 feet below the surface and extend for up to 40 miles. Drift nets catch large numbers of individuals from non-target species including sea turtles, and dolphins that often suffocate while entangled underwater in the net.

Trawler fishing: Large metal chain baskets holding nets are dragged across the ocean floor scouring the bottom for shrimp, scallops, and flounder. They scrape up just about everything on the ocean floor.

Overfishing has depleted many of the world's most abundant fisheries. Limits or bans on fishing have been implemented in most fisheries to prevent further depletion.

WHALING

Whaling is practiced by several countries including Iceland, Japan, Norway and Russia. Since whales are large and surface to breathe every few minutes, they are fairly easy to spot and kill. Whaling has subsided dramatically since the 1970s and populations of some whale populations have begun to recover.

MULTIPLE-CHOICE QUESTIONS

1. In the year 2010, a country had a population of 10 million people, a birth rate of 7.2%, and a death rate of 2.2%. If the birth and death rates remain constant, the population will be close to 40 million in
   (A) 2015
   (B) 2024
   (C) 2028
   (D) 2032
   (E) 2038

2. A country that undergoes a demographic transition will go through a period of rapid population growth, and later stabilize at
   (A) its original number
   (B) the maximum carrying capacity of the land
   (C) a population larger than before the transition
   (D) a constant, positive rate of growth
   (E) a constant, negative rate of growth

3. When compared to most developed countries, most developing countries have higher
   (A) infant mortality rates
   (B) per capita GNPs
   (C) literacy rates
   (D) rates of education among women
   (E) rates of industrialization

4. Blindness may be caused by a diet deficient in the nutrient
   (A) iodine
   (B) iron
   (C) protein
   (D) vitamin D
   (E) vitamin A

5. Which of the following best explains how a pest develops resistance to a chemical pesticide?
   (A) Natural selection takes place.
   (B) The pest develops adaptations during times of secondary pest outbreaks.
   (C) Mutation and genetic drift occur.
   (D) Geographic isolation results in the emergence of a new pest species.
   (E) Punctuated equilibrium takes place.

6. Crops genetically engineered to fix nitrogen would have which of the following advantages?
   (A) Increased disease resistance
   (B) Increased drought tolerance
   (C) Decreased need for chemical fertilizer
   (D) Decreased absorption of toxic chemicals
   (E) Increased tolerance of air pollution

7. Which of the following problems can be best addressed with contour plowing?
   (A) The failure of terracing
   (B) The excessive use of pesticides
   (C) Soil erosion
   (D) Waterlogging
   (E) Soil salinization

8. Which of the following is a feature of integrated pest management?
   (A) It makes use of the natural enemies of pests.
   (B) It makes effective use of disease transfer organisms.
   (C) It relies on the use of intermittent groundwater pumping stations.
   (D) It requires intense cultivation of marginal land.
   (E) It is most effective on land within 100 miles of the coast.

9. The connection between farming and ecological succession is best exemplified by which of the following?
   (A) Farmland is maintained permanently in a state of late succession.
   (B) Farmland is maintained permanently in a state of mid succession.
   (C) Farmland is maintained permanently in a state of primary succession.
   (D) Farmland is maintained permanently in a state of early succession.
   (E) Farmland artificially skips the first stages of succession.

10. Irrigation of farmland refers to which of the following?
    (A) The artificial addition of fertilizers
    (B) The spraying of pesticides
    (C) The crossing of one or more varieties of a species to produce a hybrid offspring with particular desired qualities
    (D) The artificial addition of water
    (E) The growing of plants in a nutrient-rich solution

11. Which of the following is the best description of hydroponics?
    (A) Monocultures that satisfy the per-capita food demand of a nation
    (B) The growing of plants in a fertilized water solution on an artificial substrate
    (C) The application of water and fertilizer to the soil from tubes that spray this mixture in the form of a fine mist
    (D) Fish farming making use of treated sewage
    (E) Anthropogenic crop cultures

12. The Green Revolution is most closely associated with the time period between
    (A) the U.S. Civil War and World War I
    (B) the beginning and the end of the Industrial Revolution
    (C) World War I and World War II
    (D) World War II and the present
    (E) the American Revolution and the U.S. Civil War

13. Where is overnutrition most common today?
    (A) In developing nations of Central Africa
    (B) In tropical nations of Asia
    (C) In Pacific and Indian Ocean island nations
    (D) In mountainous nations of South America
    (E) In developed nations of Europe and North America

14. This layer of soil is also known as the topsoil; it contains much humus.
    (A) A horizon
    (B) B horizon
    (C) C horizon
    (D) O horizon
    (E) Z horizon

15. It is determined that a soil sample is composed of 23% silt, 11% clay, and 66% sand. According to the soil triangle, which of the following is the soil texture of the soil?
    (A) Silty clay loam
    (B) Silt loam
    (C) Clay
    (D) Sandy loam
    (E) Loamy sand

FREE-RESPONSE QUESTION

The world's population grew from approximately 2.6 to 5.2 billion between 1952 and 1987. The green revolution is credited with allowing the world's food supply to keep pace with the rapid growth of human population during that time. The replacement of traditional crops with high-yielding monocultures is central to the agricultural practices associated with the green revolution.

a) Assuming that the population growth during this time period followed an exponential model, calculate the average annual population growth rate of the world between 1952 and 1987 as a percentage.

b) Describe ONE advantage and ONE environmental disadvantage associated with the farming of monocultures.

c) Another agricultural practice associated with the green revolution is the intensive irrigation of crops. Describe TWO negative environmental effects associated with intensive irrigation.

d) Other than the extensive use of monocultures and intensive irrigation, identify and describe TWO additional agricultural practices associated with the green revolution, and for each practice describe ONE environmental disadvantage associated with it.

ANSWERS

MULTIPLE-CHOICE QUESTIONS

1. **ANSWER: E.** To grow from 10 million to 40 million people, the population must double twice. With a birth rate of 7.2% and a death rate of 2.2% the population growth rate is 7.2 − 2.2 = 5%. The doubling time for the population is 70 / 5 = 14 years. To double twice it will take 14 × 2 = 28 years. 2010 + 28 = 2038 (*Living in the Environment,* 16th ed., pages G5 and G15 / 17th ed., pages G4 and G14).

2. **ANSWER: C.** The population of a country is stable before and after; however, it grows substantially during a demographic transition (*Living in the Environment,* 16th ed., pages 133–134 / 17th ed., pages 139–140).

3. **ANSWER: A.** The infant mortality rate is usually relatively low in developed nations when compared to developing nations (*Living in the Environment,* 16th ed., page 129 / 17th ed., page 133).

4. **ANSWER: E.** A deficiency in vitamin A, also known as beta-carotene, may result in blindness. Golden rice is a genetically modified crop that may reduce blindness by providing vitamin A to populations (*Living in the Environment,* 16th ed., page 275 / 17th ed., page 279).

5. **ANSWER: A.** Pest populations become resistant to pesticides when small numbers of the pest species survive an application of a pesticide and those survivors reproduce and pass their genes for resistance on to their offspring. This is the natural selection process of evolution (*Living in the Environment,* 16th ed., page 296 / 17th ed., page 299).

6. **ANSWER: C.** Since most crops cannot fix their own nitrogen, the addition of fertilizers is required to provide the plants with sufficient nitrogen in the soil. Genetically modified plants that can fix nitrogen would require less fertilizer (*Living in the Environment,* 16th ed., pages 283–284 / 17th ed., page 294).

7. **ANSWER: C.** Contour plowing follows the natural contours of the land and prevents water from accelerating down slopes, which increases soil erosion. The alternative of plowing up and down the slopes increases soil erosion (*Living in the Environment,* 16th ed., page 302 / 17th ed., pages 304–305).

8. **ANSWER: A.** Among other practices, IPM makes use of the natural enemies of a pest species to control the pest (*Living in the Environment,* 16th ed., page 300 / 17th ed., pages 302–303).

9. **ANSWER: D.** Most crop species are fast-growing, sun-tolerant annual grasses, herbs, and shrubs; plants like the early and mid-successional plants that re-populate an area by secondary succession following a disturbance (*Living in the Environment,* 16th ed., pages 116–117 / 17th ed., pages 118–119).

10. **ANSWER: D.** Irrigation is the addition of water to agricultural lands (*Living in the Environment,* 16th ed., chapter 12 / 17th ed., chapter 12).

11. **ANSWER: B.** Hydroponics is the practice of growing plants without soil in solutions or on an artificial substrate containing the nutrients needed for plant growth (*Living in the Environment,* 16th ed., pages 279–280 / 17th ed., page 282).

12. **ANSWER: D.** The Green Revolution dates back to the 1940s (*Living in the Environment,* 16th ed., page 282 / 17th ed., page 283).

13. **ANSWER: E.** Overnutrition is commonly associated with developed nations (*Living in the Environment,* 16th ed., pages 278–279 / 17th ed., page 280).

14. **ANSWER: A.** The A horizon is also known as topsoil. It is composed of mineral-containing weathered parent material and humus (*Living in the Environment,* 16th ed., page 281 / 17th ed., page 284).

15. **ANSWER: D.** Begin by extending the clay line horizontally to the right from 11% to meet the silt line coming down from 23% and the sand line coming up from 66%. They meet in the sandy

loam region of the triangle (*Living in the Environment,* 16th ed., not included / 17th ed., not included).

FREE-RESPONSE SCORING GUIDELINES

a) Assuming that the population growth during this time period followed an exponential model, calculate the average annual population growth rate of the world between 1952 an 1987 as a percentage.

2 points can be earned—1 point for a correct setup and 1 point for a correct calculation of the population growth rate of 2%

A correct setup must include the difference between 1952 and 1987.

$$1987 - 1952 = 35 \text{ years}$$

$$\frac{70}{30} = 2\% \quad \text{or} \quad \frac{70}{(1987 - 1952)} = 2\%$$

b) Describe ONE advantage and ONE environmental disadvantage associated with the farming of monocultures.

2 points can be earned—1 point for a correct advantage, and 1 point for a correct environmental disadvantage

Environmental advantage of farming monocultures:
- higher yields per acre
- uniform practices for farming reduce costs
- fertilizers and pesticides can be specifically targeted for the crop

Environmental disadvantage of farming monocultures:
- loss of genetic diversity
- loss of soil fertility due to intense farming requiring additional fertilizer that can run off into waterways causing cultural eutrophication
- pest adaptation to genetically identical crops requires larger inputs of pesticides, killing more non-target species

c) Another agricultural practice associated with the green revolution is the intensive irrigation of crops. Describe TWO negative environmental effects associated with intensive irrigation.

2 points can be earned—1 point for each correct description of a negative environmental effect of the practice of irrigating crops
- soil erosion due to irrigation water
- soil salinization resulting from evaporation

■ waterlogging due to overwatering of farmland
■ sediment pollution in waterways due to erosion
■ aquifer depletion from intense irrigation
■ diversion of water from other sources and uses

d) Other than the extensive use of monocultures and intensive irrigation, identify and describe TWO additional agricultural practices associated with the green revolution, and for each practice describe ONE environmental cost associated with it.

4 points can be earned—1 point for each correct agricultural practice identified, and 1 point for each associated environmental disadvantage

large inputs of artificial fertilizers
■ algal blooms in local waterways resulting from fertilizer runoff
■ fish kills due to low dissolved oxygen concentrations that result from the decomposition of excess organic material (cultural eutrophication)
■ formation of the greenhouse gas nitrous oxide (N_2O) leading to global warming

large inputs of pesticides
■ kill non-target species
■ fish kills result from pesticide runoff into waterways
■ air pollution resulting from spraying

large inputs of fossil fuels
■ release of carbon dioxide which contributes to global warming
■ environmental damage associated with the mining of fossil fuels
■ emission of NO_x which is a precursor to acid rain, which can lower the pH in waterways and soils killing any plants, animals, and fish that are sensitive to changes in the pH of their habitat

Answer page

ENVIRONMENTAL HAZARDS & HUMAN HEALTH

KEY CONCEPTS

- One of the greatest risks to human health is living in crowded, unsanitary, impoverished conditions. Humans are exposed to many biological hazards including transmissible and non-transmissible diseases.
- Toxicologists use a variety of methods to determine how harmful a substance is to living organisms.
- Humans produce many chemicals, some that can have negative impacts on the health of both humans and wildlife.
- Lifestyle choices can put one at greater risk for premature death.

KEY VOCABULARY

acute effect	dose-response curve
biological hazard	dysentery
biomagnification	endocrine system
carcinogens	epidemic
chemical hazard	HIV
cholera	hormonally active agent (HAA)
chronic effect	immune system
cultural hazard	infectious disease
dose	influenza

lifestyle choices

malaria

median lethal dosage (LD50)

mutagen

neurotoxin

non-transmissible disease

non-threshold dose-response

pandemic

pathogen

persistence

physical hazard

risk

risk assessment

risk management

solubility

teratogen

threshold dose-response

toxic chemical

toxicity

toxicology

transmissible disease

tuberculosis

TYPES OF MAJOR HEALTH HAZARDS

Humans take a variety of risks just by carrying out day-to-day activities. These risks include anything from driving a car to **lifestyle choices** such as smoking. In the context of this chapter, a **risk** is defined as the probability of harmful effects to human health resulting from exposure to an environmental hazard. Harmful effects can include disease, bodily injury, economic loss or damage, and even death. There are five major types of hazards humans are exposed to:

- **Biological hazards** are **pathogens** that are living organisms (protists, bacteria, fungi) and viruses that can cause human disease.
- **Chemical hazards** are in the air, soil, and water we drink and food we ingest. Some examples include pesticides, heavy metals (lead, mercury), PCBs, and asbestos.
- **Physical hazards** typically include events such as fires, earthquakes, volcanic eruptions, floods, and storms.
- **Cultural hazards** include living in areas with high crime rates, working in unsafe conditions, frequent driving on highways, and poverty.
- **Lifestyle hazards** are choices humans make that pose a health concern. Some examples are having unprotected sex, smoking, and drug use.

The process of **risk assessment** is used to determine the probability of adverse human health effects resulting from exposure to a specific hazard. According to the Environmental Protection Agency, there are four steps involved in risk assessment.

- **Step 1**—Hazard Identification: Determines whether the hazard has potential to cause human harm.
- **Step 2**—Dose-Response Assessment: Examines the probability of human harm and statistical relationships between exposure and effects.
- **Step 3**—Exposure Assessment: Explores the results of frequency, timing, and levels of contact with a hazard.

■ **Step 4**—<u>Risk Characterization</u>: Utilizes data to draw conclusions about the probability of human health risk from exposure to a specific hazard.

Risk management includes things like cost analysis of remediating the specific hazard and possibly establishing legal limits for discharge, exposure, and allowable levels of the hazard. Although the EPA can make recommendations for setting limits on pollution, it is ultimately an act of Congress that is required to create the laws for pollution control. An underlying theme to remember when thinking about pollution reduction is it is typically much easier and less costly to remove the first unit of pollution compared to the last.

BIOLOGICAL HAZARDS TO HUMAN HEALTH

According to the World Health Organization, despite vast advances in technology and medicine in the last fifty years, cardiovascular disease and infectious disease are still leading causes of death for humans worldwide. Cardiovascular (heart and blood vessel) disease is an example of a **non-transmissible disease,** one that cannot be spread from person to person. Other examples include diabetes, cancers, asthma, and malnutrition. An **infectious disease** can be spread from person to person and is therefore called a contagious or communicable disease. Examples of infectious disease include influenza, HIV, malaria, tuberculosis, and diarrheal diseases. These diseases, caused by pathogens, can spread from person to person through water, air, food, and bodily fluids. Unfortunately, where you live and your level of poverty can increase the probability of contracting some of these infectious diseases. An outbreak of an infectious disease that is limited to one area or region is known as an **epidemic**. However, if this disease spreads globally it is referred to as a **pandemic**.

know the difference between these types of diseases

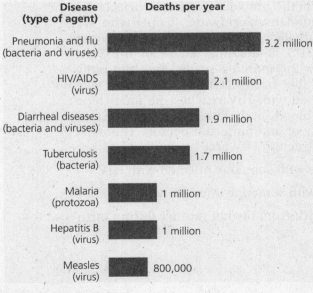

Seven deadliest infectious diseases globally

Disease (type of agent)	Deaths per year
Pneumonia and flu (bacteria and viruses)	3.2 million
HIV/AIDS (virus)	2.1 million
Diarrheal diseases (bacteria and viruses)	1.9 million
Tuberculosis (bacteria)	1.7 million
Malaria (protozoa)	1 million
Hepatitis B (virus)	1 million
Measles (virus)	800,000

© Cengage Learning 2012

INFLUENZA

Influenza is the most deadly infectious disease. This infectious disease, commonly known as the flu, is a very contagious respiratory illness caused by a virus. Each year the seasonal flu virus causes more human deaths than any other viral disease. Since influenza is viral, antibiotics cannot be used to treat it and instead people must get vaccinated in order to prevent getting the disease. The Center for Disease Control estimates 5% to 20% of the population in the United States contracts the seasonal flu virus each year. Included below are several examples of viral outbreaks of new viral strains that have emerged from animal origins. It is important to remember that while they may have received a lot of media coverage, the following viral strains are not responsible for nearly as many deaths as the regular seasonal flu virus is each year. For example, in 2008, the Avian flu was not responsible for any deaths in the United States, whereas the seasonal flu contributed to the deaths of over 36,000.

Avian Influenza (H5N1) – The Avian flu is a viral infection whose origin is from wild bird populations that naturally carry this virus in their intestines without getting sick from it. However, it has been known to spread to domesticated birds such as geese, turkeys, and chickens. Humans can contract this virus from working with infected poultry; however, those cases are rare. Since 2003, approximately 400 cases of humans infected with Avian flu have been reported, mostly in areas such as Asia, Africa, and Europe.

Swine Influenza (H1N1) – A new flu virus of swine origin emerged in the spring of 2009 in parts of Mexico and the United States. By June of 2009 the World Health Organization declared this flu a pandemic as it had spread to over 70 countries. The death toll for this virus is still low in comparison to the seasonal flu virus.

HUMAN IMMUNE DEFICIENCY VIRUS (HIV)

As you can see from the diagram on the previous page, this virus is the second most deadly disease for humans worldwide. People who are infected with HIV will eventually develop AIDS (Acquired Immunodeficiency Syndrome). AIDS is the final stage of the viral infection and so severely weakens the immune system that the body cannot defend itself from other viral or bacterial infections. It may take many years before a person infected with HIV reaches the final stage of AIDS. HIV is contracted when blood, body fluids, or breast milk of an infected person enters the body of an uninfected person. The most common activities that lead to contracting HIV are:

1. unprotected sexual intercourse with someone infected with HIV

2. sharing needles and syringes with someone infected with HIV

3. a fetus or infant can contract HIV from his/her mother during birth or through breast-feeding

<u>Treatment:</u> Although a wide range of antiviral drugs has been developed to slow the progression of AIDS in HIV patients, these medicines are very expensive and often are not a realistic solution for people in developing countries. The World Health Organization recommends the following to prevent the spread of HIV:

■ educational programs for both school-aged children and adults to encourage abstinence or condom use
■ free testing for HIV at local clinics
■ targeted education and free testing for high-risk groups such as sex workers and intravenous drug users
■ increased funding for research to develop new methods of treatment and to provide low-cost drugs to slow the progression of the disease

No cure only treatments

MALARIA

This is a mosquito-borne disease that spreads by the protozoan parasite, *Plasmodium.* The most common species of mosquito that carries this type of parasite is the *Anopheles.* Typically these mosquitoes are restricted to warmer areas near the equator, including Africa, South America, Central America, and parts of southern Asia. However, if the global climate continues to warm, the distribution of these mosquitoes, as well as the number of cases of malaria, is likely to spread. Although DDT use is controversial and banned in the United States because of its negative impact on the environment, this pesticide is effective at reducing mosquito populations and continues to be used worldwide. As of 2006, the World Health Organization continues to support the use of DDT around the equator to control malaria.

Caused by parasite

DIARRHEAL DISEASES

Most people in developed countries like the United States do not think about diarrheal diseases being a major cause of death. However, by examining the diagram on page 149, you can see that nearly 2 million people a year die from this type of infectious disease. Diarrheal disease can be caused by a host of organisms such as bacteria, viruses, or protozoa. Two common diarrheal diseases are **cholera** and **dysentery**. Cholera is caused by bacteria, whereas dysentery can be caused by bacteria, protists (often amoebas), or parasitic worms. Often people in developing countries contract these diseases from unsanitary drinking water that is contaminated with feces from runoff of human sewage or animal waste. Children in developing countries who are already malnourished and therefore have weakened immune systems are especially at risk for suffering from these types of diarrheal diseases.

TUBERCULOSIS

This bacterial disease primarily affects people in developing countries who live in crowded conditions. This respiratory disease spreads easily from person to person through the air by coughs and sneezes from infected individuals. Since this disease is bacterial, it should be possible to treat it effectively with antibiotics. However, more and more cases of antibiotic-resistant strains of TB have recently been observed in countries such as Russia, China, India, and Africa.

HEPATITIS B

The hepatitis virus is spread in the same way as HIV with the exception that infants cannot contract the disease from an infected mother through breast-feeding. Unlike HIV, people who contract Hepatitis B typically start showing symptoms within a few months. People infected with this disease can experience damage to the liver including cirrhosis and possibly cancer.

MEASLES

This is an extremely contagious respiratory disease also caused by a virus. This virus is easily spread through the air by respiratory droplets from coughs and sneezes. However, the incidence of measles in developed countries is very low due to widespread vaccinations for children.

SEVERE ACUTE RESPIRATORY SYNDROME (SARS)

This respiratory virus is spread in the same manner as hepatitis, through the air from coughs and sneezes. SARS was first reported in 2002 in an outbreak in China. According to the World Health Organization, approximately 8,500 people reported symptoms from the disease and 812 people died from the outbreak in 2002 to 2003.

WEST NILE VIRUS

West Nile Virus most commonly cycles between mosquitoes and wild bird populations. However, it can spread to humans through an infected mosquito or contact with bodily fluids of wild animals who have also been infected.

SOLUTIONS FOR REDUCING INFECTIOUS DISEASE

Due to medical advancements and increasing availability of vaccines for children in developing countries, infectious disease has seen a dramatic decline over the last 30 years. Many infectious diseases could be even further prevented by:

- improving drinking water conditions in developing countries
- decreasing malnutrition to improve immune systems to battle disease
- implementing global educational programs to prevent HIV/AIDS
- increasing availability of vaccines to children in developing countries
- reducing unnecessary use of antibiotics in humans and livestock

AP Tip

The AP exam will test your knowledge on how human activities impact the natural selection of organisms in our environment. Recently, we have seen an increase in resistance to pesticides by target insects and to antibiotics by pathogenic bacteria. How does this occur? Widespread use of pesticides or antibiotics eliminates the weaker individuals in a rapidly reproducing population such as insects or bacteria. This causes an increase in the frequency of individuals in the population who have a genetic resistance to pesticides or antibiotics because they are the ones left to rapidly reproduce. What can we do? As you learned in Chapter 4, sustainable agricultural practices can reduce the need for pesticides to control pest populations in the production of crops, and the use of free-range practices or reduced crowding in feedlot operations can lower the amount of antibiotics necessary to control disease in animals.

EVALUATING CHEMICAL HAZARDS

Humans are constantly exposed to a myriad of invisible chemical compounds. These compounds are produced from numerous human activities from burning fossil fuels for energy to the production of consumer goods. Chemicals can enter living organisms in many ways, including inhalation, ingestion, or absorption through the skin. The study of the detrimental effects these chemicals have on both humans and wildlife is known as **toxicology**. Toxicologists collect data from various resources to try and determine the effects of a particular chemical. Toxicity is the ability of that chemical to cause harm to a living organism. Some key characteristics that can cause a chemical to be toxic include:

Persistence: Some chemicals will last for long periods of time in the environment because they are not easily degraded or broken down.

Solubility: Chemicals that are fat soluble easily accumulate in the tissue of living organisms. Chemicals that are water soluble will be dissolved easily in bodies of water.

Biomagnification: Certain compounds that accumulate in body tissues can be passed from one organism to another through the food chain. Organisms on higher trophic levels, like secondary and tertiary consumers, will have the highest concentration of these materials in their bodies.

Some of our well-known toxic chemicals belong to a group of synthetic organic compounds known as chlorinated hydrocarbons. These chemicals are harmful because they persist for long periods of time in the environment, are fat soluble, and also accumulate to toxic concentrations in organisms at higher trophic levels due to biomagnification. Examples of these compounds include DDT, PCBs, and vinyl chloride.

Bald eagle example of this

When defining a harmful level, toxicologists must determine the average **dose** to which an organism is generally exposed and the effects of increasing that exposure. Toxicity of a substance can vary with the dose to which an organism is exposed and may have a threshold level below which no effects can be discerned. By plotting an organism's response to a given chemical versus the dose received, one can generate a graph known as a **dose-response curve**. The **response** is any negative health effect elicited from that particular material. An **acute effect** is an immediate response to exposure. A **chronic effect** can occur from a single dose or long-term exposure to smaller doses of a toxin. This effect causes longer-lasting or permanent damage to the body, such as liver and kidney disease or even cancer. By examining the dose-response curve, toxicologists can determine what dose would be required to be lethal for 50% of the test population. This is known as the **median lethal dosage** or LD50.

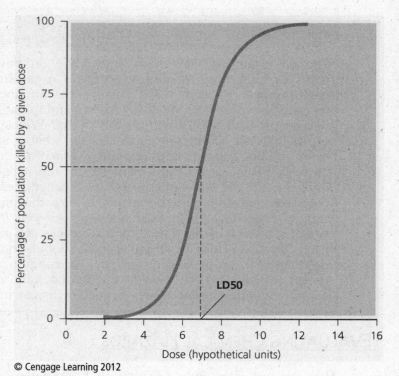

© Cengage Learning 2012

[handwritten note: LD50 = concentration not time]

If the response or effect begins at zero and increases continuously with a dosage, then it is referred to as a **non-threshold dose-response** model. In contrast, a **threshold dose-response** model shows that harmful effects do not occur until after the dose exceeds a threshold level.

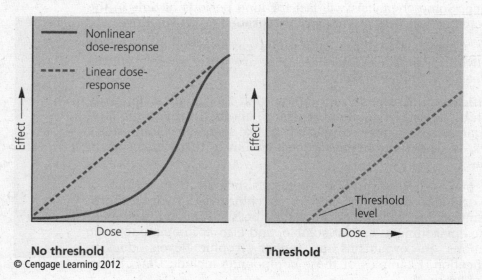

No threshold
© Cengage Learning 2012

Threshold

PROBLEMS WITH TOXICITY TESTING

There are many issues with producing accurate pictures of how chemical toxins really impact living organisms. Due to genetic variability, each individual can exhibit a different response to a given level or type of chemical exposure. Also, we typically test only for the response to one chemical at a time. However, living organisms are exposed to a wide variety of toxins at once, and understanding the synergistic effect of a combination of chemical compounds is almost impossible.

TYPES OF CHEMICAL HAZARDS

Toxic chemicals may cause short-term or permanent damage to humans or animals. There are three main categories of toxins: carcinogens, mutagens, and teratogens. Many chemicals can fall into more than one of these main categories.

> **Carcinogen:** These compounds cause or promote various types of cancer in the human body. Cancerous cells, also known as malignant cells, multiply uncontrollably and create tumors that damage body tissue and may cause death. Examples of carcinogens include benzene, poly-aromatic hydrocarbons found in tobacco smoke, formaldehyde, dioxins, and PCBs.

[handwritten: Cacin = Cancer]

> **Mutagen:** This category of chemical hazard promotes mutations or changes in DNA. These changes may also cause cancers or be passed on to future generations.

> **Teratogens:** These are chemical hazards that cause birth defects to a fetus or embryo. Examples of teratogens include heavy metals, formaldehyde, ethyl alcohol, PCBs, and phthalates.

Exposure to chemical toxins often causes damage to many of the body's systems. The **immune system**, whose role is to produce antibodies to protect against infection and disease, is often weakened by exposure to chemical toxins. This leaves the body more vulnerable to attack from pathogenic bacteria, viruses, and parasites. Also, chemical toxins can cause devastating affects on the nervous system. Toxins that cause damage to the brain, nerves, or spinal cord are known as **neurotoxins**. Some examples of neurotoxins include methyl mercury, PCBs, and lead.

[handwritten: know the immune system]

Recently, scientists have provided evidence that chemical toxins can disrupt the endocrine system in both humans and wildlife. The **endocrine system** is responsible for producing hormones that help regulate reproductive systems, growth and development, and metabolism. Some chemical toxins, known as **hormonally active agents (HAA)**, are endocrine disruptors because they either mimic estrogen (female sex hormone) or block androgens (male sex hormones) from binding to their appropriate receptor sites in the cell. These endocrine disruptors are often called "gender benders" due to their damage to sexual development, such as lower sperm counts and the presence of both male and female sex organs. Scientists are concerned that these toxins may also cause increased cases of testicular cancer in men and breast cancer in women. Examples of hormonally active agents include DDT, PCBs, and phthalates.

Case Study — Bhopal, India

In 1984 the world's most horrific industrial accident happened at a pesticide manufacturing plant in Bhopal, India. An explosion occurred in an underground storage tank that released large quantities of a highly toxic gas used to produce carbamate pesticides. This gas was converted into deadly hydrogen cyanide once in the atmosphere. Over 50,000 people suffered from permanent injuries including blindness, lung damage, and neurological disorders. The death toll from the accident is estimated between 15,000 to over 20,000 people. The AP exam will require you to know specific examples of environmental accidents such as this one. For more information on environmental toxins don't forget to see supplements in the back of your book (*Living in the Environment*, 15th ed., pages S65 and S68 / 16th ed., pages S33–S38). Also, see a full list of case studies in Part 3 of this review book.

(handwritten margin note: may show up on the test)

You will gain more knowledge of other environmental toxins and their impacts as you study the air and water pollution chapters. However, the table below is a basic introduction to common environmental toxins you will be expected to know on the AP exam.

(handwritten margin note: toxins)

Chemical Toxin	Sources	Human or Wildlife Health Impact
PCBs	■ used as electrical insulators, fire retardant materials, pesticides, and as adhesives (banned in the U.S.)	■ neurotoxin causing brain damage in fetuses ■ endocrine disruptor causing reproductive cancers
DDT	■ a commonly used pesticide in the U.S. prior to banning it in 1972 ■ still used in developing countries to control malaria and pests	■ biomagnifies in the food chain of ecosystems ■ causes reproductive damages and cancers in avian (bird) populations

Chemical Toxin	Sources	Human or Wildlife Health Impact
Phthalates	▪ group of chemicals used in the production of plastics ▪ used as solvents in many products such as vinyl flooring, adhesives, detergents, and some personal care products like soap and shampoo	▪ causes reproductive damage and cancers
Atrazine	▪ one of the most widely used pesticides in the U.S. ▪ herbicide primarily used to control weed populations in the Midwest	▪ this pesticide is currently being monitored by the EPA to determine if it is linked to endocrine cancers in humans and amphibians
Bisphenol A	▪ a chemical building block for plastic consumer goods such as water bottles, food containers, and microwaveable dishes	▪ some evidence suggests exposure can lead to neurological damage and reproductive cancers
Heavy Metals (mercury, arsenic, lead, cadmium)	▪ heavy metal pollution is often generated from smelting metals and incineration of municipal waste ▪ elemental mercury is used in batteries and fluorescent lights ▪ inorganic mercury released from coal burning is converted to toxic methyl mercury by bacteria	▪ heavy metals often biomagnify in the food chain ▪ cause neurological damage especially to fetuses ▪ can be carcinogenic
Benzene	▪ emissions from burning coal and oil and tobacco smoke	▪ short-term exposure causes dizziness and nausea ▪ long-term exposure causes damage to the liver and reproductive system, cancer, and birth defects

Know the list

toxins

toxins

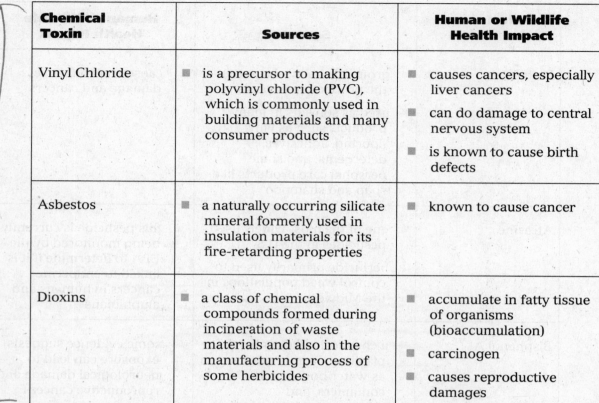

Chemical Toxin	Sources	Human or Wildlife Health Impact
Vinyl Chloride	■ is a precursor to making polyvinyl chloride (PVC), which is commonly used in building materials and many consumer products	■ causes cancers, especially liver cancers ■ can do damage to central nervous system ■ is known to cause birth defects
Asbestos	■ a naturally occurring silicate mineral formerly used in insulation materials for its fire-retarding properties	■ known to cause cancer
Dioxins	■ a class of chemical compounds formed during incineration of waste materials and also in the manufacturing process of some herbicides	■ accumulate in fatty tissue of organisms (bioaccumulation) ■ carcinogen ■ causes reproductive damages

LEGISLATION THAT REGULATES CHEMICAL TOXINS*

Know the acts well!

Federal Insecticide, Fungicide, and Rodenticide Act (FIFRA): Gives the EPA the authority to regulate the sale, packaging, distribution, and disposal of pesticides. The EPA also has the right to suspend the use of pesticides that are found to pose unreasonable risks to humans or wildlife.

Federal Food, Drug, and Cosmetic Act: Allows the EPA to set tolerance levels for pesticide residue on food for human consumption as well as on feed meant for livestock consumption.

Food Quality Protection Act of 1996: This law amended the two aforementioned laws. It outlines more requirements for assessing tolerance levels for pesticides. It also provides extra funding for the protection of infants and children.

Emergency Planning and Community Right-to-Know Act: Commonly known as the "Right-to-Know Act," this legislation requires federal, state, and local governments to improve public knowledge and access to information regarding toxic chemicals.

---

*Legislation that regulates air and water chemical toxins will be covered in Chapters 6 and 8, respectively.

CULTURAL AND LIFESTYLE HAZARDS

The greatest risk that people in developing countries face today is poverty. Poverty increases the chance of being exposed to infectious disease from living in crowded conditions with inadequate availability to sanitary conditions including clean drinking water. People in impoverished conditions also suffer from malnutrition, which increases their susceptibility to disease and death.

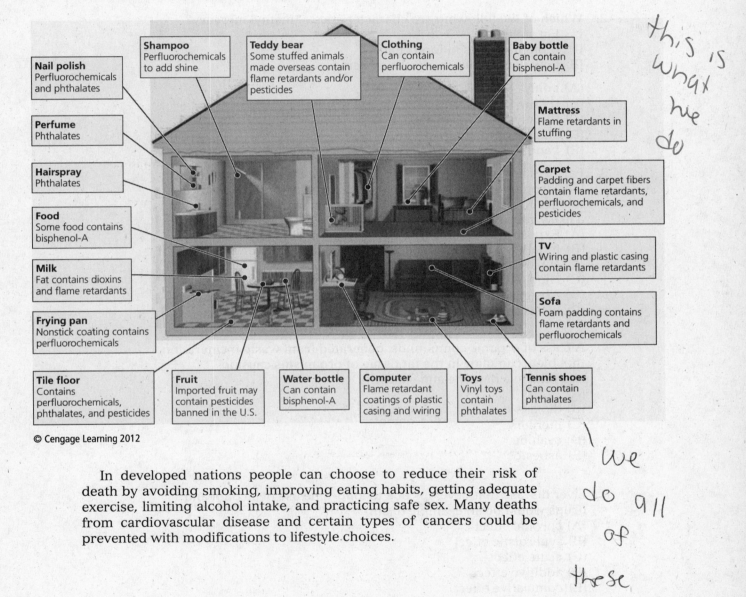

Nail polish
Perfluorochemicals and phthalates

Perfume
Phthalates

Hairspray
Phthalates

Food
Some food contains bisphenol-A

Milk
Fat contains dioxins and flame retardants

Frying pan
Nonstick coating contains perfluorochemicals

Tile floor
Contains perfluorochemicals, phthalates, and pesticides

Shampoo
Perfluorochemicals to add shine

Teddy bear
Some stuffed animals made overseas contain flame retardants and/or pesticides

Fruit
Imported fruit may contain pesticides banned in the U.S.

Water bottle
Can contain bisphenol-A

Clothing
Can contain perfluorochemicals

Computer
Flame retardant coatings of plastic casing and wiring

Baby bottle
Can contain bisphenol-A

Mattress
Flame retardants in stuffing

Carpet
Padding and carpet fibers contain flame retardants, perfluorochemicals, and pesticides

TV
Wiring and plastic casing contain flame retardants

Sofa
Foam padding contains flame retardants and perfluorochemicals

Toys
Vinyl toys contain phthalates

Tennis shoes
Can contain phthalates

© Cengage Learning 2012

In developed nations people can choose to reduce their risk of death by avoiding smoking, improving eating habits, getting adequate exercise, limiting alcohol intake, and practicing safe sex. Many deaths from cardiovascular disease and certain types of cancers could be prevented with modifications to lifestyle choices.

MULTIPLE-CHOICE QUESTIONS

1. Funding research to improve treatment of which of the following infectious diseases would decrease global death rates the most?
   (A) Avian flu
   (B) Influenza
   (C) HIV
   (D) Malaria
   (E) SARs

2. Which of the following are characteristics of methyl mercury?
   I.   Fat soluble
   II. It biomagnifies in food chain
   III. Low persistence in aquatic systems

   (A) I only
   (B) II only
   (C) III only
   (D) I and II only
   (E) I and III only

3. Farmers in the midwest United States have discovered that the local frog population is declining. Scientists determine this is due to male frogs' inability to produce sperm. Which of the following is a likely cause?
   (A) Exposure to arsenic from local metal smelting plants
   (B) Inhalation of inorganic mercury from local power plant emissions
   (C) High levels of atrazine in the water from agricultural runoff
   (D) Absorption of high levels of nitric acid through their skin
   (E) Increasing UV radiation in the Midwest

4. A class of organic compounds, generated from waste incineration, that bioaccumulate in the fat tissue of organisms causing reproductive damage and cancer is
   (A) PCBs
   (B) dioxins
   (C) mercury
   (D) cyanide
   (E) asbestos

5. Liver disease that develops due to long-time use of alcohol and drugs would be an example of a(n)
   (A) chronic effect
   (B) synergistic effect
   (C) acute effect
   (D) additive effect
   (E) cumulative effect

6. Ecologists have been studying populations in tropical regions to determine the effects of DDT on aquatic systems. Which population would you expect to show the most effects?
   (A) Phytoplankton
   (B) Small benthic fish
   (C) Zooplankton
   (D) Larger schooling fish like tuna
   (E) Predatory birds like pelicans

7. Which of the following consumer products would most likely increase your exposure to bisphenol A?
   (A) Wood paneling in the home
   (B) Imported fruit from tropical regions
   (C) Plastic food containers and water bottles
   (D) Perfumes and hairsprays
   (E) Oil-based paints

8. The reduction in coal burning to generate electricity would most likely have the biggest impact on reducing which of the following toxins?
   (A) Phthalates
   (B) Vinyl chloride
   (C) Mercury
   (D) Benzene
   (E) Radon

9. All of the following are reasons why tuberculosis (TB) is still a growing threat in developing countries EXCEPT:
   (A) It spreads rapidly from person to person.
   (B) There are very few screening and control programs.
   (C) Strains of TB bacteria have developed antibiotic resistance.
   (D) People living in crowded conditions increases the spread of the disease.
   (E) There are no effective drugs currently offered to treat TB.

10. Which statement best illustrates limitations to determining the toxicities of environmental chemicals?
    (A) Humans are not exposed to just one chemical; they are exposed to a mixture of chemicals that may produce synergistic effects.
    (B) It is too expensive to test toxins that could be harmful to humans.
    (C) The wide genetic variability of humans limits scientists' ability to determine toxicity trends for environmental chemicals.
    (D) Recent legislation has limited the amount of animal testing that can take place.
    (E) It is difficult to determine what types of chemicals humans are exposed to.

11. Scientists determined that the LD-50 for a particular chemical toxin was a dosage level of 125 milligrams per kilogram of body mass for a test population of rats. Assuming that the toxic effect observed in rats is the same for similar animals of larger size, what dosage level would be needed to kill 50% of the population of mammals who typically have a mass of 20kg?
    (A) 2.5g
    (B) 25g
    (C) 250g
    (D) 2500g
    (E) 25,000g

12. Which of the following is a likely reason why the United States could ban DDT without seeing an increase in malaria cases?
    (A) Since the United States is a developed nation there is adequate access to healthcare to prevent the disease.
    (B) Most children in the United States are vaccinated against malaria.
    (C) The United States does not typically have the genus of mosquito that carries the *Plasmodium* parasite.
    (D) The United States replaced DDT with another effective pesticide that keeps mosquito populations down.
    (E) People in developed nations have adequate access to bug spray preventatives.

13. Which of the following is an example of a non-transmissible disease that is a leading killer worldwide and in the United States?
    (A) Asthma
    (B) Liver disease
    (C) HIV
    (D) Cardiovascular disease
    (E) Genetic disorders

14. An organic chemical compound that is a known carcinogen and commonly found in tobacco smoke is
    (A) vinyl chloride
    (B) phthalate
    (C) mercury
    (D) radon
    (E) benzene

15. Of all the following solutions to reducing infectious disease seen in developing countries, which would have the most immediate impact?
    (A) An increase in availability to Hepatitis B vaccines
    (B) Funding for educational programs encouraging practicing protected sex
    (C) Government funding for medicines that treat people suffering from AIDS
    (D) Sanitation practices to provide clean drinking water
    (E) Increased use of DDT to control mosquito populations around the equator

FREE-RESPONSE QUESTION

Over the last few decades, scientists have been monitoring the beluga whale populations in the St. Lawrence River. Examinations of fat tissue in the whales have shown an accumulation of many different chemical toxins present in the waterways. Two of the toxins the scientist tested for were elemental mercury and methyl mercury.

(a) Describe how chemical toxins can accumulate to such high levels in beluga whales.

(b) Identify TWO possible chemical toxins, other than mercury, that could be found in high concentrations in the belugas' fat tissue and describe how they get into the St. Lawrence River.

(c) For one of the toxins you identified in part b, describe a human health impact that could be caused by exposure to that toxin.

(d) Explain one way to reduce the beluga whale population's possible exposure to mercury.

[handwritten: done on another pg]

ANSWERS

MULTIPLE-CHOICE QUESTIONS

1. **ANSWER: B.** Influenza is one of the leading infectious diseases worldwide. It is responsible for more deaths per year than any other viral disease. Increasing funding for treatment and availability of vaccines in developing countries would decrease the global death rate from this disease (*Living in the Environment*, 16th ed., pages 442–443 / 17th ed., page 441).

2. **ANSWER: D.** Inorganic mercury is converted into organic methylmercury by bacteria. Methylmercury is fat soluble and increases in concentration of organisms at higher trophic levels due to biomagnifications. It degrades slowly and is therefore considered a persistent chemical compound in the ecosystem (*Living in the Environment*, 16th ed., pages 450–451 / 17th ed., page 448).

3. **ANSWER: C.** Atrazine is one of the most commonly used pesticides in the United States. It is primarily used as an herbicide in the Midwest to control competing weed population. Atrazine is an endocrine disruptor and some studies have produced evidence linking it to endocrine damage of male amphibians. Endocrine damage could include lower sperm counts and the presence of female sex organs in male frogs (*Living in the Environment*, 16th ed., pages 452–453 / 17th ed., pages 448–449).

[handwritten: answers]

4. **ANSWER: B.** There are several chemicals that bioaccumulate and can be carcinogenic. Dioxins are a specific class of organic compounds that are primarily generated from waste incineration (*Living in the Environment*, 16th ed., supplement pages 448–449 / 17th ed., page 570).

5. ANSWER: **A.** Since this disease develops over a long period of exposure to toxins and has a lasting effect, it is an example of a chronic effect (*Living in the Environment*, 16th ed., page 455 / 17th ed., page 451).

6. ANSWER: **E.** DDT, although banned in the United States, is still currently being used in tropical regions around the equator to control the mosquito population that transmits malaria. This synthetic organic chlorinated hydrocarbon is fat soluble and increases in concentration at higher trophic levels due to biomagnification. Therefore, the organism at the top of the food chain will have the highest concentrations of DDT. For example, predatory birds, like pelicans, which feed on large amounts of fish will have high concentrations of DDT (*Living in the Environment*, 16th ed., pages 449, 454 / 17th ed., page 451).

7. ANSWER: **C.** Bisphenol A is a chemical building block in certain plastics, primarily polycarbonates. This chemical is a known estrogen mimic and can leach into food and water from the plastic containers they are stored in. Some studies have shown adverse effects from this toxin such as brain damage, prostate cancers, and breast cancers (*Living in the Environment*, 16th ed., page 453 / 17th ed., page 436).

8. ANSWER: **C.** Coal burning for electrical production releases elemental mercury (Hg) into the atmosphere where it is converted to inorganic mercury and organic methyl mercury. Methyl mercury is dangerous in biological systems since this toxin can increase in organisms due to biomagnification (*Living in the Environment*, 16th ed., pages 450–451 / 17th ed., page 448).

9. ANSWER: **E.** Tuberculosis is still a growing threat in developing countries for all of the reasons listed in the question except the one that says there are no effective drugs to treat the disease. The current drugs used in treatment of TB are approximately 90% effective. However, once symptoms subside within a few weeks people often stop taking the medicine, allowing TB to return easily (*Living in the Environment*, 16th ed., page 442 / 17th ed., pages 439–441),

10. ANSWER: **A.** It is often difficult to determine the toxicity level of individual environmental chemicals in humans since we are exposed to many different chemicals at one time. These chemicals may have synergistic effects once in our body. A synergistic effect occurs when exposure to more than one chemical results in more severe health effects than summing up the health effects of the individual chemicals would predict (*Living in the Environment*, 16th ed., page 457 / 17th ed., page 454).

11. ANSWER: **A.** 125mg 3 20kg = 2,500mg. However, the answer choices are given in grams. Therefore you must convert your answer: 2,500mg/1,000mg = 2.5g [1g = 1,000mg].

12. ANSWER: **C.** The United States does not typically have the genus of the mosquito that carries the Plasmodium parasite. The Anopheles

mosquito that carries the parasite is most commonly found in tropical regions around the equator such as Africa, South America, Central America, and southern Asia (*Living in the Environment*, 16th ed., pages 445–446 / 17th ed., pages 443–445).

13. **ANSWER: D.** Cardiovascular disease impacts the heart and blood vessels and is a leading killer in the United States. It is an example of a non-transmissible disease since it is not caused by a living organism and cannot be spread from person to person (*Living in the Environment*, 16th ed., pages 440–441 / 17th ed., page 438).

14. **ANSWER: E.** Benzene (C_6H_6) is a colorless, odorless organic compound that is typically found in tobacco smoke and is known to cause cancer. It is also an additive in gasoline and is an industrial solvent used to make plastics (*Living in the Environment*, 16th ed., page 448 / 17th ed., page 446).

15. **ANSWER: D.** All of those solutions could potentially decrease infectious disease in developing countries over time. However, providing means to clean drinking water would more quickly decrease the incidents of infectious disease resulting from exposure to parasites (bacterial, viral, protozoan) in water sources commonly contaminated with human and animal waste (*Living in the Environment*, 16th ed., page 448 / 17th ed., pages 445–446).

FREE-RESPONSE SCORING GUIDELINES

(a) Describe how chemical toxins can accumulate to such high levels in beluga whales.

2 points can be earned—1 point for describing the toxin being stored in fat tissue and 1 point for describing the biomagnification process

Biomagnification definition must include:
- toxins are stored in fat tissue
- some chemical toxins are fat soluble and therefore accumulate in body tissue

Process description:
- organisms in lower trophic levels will have less concentration of the toxin
- as organisms in higher trophic levels (secondary consumers) eat many organisms with the accumulation of toxins in their fat tissue, their concentration of the toxin will increase

(b) Identify TWO possible chemical toxins, other than mercury, that could be found in high concentrations in the belugas' fat tissue and describe how they get into the St. Lawrence River.

4 points can be earned—1 point for each correct answer identifying a toxin that biomagnifies and 1 point for each correct description of its source

Toxin	Source
DDT	pesticide still used in developing countries
PCBs	formerly used in electrical equipment as a dielectric fluid
Toxaphene	formerly used as a pesticide
Arsenic	used as a wood preservative in building materials
Cadmium	leaches from landfills from batteries
Lead	lead-based paint; leaded gasoline; waste incineration
Mercury	power production; waste incineration; landfills; fluorescent lights

(c) For ONE of the toxins you identified in part b, describe a human health impact that could be caused by exposure to that toxin.

2 points can be earned—1 point for correctly identifying a human health impact and 1 point for correctly linking a toxin

▪ causes cancer – arsenic, PCBs, toxaphene, cadmium, lead, mercury

▪ endocrine disruption, reproductive damage (including reproductive cancers, low sperm counts, presence of female organs in males) – DDT, PCBs

▪ birth defects (teratogens) – cadmium, PCBs, mercury

▪ neurotoxins (brain or nerve damage) – PCBs, cadmium, arsenic, toxaphene, lead, mercury

(d) Explain a way to reduce the beluga's possible exposure to mercury.

2 points can be earned—1 point for correctly identifying mercury's source and 1 point for identifying a solution

Source	Solution
Coal burning	switch to alternative energy source, remove Hg prior to burning
Waste incineration	waste reduction and recycling
Batteries	recycle batteries instead of landfilling them
Fluorescent lights	recycle light bulbs

6

WATER: GLOBAL RESOURCES AND POLLUTION

KEY CONCEPTS

- Freshwater available for human use and consumption is in limited supply.
- In some locations, groundwater is being withdrawn from aquifers at a rate faster than they can naturally replenish.
- Dams create large reservoirs of freshwater and can provide hydroelectric power, but they also disrupt ecosystems and displace people.
- Aquatic ecosystems and groundwater resources are being polluted by human activities, primarily from agricultural runoff, industrial discharge, and mining practices.
- Many lake ecosystems around the world are suffering from the effects of cultural eutrophication.
- Sewage treatment facilities help reduce water pollution in rivers and streams.

Water: global resources and pollution is discussed in depth in *Living in the Environment*, 16th ed., Chapters 13 and 20 / 17th ed., Chapters 13 and 20.

KEY VOCABULARY

aquifer	desalination
center-pivot sprinkler	distillation
cultural eutrophication	drip irrigation
dam	drought

fecal coliform bacteria

flood irrigation

floodplain

groundwater

hypoxia

land subsidence

lateral recharge

low-pressure sprinkler

natural recharge

nonpoint sources

oxygen sag curve

point sources

reservoir

reverse osmosis

septic tank

sewage treatment—primary, secondary, tertiary

sinkhole

surface runoff

surface water

water table

watershed

zone of aeration

zone of saturation

FRESHWATER RESOURCES

As you have learned, water is a vital resource that sustains life, moderates climate, shapes the earth's surface, and provides habitat for many organisms. Although water has an amazing ability to dilute and remove many pollutants, it cannot purify or disperse all the heavy concentration of contaminates resulting from the growing human population and the increasing input of toxins generated by agricultural, industrial, and residential activities. Water pollution from these activities has had a devastating impact on human health. As you recall from Chapter 5, many people in developing nations lack adequate access to clean drinking water. The World Health Organization estimates that over 1.6 million people die each year from preventable diseases contracted from contaminated drinking water.

Water resources available for human use are very limited. Much less than 1% of the global water supply is readily available as freshwater. Sources of freshwater for human use are:

GROUNDWATER

Some precipitation infiltrates the ground and percolates downward through the soil, gravel, and porous rock layers until it reaches a rock layer that is not permeable. The water that fills these underground porous spaces is known as **groundwater**. Typically, the first few layers below the earth's surface trap mostly air rather than water and are known as the **zone of aeration**. The deeper subsurface layers that fill all available porous space with water are known as the **zone of saturation**. The upper limit of this zone is known as the **water table**. The height of the water table fluctuates. It can lower in response to dry seasons or over-withdrawal by humans and it can also rise during rainy (wet) seasons. **Aquifers** are deep underground layers of porous rock material, gravel, sand, silt, or clay where groundwater flows. Groundwater in aquifers is replenished in two ways: **natural recharge** through percolation of precipitation through soil and rock layers or by **lateral recharge** through the movement of water from

aquifers biggest Ogalalla

rivers and streams. Some aquifers receive very little recharge and are therefore referred to as non-renewable aquifers. Water mining is a term used to describe withdrawals from these aquifers since eventually the supply will be depleted entirely.

SURFACE WATER

Surface water exists as rivers, lakes, wetlands, estuaries, and the ocean. Recharge to these waters is in the form of **surface runoff** from precipitation and snowmelt that does not infiltrate into the soil layers. A **watershed**, or drainage basin, is the land surrounding these bodies of water that contribute to surface runoff. Bodies of surface water are also recharged laterally from groundwater sources. Therefore, if groundwater is withdrawn faster than it is replenished this can reduce the volume of surface water in rivers, lakes, and streams.

WATER EQUITY, SHORTAGES, AND FLOODS

Globally, the main uses of groundwater and surface water are for irrigation (70%), industrial processes (20%), and the rest for human consumption. In developed nations the majority of water withdrawals goes specifically to thermoelectric power plants as coolant water. Affluent nations use large amounts of water to produce a vast array of consumer goods and food products. They also typically have easy access to water for residential needs such as flushing toilets, taking baths and showers, washing machines, and dishwashers. Unlike affluent nations, developing countries often lack access to clean drinking water. Many people in developing nations live without electricity or running water. Most of the freshwater in developing countries is used for crop production in the form of irrigation water.

A major issue facing the human population regarding freshwater resources is the disparity in its distribution. For example, Canada has 20% of the world's liquid freshwater supply but only 0.5% of the world's population. Asia has only 30% of the world's liquid freshwater supply but 60% of the world's population. Water supplies are not evenly distributed even within single nations. The western half of the United States utilizes the majority of its water withdrawals for irrigation. These states are arid or semi-arid and receive less precipitation and have higher evaporation rates than the eastern United States. Some regions also experience recurring droughts. **Droughts** are long periods of time where regions receive 30% or less of their average annual precipitation. All of these factors play a role in creating severe water shortages in the western half of the United States. In comparison, the eastern half of the United States usually does not suffer from water shortages due to the higher level of annual precipitation and the reduced evaporation rates compared to the western half of the United States.

With increasing population comes a growing demand for water resources to produce more food, supply more electricity, make more consumer goods, and for human consumption. This will continue to intensify water shortages and will escalate already heated battles over water rights. For maps highlighting water stressed regions see *Living in the Environment*, 15th ed., pages 310–311 / 16th ed., pages 318–319.

While some regions battle a lack of water, others experience heavy rains or rapidly melting snowpack. Floods are responsible for causing billions of dollars' worth of damage to infrastructure and for the loss of thousands of lives each year. **Floodplains** are flat land areas that are periodically flooded with nutrient-rich silt from the nearby rivers and streams they surround. Historically, people have settled on floodplains because of their fertile soils and readily available water supplies. When floodplains are developed, much of the water-absorbing riparian vegetation is removed, and the capacity of the wetlands to act as a natural flood barrier is destroyed. These activities are especially dangerous for densely populated areas that lie near or below sea level. For example, New Orleans experienced devastating floods from Hurricane Katrina, made worse in part by the removal of coastal wetlands.

SURFACE WATER AND GROUNDWATER DEPLETION

USING GROUNDWATER RESOURCES

Populations rely heavily on aquifer resources (groundwater) to provide irrigation and drinking water in some areas. Sustainability of aquifers depends on the rate of recharge into the groundwater system versus the rate of withdrawal by humans. Overdraft is a condition that occurs when withdrawals exceed recharge and water tables begin to fall. Overdraft from the aquifer can cause the land above the groundwater **reservoir** to sink or collapse; this is known as **land subsidence**. A type of land subsidence called a **sinkhole** occurs suddenly when the top of an underground cavern collapses. Overdraft of groundwater in coastal areas can force the flow of saltwater into freshwater aquifers. This saltwater intrusion makes the aquifer unusable for both drinking and irrigation.

Ogallala Aquifer—The freshwater resource known as the Ogallala aquifer provides almost one-third of the irrigation water to several states in the midwestern United States, helping to make them highly productive agricultural lands. The excess rate of withdrawal combined with the extremely slow recharge rate has lowered the water table in this aquifer by as much as 30 meters, thereby leading to restrictions of use. The inability to utilize this aquifer has decreased agricultural production in some states such as Texas. The reduced volume of water in the aquifer has caused land subsidence and decreased recharge into wetlands and estuaries, threatening biodiversity in these ecosystems.

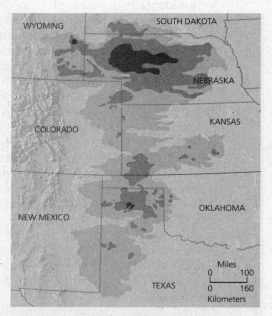

Saturated thickness of Ogallala Aquifer

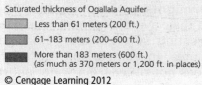

Less than 61 meters (200 ft.)

61–183 meters (200–600 ft.)

More than 183 meters (600 ft.) (as much as 370 meters or 1,200 ft. in places)

© Cengage Learning 2012

Handwritten note in left margin: know how we use ogallala

HOW TO PROTECT GROUNDWATER RESOURCES

■ subsidize water conservation strategies
■ implement water conservation practices in residential homes
■ increase the price of water to discourage waste
■ reduce the number of water-intensive crops being grown, especially in arid and semi-arid regions

USING SURFACE WATER RESOURCES

Like aquifers, surface waters (lakes, rivers, streams) around the world have provided the means for irrigation and drinking water supplies. Surface water resources are easily accessible and therefore have been utilized in a variety of ways including:

Hydroelectric Power—In many areas, fast-flowing rivers are dammed to create freshwater reservoirs and in many cases to provide hydroelectric power. Once a river is dammed the terrestrial area behind the dam will flood, creating a reservoir that stores the surface water runoff that would have once flowed directly into the river. Hydroelectric power has many advantages and disadvantages.

Advantages	Disadvantages
■ no carbon dioxide emissions	■ displaces people living behind the dam
■ provides irrigation and drinking water	■ decreases nutrient-rich silt downstream
■ can provide flood control	■ fish harvest below dam decreases
■ provides cheap electricity	■ disrupts migration patterns of some fish
■ reservoir can be used for recreation	■ loss of water by evaporation

know the list

EXAMPLES OF MAJOR DAMS

examples

Colorado River Basin—The Colorado River, flowing from Colorado to the Gulf of California, generates its water flow from annual snowmelt in the Rocky Mountains. The Colorado River provides much needed water to the southwestern United States and Mexico, an arid and semi-arid environment often plagued with recurring droughts and water shortages. The river provides drinking water to major cities like Los Angeles, San Diego, and Las Vegas. It also supplies the irrigation water to farms that produce close to 15% of our nation's crops. Government subsidies have historically increased demand for irrigation water in this area. Fourteen major dams that have been erected along the river have created water reservoirs for this desert region. Excessive withdrawals for water in this area, primarily for irrigation, have led to massive volume reductions in the river. At times, the river does not even make it to the Gulf of California, and even if it does, the residual water is so salinated from irrigation runoff that it

Understand the diagram

essentially is unusable. This has led to international disputes and has caused the United States to construct desalination plants to clean the water before releasing it to Mexico. Continued climate change may also decrease annual snowmelt, furthering water shortage problems as recharge into the river declines. Two major dams along the Colorado River are the Hoover Dam, which creates the Lake Mead reservoir, and the Glen Canyon Dam, which creates the Lake Powell reservoir.

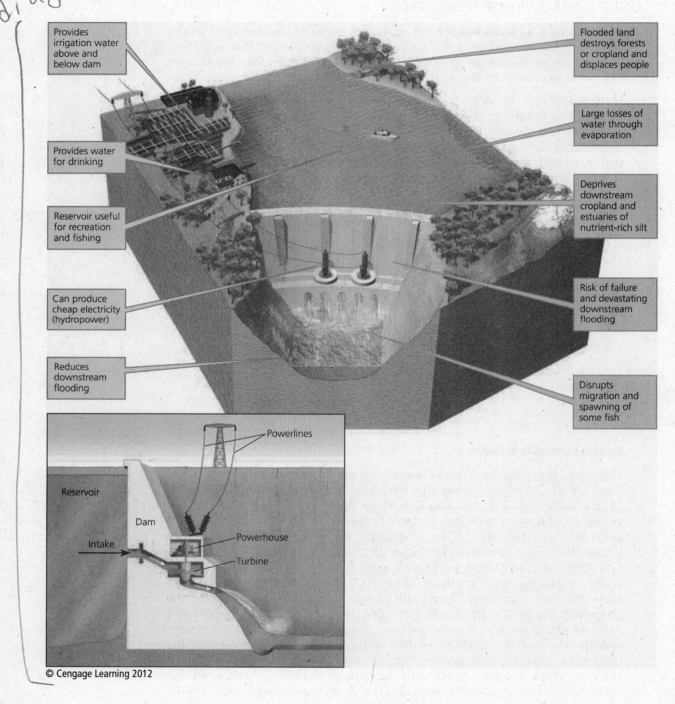

Provides irrigation water above and below dam

Provides water for drinking

Reservoir useful for recreation and fishing

Can produce cheap electricity (hydropower)

Reduces downstream flooding

Flooded land destroys forests or cropland and displaces people

Large losses of water through evaporation

Deprives downstream cropland and estuaries of nutrient-rich silt

Risk of failure and devastating downstream flooding

Disrupts migration and spawning of some fish

Powerlines

Reservoir

Dam

Intake

Powerhouse

Turbine

© Cengage Learning 2012

Three Gorges Dam—The Three Gorges Dam, built along the Yangtze River in China, is the world's largest hydroelectric dam. China has experienced massive loss of life from floods, including the 1998 flood that killed over 4,000 people. The hydroelectric dam is capable of producing the same energy output as 22 coal-burning power plants, yet does not produce the carbon dioxide emissions that coal does. However, some scientists say this savings in CO_2 emissions will be offset by methane gases being released from the decomposition of vegetation in the large reservoir.

WATER TRANSFER PROJECTS

Since water is not evenly distributed within nations, many countries and individual U.S. states have created water transfer projects to provide resources to areas limited in supply. Many of these projects have resulted in a devastating volume of water lost in ecosystems such as lakes, wetlands, and estuaries. This can result in these ecosystems being unable to support a diversity of life.

Aral Sea—The Aral Sea, located in the former Soviet Union, has been declining in volume since the 1960s. Several factors have played key roles in this shrinking. The Aral Sea is located in an area of Asia with one of the driest climates. Crop production was limited by water supplies so large irrigation canals were created to transfer water from the inland Aral Sea to outlying cotton and rice fields. However, recurring droughts, little precipitation for recharge, and high evaporation rates in this arid environment have made the transfer of water from the Aral Sea an ecological tragedy. The major loss of water volume from the sea has increased the salinity to seven times its original amount and destroyed many local wetlands. The reduction in the Aral Sea's size has also altered local climate conditions. The sea acts as a thermal buffer that moderates climate in the region. The reduction in size has reduced precipitation, and summers are now hotter and drier and winters are colder. This has had a negative impact on the region's economy by reducing commercially viable fish populations and decreasing crop production because of increased lake salinity. For satellite photos of this region showing the shrinking volume of the Aral Sea, see *Living in the Environment*, 15th ed., page 322 / 16th ed., page 331.

California Water Transfer Project—This is a massive water transfer project that uses a series of pumps, aqueducts, and dams to move water from water-rich northern California to desert regions of southern California. This is one of the world's largest water transfer projects; it has, however, come at the expense of many of the state's lake ecosystems. For example, during the 1980s, scientists discovered that Mono Lake, near Yosemite National Park, had lost over 30% of its original surface area. This elicited heated court battles that resulted in the restriction of withdrawal from Mono Lake in the 1990s. Recent measurements show the lake steadily gaining in volume.

China's Water Transfer Project—The South-North Water Transfer Project will use a series of dams, canals, and reservoirs to pump water from the southern Yangtze River basin to China's more populated northern provinces. This will also provide drinking water for major cities in China such as Beijing.

Know at least one project well.

WATER CONSERVATION

The human population has generally viewed water as a cheap, abundant, and renewable resource. However, inefficient practices and excessive withdrawals of both groundwater and surface waters are increasing the potential for dangerous water shortages around the world. The cheapest and fastest way to improve water conservation is to reduce the loss of irrigation water by evaporation and to fix residential and industrial pipe leaks.

IMPROVING IRRIGATION PRACTICES

Almost 40% of the freshwater used in the United States goes to irrigate crops. **Flood irrigation** is used in some parts of the United States and is a common practice in developing countries. This method relies on pumping large volumes of water directly onto agricultural land and allowing it to flow by gravity into ditches in the soil where crops can then absorb the water. Unfortunately, almost half of the water never reaches the intended crops, as it is lost to evaporation and surface runoff. Irrigation ditches in the field can be lined to improve efficiency. Other irrigation methods that reduce water loss are:

Drip Irrigation—Drip irrigation, also known as micro-irrigation, improves efficiency by delivering smaller volumes of water more directly to crop roots for absorption. A series of plastic pipes containing many small holes to release water are run along the crop rows or buried in the soil along the root line. This decreases the chance of evaporation and improves efficiency up to 95%. Although drip irrigation is more expensive than the traditional flood irrigation methods, it can increase crop yields from 20% to 90%.

Center Pivot—Center-pivot systems consist of numerous metal frames rolling on wheels that extend large water pipes out over the crops. **Low-pressure sprinklers** in the pipes deliver water directly to the crops, as an electric motor moves the metal frame around the field in a circular motion with the water source (such as a well) at the center. This type of sprinkler system can improve efficiency up to 80%. A low-energy precision application **(LEPA) sprinkler** system is a type of center pivot that increases efficiency up to 95% by improving direct application of water to crop roots.

OTHER METHODS OF IRRIGATION WATER CONSERVATION
- irrigate crops with treated urban wastewater
- irrigate at night to reduce water lost to evaporation
- don't grow water-thirsty crops in arid and semi-arid regions
- increase government subsidies for efficient irrigation practices
- use soil moisture monitors to irrigate only when needed
- increase use of polyculture or organic farming practices instead of monoculture
- use rainwater harvesting for smaller agricultural fields (developing countries)

drip is most effective because most of water goes to roots

IMPROVING INDUSTRIAL AND RESIDENTIAL WATER CONSERVATION

Water is a key component in many industrial processes such as petroleum refining, food processing, paper and steel production, and much more. Residential uses include water for lawn sprinkling, drinking, bathing, clothes washing, and other household uses. The largest use of domestic water comes from flushing toilets. Current U.S. standards require that toilets have no more than 1.6 gallons of water per flush. However, this is still a large waste of clean water to get rid of only a small volume of waste. According to United Nations studies, the largest source of water loss in both industrial and residential practices is leaks in pipes, valves, and water mains. There is little incentive to detect or fix leaks since water is relatively cheap when compared to other resources. Some residential homes are using grey water systems to improve water conservation. **Grey water systems** collect water from showers, bathtubs, dishwashers, and clothes washers and then reuse this water on lawns, to wash cars, or to flush toilets. Other methods of improving water conservation are:

METHODS OF WATER CONSERVATION FOR INDUSTRIAL AND RESIDENTIAL PRACTICES

- fix leaks in pipes and water mains
- increase prices for water
- require the use of water meters
- recycle water used in industrial processes
- use low-flow showerheads and low-volume toilets

We can do some of these ourselves

INCREASING FRESHWATER SUPPLIES

Many countries are looking for ways to increase their liquid freshwater supplies by utilizing an abundant resource, saltwater. **Desalination** is a process that removes dissolved salts from ocean water or from brackish seas and lakes. This can provide valuable freshwater in areas facing water shortages, especially in arid regions such as the Middle East and Northern Africa. Two methods of desalination are:

1) **reverse osmosis**—Also called microfiltration, reverse osmosis uses external pressure to push saline water through membranes that separate the solutes (salt) from the solvent (water).

2) **distillation**—This process involves heating saltwater until evaporation begins. The steam is collected and condenses as freshwater as the salts have been left behind in solid form.

While desalination provides freshwater resources to areas in short supply, it also has many drawbacks as well. Both desalination processes produce large amounts of briny wastewater that must be disposed of. It poses a risk to wildlife if dumped in ocean waters and it could potentially pollute groundwater or surface water if disposed of on land. Also, desalination is extremely expensive and not a realistic option for many developing countries.

WATER POLLUTION SOURCES AND TYPES

Water is considered polluted when any single source or larger dispersed sources make water quality unsuitable for desired uses. Water pollution is categorized as either point-source pollution or nonpoint pollution.

easily identifiable

Point-Source Pollution—Single source pollution, known as **point sources**, are discharges of pollutants from a specific location through drain pipes, ditches, or sewer lines that flow directly into a body of water. Some common examples include, but are not limited to, industries, sewage treatment plants, and oil spills from tankers. Developing countries still face problems controlling point-source pollution. However, most developed countries have laws that help control these sources as they are typically easy to identify, monitor, and therefore regulate.

You cant point at it

Nonpoint Pollution—Dispersed source pollution, known as **nonpoint sources**, are scattered and diffuse releases of pollutants that cannot be traced to any single site of discharge. The majority of surface water pollution problems stem from nonpoint pollution sources.

LEADING SOURCES OF WATER POLLUTION

1) Agriculture—Agricultural practices are the leading cause of water pollution. Surface water runoff (nonpoint sources) carries with it eroding soil sediments, excess fertilizers, and pesticides into nearby waterways. Animal wastes from feedlots also make their way into local rivers and streams by runoff.

2) Industrial—Industrial processes create large amounts of inorganic and organic wastes that often make their way into our water supplies. Common inorganic pollutants generated from industrial processes include acids, heavy metals, and fertilizers (nitrates and phosphates). Industrial organic pollutants include a wide variety of compounds such as pesticides, gasoline, motor oil, food processing wastes, PCBs, and volatile organic compounds such as solvents.

3) Mining—Mining practices expose large areas of the earth's surface to erosive forces such as wind and rain. This creates runoff of precipitation and sediments that carry with it harmful chemicals such as sulfuric acid, arsenic, and cyanide used to extract gold. Erosion can also release heavy metals from the rock layers, such as mercury.

Type and Effects	Examples	Major sources
Infectious agents (pathogens) Cause diseases	Bacteria, viruses, protozoa, parasites	Human and animal wastes
Oxygen-demanding wastes Deplete dissolved oxygen needed by aquatic species	Biodegradable animal wastes and plant debris	Sewage, animal feedlots, food processing facilities, pulp mills
Plant nutrients Cause excessive growth of algae and other species	Nitrates (NO_3^2) and phosphates (PO_4^{32})	Sewage, animal wastes, inorganic fertilizers
Organic chemicals Add toxins to aquatic systems	Oil, gasoline, plastics, pesticides, cleaning solvents	Industry, farms, households
Inorganic chemicals Add toxins to aquatic systems	Acids, bases, salts, metal compounds	Industry, households, surface runoff
Sediments Disrupt photosynthesis, food webs, other processes	Soil, silt	Land erosion
Heavy metals Cause cancer, disrupt immune and endocrine systems	Lead, mercury, arsenic	Unlined landfills, household chemicals, mining refuse, industrial discharges
Thermal Make some species vulnerable to disease	Heat	Electric power and industrial plants

Human health is at risk when exposed to infectious diseases from inadequate sanitation practices of drinking water as well as lack of water for adequate hygiene. Each year millions of people, mostly younger children, die from preventable diseases like diarrhea from unclean water used for drinking and hygiene. One method scientists use to detect the presence of infectious agents in water is to test for colonies of **fecal coliform**. Coliform bacteria, such as *E. coli*, that live in animal and human intestines, do not always cause disease but can indicate when water has come in contact with waste that could potentially carry disease-causing bacteria.

diseases

and

what

is

causing

them

Type of Organism	Disease	Effects
Bacteria	Typhoid fever	Diarrhea, severe vomiting, enlarged spleen, inflamed intestine; often fatal if untreated
	Cholera	Diarrhea, severe vomiting, dehydration; often fatal if untreated
	Bacterial dysentery	Diarrhea, bleeding; rarely fatal except in infants without proper treatment
	Enteritis	Severe stomach pain, nausea, vomiting; rarely fatal
Viruses	Infectious hepatitis (Type B)	Fever, severe headache, loss of appetite, abdominal pain, jaundice, enlarged liver; rarely fatal but may cause permanent liver damage
	Poliomyelitis	Fever, diarrhea, backache, sore throat, aches in limbs; can infect spinal cord and cause paralysis and muscle weakness
Parasitic protozoa	Amoebic dysentery	Severe diarrhea, headache, abdominal pain, chills, fever; if not treated can cause liver abscess, bowel perforation, and death
	Giardiasis	Diarrhea, abdominal cramps, flatulence, belching, fatigue
	Cryptosporidum	Severe diarrhea, cramps for up to 3 weeks, and possible death for people with weakened immune systems
Parasitic worms	Schistosomiasis	Abdominal pain, skin rash, anemia, chronic fatigue, and chronic general ill health
	Ancylostomiasis	Severe anemia and possible symptoms of bronchial infection

POLLUTION OF STREAMS, RIVERS, AND LAKES

Normally, quickly flowing rivers and streams can recover from moderate levels of degradable waste. Degradable wastes are referred to as oxygen-demanding wastes because aerobic bacteria utilize much of the dissolved oxygen in the water during decomposition. Examples of oxygen-demanding waste (as seen in the table on the previous page) include sewage, animal wastes from feedlot runoff, pulp from paper mills, and food processing wastes. An **oxygen sag curve** occurs in flowing streams as bacteria break down degradable wastes and deplete the dissolved oxygen in the process. The oxygen sag curve can also occur from an input of a large volume of heated water, since the temperature of water determines the solubility of oxygen. As water temperature increases, the solubility of oxygen decreases and therefore dissolved oxygen concentration will decrease. Thermoelectric power plants are the main source of this type of thermal pollution in surface waters.

The natural dilution ability of rivers and streams is reduced if flow is decreased by periods of drought or damming rivers, or if the concentration of degradable pollutants is too high. Moving surface waters do not have the ability to dilute slowly degradable waste, such as PCBs and pesticides, or non-degradable waste like heavy metals.

[handwritten margin note: Understand how to read this curve]

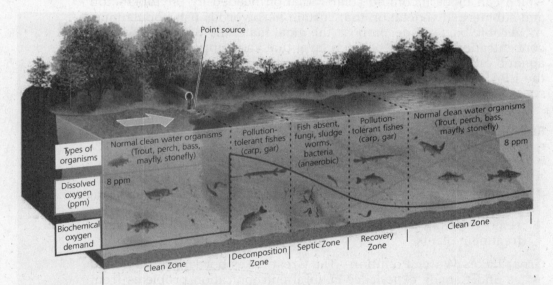

© Cengage Learning 2012

POLLUTION IN RIVERS AND STREAMS

Most developed nations, including the United States, have enacted water quality laws that monitor nonpoint sources, regulate point-source pollution from industry, and increase the number and quality of wastewater treatment plants. However, many developing countries are still discharging their untreated sewage directly into their major rivers and streams. Unfortunately, these same bodies of water are then used for drinking, bathing, and washing clothes. More than half of China's population has no form of sewage treatment and over 300 million people live without access to clean drinking water. The Ganges River in India is heavily polluted by sewage flowing directly from the major cities along the river. Also, religious beliefs dictate that bodies are to be burned in wood fires and then thrown into the Ganges. This creates oxygen-demanding wastes and increases pathogenic bacteria. India's government started building sewage treatment plants along the Ganges and also is encouraging cremation in newly constructed crematoriums rather than traditional wood-burning pyres.

POLLUTION IN FRESHWATER LAKES

Lakes are more vulnerable to contamination because they typically contain stratified layers that keep the water from mixing, and they have very little flow to dilute the pollutants. Remember from Chapter 3 that if conditions are right in the drainage basin, some lakes may become eutrophic as nutrients and sediments are added to the ecosystem over time. The natural nutrient enrichment of lakes, estuaries, or ponds is known as **eutrophication**. When human activities cause an un-natural input of plant nutrients into waters, it is known as **cultural eutrophication**. The input of excess phosphates and nitrates comes from runoff of fertilized cropland, urban lawns, animal feedlots, and the discharge of treated and untreated municipal sewage. The excess of nutrients can support large algal blooms, which can block incoming solar radiation needed by phytoplankton and submerged vegetation that sustain herbivorous fish populations. As aerobic bacteria decompose the algal mats, the dissolved oxygen concentration will drop below a level that can support most aerobic aquatic organisms (fish), and biodiversity will decline. According to the EPA, 85% of large lakes near major U.S. cities are experiencing some level of cultural eutrophication.

REMEDIATION AND PREVENTION OF CULTURAL EUTROPHICATION
- mechanical removal of excess weeds
- pumping oxygen into the water to prevent depletion
- use of herbicides and algaecides to control unwanted populations
- prevention of excess nutrients from entering water by increasing riparian buffer zones
- removal of nitrates and phosphates from wastewater in advanced treatment plants

Great Lakes Water Pollution—The Great Lakes bordering the United States and Canada experience cultural eutrophication problems from several point sources (sewage) and runoff of nonpoint sources (fertilizer and phosphate detergents). These lakes have also been bombarded by heavy inputs of industrial pollutants, such as PCBs, atmospheric deposition of mercury from coal-burning power plants, and pesticides from surrounding agricultural lands. Pollution combined with the continued removal of riparian buffer zones, such as wetlands, has caused the decline of many amphibians, birds, and fish species. Also recall from Chapter 3 that this ecosystem has been impacted by biological pollution in the form of the invasive Zebra mussel species that is threatening the health of many native species.

Lake Washington—Lake Washington is located near the popular urban area of Seattle, Washington. As urban development expanded so did the input of treated wastewater into Lake Washington. This ecosystem experienced rapid cultural eutrophication and the fish population declined sharply. Professors from the University of Washington along with concerned community leaders petitioned the city to divert the nutrient-rich effluent into Puget Sound where it could be diluted by wave activity rather than into the more stagnant Lake Washington. Within just ten years of the diversion project's completion, water clarity improved and many of the fish populations in Lake Washington have made a comeback.

WATER QUALITY TESTING TECHNIQUES

The AP Environmental Science exam will expect you to understand certain water quality tests you may have performed in laboratory activities. The following are some basic physical, chemical, and biological tests used to determine water quality in aquatic system.

PHYSICAL WATER QUALITY TESTS

Temperature—The temperature of water impacts the solubility of oxygen and the range of tolerance of aquatic organisms. Water temperature can be affected by the removal of trees along rivers and streams, which reduces shade, and by dams that decrease water depths downstream. Large inputs of heated water often come from industrial discharges and electrical power plants (both coal-burning and nuclear).

River/Stream Flow Velocity—The velocity of a river or stream will impact the ability of oxygen to diffuse into the water. Fast-flowing water can diffuse oxygen faster than slower-moving water.

Turbidity—Turbidity is the measure of the cloudiness of aquatic systems by suspended solids in the water column. Water clarity is extremely important to photosynthetic organisms, like phytoplankton and submerged vegetation, which make up the base of the food chain in most aquatic systems. Water clarity can be reduced by heavy sedimentation from erosion of the surrounding land or from algal blooms that block sunlight. Water clarity can be measured by using a Secchi disk, which is lowered into the water column until it is no longer visible.

CHEMICAL WATER QUALITY TESTS

pH—This is a test to measure the hydrogen ion concentration to determine the acidity or alkalinity of a solution. Most organisms survive best in waters with a pH between 6 and 9.

Dissolved Oxygen—This test will determine the amount of oxygen gas available in the water. Oxygen is a vital component to aerobic organisms in aquatic systems and therefore regulates biodiversity. Many aerobic organisms will begin to experience stress in water with dissolved oxygen concentrations below 5ppm. Dissolved oxygen concentrations depend on photosynthesis of primary producers, water

we did these in class so remember how to construct them.

did these at museum also

temperature, and flow rates of rivers or streams. Cold, fast-moving water will have the highest solubility of oxygen gas. This test can indicate the presence of excess fertilizers (cultural eutrophication); oxygen-demanding waste such as sewage; feedlot runoff; or thermal pollution from electrical power plants.

Nitrates/Nitrites and Phosphates—Nitrogen-containing compounds and phosphates primarily act as nutrients in aquatic ecosystems since they are limiting factors for plant and algae growth. Both types of nutrients can cause cultural eutrophication. Testing for these nutrients can indicate the presence of fertilizer runoff, municipal sewage, septic tank leaks, and animal waste from feedlot runoff.

Hardness—This test determines the presence of some common metal cations such as magnesium (Mg^{2+}) and calcium (Ca^{2+}). Increased metal ions can indicate increased solubility of heavy metals or the ability to buffer the aquatic system.

BIOLOGICAL WATER QUALITY TEST

Fecal Coliform—This assay is used to determine the possibility of fecal contamination from sewage, septic tank leaks, or animal wastes from feedlots.

Biological Assessment—Monitoring organisms can be an effective means of measuring ecosystem health since it reveals cumulative effects of water quality on organisms over a period of time. Some specific organisms may be monitored due to their sensitivity to water pollution or a specific abiotic factor. Common organisms monitored to indicate river or stream health are:

Benthic Macroinvertebrates—These organisms include aquatic insects, insect larvae, and crustaceans that live in the bottom portion of a waterway for part of their life cycle. These organisms can be used to determine water quality since some species are more sensitive to pollution than others. Sensitive organisms include mayfly, stonefly, and caddisflies. Some species of copepods are also used to determine water quality. Copepods are small plantonic or benthic crustaceans that are common to both marine and freshwater ecosystems.

Fish Species—Some fish species can be used as biological indicators due to their sensitivity for certain abiotic factors. For example, trout maybe used because of their sensitivity to dissolved oxygen concentrations. Therefore, trout are often good indicators of healthy oxygen levels present in rivers or streams.

GROUNDWATER POLLUTION

Approximately half of the United States population relies on groundwater for drinking water. Groundwater pollution sources include organic solvents, pesticides, fertilizers, gasoline, and oil that are either poured directly onto the ground or leak from buried storage containers and then seep into lower layers containing groundwater. Characteristics such as slow flow rate (1 foot per day), cold temperatures, low populations of decomposing bacteria, and lower

[handwritten margin note: Know the different tests and how to set them up]

concentrations of dissolved oxygen mean groundwater has very few methods of naturally degrading or diluting pollutants. Nondegradable wastes such as arsenic, lead, and fluoride may remain in the water permanently and slowly degradable wastes such as DDT may be there from decades to thousands of years. Specific examples of groundwater contamination include:

Arsenic—Many areas in the United States and around the world face arsenic contamination from rock and soil surrounding the aquifer. Human activities such as mining and ore processing also contribute high levels of arsenic to drinking water supplies. Such contamination is responsible for premature deaths from cancers of the skin, bladder, and lungs.

Nitrate Ions (NO_3^2)—Many rural areas depend heavily on groundwater aquifers as a source of drinking water. These aquifers can be contaminated with nitrates from fertilizers that have leached into soil layers and eventually made their way to groundwater supplies. Once in the body, nitrates are converted into nitrites and other organic compounds that have been linked to cancer. In infants, the conversion of nitrates to nitrites limits the blood's ability to effectively carry oxygen to cells and can cause death. This condition is known as blue baby syndrome.

MTBE—In 1979 the United States began using a gasoline additive known as MTBE (methyl tertiary butyl ether). It was determined in the 1990s that the additive was responsible for the contamination of many aquifers from leaking gasoline tanks. MTBE additive is a suspected carcinogen and many lawsuits have been brought against the oil companies. The United States is phasing out the use of the additives but the plumes of contaminated groundwater will last for decades.

[handwritten margin note: These are all Pollutants]

PRINCIPAL SOURCES OF GROUNDWATER CONTAMINATION

Preventing and Remediating Groundwater Pollution—If groundwater becomes contaminated it is extremely difficult and costly to remove the pollutants. Therefore, prevention of contamination is the most effective way to protect our groundwater resources. For example, hazardous waste disposal in landfills and injection wells should be banned. Also, very toxic chemicals should be stored above ground with leak detection and collection systems. If cleanup of groundwater is necessary, microorganisms sometimes can be effectively injected into aquifers to degrade pollutants. Groundwater can be pumped to the surface, cleaned, and then returned to the aquifer. However, this type of cleanup effort is extremely expensive.

Providing Clean Drinking Water—Most developed nations have laws that regulate and monitor drinking water supplies. Some arid parts of the United States such as California and Texas are recycling and purifying wastewater to provide drinking water. Developing countries are being encouraged to collect drinking water in clear containers and expose it to sunlight for several hours to allow the UV radiation and heat to kill pathogens in the water. Also, scientists have developed several nanofilters that are placed in water bottles, or large plastic straws that filter water prior to drinking. Most developed nations are recognizing that the cheapest way to provide clean drinking water sources is to use the earth's natural filtration systems of forests and wetlands for the hydrologic cycle.

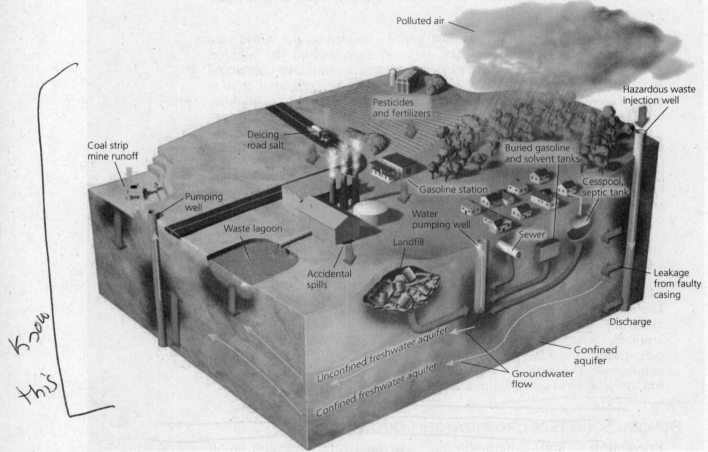

© Cengage Learning 2012

OCEAN POLLUTION

Typically oceans can dilute, disperse, and degrade large quantities of degradable contaminants. As you learned in Chapter 4, over half of the world lives within 50 miles of the coast. Therefore the coastal areas such as mangroves, estuaries, and coral reefs are seeing much of the major impacts of pollution as a result of human activities. In many developing countries and some developed countries, coastal municipal sewage and industrial waste is dumped into the surrounding coastal zones without any treatment. Studies along U.S. coastal waters have found extensive colonies of viruses, which may account for the numerous ear infections, sore throats, eye irritations, and respiratory diseases experienced by people using beaches in these areas. Many "floatables" such as plastics are also making their way into the oceans from runoff and storm drains that carry trash into ocean waters. These plastics can cause physical injury to animals and slowly degrade over time, leaching harmful chemicals into the water. Runoff of sewage and agricultural waste along coastal areas is responsible for harmful algal blooms such as red tides. Excess nutrients also cause eutrophic conditions and lower concentrations of dissolved oxygen, known as **hypoxia**, along the coast. Very few oxygen-consuming fish and bottom-dwelling organisms can live in these hypoxic conditions. Decomposing bacteria, however, thrive here.

Sources of Ocean Pollution

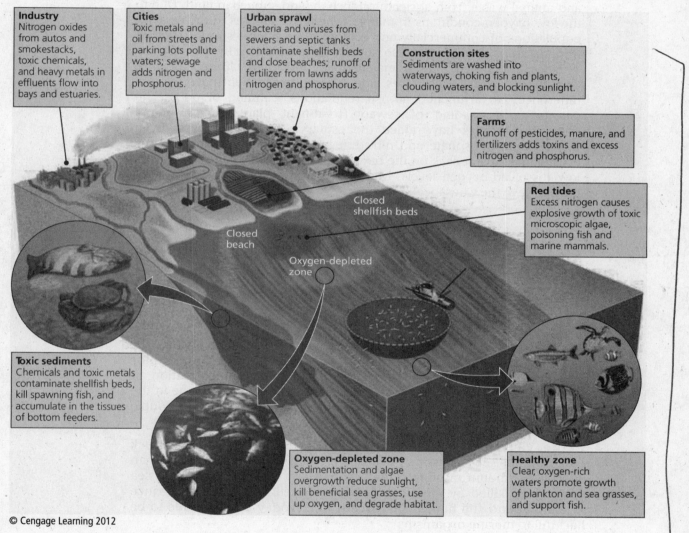

Industry
Nitrogen oxides from autos and smokestacks, toxic chemicals, and heavy metals in effluents flow into bays and estuaries.

Cities
Toxic metals and oil from streets and parking lots pollute waters; sewage adds nitrogen and phosphorus.

Urban sprawl
Bacteria and viruses from sewers and septic tanks contaminate shellfish beds and close beaches; runoff of fertilizer from lawns adds nitrogen and phosphorus.

Construction sites
Sediments are washed into waterways, choking fish and plants, clouding waters, and blocking sunlight.

Farms
Runoff of pesticides, manure, and fertilizers adds toxins and excess nitrogen and phosphorus.

Red tides
Excess nitrogen causes explosive growth of toxic microscopic algae, poisoning fish and marine mammals.

Closed shellfish beds

Closed beach

Oxygen-depleted zone

Toxic sediments
Chemicals and toxic metals contaminate shellfish beds, kill spawning fish, and accumulate in the tissues of bottom feeders.

Oxygen-depleted zone
Sedimentation and algae overgrowth reduce sunlight, kill beneficial sea grasses, use up oxygen, and degrade habitat.

Healthy zone
Clear, oxygen-rich waters promote growth of plankton and sea grasses, and support fish.

© Cengage Learning 2012

CASE STUDY: The Chesapeake Bay

The Chesapeake Bay is the largest estuary in the United States and has close to 17 million people living in the watershed area. The estuary receives point and nonpoint-source pollution from the surrounding areas that is input into the bay through nine major rivers and 141 tributaries. Much of the phosphate pollution comes from point sources such as sewage treatment plants and industrial plants. The nitrate pollution originates from nonpoint sources such as runoff of fertilizers and animal waste from agricultural, urban, and suburban land. Due to the low oxygen conditions in many of the input sources to the estuary, populations of commercially and ecologically valuable species such as oysters, crabs, and several fish species have declined. In the past few decades, integrated coastal management including citizen's groups, communities, state legislatures, and federal government have made a difference. Government land-use regulations, banning of phosphate detergents, upgrading of sewage treatment plants, and wetland restoration efforts have aided the estuary's healing process. Even though both phosphate and nitrate levels have dropped and grasses are making a comeback on the bay's floor, the estuary still suffers from low dissolved-oxygen levels. Many diverse groups continue to work hard to save the Chesapeake Bay.

OIL POLLUTION IN OCEAN WATERS

There are many sources of leaks or spills of crude oil (from the ground) and refined petroleum (gasoline). Although large oil spills from tankers attract a lot of media attention, the largest source of ocean oil pollution is urban and industrial runoff from land. **VOCs (volatile organic compounds)** in oil immediately kill many larval forms of ocean organisms. The oil reduces buoyancy and insulation in marine mammals and sea birds and can cause death from loss of body heat or drowning. Preventative methods for reducing oil contamination in ocean water include banning the dumping of waste and sewage in the open ocean, regulation of coastal development, and requiring double hulls for oil tankers.

Exxon Valdez—In 1989, the Exxon Valdez collided with some rock outcroppings in Alaska's Prince William Sound, releasing an enormous amount of oil into the ocean. Many sea birds, fish, and sea otters were killed by the oil spill. Some shoreline areas of the Prince William Sound still have toxic patches of oil today and continue to be harmful to marine organisms.

PREVENTING AND REDUCING WATER POLLUTION

As mentioned earlier, the three leading causes of water pollution are agriculture, industrial, and mining practices. Nonpoint sources are primarily responsible for much of the water pollution problems seen today. Methods for reducing nonpoint-source pollution include:
- reducing soil erosion by keeping cropland covered with vegetation

- reducing the amount of fertilizers used by using slow-releasing fertilizers and practicing polyculture or organic farming
- applying pesticides only when needed and using integrated pest management practices
- moving animal feedlots away from steeply sloping land and flood zones
- protecting natural water filtration systems such as wetlands and riparian buffer zones
- increasing use of alternative energy sources to reduce mercury emissions from coal-burning power plants

Prevention

Another method of reducing water pollution is providing improved treatment of human wastewater systems. Many developing countries lack any type of formal sewage treatment, especially in rural areas. Urban areas in most developed countries rely on primary and secondary treatment of sewage (see diagram below).

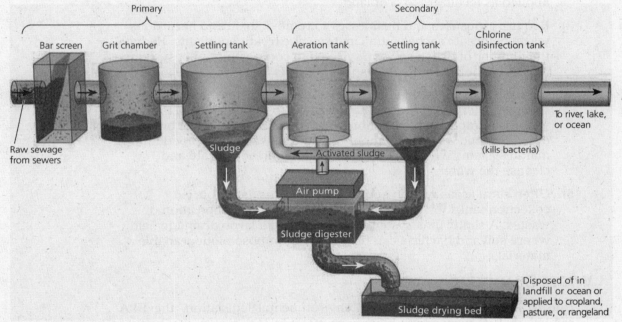

© Cengage Learning 2012

Primary sewage treatment—Primary sewage treatment is a physical process that uses screens and a grit tank to remove large floating debris and allows solids to settle out as sludge.

Secondary sewage treatment—Secondary sewage treatment is a biological process in which aerobic bacteria remove dissolved and biodegradable oxygen-demanding waste in aeration tanks. Settable solids are removed as sludge. Before discharge, water is bleached and treated with some method of disinfection to remove infectious agents. One of the more common methods used for disinfecting water is chlorination, but chlorine can react to form chlorinated hydrocarbons, which have been linked to human endocrine and nervous system damage. Alternatives to chlorine disinfection include treatment with ozone and ultraviolet light.

Advanced or tertiary sewage treatment—Advanced or tertiary sewage treatment is a physical and chemical process to remove specific pollutants left in the water after primary and secondary treatment. For example, this process could remove excess nitrates from water contaminated with excess fertilizers.

FURTHER RECOMMENDATIONS FOR SEWAGE TREATMENT

1) Use a separate network of pipes for carrying runoff of storm water from urban areas and sewage lines. Often municipal areas have combined these two systems to save money. Heavy rains can cause the combined lines to overflow and discharge untreated (raw) sewage directly into surface waters.

2) Sludge from sewage treatment facilities needs to be treated for harmful bacteria, toxic metals, and organic chemicals before it is applied as fertilizers to cropland.

3) Require industries and businesses to remove toxic and hazardous waste before it reaches municipal sewage treatment plants. Reduce the number of urban sewage systems to composting toilet systems to reduce the amount of sewage that needs to be treated.

4) Increase use of natural and artificial wetland systems to treat sewage. After using sedimentation tanks to remove solids, the water is pumped into oxidation ponds where bacteria will break down organic waste for a month. Next, the water is pumped into marsh systems where plants and bacteria further filtrate and cleanse the water.

5) Often rural areas rely on **septic tank** systems, large buried collection tanks for waste that allow bacterial decomposition of wastes. A septic tank system should include a large drainage field where soil and bacteria can filter and decompose biodegradable materials.

WATER QUALITY LEGISLATION

Due to increased education and environmental legislation, the EPA reports that improvements have been made in U.S. water quality over the past decade. However, there are still major water quality issues that face the United States today.

Clean Water Act—The Federal Water Pollution Control Act of 1972 was amended and renamed the Clean Water Act in 1977. This act primarily deals in regulating point-source pollution from municipal sewage facilities and industries and financing wastewater treatment systems. The Clean Water Act has had many positive effects on water quality in the United States, including decreasing annual wetland losses and increasing the percent of the U.S. population served by sewage treatment plants. Great strides have been made since the 1970s to improve U.S. water quality, but there is still room for improvement. A 2006 report from the EPA found that 45% of the United States' lakes and 40% of the streams are still unfit for fishing and swimming.

Water Quality Act—This amendment to the Clean Water Act was enacted in 1987. This amendment was to encourage the separation of storm water and sewer water lines.

U.S. Safe Drinking Water Act—In 1974, the United States passed the Safe Drinking Water Act. This act requires the EPA to set standards of maximum containment levels for water pollutants that have negative health impacts for humans.

Public Health Security and Bioterrorism Preparedness and Response Act of 2002—This act is to assess community water systems' infrastructure for any possible vulnerability to a terrorist or other intentional attack that would disrupt the ability to provide a clean, safe supply of water.

know the acts well

MULTIPLE-CHOICE QUESTIONS

1. The process of human activities near urban or agricultural areas that input excess plant nutrients into lakes is known as
   (A) artificial fertilization
   (B) cultural eutrophication
   (C) thermal pollution
   (D) lake stratification
   (E) synthetic primary productivity

2. Of the following, which constitutes the greatest percent of use for water withdrawn in the world today?
   (A) Flushing toilets in residential homes
   (B) Drinking water for human consumption
   (C) Smelting of metal in manufacturing
   (D) Irrigation for food production
   (E) Coolant water for electricity produced from coal

3. The federal legislation that set maximum containment levels for pollutants that cause adverse health effects in humans is the
   (A) Water Quality Act
   (B) Clean Water Act
   (C) Pollution Prevention Act
   (D) National Environmental Policy Act
   (E) Safe Drinking Water Act

4. Which water quality test will best determine the disruption of photosynthesis caused by cloudy water conditions from sedimentation?
   (A) Temperature
   (B) Salinity
   (C) Dissolved oxygen
   (D) pH
   (E) Turbidity

5. Coal-burning power plants and nuclear power plants producing electricity both release a large amount of
   (A) nitrogen compounds
   (B) arsenic contaminates
   (C) thermal pollution
   (D) infectious agents
   (E) oxygen-demanding wastes

6. Which of the following would least likely reduce the nutrient loading into the Chesapeake Bay estuary?
   (A) Replanting of riparian zones and sea grass beds
   (B) Upgrade of current sewage treatment plants
   (C) Improvement of manure containment lagoons in feedlots
   (D) Government subsidies for cotton crops
   (E) Re-introduction of native oyster beds

7. The largest source of oil pollution found in the oceans is from
   (A) urban and industrial runoff from the land
   (B) oil tanker accidents transporting oil between port cities
   (C) offshore drilling rigs in the Gulf of Mexico
   (D) pipeline leaks near coastal areas
   (E) the Alaskan pipeline

8. Although PCBs have been banned in the United States since 1977, they are still causing damage in the Great Lakes because
   (A) they are still being produced in Canada today
   (B) fishermen are illegally dumping PCBs
   (C) PCBs are persistent pollutants that do not degrade easily
   (D) they are water soluble and therefore make their way into aquatic systems
   (E) they are examples of heavy metals that are nondegradable

9. A type of wastewater treatment that includes some form of physical cleaning is
   I. primary treatment
   II. secondary treatment
   III. tertiary treatment

   (A) I only
   (B) II only
   (C) III only
   (D) I and III
   (E) I, II, and III

10. Which of the following is NOT a nonpoint-source pollutant?
    (A) Sediment loading from erosion
    (B) Runoff of pesticides from cropland
    (C) Animal wastes from feedlots
    (D) Fertilizer runoff from urban lawns
    (E) A sewage treatment plant effluent pipe

11. Which of the following would most likely cause metabolic stress in aerobic lake organisms?
(A) Variation in conductivity
(B) Dissolved oxygen levels at 2 to 3ppm
(C) Influx of dissolved solids
(D) A 1- to 2-degree change in water temperature
(E) An increase in pH from 6 to 7

12. The loss of riparian land along a river would cause which of the following?
I.   Increased flooding
II. Decreased turbidity
III. Increased nonpoint-source pollution

(A) I only
(B) II only
(C) III only
(D) I and III
(E) I, II, and III

13. Stronger regulations for coal-burning power plant emissions are likely to reduce which of the following aquatic pollutants?
(A) Arsenic
(B) DDT
(C) Mercury
(D) Atrazine
(E) Cadmium

14. Which of the following river conditions would yield the highest dissolved oxygen content?
(A) Fast-moving cold water, large amounts of submerged vegetative biomass
(B) Slow-moving cool waters, large amounts of emergent vegetative biomass
(C) Slow-moving warm waters, low amounts of submerged vegetative biomass
(D) Stagnant, warm water with large clumps of algae
(E) Warm water with little vegetative biomass

15. In coastal areas, withdrawing groundwater to the point where lateral recharge into the oceans becomes limited can cause
(A) hypoxic conditions
(B) increased vertical recharge
(C) saltwater intrusion
(D) change in the zone of aeration
(E) drought

FREE-RESPONSE QUESTION

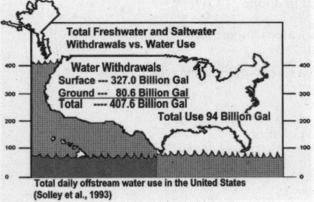

Total Freshwater and Saltwater
Withdrawals vs. Water Use

Water Withdrawals
Surface --- 327.0 Billion Gal
Ground --- 80.6 Billion Gal
Total ---- 407.6 Billion Gal

Total Use 94 Billion Gal

Total daily offstream water use in the United States
(Solley et al., 1993)

http://www.epa.gov/watrhome/you/chap1.html

done on seperate paper

1. a) Calculate the following by using statistics given in the table.
    i.   How many gallons of water, based on total use, would be available to each U.S. citizen? (U.S. population approximately 300 million)
    ii. The total withdrawal of groundwater represents what percent of the total water withdrawal?
    b) Identify TWO economic uses of surface water supplies that are withdrawn.
    c) Explain how sources of ground water could become unfit for human consumption.
    d) Excess nutrients often enter surface waters from surrounding agricultural land. Identify where these nutrients are generated from and discuss a preventative measure for nutrient loading into waterways.
    e) Identify and describe one federal law used to protect the quality of water resources in the United States.

ANSWERS

MULTIPLE-CHOICE QUESTIONS

1. **ANSWER: B.** Cultural eutrophication occurs from the input of excess nutrients such as nitrates and phosphates into aquatic ecosystems. The reduction in dissolved oxygen from aerobic bacterial decomposition leads to fish kills (*Living in the Environment,* 16th ed., page 539 / 17th ed., pages 536–537).

2. **ANSWER: D.** Approximately 70% of the water withdrawn each year is used for irrigation of crops. Industry is the second leading user of water supplies (*Living in the Environment,* 16th ed., pages 308–317 / 17th ed., page 320).

3. **ANSWER: E.** The United States Safe Drinking Water Act is federal legislation that sets maximum containment levels for pollutants

that cause adverse health effect in humans (*Living in the Environment*, 15th ed., page 546 / 16th ed., pages 542–543).

4. **ANSWER: E.** Turbidity is the measure of cloudiness in the water column. Water clarity affects phytoplankton and submerged vegetation populations, as UV radiation necessary for photosynthesis is blocked by suspended solids (*Living in the Environment*, 16th ed., page 534 / 17th ed., page 533).

5. **ANSWER: C.** Electric power plants release large amounts of heated water that has been used as coolant water back into rivers, lakes, and streams. (*Living in the Environment*, 16th ed., page 534 / 17th ed., page 532).

6. **ANSWER: D.** The Chesapeake Bay estuary, the largest in the United States, has experienced devastating biodiversity loss due to increased nutrients. The primary sources of these phosphates and nitrates are faulty sewer lines and agricultural feedlots. Encouraging increased agriculture through government subsidies will not reduce the nutrient loading in this area (*Living in the Environment*, 16th ed., pages 172–173 / 17th ed., pages 179–180).

7. **ANSWER: A.** Although major oil spills like the Exxon Valdez get the most media attention, everyday urban and industrial runoff creates the largest input of oil into the oceans (*Living in the Environment*, 16th ed., pages 549–550 / 17th ed., pages 547–548).

8. **ANSWER: C.** PCBs belong to a group of synthetic organic chlorinated hydrocarbon toxins. These toxins are fat soluble and therefore experience biomagnifications in the food chain. They also are slowly degraded in the environment and therefore are persistent chemicals found in ecosystems (*Living in the Environment*, 16th ed., page 495 / 17th ed., pages 536, 446).

9. **ANSWER: D.** Both primary treatment and tertiary (advanced) use forms of physical cleaning methods such as screens or filters to remove pollutants from wastewater (*Living in the Environment*, 16th ed., page 554 / 17th ed., pages 550–554).

10. **ANSWER: E.** A nonpoint source is one that enters the water from broad, diffuse sources such as runoff or atmospheric deposition of chemicals. Sewage treatment plants often have effluent pipes that return treated wastewater to surface waters. This is an example of a point-source pollutant—**not** a nonpoint-source pollutant (*Living in the Environment*, 16th ed., pages 532–533 / 17th ed., pages 529–530).

11. **ANSWER: B.** Decreasing the level of dissolved oxygen below 5 ppm typically causes metabolic stress in most aerobic consumers (*Living in the Environment*, 16th ed., pages 58, 535 / 17th ed., page 533).

12. **ANSWER: D.** Riparian land is vegetation that lies along aquatic ecosystems. This vegetation serves as a natural sponge for floodwaters and can also soak up nonpoint pollutants prior to

entering waterways. Therefore removing these buffers will increase flooding and the chance for nonpoint-source pollution to enter waterways (*Living in the Environment*, 16th ed., page 546 / 17th ed., pages 340–341).

13. **ANSWER: C.** Mercury enters aquatic ecosystems from atmospheric deposition of coal-burning emissions. After it enters surface waters it is converted to methylmercury by bacteria and can become stored in the fat of organisms and increase through the food chain (biomagnification) (*Living in the Environment*, 16th ed., page 534 / 17th ed., page 448).

14. **ANSWER: A.** The solubility of oxygen is determined by water temperature. Colder water enables a higher solubility of oxygen gas, and the faster the water flows the more easily it can diffuse into the water (*Living in the Environment*, 16th ed., pages 58 and 535 / 17th ed., page 533).

15. **ANSWER: C.** In coastal areas near the shore, natural groundwater serves as lateral recharge into ocean systems. However, if this recharge is limited and does not make its way to the ocean, saltwater will back up into groundwater reserves. This can contaminate sources of drinking water with salt (*Living in the Environment*, 16th ed., pages 323–324 / 17th ed., pages 326–327).

FREE-RESPONSE SCORING GUIDELINES

a) i. How many gallons of water, based on total use, would be available to each U.S. citizen? (U.S. population approximately 300 million)

2 points can be earned—1 point for a correct setup and 1 point for the correct answer of 300 gal to 320 gals

$$\frac{94 \text{ billion gallons}}{300 \text{ million people}} \text{ or } \frac{9.4 \times 10^{10}}{3.0 \times 10^{8}} = 313 \frac{\text{gallons}}{\text{person}} \text{ (300 to 320 accepted)}$$

ii. The total withdrawal of groundwater represents what percent of the total water withdrawal?

2 points can be earned—1 point for a correct setup and 1 point for the correct answer of 20%

$$\frac{80.6 \text{ billion gallons (groundwater)}}{407.6 \text{ billion gallons (total water withdrawal)}} \times 100 = 20\%$$

b) Identify TWO economic uses of surface water supplies that are withdrawn.

2 points can be earned—1 point for each correct identification of water use—note: this must be an economic use which must tie into making money for the economy or individual
   - as a coolant in coal-burning and nuclear power plants that generate electricity
   - in metal extraction and mining processes

- as water to feed livestock
- in aquaculture processes
- in industrial processes that manufacture consumer goods
- as irrigation water for crops
- in industrial processes that produce food (meat industry, food processing)

c) Explain how sources of groundwater could become unfit for human consumption.

1 point can be earned for a correct identification of a groundwater pollutant and description of source

Sources of groundwater contamination
- saltwater intrusion due to excess withdrawal of groundwater near coastal areas
- fecal contamination by leaking septic tanks
- animal waste contamination by overflows of waste lagoons on feedlots
- hazardous waste leaking from deep well injection sites
- toxins from mining practices that leach into soil layers
- leachate from landfills
- excess pesticides and fertilizers that leach into soil layers
- buried gasoline and solvent drums that leak into surrounding soil layers
- salts from de-icing roadways

d) Excess nutrients often enter surface waters from surrounding agricultural land. Identify where these nutrients are generated from and discuss a preventative measure for nutrient loading into waterways.

2 points can be earned—1 point for a correct identification of where the nutrients are generated from and 1 point for describing a linked preventative method

Sources of excess nutrients
- fertilizers like phosphates and nitrates sprayed on cropland
- animal waste runoff from feedlots
- pulp from paper mills
- food waste from food processing plants
- sewage effluent from urban areas

Preventative measures
- protection of current wetlands and forests that naturally remove toxins
- planting of vegetative buffers (increasing riparian zones)
- polyculture practices to reduce fertilizer needs
- organic farming practices to reduce fertilizer needs
- composting of logging, paper mill, and food processing wastes

Answer

Page

e) Identify and describe one federal law used to protect the quality of our water resources in the United States.

1 point can be earned for correctly naming and describing one of the following laws:

Clean Water Act—The Federal Water Pollution Control Act of 1972 was amended and renamed the Clean Water Act in 1977. This act primarily deals in regulating point-source pollution from municipal sewage facilities and industries and financing wastewater treatment systems.

Water Quality Act—This amendment to the Clean Water Act was enacted in 1987. This amendment was to encourage the separation of storm water and sewer water lines.

Safe Drinking Water Act—First enacted in 1974 and amended in 1986 and 1996, this law requires the EPA to establish National Primary Drinking Water Regulations (NPDWRs) for contaminants in sources used for drinking water that may cause adverse public health effects.

MINERAL AND ENERGY RESOURCES

KEY CONCEPTS

- The mining and processing of geologic resources result in considerable environmental and societal costs.
- The surface of the earth is in constant motion.
- Mineral resources are not evenly distributed across the earth.
- Fossil fuels provide most of the world's energy, and their supply is limited.
- Conservation is a simple strategy for extending the lifetime of limited resources and for reducing the environmental impact from resource extraction and use.
- Alternate sources of energy also have environmental and societal costs.
- It will take several alternate sources of energy used in concert to supply the future energy needs of the world.

Mineral and energy resources are discussed in depth in *Living in the Environment*, 16th ed., Chapters 14, 15, & 16 / 17th ed., Chapters 14, 15, & 16.

KEY VOCABULARY

acid mine drainage	ANWR
active solar energy	bauxite
advanced light-water reactors	biodiesel fuel
anthracite coal	biomass energy

control rod

bituminous coal

CAFE standards

chain reaction

Chernobyl, Ukraine

cogeneration

boundary

crude oil

crust

divergent plate boundary

energy conservation

energy efficiency

fossil fuels

fractional distillation

fuel rod

General Mining Law of 1872

geothermal energy

high-level radioactive waste

hydrogen fuel cell

light-water nuclear reactor

lignite

liquefied natural gas (LNG)

mineral

moderator

mountaintop removal

multi-paned windows

natural gas

nuclear fusion

oil refinery

oil shale

OPEC

open-pit mining

ore

overburden

passive solar energy

peat

pebble-bed modular reactors

petrochemicals

photovoltaic cell

reserve

resource

smelting

solution mining

subsurface mining

surface (strip) mining

Surface Mining Control and Reclamation Act of 1977

solar power tower

synfuels

tar sands

tectonic plate

Three Mile Island

transform fault

wind power

Yucca Mountain, Nevada

Vocab list (handwritten)

MINING

Minerals and **fossil fuels** are mined from the earth's crust. The method of removing a resource is selected based on factors such as the depth at which the resource is located, the amount and stability of the material that must be removed to reach the mineral (**overburden**), the topography of the area, safety, and economics. The most common mining techniques for removing materials from the earth are listed below.

Surface (Strip) Mining—Used to remove deposits that lie in horizontal beds close to the earth's surface. First, the land is clear-cut, and the overburden is removed and set aside with explosives and heavy equipment. The deposit is then removed with huge power shovels, and the overburden is replaced. Surface mining, even when the land is reclaimed, results in long-term environmental damage.

Mountaintop Removal—A type of surface mining in which coal seams are exposed by removing the top of a mountain using explosives and/or heavy equipment. The material removed is dumped into adjacent valleys, sometimes burying forests, rivers and streams. The coal is then removed with power shovels or bulldozers. Although federal law requires the land to be reclaimed, the topology of the land cannot be fully restored and the original forests, rivers, and streams often remain permanently buried beneath the former mountaintop.

Open-Pit Mining—A huge hole is dug using explosives and heavy equipment, and the deposit is removed. After a pit is abandoned, it often fills with water, which becomes acidic and polluted with heavy metals due to the mine waste that was left behind.

Subsurface Mining—Deep vertical mine shafts with horizontal tunnels branching off are blasted into the earth to remove deposits that are too far underground to reach by surface mining. While there is less habitat destruction on the surface, subsurface mining is dangerous. When mineshafts cave in, the ground above it can collapse or subside. Methane and coal dust can cause underground explosions, poisonous gases can fill the tunnels, and mineshafts can be flooded. Additionally, in the case of subsurface mining for coal, miners develop black lung disease, which is caused by long-term exposure to coal dust.

Drilling—To remove liquids and gases (oil, natural gas and steam), deep shafts are drilled into the earth to reach the geologic formation containing the desired material. Normally, pressure in the formation forces the liquid or gas to the surface, but if natural pressure is not sufficient, water, steam, or other fluids sometimes can be injected to force the material out. A drilling platform or pad is required that destroys habitat on the surface. Liquids are susceptible to leaking and spilling during extraction, storage, and transportation, contaminating land and water. The construction of pipelines that carry gases and liquids result in habitat loss and fragmentation (pipelines can be thousands of miles long). Offshore drilling rigs and oil tankers can also spill and leak into ocean waters.

ENVIRONMENTAL COSTS OF MINING

Mining operations cause significant damage to the environment. The first step of a mining operation requires that the habitat above the deposit be destroyed by clear-cutting forests and removing native vegetation. Even after overburden is replaced, soils will no longer be layered into the soil horizons that would allow true restoration of the native habitat. Streams and rivers in the area are clouded by sediment and in some cases are buried. Wastewater that flows into local waterways is contaminated with hazardous chemicals leached from mine waste. Mining produces a huge volume of solid waste. In the United States, 75% of all solid waste comes from mining operations. The dust and emissions created in mines is usually hazardous. Mining in the United States produces more hazardous emissions than any other activity.

Acid mine drainage occurs when sulfur compounds in mine waste are exposed to air, oxidize, and dissolve in rainwater to form a sulfuric acid solution. The acidic runoff enters waterways, causing significant ecological damage similar to that of acid rain.

U.S. MINING LAWS

Know the laws and acts

The General Mining Law of 1872—This U.S. law was enacted to encourage the exploration and mining of mineral resources. Currently, it enables corporations to acquire large tracts of public lands at far below market prices. A few modifications have been made to the law since 1990, but critics still claim that it allows corporations to remove valuable minerals from public lands without paying adequate royalties or requiring sufficient cleanup of mining sites.

The Surface Mining Control and Reclamation Act of 1977—This requires that mined land be restored to its pre-mining state. This includes disposal of all mining waste, re-contouring the land as closely as possible to its original topography, and replanting native vegetation.

MINERAL RESOURCES

Modern societies rely on a constant supply of mineral resources that are extracted from the earth's crust. Metallic minerals are extracted as **ores**. High-grade ore has a significant concentration of the desired mineral that can be recovered economically, while low-grade ore may have only trace amounts that are too expensive to recover. Some of the metallic mineral resources that are mined extensively include aluminum, iron, lead, chromium, manganese, nickel, silver, and gold. Nonmetal mineral resources include sand, gravel, limestone, clay, asbestos, talc, and salt. The standard of living in a country is directly related to its ability to access these resources. Mineral resources are nonrenewable, their availability is limited, and their extraction, use, and disposal results in significant environmental and societal costs.

PLATE TECTONICS

The material that makes up the earth's crust is in constant motion, and it is covered with an array of thick massive slabs, or **tectonic plates**, that move slowly across the surface. The movement of these tectonic plates forms mountain ranges and causes environmental hazards such as earthquakes, volcanic eruptions, tsunamis, and landslides. The movement of tectonic plates has also caused geologic resources to accumulate unevenly across the earth's surface. Tectonic plates meet at three types of plate boundaries.

Divergent Plate Boundary—This is a plate boundary where two oceanic plates are separating, and molten rock flows up into the void that is created between the plates. An example is the Mid-Atlantic Ridge.

Convergent Plate Boundary—This is a plate boundary where two plates are colliding with one another. When an oceanic plate and a continental plate converge, the denser oceanic plate usually goes under the continental plate. Volcanoes are often located on the upper continental plate. For example, the plate boundaries in the Western Pacific Ocean have resulted in the formation of numerous volcanoes and caused large earthquakes in the region, including the earthquake that led to the deadly tsunami that devastated Indonesia in 2004. When two continental plates converge they push up a range of mountains. For example, the boundary between India and China where the Himalayas are rising was caused by such a collision.

Transform Fault—This is a plate boundary where the plates are sliding past one another. For example, the San Andreas Fault in California represents such a boundary and is the cause of frequent earthquakes in that area.

MINERAL DEPOSITS

The movement of tectonic plates can concentrate minerals. At divergent plate boundaries, where new crustal material is emerging, minerals may be transported by heated water that dissolves metals as they emerge from the earth's crust and deposits them nearby upon cooling. In addition, as molten rock cools, heavier minerals may solidify early and sink to the bottom of the liquid, where they become more concentrated, before the rock hardens completely. At convergent plate boundaries, the intense heat and pressure that occur when plates collide can melt metallic minerals that then flow and accumulate in cooler areas of the crust. Physical processes like weathering and erosion (a great deal of which occurs along transform faults) along with transport by water, wind, and gravity also separate minerals based on size and density, thereby producing varied mineral deposits.

MINERAL PROCESSING

The removal of metals from ores, in some cases, can cause more damage to the environment than the mining of the ore, and in many cases mineral processing is a much greater hazard to human health.

Smelting—The heating of ores to remove metals produces air pollution that includes heavy metals, particulate matter, and sulfur dioxide, which is a precursor to acid rain.

Cyanide Solution Mining or Heap-Leach Extraction—The practice of spraying cyanide solutions on piles of crushed ore to dissolve and extract gold creates holding ponds of cyanide-laced water that may seep into groundwater and run off along the surface to poison local waterways.

RECYCLING AND MINERAL RESERVES

The massive amount of energy required, in addition to the environmental, social, and economic costs of mining and processing minerals from their ore, makes recycling a sensible means of prolonging the useful life of a mineral. For example, recycling aluminum cans consumes about 5% of the energy and eliminates most of the environmental costs associated with mining and smelting the aluminum ore **(bauxite)**. Other minerals that are commonly recycled include copper, steel, platinum, silver, gold, and glass.

By definition, nonrenewable resources can be exhausted. However, since the consumption of a resource like aluminum does not transform aluminum atoms into other atoms, given enough technology, energy and time, all aluminum theoretically could be recycled. However, collecting every piece of aluminum ever used and discarded from the thousands of landfills and other disposal sites, for all practical purposes, is impossible. As a result, we rely on reserves from which we can extract additional minerals. A **reserve** is a location from which a mineral can be extracted in an economically viable manner. Probable, hypothetical or speculative resources may become reserves if exploration and market prices establish that they are economically viable to extract.

FOSSIL FUELS

The term fossil fuel refers to solid, liquid, and gaseous forms of ancient vegetation or animal matter that can be found buried inside the earth's crust. Although fossil fuels are geologic resources, they are organic, and as a result not classified as minerals, which are usually defined as inorganic compounds. Nonetheless, coal is extracted by the same mining processes used to extract mineral resources.

COAL

Coal is the most abundant fossil fuel, and is used to produce most of the world's electricity. In a coal-burning power plant, coal is pulverized into small pellets and burned to produce steam. The steam is directed across the blades of a turbine to rotate it and a generator that generates electricity. The environmental costs of mining and burning coal are severe. In addition to the environmental costs of mining listed above, burning coal produces large quantities of air pollution including heavy metals, particulate matter, and sulfur dioxide. Burning coal also produces more carbon dioxide than other fossil fuels. Because of its abundance in China, India, and other developing countries, coal use and the associated environmental cost are likely to increase in the future.

Coal formation begins with **peat**, which forms from an accumulation of partially decomposed plant debris in waterlogged, anaerobic conditions. After being buried by millions of years of sediment accumulation, heat and pressure squeeze the water from the peat, and initiates a series of transformations into the ranks of coal. In order from youngest to oldest, after the formation of peat, the ranks of coal are **lignite**, **sub-bituminous coal**, **bituminous coal**, and **anthracite coal**. Anthracite coal has the highest energy content by weight, or energy density, followed in reverse order of formation by bituminous coal, sub-bituminous coal, and lignite. Although peat has the lowest energy content by weight and emits noxious smoke when burned, it is still used for fuel in some areas.

CRUDE OIL OR PETROLEUM

Crude oil is formed from the remains of ancient marine organisms that were buried beneath sediments and subjected to high temperatures and pressure. Oil is a mixture of many different liquids and gases, whose components are used to provide energy for a variety of purposes. Its liquid components such as fuel oil and gasoline, are used for home heating and transportation in cars, airplanes, trucks, and train engines. Gaseous components such as propane and butane are used for cooking and heating. The solid components include grease, wax, petroleum jelly, and asphalt.

Because of the United States' intense dependence on petroleum, and because most of the reserves of oil are in the Middle East and controlled by the Organization of Petroleum Exporting Countries (**OPEC**), there is concern over the reliance on politically unstable governments for such an important energy resource. These concerns have led some to call for renewed oil exploration and drilling in environmentally sensitive areas such as offshore and in the Arctic National Wildlife Refuge (**ANWR**). However, most experts agree that it is not possible to solve the nation's energy problem in the long run through increased petroleum production. Rather, we must seek alternative fuels and focus on improved energy efficiency.

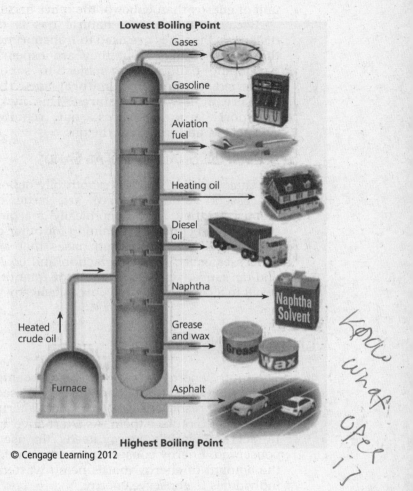

© Cengage Learning 2012

Because it is a mixture of liquids, crude oil requires a separation and purification step between extraction and use that is not required of the other fossil fuels. This step takes place at an **oil refinery** and it makes use of a process called **fractional distillation**, which separates liquids based on differences in their boiling points. The refining of oil produces many different products in addition to those listed above, including **petrochemicals** that can be made, among other things, into synthetic fibers for clothing, plastics, pesticides, cleaning fluids, paints, and medicines.

NATURAL GAS

Mostly methane (CH_4) in composition, natural gas is formed and found alongside crude oil and coal. Like coal, it can be used in power plants to produce electricity, and it is also commonly used for cooking, and space heating. Burning natural gas produces less carbon dioxide per unit of energy than either of the other fossil fuels.

Because it is a gas, natural gas is difficult to transport great distances. Pipelines are used to transport natural gas over hundreds or thousands of miles, but they are expensive, unaffordable in many developing nations, and subject to sabotage. Natural gas can be converted to **liquefied natural gas (LNG)** when placed under pressure at low temperatures. This makes it more convenient to transport large distances, but requires energy to compress, refrigerate, and transport the gas.

SYNFUELS, OIL SHALE, AND TAR SANDS

Oil shale and tar sands are both oily deposits that can yield oil when processed. Although there are large reserves of these energy resources, they are economically marginal and require the same destructive techniques as mining for other geologic resources.

Synfuels are liquids and gases that are produced from coal by processes called coal liquefaction and coal gasification. Like oil shale and tar sands, synfuels take a large quantity of energy to produce and result in a correspondingly low net energy yield.

ENERGY CONSERVATION

The future energy needs of the earth cannot be met with fossil fuels. Their limited supply, and the increased cost of exploiting less accessible resources, dictate that alternative energy sources be developed to replace them. As alternative energy sources are scaled up to meet the world's energy needs, the use of fossil fuels must also be conserved. Energy conservation simply refers to strategies that reduce the amount of energy that is being wasted. There are many ways for individuals to conserve energy.

Decrease energy for transportation—Reduce driving by using mass transit, walking, or riding a bike. Join a carpool. Walk up and down stairs instead of using an elevator. Buy locally grown food and locally made products to reduce the energy required to transport goods to market. Replace a gas-guzzling car with a hybrid-electric or electric vehicle.

Decrease energy for heating—Decrease the thermostat setting when it is cold and wear warmer clothing while indoors. Use less hot water and take cooler, shorter showers. Increase the amount of insulation in a home to reduce heat loss. Replace single-paned with **multi-paned windows**. Reduce heat loss by improving the seals around windows and doors. Replace a hot water heater that stores hot water in a tank with a tankless hot water heater. Install an active solar energy system to replace a furnace and hot water heater.

Decrease electricity use—Turn off lights when leaving a room. Increase the thermostat setting when it is hot to reduce the use of an air conditioner. Replace incandescent light bulbs with fluorescent bulbs. Unplug electronics that have a standby mode when they are not in use, or plug them into a power strip and turn off the power strip when appliances are not in use. Install photovoltaic solar panels to provide electricity.

> ## AP Tip
>
> A common prompt in the free-response section of the APES exam is to request a description of ways to reduce the environmental costs associated with an activity like burning coal. Often the best way to respond to such a prompt is by invoking conservation. By using conservation strategies like those listed above, you may be able to avoid a lengthy description of a complicated technology.
>
> For example, it is easier to describe the act of turning off the lights when leaving a room to lower electricity consumption and eliminate sulfur dioxide emissions than it is to describe the operation of a wet scrubber on a coal-fired power plant to eliminate those same emissions.

read this on AP day understand this

ENERGY EFFICIENCY

Several of the conservation measures listed above are effective because they increase the energy efficiency of an action. For example, incandescent light bulbs have efficiencies of approximately 5% compared to 25% for fluorescent bulbs. The second law of thermodynamics establishes that no energy transformation can be 100% efficient and that some waste heat must be produced when energy is converted from one form to another. Efficiency is the ratio of the quantity of work or energy that is produced to the quantity of energy that was used. For example, if 500 Btu of electric energy is produced from 5,000 Btu of potential energy in a fuel, the efficiency is 500/5,000 = 0.1 or 10%. While about 40% of the energy generated in the United States is unavoidably lost due to the second law of thermodynamics, estimates are that another 40% or so of the energy generated in the United States is unnecessarily wasted.

OTHER CONSERVATION STRATEGIES

In addition to many of the same strategies for individuals, some industries can conserve energy by using a process called **cogeneration**. Large companies and power plants that burn fuel often waste excess heat by expelling it into the surroundings. In some cases, that excess heat can be used to produce steam that can generate electricity. If the excess heat is insufficient for generating electricity, it can be used to heat nearby buildings, thereby reducing the need to burn additional fuel.

Governments can help conserve energy by mandating energy standards. In the United States, for example, the Corporate Average Fuel Economy (**CAFE**) Standards were first enacted by Congress in 1975 to require automobile manufacturers to produce cars that meet a minimum fuel efficiency standard. CAFE standards were effective in raising the average mileage for U.S. cars from 13 miles per gallon (mpg) in 1973 to 22 mpg in 1985. But a relaxation of standards in the mid-80s coupled with loopholes in the law and a changed mix of vehicles in the national fleet kept the average at 22 mpg until 2008 when new legislation was passed that will raise the standard to 35 mpg by 2020.

HYBRID-ELECTRIC VEHICLES

This is very needed

Hybrid-electric vehicles are becoming more common. These cars use a relatively small amount of gasoline by combining an electric motor with a small gasoline engine for vehicle propulsion. Some of the kinetic energy of the car is used to drive an alternator that charges the batteries needed to power the electric motor. Hybrid-electric vehicles can have efficiencies several times that of a typical automobile getting up to 40–50 mpg.

Electric vehicles and plug-in hybrid vehicles both use electricity to charge batteries in the car. This likely utilizes electricity from an electric grid. Ideally, this electricity would be generated using an alternative energy source like solar or wind; however, if the electricity was produced by a coal or natural gas fired power plant, fossil fuels would still be being consumed, albeit indirectly, to power the vehicle. By diverting the energy generation from the internal combustion engine of the car to a power plant, the consumer is trading off some of the environmental costs of operating a gasoline vehicle with those of operating the power plant. It will reduce the environmental costs of operating the vehicle either way, but using alternate energy sources to provide the electricity for an electric car is the best option for conserving fossil fuels as well.

ALTERNATE ENERGY SOURCES

Alt Energy

Replacing fossil fuels as a source of energy must be done. There are many different alternatives to the use of fossil fuels, both renewable and nonrenewable. Some make use of new technology and some make use of mature technology. However, in either case, new research is continuously improving technologies to make these alternatives more and more viable. The different energy needs—electricity, transportation, and heating—will require different alternatives. As a result, the solution will not be a single alternative, but many used in concert to supply the future energy needs of the world.

Keep in mind that while alternates to fossil fuels will reduce or eliminate some of the environmental costs associated with them, those costs will not be eliminated entirely, and in some cases new problems will replace the problems that are being solved.

NUCLEAR ENERGY

Like fossil fuels, nuclear energy is a nonrenewable resource. Huge environmental and social costs are associated with the extraction, processing, use, and disposal of radioactive nuclear fuel. In the 1950s, nuclear power was thought to be the solution to the world's energy needs, but safety concerns and unanticipated economic, environmental, and social costs undermined that dream. Nonetheless, nuclear energy still comprises 5–10% of world and U.S. energy supplies, all of which is electricity. A few countries generate far more of their electricity from nuclear energy than others; for example, France generates about 75% of its electricity from nuclear power.

Nuclear power plants use the same method as those fired by fossil fuels to generate electricity, namely by heating water to produce steam, which rotates a turbine connected to a generator to produce electricity. Nuclear power plants use the process of nuclear fission rather than combustion of coal to heat the water that becomes steam. The most commonly used nuclear fuel is uranium, a radioactive element that is mined from the earth and enriched to increase the concentration of the fissionable U-235 isotope to about 3% from a naturally occurring abundance of less than 1%. Enriched uranium is pelletized and packed into **fuel rods** that are placed into the reactor core, along with a **moderator** that is used to slow down neutrons that are released during the fission reactions. **Control rods**, usually containing pure carbon as graphite, are interspersed with the fuel rods to absorb neutrons and regulate the rate of the fission reactions and the amount of energy produced.

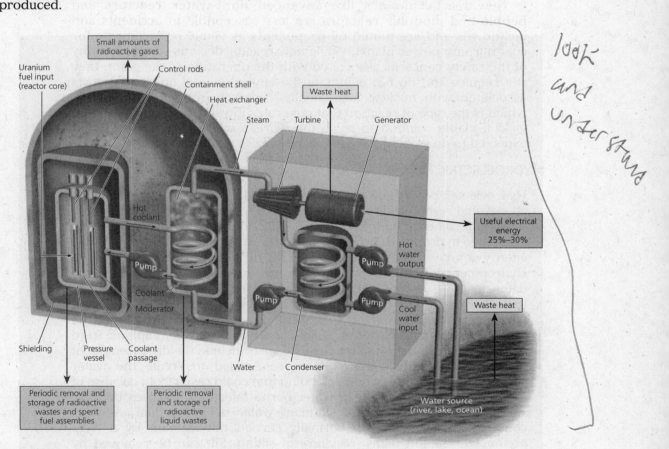

© Cengage Learning 2012

After the used fuel rods are removed from the reactor core they are stored onsite in water-filled tanks. There is no long-term disposal site presently available for spent nuclear fuel rods and other waste, which is classified as **high-level radioactive waste**. A proposal to open the first high-level radioactive waste repository in the world at **Yucca Mountain, Nevada** has been delayed due to safety and security concerns and probably will not be opened any time soon.

The environmental costs of nuclear power include the waste, runoff, air pollution, and land damage that result from the mining, processing, and transportation of uranium; the ecological damage due to the accidental release of radioactive materials; and thermal pollution in bodies of water being used as coolant for nuclear power plants. Other concerns include the lack of long-term storage for nuclear waste, the economic and environmental costs of decommissioning old nuclear power plants, the threat of terrorist attack and sabotage at nuclear power plants, and the safety of operating nuclear power plants near large populations. In **Chernobyl, Ukraine**, a meltdown in 1986 exposed millions of people across Europe to dangerous levels of radiation. At the **Three Mile Island** nuclear power plant in Pennsylvania, a meltdown was narrowly averted in 1979 that could have exposed the population on the East Coast of the United States to nuclear fallout.

New reactor designs like **advanced light-water reactors** and **pebble-bed modular reactors** are less susceptible to accidents and meltdowns and are touted by proponents as viable replacements for coal-burning power plants. While new reactor designs eliminate many of the safety concerns associated with the operation of the plant, they still require and do not eliminate the environmental and social costs associated with nuclear fuel. Finally, research into **nuclear fusion**, which is the type of reaction that generates the sun's energy, has yet to yield a viable solution to solve the world's energy needs and is not expected to do so before fossil fuel resources are exhausted.

HYDROELECTRIC POWER

Hydroelectric power makes use of the potential energy of water stored in an elevated reservoir. Water released from the reservoir is made to flow through turbines that are connected to generators to produce electricity. Currently, hydropower produces more energy than any other renewable energy source in the world—about 25% of the world's electricity. The environmental costs of hydroelectric power are associated with the large dams that are needed to store water for reliable energy production. Impacts include the flooding of habitat upstream from the dam and fragmentation of the river ecosystem. Fragmentation prevents large ranging or migratory species, such as salmon and river dolphins, from accessing part of their habitat. Societal costs include the displacement of human communities when homes are flooded to create the water storage reservoir, catastrophic flooding that could result from collapse of the dam, and an increase in water-borne infectious diseases that are spread in slow-moving and stagnant water behind a dam. Another concern is that sediments normally carried downstream by a river accumulate behind dams, resulting in silting. Silt can be removed by dredging; if the sediments are not removed, they will accumulate until the dam is no longer functional.

SOLAR ENERGY

For thousands of years, people have built and oriented their homes to make use of the sun's energy. **Passive solar energy** systems make direct use of sunlight to heat a building. Since the path of the sun is predictable, a building can be positioned to maximize its utilization of the sun's energy. In the northern hemisphere, for example, windows placed along the south side of a building will allow sunlight to enter year-round and heat the interior. The heat can be stored in building materials like stone, concrete, or adobe, and in large tanks of water. Heat stored during the day can be released slowly during non-daylight hours. Passive solar energy is more effective when it is used in combination with energy conservation measures such as thick or high r-value insulation and well-sealed, multi-paned windows.

In order to reduce cooling costs and avoid overheating buildings that use passive solar energy systems during the summer, overhangs can be used that block out high-angle summer sunlight while allowing low-angle winter sunlight to enter. Deciduous trees can be planted where they shade the building in the summer while allowing winter sunlight to pass through their leafless branches.

[handwritten margin note: effective with solar panels]

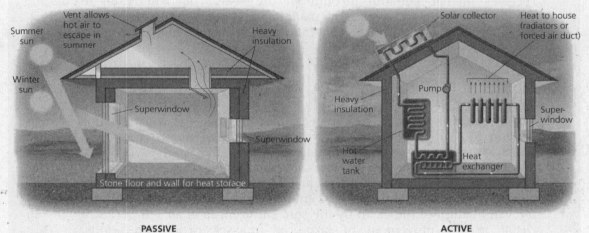

PASSIVE

ACTIVE

© Cengage Learning 2012

Active solar energy systems make use of pumps to move water or a fluid-like antifreeze through solar collectors, where it is heated by the sun and then pumped throughout a building to provide heat. An active solar energy system can also store the hot fluid and allow it to slowly release its heat throughout non-daylight hours. These systems can also be used to heat water and replace conventional hot water heaters.

Photovoltaic cells (PV or solar cells) convert sunlight directly into electricity by making use of the electrical properties of the semiconducting element silicon. Solar cells can be used to generate electricity in remote locations far from an electrical grid. In these "off-the-grid" applications, excess electricity can be used to charge batteries that will provide electricity whenever sunlight is not available. Solar cells can be used on buildings that are connected to an electrical grid in such a way that the excess electricity they generate is fed into the grid, decreasing the need to generate electricity by other means. A big drawback to photovoltaic cells is their high cost. For example, the installation of an array of solar cells sufficient to power a home in the southwestern United States currently takes 10 to 20 years to pay back with savings from energy bills—a price most consumers are unable or unwilling to pay—and this is in the most advantageous area of the United States for solar energy use. PV cells are a far less feasible alternative at more northern latitudes where sunlight is less intense.

Solar power plants use sunlight to provide electricity for cities. A **solar power tower** makes use of an array of mirrors that focus sunlight to a single point where the concentrated solar energy is used to heat a fluid that heats water to produce the steam necessary to rotate a turbine attached to a generator that produces electricity. Another type of solar power plant uses long parabolic mirrors that have a fluid-filled pipe running along the focus of each mirror that is heated by the concentrated sunlight. The heated fluid is pumped to a boiler where it heats water to produce the steam necessary to generate electricity. In both of these examples the mirrors are mounted and use motors in such a way that they track the sun during daylight hours. A solar power plant requires a large area of land in an arid location that receives intense sunlight throughout the year. This will result in habitat loss in the area where the plant is built and limits the regions of the earth where such power generation is feasible primarily to desert biomes.

Wind Energy

Wind power has been used for centuries to push the sails of ships around the world and to the turn windmills that pump water and make flour. The modern windmills of today are used to produce electricity, and when all of the environmental costs of resource extraction and pollution cleanup are factored in, wind energy is an inexpensive renewable source of energy. Winds are the result of the uneven heating of the earth by the sun. Differences in air temperature result in the movement of large air masses producing winds. Mountain ridges and passes are locations with concentrated reliable winds, and many wind farms have been built in these areas around the world. Offshore wind farms are currently being considered as a way of increasing the generation of electricity from wind. This also reduces the complaint of some who consider the wind farms that occupy ridges and passes to be a visual blight. Other concerns over wind energy include the noise produced by windmills, interference with bird migration, and that even in the windiest places on earth, the strength and direction of wind are too unreliable to depend entirely on winds for energy without substantial backup systems.

only down Side is Nimby

GEOTHERMAL ENERGY

Geothermal energy makes use of the earth's internal temperature by tapping into high-temperature, high-pressure steam that exists below the earth's surface in some areas. Limited to use in areas where such conditions exist, usually near tectonic plate boundaries, some countries, notably Iceland (which sits atop the Mid-Atlantic Ridge), have made extensive use of geothermal energy. The heat is used to heat buildings and to generate electricity.

BIOFUELS

Biofuels are a collection of different energy sources that all involve obtaining fuel from plant matter and animal waste. Burning wood, dung, crop wastes and other **biomass** has supplied humans with energy for thousands of years. Because wood can be harvested sustainably and since dung and crop wastes otherwise will be discarded, these are attractive and inexpensive sources of energy. However, the smoke from fires using biomass contains poisonous carbon monoxide, as well as ash, soot, and hydrocarbons, which are hazardous and may be carcinogenic.

Methane digesters can be used to convert animal waste from feedlots and factory farms into methane. Landfills and wastewater treatment facilities can collect the methane that is produced during decomposition. The methane from either source can be used, like natural gas, to produce electricity, for cooking, or to heat buildings.

Sugar cane, corn, and other crops can be fermented into ethanol that can be used in automobiles. While there is concern that using food crops like corn and sugar cane to produce energy may increase food shortages in the world, the use of a nonfood alternative like switch grass may reduce such concerns. Ethanol produced from corn is also controversial because of the large inputs of fossil fuel energy currently required to produce it.

Biodiesel fuel is made from sources like used frying oil, waste products from meat processing, vegetable oil, and oil squeezed from algae. Biodiesel fuel replaces traditional diesel fuel, which is produced from crude oil, in automobiles whose diesel engines have been modified.

HYDROGEN FUEL CELLS

Fuel cells use chemical reactions to produce electric current as it is needed. The most common fuel cells use hydrogen and oxygen as reactants and produce drinkable water as the only product. They are used in similar applications to batteries and the reactants in the chemical reaction can be replenished as needed. For hydrogen fuel cells, the oxygen in ambient air can be used, but hydrogen must be supplied as a gas or liquid. Obtaining and storing this hydrogen is in itself energy intensive, so a fuel cell may not be a net producer of energy unless alternate methods such as solar energy are used to electrolyze water and generate the fuel.

© 2012 Cengage Learning. All Rights Reserved. May not be copied, scanned, or duplicated, in whole or in part, except for use as permitted in a license distributed with a certain product or service or otherwise on a password-protected website for classroom use.

> ## AP Tip
>
> Many questions on the APES exam have tested student knowledge of alternate energy. Practice the APES FRQs that are available in the student section of the College Board's website. The topics covered in past questions include hydroelectric dams, wind power, active and passive energy, biofuels, methane digesters, and electric cars.

Ocean Waves and Tidal Energy

The rise and fall of ocean tides and waves involves an enormous amount of energy. The currents that flow during the constantly changing tides can be used to turn turbines and generate electricity. Currently, these technologies do not provide much energy, but they hold promise for the future, especially in coastal areas, and in regions with large differentials between the high and low tides.

Multiple-Choice Questions

1. The San Andreas tectonic feature in southern California is an example of a
   (A) convergent plate boundary
   (B) mid-plate hot spot
   (C) divergent plate boundary
   (D) sub-bituminous plate fault
   (E) transform fault

2. In which of the following environments is it most likely that coal deposits originated?
   (A) Ocean trenches
   (B) Deserts
   (C) Swamps
   (D) Mountain peaks
   (E) Rivers

3. Which of the following possesses the highest energy content?
   (A) Lignite
   (B) Anthracite coal
   (C) Biomass
   (D) Peat
   (E) Bituminous coal

4. Which of the choices below lists the steps of coal formation in order of youngest to oldest material?
   (A) Peat–lignite–bituminous–anthracite
   (B) Peat–bituminous–lignite–anthracite
   (C) Anthracite–lignite–bituminous–peat
   (D) Anthracite–bituminous–lignite–peat
   (E) Peat–anthracite–bituminous–lignite

5. Which of the following toxic heavy metals is released in significant quantities during the burning of coal?
(A) Nickel
(B) Mercury
(C) Lead
(D) Uranium
(E) Plutonium

6. Nuclear reactors produce energy through the process of
(A) incineration
(B) transmutation
(C) fusion
(D) breeding
(E) fission

7. Of the following, the most common fuel for nuclear fission is
(A) radium
(B) magnesium
(C) hydrogen
(D) sodium
(E) uranium

8. Which of the following is the most cost-efficient method of space heating?
(A) Passive solar heat
(B) Electricity
(C) A natural gas furnace
(D) An oil furnace
(E) A geothermal heat pump

9. Which of the following is the most efficient water heater?
(A) A water tank wrapped in electric coils
(B) A natural gas water heater with an insulated tank
(C) A propane water heater with an insulated tank
(D) An oil water heater with a non-insulated tank
(E) A tankless instant water heater fired by natural gas

10. Which of the following are features of passive solar design?
(A) Adobe walls for heat storage
(B) Coniferous trees to block the sun
(C) Photovoltaic cells to generate electricity
(D) Compact fluorescent light bulbs
(E) Energy efficient appliances

11. Often, large projects provide people with opportunities for recreational activities. Which of the following is most likely to result in creating such opportunities?
(A) Wind power
(B) Passive solar energy
(C) Hydroelectric power
(D) Photovoltaic cells
(E) Geothermal energy

12. What might result in a decline in the population of certain species
of migratory birds?
(A) Wind power
(B) Passive solar energy
(C) Hydroelectric power
(D) Photovoltaic cells
(E) Geothermal energy

13. Of the following, which is currently the most expensive method of
generating electricity?
(A) Wind power
(B) Passive solar energy
(C) Hydroelectric power
(D) Photovoltaic cells
(E) Geothermal energy

14. The site of one of the most ecologically destructive oil spills in
history is
(A) Chernobyl, Ukraine
(B) Valdez, Alaska
(C) Yucca Mountain, Nevada
(D) Kuwait City, Kuwait
(E) Shanghai, China

15. Of the following, the best example of obtaining energy from
biomass is
(A) burning coal in a boiler
(B) generating electricity with hydroelectric power
(C) an elephant running on a treadmill
(D) driving a gas-electric hybrid car
(E) burning wood in a stove

FREE-RESPONSE QUESTIONS

Bill and Angela are in an APES class together at Fremont High School
and both of their families are getting a new car. Bill's family is
purchasing a $21,000 car that will get an average of 30 miles per
gallon, taking into account their typical combination of city and
highway driving, while Angela's family is purchasing a $24,000 hybrid
car that gets 50 miles per gallon based on their driving habits. The car
Bill's family purchased has an annual estimated maintenance cost of
$900, while, because of the projected need to replace the batteries
approximately every 10 years, the estimated annual maintenance cost
of the hybrid Angela's family purchased is $1500.

a) If both cars are driven an average of 15,000 miles per year,
estimate the annual costs of operating both cars when gas prices
are
i) $3 per gallon
ii) $5 per gallon

b) When gas prices are $5 per gallon, calculate the time in years that
it will take for the total costs of both cars to be equal.

c) Describe ONE environmental benefit and ONE environmental cost of hybrid vehicles.

d) It has been estimated that the true cost of gasoline, once all of the hidden costs are added to the price at the pump, could be as high as $16 per gallon. Describe TWO of the hidden costs that contribute to the true cost of gasoline.

ANSWERS

MULTIPLE-CHOICE QUESTIONS

1. ANSWER: E. The San Andreas Fault is a transform fault that marks the boundary between the North American and Pacific plates (*Living in the Environment*, 16th ed., page 348 / 17th ed., page 349).

2. ANSWER: C. Coal is formed from partially decayed plant matter in moist anaerobic conditions, the conditions that would be found in bogs, marshes, and swamps (*Living in the Environment*, 16th ed., page 382 / 17th ed., pages 381–382).

3. ANSWER: B. Anthracite coal has the highest density of the energy sources listed (*Living in the Environment*, 16th ed., page 383 / 17th ed., page 382).

4. ANSWER: A. Peat–lignite–bituminous–anthracite is the correct order from youngest (peat) to oldest (anthracite) (*Living in the Environment*, 16th ed., page 383 / 17th ed., page 382).

5. ANSWER: B. Mercury is released in significant quantities during the burning of coal (*Living in the Environment*, 16th ed., page 384 / 17th ed., page 383).

6. ANSWER: E. Nuclear fission reactions are used as the energy source in nuclear power plants (*Living in the Environment*, 16th ed., pages 386–387 / 17th ed., page 386).

7. ANSWER: E. Uranium is the fuel used for nuclear fission in nuclear power plants (*Living in the Environment*, 16th ed., page 386 / 17th ed., page 386).

8. ANSWER: A. Passive solar energy is free after the initial costs, which will not significantly differ from the initial costs of the other options, all of which also have ongoing costs (*Living in the Environment*, 16th ed., page 408 / 17th ed., page 409).

9. ANSWER: E. Tankless water heaters provide hot water on demand, heating only what is needed and eliminating the need to store hot water (*Living in the Environment*, 16th ed., page 408 / 17th ed., page 409).

10. ANSWER: A. One passive solar energy technique is to store heat from the sun in large heat storage containers to be released slowly during the night to keep the area around it warm. Unlike

deciduous trees, coniferous trees do not lose their leaves in the winter and thus do not allow the sun to pass through their branches (*Living in the Environment*, 16th ed., page 411 / 17th ed., pages 410–411).

11. ANSWER: **C.** Large-scale hydroelectric power generation requires large water storage reservoirs, which can provide recreational activities such as swimming, boating, and fishing (*Living in the Environment*, 16th ed., page 418 / 17th ed., page 415).

12. ANSWER: **A.** The use of wind turbines to generate electricity may result in the inadvertent killing of some species of birds if the turbines are placed along their traditional migratory paths (*Living in the Environment*, 16th ed., page 421 / 17th ed., page 418).

13. ANSWER: **D.** Photovoltaic cells are still the most expensive method of generating electricity of those listed (*Living in the Environment*, 16th ed., page 416 / 17th ed., pages 412–413).

14. ANSWER: **B.** The 1987 oil spill from the Exxon Valdez oil tanker into Prince Edward Sound off the coast of Valdez, Alaska, killed a massive amount of marine life (*Living in the Environment*, 16th ed., pages 549–551 / 17th ed., page 548).

15. ANSWER: **E.** Burning wood in a stove is an example of using biomass (wood) for energy (heat) (*Living in the Environment*, 15th ed., page 422 / 16th ed., pages 419–420).

FREE-RESPONSE SCORING GUIDELINES

a) If both cars are driven an average of 15,000 miles per year estimate the annual costs of operating both cars when gas prices are

i) $3 per gallon

ii) $5 per gallon

4 points can be earned—1 point for each correct setup and correct calculation of the annual costs for each car when gas is $3 per gallon and $5 per gallon

i) Bill's car: $15,000 \text{ mi} \times \dfrac{1 \text{ gal}}{30 \text{ mi}} \times \dfrac{\$3}{1 \text{ gal}} = \$1500 + \$900 = \$2100$

Angela's car: $15,000 \text{ mi} \times \dfrac{1 \text{ gal}}{50 \text{ mi}} \times \dfrac{\$3}{1 \text{ gal}} = \$900 + \$1500 = \$2100$

ii) Bill's car: $15,000 \text{ mi} \times \dfrac{1 \text{ gal}}{30 \text{ mi}} \times \dfrac{\$3}{1 \text{ gal}} = \$2500 + \$900 = \$3400$

Angela's car: $15,000 \text{ mi} \times \dfrac{1 \text{ gal}}{50 \text{ mi}} \times \dfrac{\$5}{1 \text{ gal}} = \$1500 + \$1500 = \$3000$

b) When gas prices are $5 per gallon, calculate the time in years that it will take for the total costs of both cars to be equal.

2 points can be earned—1 point for a correct setup and 1 point for the correct answer: 10 years

The additional cost of operating Bill's car = $3400—$3000 = $400 per year

Angela's car was $24000—$20000 = $4000 more expensive

At $400 per year the total costs will be equal in $\frac{\$4000}{\$400} = 10$ years.

c) Describe ONE environmental benefit and describe ONE environmental cost of hybrid vehicles.

2 points can be earned—1 point for a correct environmental benefit and 1 point for a correct environmental cost

Environmental Benefits

- Hybrid vehicles emit less carbon dioxide, with a lower contribution to global warming.
- Hybrid vehicles emit less NO_x, thus reducing acid rain.
- Hybrid vehicles emit less carbon monoxide, reducing respiratory problems.
- Hybrid vehicles use less gasoline, reducing the need to drill for oil, and reducing habitat destruction, land subsidence, and oil spills.

Environmental Costs

- Environmental damage results from mining the additional minerals needed to manufacture the added batteries.
- Environmental damage results from mining the additional minerals needed to manufacture the electric motor.
- Waste is produced during the production and disposal of the added batteries.

d) It has been estimated that the true cost of gasoline, once all of the hidden costs are added to the price at the pump, could be as high as $16 per gallon. Describe TWO of the hidden costs that contribute to the true cost of gasoline.

2 points can be earned—1 point for each description of a hidden cost

- the cost of government subsidies and tax breaks to oil companies, car manufacturers and road builders
- the costs of air pollution control and cleanup
- the costs of water pollution control and cleanup resulting from oil spills and leaking underground storage tanks
- increased healthcare or insurance costs associated with respiratory problems from breathing polluted air
- increased healthcare or insurance costs associated with the contamination of water supplies with oil from spills
- increased healthcare or insurance costs associated with the contamination of groundwater by gasoline

Answers

and gasoline additives that leaked from underground storage tanks.

◾ the cost of military protection of oil supplies and access to oil supplies

◾ the costs associated with climate change (water shortages, food shortages, rising sea levels, increased storm damage, etc.)

AIR POLLUTION

KEY CONCEPTS

- Air pollution creates some of the most critical environmental problems.
- Photochemical smog is a health hazard anywhere there are cars and sunlight.
- Acid deposition causes damage to ecosystems all over the world.
- Indoor air pollution is often a more significant health hazard than outdoor air pollution.
- Human activities are causing global climate change, which is having profound effects on the earth's systems.
- The earth's protective ozone layer has been damaged and will take a long time to heal.

Air pollution is discussed in depth in *Living in the Environment*, 16th ed., Chapters 18 and 19 / 17th ed., Chapters 18 and 19.

KEY VOCABULARY

acid deposition

aldehydes

buffer

catalytic converter

chlorofluorocarbon (CFC)

Clean Air Act

Dobson units

electrostatic precipitator

global climate change

greenhouse gases

halons

heat island effect

hydrochlorofluorocarbon (HCFC)

hydrofluorocarbon (HFC)

indoor air pollution

Kyoto Protocol

mesosphere

methyl bromide

Montreal Protocol

oxides of nitrogen (NO_x)

oxides of sulfur (SO_x)

ozone

ozone depletion

ozone hole

ozone layer

particulate matter

peroxyacyl nitrates (PANs)

photochemical smog

polar stratospheric clouds

primary pollutant

radon

Rowland & Molina

scrubber

secondary pollutant

sick-building syndrome

stratosphere

temperature inversion

thermosphere

troposphere

volatile organic compound (VOC)

THE ATMOSPHERE

The atmosphere is a thin layer of gases that are held close to the earth by the force of gravity. The rotation of the earth around its axis causes the atmosphere to be thinner at the poles and thicker at the equator. The two largest components of the atmosphere are nitrogen (N_2) at 78% and oxygen (O_2) at 21%. The remaining one percent of the atmosphere is argon and several other trace gases. Carbon dioxide and water vapor are also present in small percentages that depend on local conditions.

Structurally, the atmosphere is divided into layers that are determined by changes in the temperature gradient of the atmosphere as it changes with altitude. The **troposphere** is the first layer of the atmosphere and is adjacent to the surface of the earth. The temperature in the troposphere decreases with increasing altitude and it extends to an altitude of about ten miles. All life on earth exists in the troposphere, and the troposphere is responsible for the greenhouse effect and for most weather phenomena. The second layer of the atmosphere is called the **stratosphere** and it extends from the top of the troposphere to about 30 miles above the surface of the

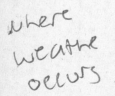
where weather occurs

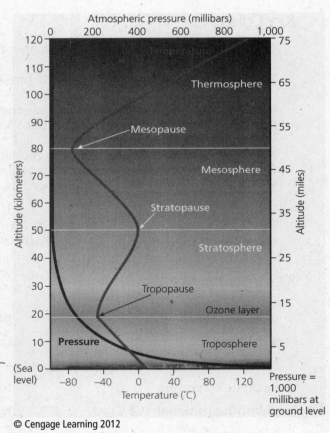

© Cengage Learning 2012

earth. The protective **ozone layer** is in the lower portion of the stratosphere. The temperature in the stratosphere increases with increasing altitude due to a series of reactions that occur between oxygen, **ozone** (O_3), and UV radiation in the stratospheric ozone layer. The third layer of the atmosphere is called the **mesosphere**, where the temperature again decreases with altitude. Finally, the **thermosphere** extends to outer space, about 300 miles above the surface of the earth. Because humans and the rest of life on earth depend on, interact with, and impact primarily the first two layers of the atmosphere, they receive the most attention in the study of environmental science.

all the layers = need to know

AIR POLLUTION

Global climate change, ozone depletion, acid rain, photochemical smog, and indoor air pollution are some of the most significant environmental problems faced by humanity. The fact that all of these problems relate to the atmosphere illustrates how important air pollution is to the study of environmental science. Air pollutants are categorized in many ways; one way is based on their source.

Primary air pollutants—air pollutants that are released directly from their source into the atmosphere

Secondary air pollutants—air pollutants that form as the products of chemical reactions that occur among primary pollutants and other chemicals present in the atmosphere

---

AP Tip

Pollution is a much-abused word in environmental science and also on the APES exam. Simply stating that an activity "causes pollution" is unlikely to earn points on the exam. Rather, graders are looking for a deeper understanding of issues. At least state whether the activity causes *air* pollution" or "*water* pollution." But, more than likely, graders will only accept specific information, for example, a statement that an activity "releases *sulfur dioxide* into the atmosphere." So, be specific!

MAJOR AIR POLLUTANTS

The U.S. Congress passed the **Clean Air Act** in 1970 and amended and renewed it in 1977 and 1990. The Clean Air Act establishes national standards for the allowable outdoor concentration of six criteria air pollutants to protect human health. It also establishes industrial emission standards for 189 hazardous air pollutants (mostly known and suspected carcinogens) that pose a serious hazard to human health or the environment. The U.S. Environmental Protection Agency (EPA) is charged with the enforcement of the Clean Air Act. The six criteria air pollutants are identified and described below, along with their sources, effects, and a few reduction strategies.

Carbon monoxide (CO)—A primary pollutant that is the product of incomplete combustion reactions during the burning of fossil fuels. Over half of the carbon monoxide released in the United States is emitted by motor vehicles. Its health effects include preventing hemoglobin in red blood cells from binding with oxygen, which can cause headaches and even death if ingested in high concentrations. **Catalytic converters** remove carbon monoxide from motor vehicle exhaust. Carbon monoxide can also be reduced by improving motor vehicle technology to produce cleaner-burning engines and through conservation.

Nitrogen dioxide (NO_2)—A primary pollutant that is formed as a product of the reaction between nitrogen and oxygen in the high-temperature environment of fossil fuel combustion. Nitric oxide (NO) forms first, and is oxidized to NO_2. Together these two compounds are also known as **oxides of nitrogen**, nitrogen oxides, or NO_x. Nitrogen dioxide is a reddish-brown gas; it plays a central role in the formation of photochemical smog (and tropospheric ozone), and it is a precursor to the atmospheric formation of the nitric acid (HNO_3) that falls to the earth as acid rain. A few of the health and environmental effects of nitrogen dioxide are irritation of the respiratory system, aggravation of asthma and bronchitis, impaired plant growth, and decreased visibility. Catalytic converters remove nitrogen dioxide from motor vehicle exhaust. Nitrogen dioxide can also be reduced by improving motor vehicle technology to produce cleaner burning engines and through conservation.

Both are Pollutants

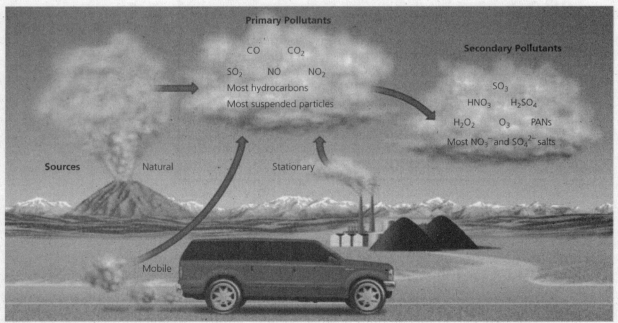

© Cengage Learning 2012

Sulfur dioxide (SO₂)—A primary pollutant that is formed as a product of the reaction between sulfur and oxygen during the combustion of coal. Sulfur dioxide is further oxidized in the atmosphere to sulfur trioxide (SO_3). Together, these two compounds are also known as **oxides of sulfur**, sulfur oxides, or SO_x. Sulfur trioxide reacts with water to form the sulfuric acid (H_2SO_4) that falls back to the earth as acid rain. The health and environmental effects of sulfur dioxide include aggravation of breathing problems, plant damage, and reduced visibility. Sulfur dioxide can be removed from coal smoke with **scrubbers** that use fine mists of a calcium carbonate ($CaCO_3$) or calcium oxide (CaO) solution to wash the pollutants out of the smoke. The resulting sludge must then be removed to a landfill. Sulfur dioxide emissions can also be reduced by burning low-sulfur coal, removing the sulfur before burning coal, by converting to natural gas, or by replacing coal with alternate energy sources.

Tropospheric or Ground-Level Ozone (O_3)—A secondary pollutant that is the major component of photochemical smog. Its formation is described in the following section on photochemical smog. Ozone is an unstable molecule and a strong oxidant. It readily reacts to shed a single oxygen atom, which transforms it to a more stable oxygen (O_2) molecule. Its health and environmental effects include irritation of the respiratory system and eyes, plant damage, and disintegration of plastic and rubber products.

Particulate matter (PM-10)—A category of primary pollutants that includes a variety of particulates, both solid and liquid, that are emitted from coal-fired power plants, agricultural operations such as the plowing of fields and harvesting of crops, tobacco smoke, construction, and motor vehicles. Particulate matter with an average diameter of 10 millimeters or less is classified as PM-10. Particulate matter can irritate the respiratory system, aggravate asthma and bronchitis, and depending on the composition of the particulates, can cause mutations or cancer. For example, lead, which is a carcinogen, is a common component of particulates in older homes and in motor vehicle exhaust in developing countries that still use lead additives in gasoline. Mercury and cadmium are other examples of toxic heavy metals that can be found in particulate matter. Particulate matter also reduces visibility, and corrodes metals. Particulates can be removed from smoke by filtering them out or by using a device called an **electrostatic precipitator** that removes the particles by imparting a negative charge on them and attracting them to positively-charged plates where they are scraped off and removed to a landfill.

Lead—A primary pollutant, some of which is released as a result of the use of leaded gasoline and the peeling of lead-based paint in older homes. Leaded gasoline uses the additive tetraethyl lead to improve the performance of internal combustion engines, and although it was banned in the United States in 1976, it will persist in the environment for decades. The lead additive is still in use in some developing countries. Lead paint has also been banned in the United States since the 1970s, but it is still present in homes built before the ban, and is still imported on some painted materials. Recently, for example, painted toys from China were found to contain lead-based paints. Health effects of lead are most severe in children and include brain damage, partial paralysis, blindness, and mental retardation. Careful removal and disposal of lead-based paints, and a global ban of lead additives in gasoline and lead paint will reduce the amount airborne lead in the environment.

It is important to be aware of the following air pollutants as well as those listed above.

Nitric oxide or Nitrogen monoxide (NO)—A primary pollutant involved in the formation of photochemical smog and a precursor to acid rain is nitrogen oxide or NO$_x$. Nitric oxide is formed as a product of the reaction between nitrogen and oxygen in the high-temperature environment of fossil fuel combustion. It reacts quickly in air to form nitrogen dioxide, which is one of the EPA's criteria air pollutants described above. Catalytic converters remove nitric oxide from motor vehicle exhaust. It can also be reduced by improving motor vehicle technology to produce cleaner burning engines and through conservation.

Volatile Organic Compounds (VOCs)—A category of primary pollutants that includes many different hydrocarbons, both man-made and naturally occurring. Many VOCs are involved in the formation of photochemical smog. Anthropogenic sources of VOCs include leaks from fossil fuel production, gas pumps, dry cleaning, and industrial solvents. VOCs are also formed and released naturally by some tree species. Many VOCs are among the 189 hazardous air pollutants that are monitored according to the Clean Air Act. They include many mutagens and carcinogens. A few ways to reduce anthropogenic VOC levels are by sealing leaks, switching to alternative dry-cleaning methods, capturing solvents for reuse, and preventing the vaporization of gasoline during fueling.

PHOTOCHEMICAL SMOG—CAUSES AND EFFECTS

The unpleasant brown-air pollution that sits over most large cities on warm, sunny days is a familiar sight to most people. Also known as photochemical smog, the characteristic brown haze is so abundant that it is even known to drift over the Arctic Circle. The formation of photochemical smog requires cars and sunlight. Morning traffic releases nitrogen oxides and VOCs into the air. The ultraviolet radiation in sunlight promotes a series of reactions that result in the formation of as many as 100 different compounds including ozone— the most abundant. Also present are other photochemical oxidants like nitrogen dioxide, **peroxyacyl nitrates (PANs)**, and **aldehydes**, all of which irritate the respiratory system and eyes, and damage living tissues. Warmer air temperatures increase the rate of the reactions that form smog; as a result, cities with warm, arid climates and lots of cars have the most dangerous photochemical smog.

The concentration of ozone, PANs, aldehydes, and other secondary pollutants peak when the sun is at its highest, around noon. Their levels drop off during the afternoon and evening, fall back to near zero overnight, and then start all over again the next morning. Nitrogen oxide concentrations, on the other hand, are highest in the late morning and then drop as the sun gets higher in the sky and secondary pollutants are formed.

Photochemical smog can become even worse over cities due to the presence of the city itself. Because of the heat-absorbing properties of the materials used to construct them, the presence of tall buildings that block cooling winds, and the operation of heat-generating cars, power plants, and other machinery, the temperature of a city is typically several degrees warmer than the surrounding natural areas. Because of this **heat island effect**, the heat-loving reactions that form photochemical smog are made worse than they might have otherwise been. Another troublesome factor for some cities is the geography of the surrounding area. Cities that are built in valleys and areas that are surrounded by mountains are subject to **temperature inversions** that can trap pollutants over a city for several days or weeks. A temperature inversion occurs when a layer of warm air sits atop cooler polluted air over a city and prevents the cool air from rising and dispersing its pollutants.

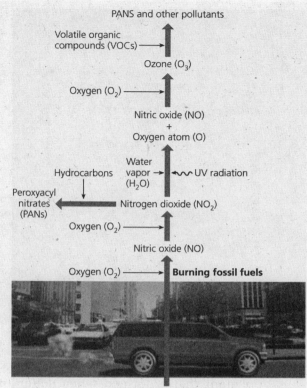

© Cengage Learning 2012

this is important

Acid Deposition—Causes, Effects, and Remediation Strategies

The oxides of sulfur and nitrogen can be further oxidized in the atmosphere, and react with water to form acids, which then fall back to the earth as acid rain, snow, fog, hail, sleet, and the dry deposition of acidic particulates. Acid deposition is not usually a serious problem near the source of the primary pollutants that react to form it; instead, the acidic fallout can occur as much as hundreds or thousands of miles downwind from the pollution sources. Oxides of sulfur and nitrogen are the primary pollutants that react in the atmosphere to form acidic molecules.

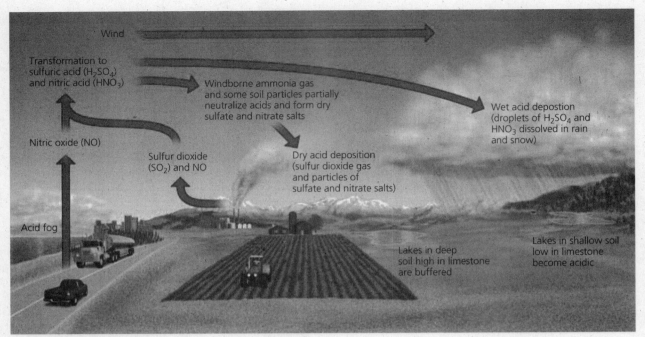

Wind

Transformation to sulfuric acid (H_2SO_4) and nitric acid (HNO_3)

Nitric oxide (NO)

Windborne ammonia gas and some soil particles partially neutralize acids and form dry sulfate and nitrate salts

Wet acid depostion (droplets of H_2SO_4 and HNO_3 dissolved in rain and snow)

Sulfur dioxide (SO_2) and NO

Dry acid deposition (sulfur dioxide gas and particles of sulfate and nitrate salts)

Acid fog

Lakes in deep soil high in limestone are buffered

Lakes in shallow soil low in limestone become acidic

© Cengage Learning 2012

Pollutants

Sulfuric acid and sulfate salts (H_2SO_4 or SO_4^{22})—A secondary pollutant that is formed when sulfur oxides react with water in the atmosphere. The health and environmental effects are listed on the next page. The reduction strategies are the same as those for reducing emissions of sulfur dioxide.

Nitric acid and nitrate salts (HNO_3 or NO_3^2)—A secondary pollutant that is formed when nitrogen oxides react with water in the atmosphere. The health and environmental effects are listed on the next page. The reduction strategies are the same as those for reducing emissions of NO_x.

Acid deposition causes many environmental problems. The acids leach calcium and magnesium from soils, reducing the availability of those important nutrients while releasing toxic ions of aluminum, lead, cadmium, and mercury, thus resulting in reduced plant growth. The loss of nutrients and presence of toxins in the soil, along with the direct damage to their leaves by the acids, increases the vulnerability of trees to damage and death from disease, pests, drought, and extreme weather conditions. Acidified waterways are subject to fish kills resulting from acids releasing aluminum ions, which are toxic to fish in high concentrations. Thousands of lakes in Canada and Scandinavia have few or no fish as a result of acid deposition. Acid deposition also irritates and damages the human respiratory system and accelerates the erosion and degradation of building materials and finishes by dissolving them.

Some soils contain lime (calcium oxide or CaO) or limestone (calcium carbonate or $CaCO_3$) in sufficient quantities to serve as a natural **buffer** that neutralizes the acids and minimizes ecosystem damage. Although it is expensive and difficult to determine exactly how much is needed, lime and limestone can also be added to soils to reduce the effects of acid deposition. Reducing acid deposition at the source can be accomplished by reducing or eliminating sulfur in coal before it is burned, or by not burning coal. Catalytic converters, efficiency improvements, and conservation can also reduce the emission of NO_x and SO_x.

Because acid deposition does not usually fall in the same area from which the pollutants are released, cleanup can be a political challenge. Often the affected area is in a different state or country than the source of the pollution that caused it. As a result, cities, states, and countries are reluctant to pass legislation to prevent something that they may not perceive to be their problem, but that will likely cost them money and jobs.

INDOOR AIR POLLUTION

Many people in developed countries spend most of their time in enclosed space either inside buildings or automobiles. Due to poor ventilation, indoor air pollutants can accumulate and increase in concentration until they are far more concentrated than they are in outdoor air. Take cigarette smoke for example; outdoors, cigarette smoke dissipates quickly and does not build up to great concentrations, indoors, however, the smoke accumulates and can become overwhelming, especially in poorly ventilated rooms with many smokers. Most indoor air pollutants have no odor, which makes them impossible to notice in high concentrations like cigarette smoke, but they still increase in concentration, especially in poorly ventilated spaces. Descriptions of a few of the major indoor air pollutants are listed below.

Cigarette Smoke—One of the most hazardous indoor air pollutants, exposure to second-hand smoke is one of the most substantial risks to human health. The risk is multiplied when the smoke is trapped and concentrated in enclosed places like inside buildings or automobiles. Cigarette smoke causes cancer, heart disease, birth defects, and emphysema. To reduce cigarette smoke, smokers can quit smoking, smoking can be banned in buildings, and ventilation can be improved in buildings.

Formaldehyde—A chemical that is present in materials found throughout most indoor environments including plywood, particleboard, carpet, wallpaper, furniture, and drapes. Formaldehyde is one of the most hazardous indoor air pollutants. Health effects include headaches, respiratory tract irritation, eye irritation, sore throats, skin rashes, dizziness, nausea, and cancer. To reduce its concentration, formaldehyde-free materials can be substituted for conventional materials that contain formaldehyde, and ventilation can be increased in the buildings.

Radon—A naturally occurring radioactive gas that seeps into buildings from underground deposits. When present, it will accumulate to dangerous levels without adequate ventilation. When inhaled, the alpha particles emitted by radon damage lung tissues and other tissues in the respiratory tract. This increases the risk of lung cancer. Radon and cigarette smoke have been found to interact synergistically greatly increasing the risk of lung cancer. Radon can be detected and, if present, cracks in the foundation and walls of the

We have these in our homes

building can be sealed. Ventilation can also be increased to remove radon before it accumulates to dangerous levels.

Bacteria, Viruses, Pollen, Dust Mites, Mildew, Mold, and Yeast—A collection of living organisms that can become airborne and circulate through a building in the heating, ventilation, and air conditioning systems. Health effects include infectious diseases, allergic reactions, headaches, respiratory tract irritation, and aggravated asthma. The presence of these living organisms in a building can result in **sick-building syndrome**, a condition that causes an abnormally high incidence of headaches, coughing, sneezing, burning eyes, and illness among the employees or residents of the building. The heating, ventilation and air conditioning systems must be disinfected or replaced. In extreme cases the building may be condemned.

Carbon monoxide—An asphyxiant at high concentrations, carbon monoxide can accumulate in an enclosed space and suffocate the occupants. At lower concentrations, carbon monoxide causes headaches and drowsiness. Carbon monoxide monitors are available to warn the occupants of a building if carbon monoxide concentrations are building up to lethal levels. Furnace burners and stoves should be kept clean to ensure efficient combustion takes place. Fires should not be lit indoors without adequate ventilation. Barbeque grills should not be used indoors to cook or to provide heat.

Asbestos—A mineral that was once widely used to insulate buildings, and to manufacture acoustical ceilings and floor tiles. Asbestos fibers cause skin irritation and lung cancer. Asbestos can be removed from buildings by professionals. It is a serious problem for workers and nearby residents during the demolition of older buildings.

GLOBAL CLIMATE CHANGE

As explained in Chapter 2, the earth absorbs energy from the sun, and when that energy is released by the earth, gases in the troposphere including water vapor in clouds, carbon dioxide and other gases trap some of the heat, and it is this greenhouse effect that warms the atmosphere and the earth's surface. Without the natural greenhouse effect, the average temperature on earth would be about $-18°C$ ($0°F$), below the freezing point of water and not hospitable to life. Human activities that release **greenhouse gases** increase the amount of heat that is trapped in the atmosphere, which results in an enhancement of the natural greenhouse effect. The four major anthropogenic greenhouse gases—carbon dioxide, nitrous oxide, methane, and chlorofluorocarbons—are described below.

Carbon dioxide (CO_2)—a natural product of the combustion of hydrocarbons. Carbon dioxide is the greenhouse gas that contributes more to the human enhancement of the greenhouse effect than any other. It can be reduced through conservation, by switching to alternate energy sources, by planting trees, or by burying (sequestering) carbon dioxide in cavities deep within the earth's crust. Carbon dioxide is removed from the atmosphere by photosynthesis, which is reduced by the cutting of forests; as a result, the reduction of deforestation will also reduce carbon dioxide in the atmosphere.

Nitrous oxide (N_2O)—A primary pollutant that is released as a result of intensive use of inorganic fertilizers, the burning of fossil fuels, animal waste management, and sewage treatment. The decomposition of fertilizers, and human and animal wastes release nitrous oxide. Nitrous oxide has a long residence time in the atmosphere. Nitrous oxide emissions can be reduced by decreasing the use of inorganic fertilizers and reducing fossil fuel use.

Methane (CH_4)—A primary pollutant and VOC. Methane is released into the atmosphere from cattle, losses during fossil fuel mining production, landfills, wastewater treatment, and rice cultivation. Methane emissions can be reduced by capturing them and using them for fuel, or by simply burning them. While both of these solutions replace methane with carbon dioxide, methane is a more potent greenhouse gas than carbon dioxide.

Chlorofluorocarbons (CFCs)—A category of manmade primary pollutants that includes the variety of inert, stable molecules that are made of a combination of chlorine and fluorine atoms attached to a carbon backbone. CFCs were once used as coolants in refrigerators and air conditioners, to clean electronics, as fumigants, as foam-blowing agents, and as propellants in aerosol cans. CFCs have a long residence time in the atmosphere, and they are also ozone-depleting chemicals. The **Montreal Protocol** greatly reduced the production and release of CFCs to prevent them from destroying stratospheric ozone molecules; however, there are still as many as 5 billion tons of CFCs in the troposphere, and their replacements, hydrochlorofluorocarbons and hydrofluorocarbons, are also greenhouse gases.

[handwritten margin note: These affect ozone]

AP Tip

Be careful that you don't state, in answering a free-response question, that an air pollutant is bad because it is a greenhouse gas. Remember that without greenhouse gases the temperature on earth would be below the freezing point of water. Life needs the greenhouse effect; what most living things do not need is more of it. The addition of anthropogenic greenhouse gases is bad because they enhance the natural greenhouse effect, causing global warming and climate change.

IMPACTS AND CONSEQUENCES OF GLOBAL CLIMATE CHANGE

There are many consequences of global climate change.

Sea Level Rise—The thermal expansion of water and the melting of land-based glaciers both contribute to rising sea levels. Sea level rise will cause the destruction and degradation of coastal wetlands and estuaries, damage to coral reefs and fisheries, the flooding of low-lying coastal areas, submergence of small islands, and the contamination of freshwater supplies with saltwater. Furthermore, as snow or ice melts, it exposes more soil or water, both of which absorb more energy than snow or ice, which causes temperatures to rise, exposing more soil or water, and so on. This positive feedback loop will accelerate the rate of loss of glacial ice.

Melting of Permafrost—The frozen ground under arctic tundra that was once thought to be permanently frozen has massive quantities of methane and carbon dioxide trapped in it. If it melts, that methane and carbon dioxide will be released, which will increase warming causing additional permafrost to melt, and so on. This is an example of another positive feedback loop that has great potential to accelerate global warming. Permafrost is already beginning to thaw; in fact, the Trans-Alaska pipeline, which is built on permafrost, has sustained damage due to thawing.

Extreme Weather—Severe drought and heat waves will result in less moisture in soils, more devastating forest fires, expansion of deserts, and reduced plant growth. Since plants absorb carbon dioxide, fewer plants will result in less carbon dioxide removed from the atmosphere, resulting in fewer plants, and so on; another positive feedback loop.

Changes in Ocean Currents—Ocean currents are not well understood, but it is reasonable to predict that the addition of massive amounts of freshwater from melting glaciers in the Arctic Circle could disrupt the conveyor belt of currents in the North Atlantic, with potentially devastating effects in Europe, where the climate is regulated by the warm ocean water carried north by the Gulf Stream.

Changing Vegetative Zones—An increase in average temperature will shift vegetative zones northward. Species that occupy habitat islands will face extinction if the temperature rises beyond their tolerance limit. This will also affect crops. As temperatures increase, farmers will face the challenge of either growing new crops that are adapted to a warmer climate, moving their entire operation northward, or giving up farming.

Biodiversity Loss—In addition to the loss of plant species due to the changing vegetative zones, as described above, the animals that relied on those plants for food and shelter will also need to migrate or face extinction. In the case of Arctic species, they will face extinction at a greater rate due to the fact that they will have nowhere to which they can migrate.

ATMOSPHERE–OCEAN INTERACTIONS

Carbon dioxide is soluble in water, and the oceans dissolve it in huge quantities—about half of all the carbon dioxide released since the beginning of the industrial revolution is dissolved in the world's oceans. Carbon dioxide forms carbonic acid when it dissolves in water, so as more is dissolved in the oceans, the acidity of the oceans increases. Increased acidity inhibits the ability of coral and shellfish to make shells, which has a devastating effect on their populations.

The solubility of most gases, including carbon dioxide, decreases with a rise in temperature. As a result, warmer oceans will also absorb less carbon dioxide. Some carbon dioxide could bubble out of the oceans as they warm, adding it back to the atmosphere, increasing warming and causing more carbon dioxide to bubble out of the oceans, and so on; another example of a positive feedback loop.

REDUCING CLIMATE CHANGE

Climate change is a global problem, and reaching consensus on how to address it has proven to be a challenge. In 1988, the Intergovernmental Panel on Climate Change (IPCC) was formed to confront the challenge of understanding the causes and impact of climate change, as well as assessing possible solutions. Much of the current understanding of the effects of climate change is a result of the work of the IPCC.

International efforts to reduce climate change have usually ended in disagreement. The **Kyoto Protocol** is an example of such an effort. Negotiated in 1997 and enacted in 2005, it requires industrialized countries to reduce their greenhouse gas emissions to 5% below their 1990 levels between 2008 and 2012. The United States and Australia did not agree to the treaty because of its potential economic impact and because it does not require developing countries like China and India to reduce greenhouse gas emissions. In 2009, delegates met in Copenhagen, Denmark, but after two weeks of negotiations, disagreement over the responsibilities of developed and developing nations to curb global warming once again stifled efforts at reaching an agreement that would make substantial changes in future greenhouse gases emissions.

There are actions that individuals can take to reduce climate change. All of the energy conservation strategies listed in Chapter 7 also reduce greenhouse gas emissions.

STRATOSPHERIC OZONE

The stratospheric ozone layer prevents the most damaging ultraviolet radiation (UV-B) from reaching the surface of the earth. The ozone layer is formed by the chemical reactions that also protect life on earth from UV radiation. Oxygen molecules (O_2) are broken down into two free oxygen atoms when they absorb UV radiation. The free oxygen atoms then react with oxygen molecules to form ozone (O_3). The ozone then absorbs more UV radiation and breaks down to reform an oxygen atom and an oxygen molecule. This back and forth exchange between oxygen and ozone molecules in the stratosphere is what shields the earth from UV radiation. The destruction of stratospheric ozone by man-made chemicals eliminates this protective shield.

understand this

Ozone layer

> ## AP Tip
>
> Stratospheric ozone depletion and global climate change are two different processes that are often confused with one another. The confusion is rooted in the fact that the newspapers and magazines we read, the television shows we watch, and some of the people we encounter in our everyday lives confuse the two processes. The chances are that your APES teacher spent much time teaching you to differentiate between these two global environmental concerns, and he or she was correct in doing so, because it will likely be worth a few points on your APES exam to understand the similarities and differences between stratospheric ozone depletion and global climate change.

STRATOSPHERIC OZONE DEPLETION

In 1974, **F. Sherwood Rowland** and **Mario Molina** proposed the hypothesis that increased chlorofluorocarbon concentrations in the stratosphere are responsible for depleting the stratospheric ozone layer. The work of Rowland and Molina was met with shock and skepticism over the concern that human activities could damage something as distant and mysterious as the earth's ozone layer.

Chlorofluorocarbons came into wide use after their discovery in the early 20th century because of the desirable property that they seemed to be completely inert. They are unreactive, insoluble in water, nonflammable, noncorrosive, odorless, and nontoxic, while possessing desirable properties as refrigerants, solvents, fumigants, and propellants. They seemed to be dream chemicals with no adverse human health or environmental effects, and they were used as coolants in refrigerators and air conditioners, to clean electronics, as fumigants, as foam-blowing agents, and as propellants in aerosol cans.

Ironically, the problem with CFCs arises from one of the same characteristics that made them desirable, namely their low reactivity. For decades, the unreactive CFCs drift around the troposphere trapping heat like other greenhouse gases until, eventually, they reach the stratosphere. Once in the stratosphere, they absorb enough energy from UV radiation to break off a chlorine atom. The freed chlorine atom, which is highly reactive, is released directly in the stratosphere where ozone is most prevalent and breaks down an ozone molecule by reacting with it to form an oxygen molecule and chlorine monoxide (ClO) molecule. Chlorine monoxide then reacts with a free oxygen molecule to form another molecule of oxygen and return the single chlorine atom to start the process over again with another ozone molecule. Because the chlorine atom acts as a catalyst (it is unchanged at the end of the reaction), one chlorine atom may react with and destroy numerous ozone molecules—estimates are as high as one hundred thousand ozone molecules per chlorine atom.

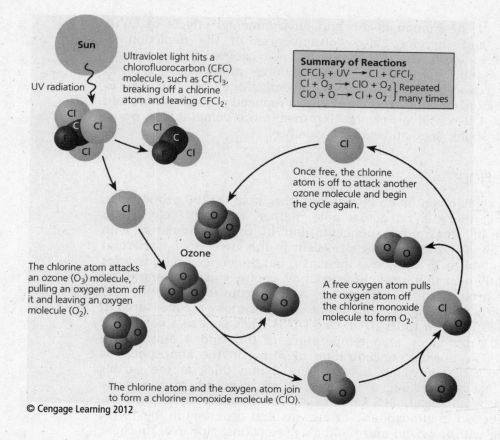

Sun

UV radiation

Ultraviolet light hits a chlorofluorocarbon (CFC) molecule, such as CFCl₃, breaking off a chlorine atom and leaving CFCl₂.

Cl
C
Cl
Cl

Cl
C
Cl

Summary of Reactions
$CFCl_3 + UV \longrightarrow Cl + CFCl_2$
$Cl + O_3 \longrightarrow ClO + O_2$ ⎤ Repeated
$ClO + O \longrightarrow Cl + O_2$ ⎦ many times

Cl

Once free, the chlorine atom is off to attack another ozone molecule and begin the cycle again.

Cl

O
O

Ozone

The chlorine atom attacks an ozone (O_3) molecule, pulling an oxygen atom off it and leaving an oxygen molecule (O_2).

O
O
O

O
O
O

O
O

O
O

A free oxygen atom pulls the oxygen atom off the chlorine monoxide molecule to form O_2.

Cl

Cl

Cl
O

O

The chlorine atom and the oxygen atom join to form a chlorine monoxide molecule (ClO).

© Cengage Learning 2012

There are many other ozone-depleting chemicals, including nitrogen oxides that are released from jet planes, **halons**, which are chemicals that are used in fire extinguishers, and **methyl bromide**, which is a fumigant used to disinfect soils. In the latter cases, the element bromine replaces chlorine in the role of the catalyst in the ozone depleting reactions. The Montreal Protocol also called for reduced production and use of these chemicals.

Ultraviolet Radiation

Ultraviolet radiation is categorized as UV-A, UV-B, and UV-C. Ultraviolet A has the least energy, has low potential to harm life, and is not absorbed by the ozone layer. Ultraviolet C has the most energy and the most potential to harm life. Ultraviolet C is the only type of UV radiation with sufficient energy to break down oxygen molecules, and as a result, even with no ozone layer, it would still be absorbed by oxygen in the atmosphere and little or no UV-C would reach the surface of the earth. Ultraviolet B has more energy than UV-A and less energy than UV-C. Ultraviolet B can do considerable harm to life, and it is strongly absorbed by the ozone layer. Ultraviolet B is absorbed only by ozone molecules, and as a result the concern over the destruction of stratospheric ozone is primarily about protecting life from UV-B radiation.

A few of the human health and environmental effects of UV-B radiation, and therefore also consequences of the depletion of stratospheric ozone, include sunburns, eye cataracts, skin cancer, immune system suppression, reduced food supply due to crop damage, reduced productivity in oceans due to damage to phytoplankton, damage to fisheries due to reduced phytoplankton, and damage to UV-sensitive trees making them more vulnerable to pests, disease, drought, fires, and extreme weather.

THE OZONE HOLE

The media has given much attention to the "hole" in the ozone layer, but in fact there is no actual hole. Rather, the term refers to a reduction in atmospheric concentration of ozone compared with normal values. Ozone is most prevalent in the lower stratosphere at altitudes of 15 to 35 km above the earth, but the concentration varies significantly over this range. Accordingly, ozone is usually monitored from the ground and is reported in terms of the total amount in a column directly overhead. Total ozone concentrations are measured in units called **Dobson units** (DU). One DU is equivalent to a column of ozone 0.01 mm thick at a temperature of 0°C and 1 atmosphere pressure. The normal concentration of ozone in the atmosphere is about 300 DU, equivalent to a column 3 mm thick at the earth's surface. In comparison, a column of air reduced to the same conditions would be about 8 km thick.

A reduction in atmospheric ozone was first observed in the 1970s, consistent with Rowland and Molina's predictions. However, because of statistical uncertainty in the data and problems with calibration of monitoring equipment, the depletion was not universally accepted until 1985 when a 30% reduction appeared over Antarctica in October (the beginning of spring in the southern hemisphere). The "hole" grew in size every year until the mid-1990s when it stopped increasing in area. The ozone depletion over Antarctica is a result of clouds that form in the stratosphere over the South Pole when it is extremely cold because of the lack of sunlight during the winter (June–September). The air mass that these clouds occupy is isolated from the rest of the atmosphere during the polar winter, and rotates in a counterclockwise direction around the South Pole. Once the sun reappears in the spring, and ozone-depleting reactions begin again, these **polar stratospheric clouds** facilitate conditions that allow those ozone-depleting reactions to destroy ozone at an unusually high rate. The amplified ozone-depletion reactions consume ozone at such a rapid rate that the "ozone hole" makes its most dramatic appearance in October or November each year.

> ## AP Tip
>
> While they are the same structural molecule, remember that ozone in the stratosphere plays a different role from that in the troposphere. Stratospheric ozone is the so-called "good" ozone that protects life from the sun's ultraviolet radiation. Tropospheric ozone is the "bad" ozone that irritates our eyes and our respiratory systems, causes crop damage, etc. The instability of ozone molecules is necessary for both roles: good (destroying UV radiation) and bad (destroying cells in living organisms).

REDUCING OZONE DEPLETION

Like acid deposition and global climate change, reducing stratospheric ozone depletion requires international cooperation. In 1987, the Montreal Protocol was negotiated. This international agreement, along with a few follow-up amendments, has significantly reduced the production and use of ozone-depleting chemicals. The Montreal Protocol is considered a success story in the short history of international environmental problem solving; however, it is not without its drawbacks. Some poorer nations along with China and India do not participate in the protocol, and a black-market trade in CFCs continues their production and use.

this is a success story

One of the keys to successfully reducing CFC use was that substitutes were quickly made available. Hydrochlorofluorocarbons and hydrofluorocarbons, although more expensive, have successfully replaced most CFCs. Both of these substitutes are slightly less stable due to the addition of a hydrogen atom that causes them to break down in the troposphere, and although they will still deplete the stratospheric ozone layer upon reaching it, relatively small amounts of these compounds persist in the atmosphere long enough to reach it. Although they are no longer being released in significant amounts, as many as 5 billion tons of CFCs that were previously released are still moving slowly toward the stratospheric ozone layer. It is predicted that it will take until 2068 for the ozone layer to return to 1980 levels, and until 2108 to return to 1950 levels.

MULTIPLE-CHOICE QUESTIONS

1. Which of the following is used as insulation and is known to cause lung cancer?
    (A) Asbestos
    (B) Sulfur dioxide
    (C) Formaldehyde
    (D) Fiberglass
    (E) Vermiculite

2. Much of the radiation emitted by the earth is captured and trapped in the
   (A) stratosphere
   (B) lithosphere
   (C) aethenosphere
   (D) troposphere
   (E) mesosphere

3. Of these, the furthest from the center of the earth is the
   (A) stratosphere
   (B) lithosphere
   (C) aethenosphere
   (D) troposphere
   (E) mesosphere

4. Which of the following is a naturally occurring indoor air pollutant?
   (A) Carbon monoxide
   (B) Methane
   (C) Formaldehyde
   (D) Radon
   (E) Ozone

5. Which of the following is a secondary pollutant and major component of photochemical smog?
   (A) Carbon monoxide
   (B) Methane
   (C) Formaldehyde
   (D) Radon
   (E) Ozone

6. Which of the following is a colorless and odorless gas that binds to hemoglobin in blood?
   (A) Carbon monoxide
   (B) Methane
   (C) Formaldehyde
   (D) Radon
   (E) Ozone

7. Which of the following is a primary pollutant?
   (A) PANs
   (B) Sulfuric acid
   (C) Nitric acid
   (D) Ozone
   (E) Carbon monoxide

8. Which of the following is a strategy for reducing the effects of acid rain?
   (A) Applying a layer of granite under lakes
   (B) Reducing the depth of soils
   (C) Adding methyl mercury to lakes
   (D) Adding calcium carbonate to soils
   (E) Increasing electricity use

9. Which of the following is the layer of the atmosphere in which photochemical smog forms?
   (A) Mesosphere
   (B) Lithosphere
   (C) Stratosphere
   (D) Troposphere
   (E) Thermosphere

10. Which of the following is most likely to occur during the development of photochemical smog on a typical hot, sunny day in a big city?
   (A) Nitrogen oxide reaches its peak concentration around 6 p.m.
   (B) Ozone reaches its peak concentration around 8 a.m.
   (C) Nitrogen dioxide reaches its peak concentration around 3 p.m.
   (D) Ozone reaches its lowest concentration around 11 a.m.
   (E) Nitric oxide reaches its lowest concentration around 12 noon.

11. Which of the following is commonly used to remove sulfur dioxide from the exhaust of a coal-fired power plant?
   (A) A baghouse filter
   (B) A catalytic converter
   (C) A scrubber
   (D) An electrostatic precipitator
   (E) A cyclone separator

12. A temperature inversion is the result of
   (A) a lid of warm air on top of cooler air
   (B) precipitation
   (C) a cold blanket of air that prevents warm air from rising
   (D) ocean currents
   (E) a steady decrease in air temperature with altitude

13. Which of the following is NOT correct?
   (A) Increased atmospheric CO_2 leads to an increased greenhouse effect.
   (B) Increased glacial melting leads to decreased albedo.
   (C) Decrease in cloud albedo leads to increased atmospheric temperature.
   (D) Decreased atmospheric H_2O leads to an increased greenhouse effect.
   (E) Increased surface temperature leads to increased evaporation.

14. Of the following, which is the main reason that CFCs have a long residence time in the atmosphere?
   (A) They react shortly after entering the atmosphere to form unreactive secondary molecules.
   (B) They are always present in marine aerosols.
   (C) They are never destroyed, and cycle through the atmosphere as catalysts.
   (D) They are insoluble in water and chemically unreactive in the troposphere.
   (E) They are transparent to most wavelengths of light and resist photochemical break-up.

15. Which of the following is NOT a significant effect of increased ultraviolet radiation?
    (A) Sea level rise
    (B) Destruction of phytoplankton in the ocean
    (C) Vision impairment in humans
    (D) Decreased crop yields
    (E) Increase in skin cancer

FREE-RESPONSE QUESTION

Two of the most significant global environmental problems are global climate change and the destruction of the earth's protective ozone layer. The roots of these two problems lie in the industrialization that has taken place during the past two to three hundred years in what is now considered the developed world.

a) Identify and describe the layer of the atmosphere in which the greenhouse effect occurs and the layer of the atmosphere that contains the protective ozone layer.

b) List ONE major anthropogenic greenhouse gas, and ONE major ozone-depleting chemical. For each selection, identify a major source, and describe a method that is effective at reducing its emissions.

Early in 2005, the Kyoto Protocol went into effect.

c) Describe ONE of the goals of the Kyoto Protocol.
   Opponents claimed that the Kyoto Protocol pitted developed nations against developing nations. This was one of the most controversial elements of the Kyoto Protocol and it led to the failure of attempts to ratify it in the United States and Australia.

d) Discuss the assertion that developed nations should bear more responsibility than developing nations for the cleanup of global environmental problems.

ANSWERS

MULTIPLE-CHOICE QUESTIONS

1. **ANSWER: A.** Asbestos is a mineral that is used as insulation and is a known carcinogen (*Living in the Environment*, 16th ed., page 484 / 17th ed., page 482).

2. **ANSWER: D.** The only layer of the atmosphere that captures and traps the radiation that is emitted by the earth is the troposphere, where the greenhouse effect occurs (*Living in the Environment*, 16th ed., pages 498–499 / 17th ed., page 500).

3. **ANSWER: E.** Of the layers of the earth system listed, two are layers of the earth itself (aethenosphere and lithosphere). Of the layers of the atmosphere listed, the mesosphere is the furthest from the surface of the earth and also, therefore, from the center (*Living in the Environment*, 16th ed., page 470 / 17th ed., page 467).

4. **ANSWER: D.** Radon is a naturally occurring radioactive gas that seeps into buildings through cracks in the building foundation and walls (*Living in the Environment*, 16th ed., pages 485–486 / 17th ed., page 482).

5. **ANSWER: E.** Ozone is a secondary pollutant and the major component of photochemical smog (*Living in the Environment*, 16th ed., page 476 / 17th ed., page 474).

6. **ANSWER: A.** Carbon monoxide is a dangerous air pollutant both indoors and outdoors; it can bind to hemoglobin in red blood cells inhibiting their ability to transport oxygen through the body (*Living in the Environment*, 16th ed., pages 472–473 / 17th ed., page 470).

7. **ANSWER: E.** Carbon monoxide is a primary air pollutant (*Living in the Environment*, 16th ed., page 472 / 17th ed., page 469).

8. **ANSWER: D.** The addition of calcium carbonate (limestone) neutralizes acid rain (*Living in the Environment*, 16th ed., pages 482–483 / 17th ed., page 477).

9. **ANSWER: D.** Photochemical smog forms in the troposphere (*Living in the Environment*, 16th ed., page 470 / 17th ed., page 474).

10. **ANSWER: E.** During a typical day, the pattern of change for the reactants and products of the reactions that form photochemical smog will be that the reactants, NO_x and VOCs, are highest in the morning and lowest when the sun is strongest, around noon; the products of the reactions, ozone, and other photochemical oxidants, are highest when the sun is at its strongest, around noon, and lowest in the morning and evening. Therefore, of those listed, E is the best option (*Living in the Environment*, 16th ed., pages 476–477 / 17th ed., pages 474–475).

11. **ANSWER: C.** Sulfur dioxide is most commonly removed from smoke or exhaust by a scrubber that sprays a fine mist of a neutralizing solution, like calcium carbonate, through the smoke (*Living in the Environment*, 16th ed., page 491 / 17th ed., pages 486–487).

12. **ANSWER: A.** A temperature inversion occurs when cooler polluted air over a city is trapped by mountains to the sides and a lid of warmer air on top. Temperature inversions can trap pollutants over a city for weeks (*Living in the Environment*, 16th ed., page 478 / 17th ed., page 476).

13. **ANSWER: D.** This is a negative-stem question. It has four correct options and one incorrect option. Treating each option as a true/false question (as suggested in Section I of this review guide), D emerges as the only false answer. Since water is a greenhouse gas, decreasing water in the atmosphere would decrease, not increase the greenhouse effect (*Living in the Environment*, 16th ed., pages 505–508 / 17th ed., pages 495–500).

14. **ANSWER: D.** Chlorofluorocarbons are insoluble in water, preventing them from being washed out of the troposphere in rain, and they are unreactive, allowing them to pass through the troposphere chemically unchanged (*Living in the Environment*, 16th ed., page 524 / 17th ed., pages 521–522).

15. **ANSWER: A.** Increased UV radiation will not contribute significantly to sea level rise. The other four options are all serious hazards associated with increased UV radiation (*Living in the Environment*, 15th ed., pages 524–525 / 16th ed., pages 522–523).

FREE-RESPONSE SCORING GUIDELINES

(a) Identify and describe the layer of the atmosphere in which the greenhouse effect occurs and the layer of the atmosphere that contains the protective ozone layer.

2 points can be earned—1 point for each correct identification <u>and</u> description

The greenhouse effect occurs in the troposphere (identification).

<u>And</u> one of the following descriptions:
■ it is the first or lowest layer of the atmosphere
■ the composition is approximately 78% nitrogen, 21% oxygen
■ it extends from 0 to 5 or 10 miles above the earth
■ air temperature decreases with increasing altitude

The protective ozone layer is in the stratosphere (identification).

<u>And</u> one of the following descriptions:
■ it is the second layer of the atmosphere
■ it extends from 5 to 10 miles to approximately 30 miles above the earth
■ air temperature increases with increasing altitude

b) List ONE major anthropogenic greenhouse gas, and ONE major ozone-depleting chemical. For each selection, identify a major source, and describe a method that is effective at reducing its emissions.

6 points can be earned—1 point for each correct gas identified (one greenhouse gas and one ozone-depleting chemical), 1 point for a major source, and 1 point for a correct reduction method

Greenhouse Gas	Major Source	Reduction Method
Carbon dioxide Or CO_2	Burning of fossil fuels	Reduce fossil fuel use Plant trees Sequester carbon
Nitrous oxide Or N_2O	Use of inorganic fertilizers Burning of fossil fuels Animal waste Sewage treatment	Use less inorganic fertilizer Reduce fossil fuel use
Methane Or CH_4	Cattle production Leaks in fossil fuel mining operations Landfills Wastewater treatment Rice cultivation	Capture and use to produce energy Burn it off at the source
Carbon dioxide Or CO_2	Burning of fossil fuels	Reduce fossil fuel use Plant trees Sequester carbon
Nitrous oxide Or N_2O	Use of inorganic fertilizers Burning of fossil fuels Animal waste Sewage treatment	Use less inorganic fertilizer Reduce fossil fuel use
Methane Or CH_4	Cattle production Leaks in fossil fuel mining operations Landfills Wastewater treatment Rice cultivation	Capture and use to produce energy Burn it off at the source
Chlorofluorocarbons	Refrigerators Air conditioners Cleaning electronics Fumigation Foam blowing Propellants in aerosol cans	Replacement with substitutes (HCFCs, HFCs) Capture and recycle chemicals rather than emitting them Enforce the Montreal Protocol
Chlorofluorocarbons	Refrigerators Air conditioners Cleaning electronics Fumigation Foam blowing Propellants in aerosol cans	Replacement with substitutes (HCFCs, HFCs) Capture and recycle chemicals rather than emitting them Enforce the Montreal Protocol
Halons	Fire extinguishers or suppression equipment	Use non-ozone-depleting substitutes
Methyl bromide	Fumigant for disinfecting soils	Use non-ozone-depleting substitutes

Note: Only the first identified greenhouse gas and the first identified ozone-depleting chemical may be graded.

c) Describe ONE of the goals of the Kyoto Protocol.

1 point can be earned for a correct description of a goal of the Kyoto Protocol

Note: Only the first description may be graded.
- reduce greenhouse gas emissions
- reduce global warming
- reduce or stabilize sea level rise
- reduce or stabilize the melting of permafrost
- reduce or stabilize the melting of ice
- avoid biodiversity loss
- maintain predictable ocean currents
- stabilize vegetative zones
- maintain or reduce carbon dioxide concentrations in the oceans

d) Discuss the assertion that developed nations should bear more responsibility than developing nations for the cleanup of global environmental problems.

2 points can be earned—1 point for each correct discussion of a position on the issue

Note: One or both sides of the issue can be addressed in a correct discussion
- Developed nations emit most of the greenhouse gases; therefore they should be more responsible for reducing greenhouse gas emissions.
- Historically, developed nations emitted most of the greenhouse gases that caused global climate change; therefore they should be responsible for remediation.
- Developing nations must be free to pursue economic well-being before reducing greenhouse gas emissions.
- Developing nations will soon emit most of the world's greenhouse gases; therefore they must share the responsibility for reducing greenhouse gas emissions.

Answer Page

SOLID AND HAZARDOUS WASTE PRODUCTION

KEY CONCEPTS

- The human population, especially in developed nations, generates large amounts of solid waste, amounting to about 5 pounds per person in the United States.
- Some waste is hazardous and can pollute water resources and cause human health problems.
- Most <u>industrial</u> solid waste generated in the United States comes from mining operations.
- Solid waste can be managed by reducing consumption, reusing consumer products, and recycling.
- Integrated management practices for dealing with hazardous waste include producing less of it, recycling, reusing, and converting it to less hazardous materials.

Solid and hazardous waste disposal is discussed in depth in *Living in the Environment*, 16th ed., Chapter 21 / 17th ed., Chapter 21.

KEY VOCABULARY

bioremediation

cradle-to-grave system

deep-well injection

hazardous waste

hazardous waste landfill

industrial solid waste

leachate

municipal solid waste

open dumps

phytoremediation

primary or closed-loop recycling

sanitary landfills

secondary recycling

solid waste

surface impoundment

CHARACTERISTICS OF SUSTAINABLE SOCIETIES

Sustainable societies are ones that utilize earth's natural capital (resources) in a manner that ensures its continued use for future generations. As the human population continues to grow, increasing pressures will be placed on the earth's resources. Therefore, sustainability is an underlying theme throughout your course of study in AP Environmental Science. You have already learned many sustainable practices for agriculture, energy resources, and water resources in previous chapters. In this chapter we will focus on ways to reduce and deal with waste to improve the sustainability of life.

METHODS OF SOLID WASTE DISPOSAL

Understand
Waste
types

The human population produces large amounts of unwanted, discarded products known as **solid waste**. Sustainable societies must have in place waste disposal practices that protect natural resources from degradation and pollution. Solid waste generated by agricultural, mining, and manufacturing activities are referred to as **industrial solid wastes**. Most of the solid waste generated in the United States comes from mining activities. As you learned in Chapter 7, mining activities provide many raw materials for both consumer products and industrial products. What is typically referred to as trash or garbage that is thrown out by residential or commercial buildings is known as **municipal solid waste (MSW)**.

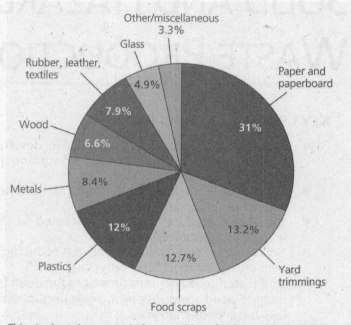

This pie chart shows a typical composition of U.S. municipal solid waste (MSW) in 2008. (Data from U.S. Environmental Protection Agency, 2009)

© Cengage Learning 2012

The United States is the world leader in producing solid waste, generating nearly 5 pounds of waste per person per year. As you can see in the diagram below, the largest source of municipal solid waste in the United States is paper products.

The United States produces more trash per person than any other person in the world. How do we deal with this large volume of solid waste? In the United States, about 25% of municipal solid waste currently is recycled, and another 54% is buried in landfills. The remainder is incinerated. Heat from waste incineration sometimes is used to produce steam and generate electricity.

OPEN DUMPING

In developing countries it is a common practice to dispose of waste in open dumps. **Open dumps** are simply large fields or holes in the ground where garbage is deposited and often burned. Such dumps create significant environmental hazards through the uncontrolled release of harmful materials and the attraction of rodents and other vermin. Open dumping is forbidden in most developed countries.

SANITARY LANDFILLS

More than half of municipal solid waste in the United States is buried in sanitary landfills. **Sanitary landfills** are specially prepared facilities that must meet specific federal requirements mandated by the Resource Conservation and Recovery Act for location, design, operation, closure, monitoring, and financial assurance. Landfills must be constructed with special liners and impermeable soil layers to prevent release of materials to the environment, and procedures must be in place to monitor and control leaks (leachate) that could contaminate local water supplies. Wastes brought to landfills are spread out daily and covered with a layer of either clay or plastic foam. Most modern landfills can handle large amounts of waste, have limited odors, and relatively low-operating costs. However, they are not sustainable over long periods of time for the following reasons:

SANITARY LANDFILL DISADVANTAGES
- Landfills release greenhouse gases (methane and CO_2) as wastes decompose.
- Toxic materials leach out of landfills as liquid moves downward through the layers. This liquid is known as **leachate** and can make its way to groundwater supplies if not carefully monitored and controlled.
- Air pollution is generated from both the landfill and trucks transporting waste.

WAYS TO MAKE SANITARY LANDFILLS MORE SUSTAINABLE
- use clay and plastic liners to prevent leaks
- use pipes that collect leachate, liquid draining from the landfill, from the bottom of the landfill
- have leachate storage tanks and treatment systems in place
- collect methane gas on site for use as fuel for electrical generation
- use groundwater stations to monitor for toxins from leachate

A major drawback to landfilling waste is find suitable locations to put them. Most waste is generated in areas of high population density, such as cities. However, in most cities land is scarce and often expensive, which makes finding areas for landfills difficult. Some cities must transport their trash across state lines to neighboring states to utilize their landfill space. For example, since 2001, New York has been sending most of its trash to landfills in New Jersey, Virginia, and Pennsylvania. Canada, the second-leading world producer of trash per person, started sending trash generated in Toronto to landfills in nearby Michigan beginning in 2002. Shipping trash to surrounding areas is not only expensive but also releases air pollutants such as nitric and sulfur oxides and carbon dioxide from the trucks used to transport the waste.

INCINERATION OF WASTE

Some municipal solid waste is sent to waste-to-energy incinerators. These incinerators can reduce the volume of solid waste up to 90%. Waste incineration can be used to produce steam to create electrical energy. In Chapter 7 you learned about air pollution controls, such as scrubbers, that remove air pollutants from the combustion process in coal-burning power plants. These same controls are also used in waste incinerators.

INCINERATION DISADVANTAGES
- creates greenhouse gas emissions of CO_2
- releases air pollutants such as nitrogen oxides, sulfur dioxides, mercury, and dioxins
- creates large amounts of fly ash that must be stored in hazardous waste landfills
- expensive to build and operate; incineration typically costs twice as much as landfilling

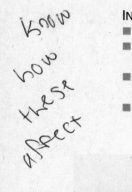

Know how these affect

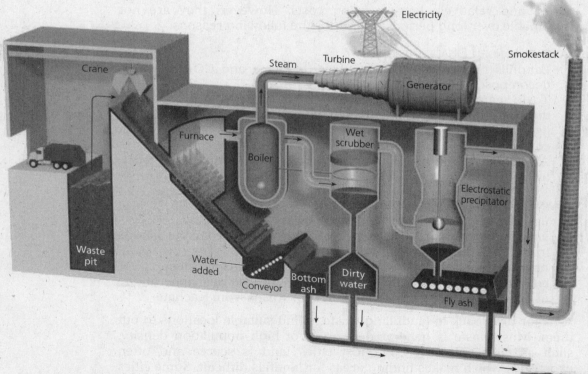

Ash for treatment, disposal in landfill, or use as landfill cover

© Cengage Learning 2012

METHODS FOR REDUCING SOLID WASTE PRODUCTION

Understanding how our society can become more sustainable in its solid waste production is not much different than what you have already learned about sustainable agriculture or energy practices. The underlying theme in sustainable societies is to utilize practices that accomplish the same tasks or produce the same yield with less input of energy. It is more cost effective and therefore more sustainable to reduce the input or production of wastes and pollutants rather than to create ways to remediate or store them later. You have probably heard of the three Rs—reduce, reuse, and recycle. These three methods of reducing our overall input of waste into the environment can also reduce the amount of energy used and the greenhouse gas emissions released.

Reduce—An important part of reducing the overall solid waste production is to look for ways to reduce consumption of consumer products and energy. Simple ways to reduce consumption may be to walk, bike, or carpool to work, read newspapers or magazines online, and buy items secondhand. Reducing consumption requires less raw material input and therefore is a preventive measure, avoiding the production of waste from mining processes and air pollutants from energy production.

Reuse—This term refers to using reusable materials rather than relying on the production of "one-time use" items. For example, many consumers are now using refillable water containers rather than buying single-use plastic water bottles that are thrown out when finished. Plastics are made from a petroleum by-product and can take up to 1,000 years to break down. Over two million plastic bottles are thrown away in the United States every hour! So, reducing plastic consumption helps reduce not only solid waste but also the energy used in production and air and water pollution by-products from fossil fuel use. There are numerous examples of reusable items that can replace common consumer products such as cloth grocery bags instead of plastic, rechargeable batteries, and cloth napkins rather than paper.

Recycling—The United States currently recycles between 25–30% of its municipal solid waste. Materials like paper, steel, aluminum, glass, and some plastics are reprocessed to provide materials for new products. Two types of processing are primary, or closed-loop recycling, and secondary recycling. In **primary**, or **closed-loop recycling**, materials are converted into new products of the same type. For example, recycling an aluminum can in primary recycling will convert a used can into a new one. In **secondary recycling**, materials can be converted into a different type of product. For example, secondary recycling will convert rubber tires into rubberized road surfacing materials. Most wastes that can be recycled are actually generated during the manufacturing process and are known as pre-consumer or internal waste products. **Composting** is a type of recycling that utilizes the natural role of decomposing bacteria and fungi to convert biodegradable waste into usable soil amendments. Yard trimming and food scraps (primarily vegetable-based) are all easily composted. Over time these decomposing microorganisms convert these wastes into nutrient rich organic soil fertilizer.

good table

Recycling Advantages	Recycling Disadvantages
Reduces greenhouse gas emission Reduces need for mining of minerals Decreases water pollution Reduces solid waste production and disposal	Decreases jobs and profits at landfills and incinerator facilities Can be expensive when compared to a landfill Money generated from glass and plastics is reduced

Case Study: Paper Recycling

Over half of the tree harvest worldwide goes to produce paper. As you saw in the diagram earlier, paper represents over 30% of our MSW in the United States. The production of paper requires large amounts of energy and water. In the United States, paper production is the third-leading industrial producer of pollutants and energy consumption. Paper production releases into the environment harmful chlorine compounds that are used to bleach the cellulosic fibers. Making recycled paper uses 64% less energy and produces much less air and water pollution. However, recycled paper is more expensive to produce than virgin paper.

METHODS OF HAZARDOUS WASTE DISPOSAL

Any waste that poses potential harm to human health due to its toxicity is known as **hazardous waste**. Hazardous waste is often corrosive, flammable, or dangerously chemically reactive. The two main categories of hazardous waste are synthetic organic compounds (pesticides, PCBs) and heavy metals (mercury, lead). Developed countries are responsible for the large majority of the hazardous waste produced worldwide. Many developed nations do not have adequate procedures for dealing with hazardous waste materials, which often are simply mixed with household garbage and sent to landfills. Households in the United States alone generate over one million tons of hazardous waste each year.

Common Sources of Hazardous Waste

Source	Hazardous Waste
Household	paints, pesticides, solvents, batteries, oil, antifreeze
Medical	used bandages, surgical gloves, syringes, culture dishes, surgical instruments
Nuclear	spent uranium fuel rods and nuclear weapons
Industry	solvents, mercury, lead, PCBs, dioxins

INTEGRATED MANAGEMENT OF HAZARDOUS WASTE

Integrated management of hazardous waste includes producing less, recycling or reusing the waste, or converting it to a less hazardous material. Unfortunately, the most common method of dealing with hazardous waste is simply storing it.

Producing Less and Recycling—Producing less hazardous waste will require industries to actively search for alternatives to commonly used hazardous materials. Some types of hazardous waste can be recycled to become the raw materials for other industrial processes. Examples of hazardous waste that can be recycled are metals and solvents. In 2007, the United States recycled less than 5% of the total hazardous waste managed (http://www.epa.gov/epawaste/hazard/recycling/index.htm).

Converting to Less Hazardous Substances—Methods of detoxifying hazardous wastes include the following:

1) Chemical methods—Some types of hazardous waste can be remediated by chemical reactions that convert the waste into compounds that are less toxic. Examples include using cyclodextrin, sugar made from cornstarch, to remove solvents and pesticides from soils and groundwater resources.

2) Physical methods—Hazardous waste can also be physically removed by distilling liquid mixtures to remove toxic compounds and by using charcoal or resins to filter out solid hazardous wastes.

3) Biological methods—**Bioremediation** includes the use of organisms, such as bacteria or other microorganisms, to remove contaminants from solid or liquid hazardous waste. **Phytoremediation** utilizes natural plant species or genetically engineered plants to absorb contaminants such as mercury, lead, pesticides, or organic solvents from soils and water. The diagram below describes the various methods of phytoremediation.

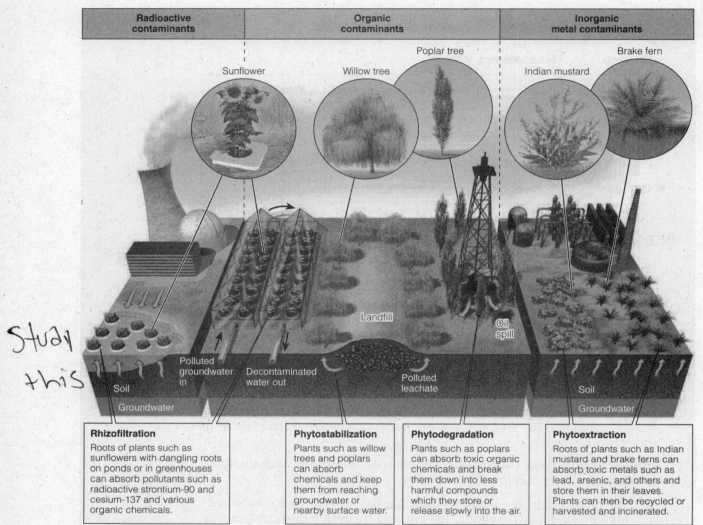

| Radioactive contaminants | Organic contaminants | Inorganic metal contaminants |

Sunflower
Willow tree
Poplar tree
Indian mustard
Brake fern

Landfill
Oil spill

Polluted groundwater in
Decontaminated water out
Polluted leachate

Soil
Groundwater
Soil
Groundwater

Rhizofiltration
Roots of plants such as sunflowers with dangling roots on ponds or in greenhouses can absorb pollutants such as radioactive strontium-90 and cesium-137 and various organic chemicals.

Phytostabilization
Plants such as willow trees and poplars can absorb chemicals and keep them from reaching groundwater or nearby surface water.

Phytodegradation
Plants such as poplars can absorb toxic organic chemicals and break them down into less harmful compounds which they store or release slowly into the air.

Phytoextraction
Roots of plants such as Indian mustard and brake ferns can absorb toxic metals such as lead, arsenic, and others and store them in their leaves. Plants can then be recycled or harvested and incinerated.

© Cengage Learning 2012

4) <u>Incineration</u>—Much like solid waste incineration, hazardous waste can also be broken down in high temperature incinerators that convert the waste to less toxic materials. A major disadvantage to incineration is the creation of toxic ash that must be stored in a hazardous waste landfill site.

5) <u>Plasma Arc Torch</u>—This device generates plasma by passing an electrical current through a gas at very high temperatures. This process converts solid or liquid hazardous waste into a synthetic gas that can be utilized to make fuels such as natural gas and ethanol. This process, however, is relatively expensive compared to other disposal methods. It also produces carbon dioxide gas and can release toxic metals and radioactive elements.

STORING HAZARDOUS WASTE

Currently, the least expensive method of disposal of hazardous waste is simple burial on land and therefore this is the predominant method used in the United States. It is also a common practice for the United

States to ship some solid hazardous waste, such as electronics, to other countries for disposal. Much of the global share of electronic waste ends up in developing countries and increases residents' exposure to toxic heavy metals.

1. **Deep-Well Disposal (Injection)**—This is the most common form of storing liquid hazardous waste. Liquid wastes are pumped through pipes into permeable injection zones that are beneath aquifers and ideally sealed off by impermeable vertical rock layers above the injection zone. Although this method is relatively safe and inexpensive, it is possible for leaks to occur, especially in areas that experience earthquake activity. These leaks can contaminate groundwater with hazardous waste. Also, there are limited areas that have the appropriate geologic structure to be a deep-well disposal site.

2. **Surface Impoundment**—Some liquid hazardous waste is simply stored in natural topographic depressions in the earth or man-made lagoons or ponds. Unfortunately, many of these waste lagoons lack adequate liners and therefore leach toxins into groundwater. These lagoons can also overflow with heavy rains and contaminate soil and nearby waterways.

3. **Hazardous Waste Landfill**—Solid or liquid hazardous waste can also be placed in drums or barrels that are sealed and buried in special hazardous waste landfill facilities. This method is used infrequently due to the cost of building and maintaining these types of facilities.

AP Tip

In the early 1940s and 1950s, the Hooker Chemical Company buried at least 200 drums of hazardous waste at a location called Love Canal near Niagara Falls, New York. The company then sold this property to the local school board where many homes and an elementary school were built. In the 1970s, the storage drums began leaking and hazardous waste entered storm sewers, basements, and school playgrounds. Many cases of cancer were linked to this contamination, and all residents were affected financially because of the loss of property value. The entire area ultimately had to be evacuated. In order to remediate the site, all leaking drums had to be located and removed as well as the surrounding soil. This case sparked the creation of CERCLA and superfund law (described on the next page). The contamination of toxic waste that occurred in Love Canal, NY, is an example of just one of the many well-known environmental case studies the AP exam will expect you to know. Make sure you pay close attention to these case studies as you read your textbook. See a list of well-known case studies in the supplement section of this review book.

HAZARDOUS WASTE LEGISLATION IN THE UNITED STATES

Resource Conservation and Recovery Act (RCRA)—This act allows the EPA to set standards for management of several types of hazardous waste produced. The EPA issues permits to companies that have developed a plan for hazardous waste from the initial generation of the waste to the end disposal. This is known as a **cradle-to-grave system** to track hazardous waste disposal. Although this is valuable legislation for controlling hazardous waste disposal, it is important to remember that this law regulates less than 5% of the hazardous waste produced in the United States.

Comprehensive Environmental Response, Compensation, and Liability Act (CERCLA or Superfund Act)—This act identifies areas that have been contaminated with hazardous waste. These areas, known as superfund sites, are placed on the national priorities list for cleanup. The law also allows for citizens to be made aware of the hazardous waste being stored or released in their communities. Initially, the law was designed to have the companies responsible for the contamination to pay to clean up the site. The U.S. government, state legislatures, and local agencies are passing laws and providing incentives for the cleanup of abandoned industrial and commercial sites known as **brownfields**. These areas are often converted into living, office, or retail space in downtown urban areas.

Basel Convention—This international treaty was drafted as a result of hazardous waste, including e-waste, from developed nations being shipped overseas to developing countries without their permission. It now requires that developing countries must give full permission to accept the hazardous waste. As of 2009, this treaty has been signed by 172 countries, but not by the United States.

Persistent Organic Pollutants (POPs) treaty—This treaty originated at the Stockholm convention. It is an international agreement to phase out 12 organic persistent pollutants, also known as the "dirty dozen," such as DDT and PCBs. As of 2009, 162 countries and the European Union have ratified this treaty. The United States has yet to ratify this treaty or enact any legislation toward doing so.

MULTIPLE-CHOICE QUESTIONS

1. Which of the following methods best illustrates how the United States deals with over half of its solid waste?
   (A) Deep-well injection
   (B) Plasma arc torch
   (C) Phytoremediation
   (D) Landfills
   (E) Composting

2. The U.S. legislation that requires industry producing hazardous waste to develop a cradle-to-grave plan for disposal is
(A) CERCLA
(B) Kyoto treaty
(C) Montreal protocol
(D) National Environmental Policy Act (NEPA)
(E) Resource Conservation and Recovery Act

3. Which of the following is most likely to be released from electronic waste and can cause adverse human health impacts?
(A) Uranium
(B) Heavy metals
(C) Radon-222
(D) Chlorine
(E) Cyclodextrin

4. The use of various types of plants to absorb organic compounds and toxic metals is known as
(A) composting
(B) nanomagnet sorting
(C) phytoremediation
(D) resin filtration
(E) leachate treatment

5. Which statement is incorrect concerning benefits to recycling solid waste?
(A) It is a cheaper method of disposing of solid waste materials.
(B) It reduces the amount of air and water pollution associated with conventional waste disposal methods.
(C) It can save land space needed for landfill areas.
(D) It decreases the demand for mining for resources such as aluminum.
(E) It can require less energy to make materials from recycled products.

6. Which of the following activities best illustrates how the majority of solid waste in the United States is produced?
(A) Agricultural practices
(B) Industrial manufacturing
(C) Mining processes
(D) Residential use of products
(E) Use of electronics

7. Many cities have offered financial incentives to developers to convert abandoned, industrial hazardous waste sites into useful urban areas such as living space or retail areas. These areas are known as
(A) brownfields
(B) superfund sites
(C) urban heat islands
(D) industrial parks
(E) eco-townships

8. Of the following household waste products, which is NOT considered to be hazardous?
   (A) Antifreeze
   (B) Weed killer
   (C) Paint remover
   (D) Batteries
   (E) Aluminum cans

9. All of the following environmental toxins were included in the POPs treaty EXCEPT
   (A) DDT
   (B) furans
   (C) mercury
   (D) PCBs
   (E) dioxins

10. Which of the following consumer products constitutes the largest percent of municipal solid waste?
    (A) Paper
    (B) Plastic
    (C) Aluminum
    (D) Glass
    (E) Batteries

11. On average, the typical U.S. citizen produces 5 pounds of solid waste per day. About how many pounds of waste per year would the approximately 300 million United States citizens produce?
    (A) 5.5×10^{10}
    (B) 5.5×10^{11}
    (C) 5.5×10^{12}
    (D) 5.5×10^{13}
    (E) 5.5×10^{14}

12. Which of the following methods of solid or hazardous waste disposal would contribute the least to the increasing global climate?
    (A) Plasma arc torch
    (B) Open dumps
    (C) Incineration
    (D) Deep-well injection
    (E) Sanitary landfills

13. Chlorine dioxide is a toxic compound that is corrosive to machinery, hazardous to workers, and harmful when released into the environment. Reducing the use of which of the following products will decrease the amount of chlorine dioxide produced?
    (A) Plastics
    (B) Gold
    (C) Glass
    (D) Aluminum
    (E) Paper

14. A plastic bottle is sent to a recycling facility, where it is converted into the raw materials used to make a new plastic food container. This is an example of
 (A) open-loop recycling
 (B) tertiary recycling
 (C) secondary recycling
 (D) closed-loop recycling
 (E) advanced recycling

15. A large amount of toxic ash that must be disposed of in a hazardous waste landfill is created during the process of
 (A) composting of biodegradable waste
 (B) deep-well injection of hazardous waste
 (C) incineration of non-hazardous solid waste
 (D) phytoremediation of heavy metals
 (E) plasma arc torches used to make syngas from waste

FREE-RESPONSE QUESTION

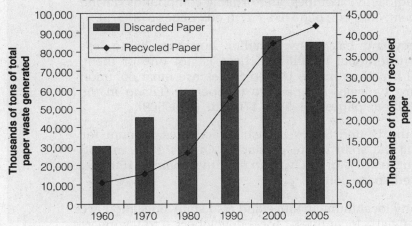

US Production of Paper in Municipal Waste Stream

(a) (i) What is the percent increase in total discarded paper waste production in the United States from 1960 to 1980?
 (ii) What percent of the total paper discarded in 1990 was recycled?
(b) Other than recycling, identify and describe a possible reason why solid waste production of paper declined in 2005.
(c) Discuss why it is beneficial to produce paper products from recycled materials rather than from wood.
(d) Explain TWO environmental consequences to conventional landfill or incineration practices for solid waste material.

done on seperate sheet

ANSWERS

MULTIPLE-CHOICE

1. **ANSWER: D.** Although the United States uses a variety of methods to dispose of waste, over half of it is sent to sanitary landfills (*Living in the Environment*, 16th ed., page 574 / 17th ed., page 570).

2. **ANSWER: E.** Resource Conservation and Recovery Act—this act was meant to force industry to create a cradle-to-grave system for hazardous waste disposal (*Living in the Environment*, 16th ed., page 582 / 17th ed., page 578).

3. **ANSWER: B.** Heavy metals are commonly released from electronic waste in landfills. Common metals released are lead, mercury, and cadmium (dry-cell batteries) (*Living in the Environment*, 16th ed., page 560 / 17th ed., page 557).

4. **ANSWER: C.** Phytoremediation utilizes various species of plants to remediate a variety of toxic compounds. They are used to absorb heavy metals, radioactive isotopes, and organic compounds (*Living in the Environment*, 16th ed., page 579 / 17th ed., pages 574–575).

5. **ANSWER: A.** Recycling has many benefits; however, being less expensive than traditional landfill practices is not one of them. Sanitary landfill practices in the United States are most common because they are typically inexpensive to operate (*Living in the Environment*, 16th ed., pages 574–580 / 17th ed., page 568).

6. **ANSWER: C.** In the United States industrial activities account for about 98% of all the solid waste produced. Of this 98%, mining practices account for 76% of it (*Living in the Environment*, 15th ed., page 563 / 16th ed., page 559).

7. **ANSWER: A.** Many local municipalities and also state legislation are providing financial incentives for developers to convert brownfields into usable living and working space in cities. Brownfields are abandoned industrial areas that are typically contaminated with hazardous waste materials. Examples could include abandoned gas stations with buried gas drums or old factory sites with buried hazardous waste (*Living in the Environment*, 16th ed., page 583 / 17th ed., page 579).

8. **ANSWER: E.** All of those items are considered common household hazardous waste except for aluminum cans. Aluminum cans can enter the regular municipal solid waste stream or be recycled (*Living in the Environment*, 16th ed., page 562 / 17th ed., page 559).

9. **ANSWER: C.** The POPs treaty stands for persistent organic pollutants. This is also called the list of the dirty dozen. Mercury is an inorganic heavy metal and therefore is not on this list. Examples of toxins on the POPs list are PCBs, dioxins, furans, and DDT (*Living in the Environment*, 16th ed., page 584 / 17th ed., page 580).

10. **ANSWER: A.** In the United States, paper products make up the largest percent of our municipal solid waste. This includes things like computer paper, mail, cardboard, paper towels, cups, and plates (*Living in the Environment*, 16th ed., page 563 / 17th ed., page 560).

11. **ANSWER: B.** $5 \text{ lbs} \times 3.0 \times 10^8 = 1.5 \times 10^9 \times 365 \text{ days} = 5.5 \times 10^{11}$ lbs/year (*Living in the Environment*, 16th ed., page 563 / 17th ed., page 560).

12. **ANSWER: D.** All of those choices except deep-well injection either release greenhouse gases such as carbon dioxide or methane (landfill only). Both of those gases contribute to global climate change (*Living in the Environment*, 16th ed., pages 574–580 / 17th ed., pages 575–577).

13. **ANSWER: E.** The production of paper often includes a bleach process to whiten the fibers. This process typically uses chlorine as the bleach and therefore releases chlorine dioxide as a waste product. However, some companies have switched to the less harmful hydrogen peroxide (*Living in the Environment*, 16th ed., page 571 / 17th ed., page 567).

14. **ANSWER: D.** Closed-loop recycling, or primary recycling, is when a product is made into something of the same type (*Living in the Environment*, 16th ed., page 569 / 17th ed., pages 565–566).

15. **ANSWER: C.** Incinerators produce a large amount of toxic fly ash that has been collected from the combustion process. Although the removal of the fly ash reduces air pollution, it still must be collected and sent to a hazardous waste landfill to be stored (*Living in the Environment*, 16th ed., pages 574–580 / 17th ed., pages 570–571).

FREE-RESPONSE SCORING GUIDELINES

(a) (i) What is the percent increase in total discarded paper waste production in the United States from 1960 to 1980?

2 points can be earned—1 point for a correct set-up and 1 point for a correct answer

1980—60,000 tons
1960—30,000 tons

$$\frac{60,000 \text{ tons} - 30,000 \text{ tons}}{30,000 \text{ tons}} = 1.0 \times 100 \times 100\% \text{ increase}$$

(ii) What percent of the total paper discarded in 1990 was recycled?

2 points can be earned—1 point for correct set-up and 1 point for correct answer

$\dfrac{25,000 \text{ tons recycled}}{75,000 \text{ tons discarded}} = 0.33 \times 100 = 33\%$ (accepted range 30–35%)

(b) Other than recycling, identify and describe a possible reason why solid waste production of paper declined in 2005.

2 points can be earned—1 point for each correct identified method
- ▨ <u>Reusing consumer products to replace paper</u>—examples can include but are not limited to: cloth bags for groceries, plastic or metal coffee cups, plastic or metal food containers, use of email or cell phones over regular mail, etc.
- ▨ <u>Reducing demand for consumer paper products</u>—not replacing paper goods as often, utilizing fewer paper products

(c) Discuss why it is beneficial to produce paper products from recycled materials rather than from wood.

2 points can be earned—1 point for each correct benefit with a description
- ▨ Requires less energy to produce products from recycled paper rather than from wood
- ▨ Reduces the amount of air pollution that is released from paper mills using wood products
- ▨ Reduces the amount of water pollution that is released from paper mills using wood products
- ▨ Protects forests by decreasing overall demand for wood products

(d) Explain TWO environmental consequences to conventional landfill or incineration practices for solid waste material.

2 points can be earned—1 point for each correct environmental consequence

Landfill	**Incineration**
Trucks hauling waste to landfill produce air pollution which leads to smog or climate change	Creates toxic ash which must be sent to a landfill
Landfill releases methane and CO_2 which causes climate change	Produces CO_2 which leads to climate change
Leachate can contaminate soils and groundwater	Air pollution such as fly ash can be generated
Dust can blow off soil caps and creates air pollution	
Requires allocation of land that could be put to other societal or environmental purposes	

Part III

Supplements

PEOPLE IN ENVIRONMENTAL SCIENCE HISTORY

The AP Environmental Science exam may include a few questions about specific people and their contribution to the field of environmental science or conservation. It is important to not only know who the person is, but to be able to identify his or her major contributions to the field of environmental science. This can include anything from literary works such as books and journal articles to scientific discoveries that have earned the Nobel Prize. The following are key people to know in alphabetical order by last name.

1. **Rachel Carson**: published *Silent Spring* in 1962; documented the environmental damage done by DDT and other pesticides. This book heightened public awareness at the start of the modern environmental movement.

2. **Paul Ehrlich**: a biologist who published *The Population Bomb* in 1968; discussed overpopulation and food production issues for future generations.

3. **Garrett Hardin**: published "The Tragedy of the Commons" in the journal *Science* in 1968; argued that rational people will exploit shared resources (commons).

4. **Aldo Leopold**: wrote A *Sand County Almanac*, published a year after his death in 1948; promoted a "Land Ethic" in which humans are ethically responsible for serving as the protectors of nature.

5. **Wangari Maathai**: won the 2004 Nobel Peace Prize for "Green Belt" movement – planting trees in Kenya that provided food and fuel, and improved soil erosion and desertification.

6. **Thomas Malthus**: a British Economist who said, "human population cannot continue to increase. Consequences will be war, famine & pestilence (disease)."

7. **John Muir**: founded Sierra Club in 1892; fought unsuccessfully to prevent the damming of the Hetch Hetchy Valley in Yosemite National Park.

8. **Gifford Pinchot**: first chief of the United States Forest Service; advocated managing resources for multiple use using principles of sustainable yield.

9. **Theodore Roosevelt**: president of the United States from 1901 to 1909, well-known for his conservation efforts. He established the first National Wildlife Refuge at Pelican Island.

10. **Sherwood Rowland and Mario Molina**: in 1974, determined that CFCs destroy stratospheric (good) ozone.

11. **E.O. Wilson**: biologist who co-coined, with Robert MacArthur, the theory of island biogeography, which identifies factors that regulate species richness on islands.

Know their impact

275

Summary of Well-Known Case Studies in Environmental Science

There are several case studies in environmental science that have had a significant impact on public perception about the environment, and have influenced policy decisions and/or legislation. While it is important to also be familiar with your local or regional case studies, because the APES exam will be taken by students from all over the world, it will only include case studies that have had national or international significance. The following are brief synopses of several case studies to jog your memory; you may consult your textbook for more details.

Aral Sea, Uzbekistan/Kazakhstan (former Soviet Union) and Mono Lake, California: a large inland sea that is drying up; its salinity is rising as a result of water diversion for irrigating crops.

Ogallala Aquifer: the world's largest aquifer; under parts of Wyoming, South Dakota, Nebraska, Kansas, Colorado, Oklahoma, New Mexico, and Texas (the Midwestern United States). It holds enough water to cover the United States with 1.5 feet of water. It is being depleted for agricultural and urban use.

Minamata, Japan: mental impairments, birth defects, and deaths caused by mercury dumped in Minamata Bay by a factory. The mercury was converted to methylmercury, bioaccumulated in fish, and biomagnified through food chains. Mercury entered humans who ate a traditional fish-based diet.

Aswan High Dam, Egypt: the silt that made the Nile region fertile fills the reservoir. Lack of irrigation controls causes waterlogging and salinization. The parasitic disease schistosomiasis thrives in the stagnant water of the reservoir.

Chesapeake Bay, Maryland/Virginia: the largest estuary in the United States; lies off the Atlantic Ocean between Maryland and Virginia, and was declared a dead zone in the 1970s due to hypoxic conditions created from nutrient loading by fertilizers, which caused cultural eutrophication.

Love Canal Housing Development, Niagara Falls, New York: hazardous chemicals buried in an old canal leaked into homes and school yards. Led to the passage of the Comprehensive Environment Response, Compensation, and Liability Act (CERCLA), also known as the Superfund Act.

Three-Mile Island, Pennsylvania: on March 29, 1979, the emergency cooling system of a nuclear reactor was shut down erroneously by an operator. This led to a partial core meltdown. The containment structure worked well to retain all radioactive materials, but eventually some radioactive gas was purposely released to reduce pressure in the containment structure and avoid a more serious accident.

Bhopal, India: on December 2,1984, poisonous methyl isocyanate gas was released accidentally by a Union Carbide pesticide plant killing about 5,000 people and causing serious health effects for 50,000–60,000.

Chernobyl, Ukraine: on April 26, 1986, an unauthorized safety test led to a fire and explosion at a nuclear power plant—as a result, millions of people in Europe are exposed to unsafe levels of radiation.

Valdez, Alaska: on March 24, 1989, the oil tanker Exxon Valdez hit a reef in Prince William Sound spilling 260,000 barrels of oil. It was the largest oil spill ever in U.S. waters.

Yucca Mountain, Nevada: the proposed site for permanent storage of high-level nuclear waste, 70 miles northwest of Las Vegas. Critics are concerned about the safety of transporting high-level radioactive waste to the site and the proximity of the site to a volcano and earthquake faults.

Three Gorges Dam, China: the world's largest dam on Yangtze River submerged ecosystems, cities, archeological sites, displaced two million people, and fragmented the river habitat.

Clinch River, Tennessee: the Tennessee Valley Authority's power plant near Knoxville had a wall breached in a retention pond holding sludge from the coal burning power plant. This released up to 1 billion gallons of mercury- and arsenic-containing sludge into the nearby Clinch River watershed.

Summary of Environmental Laws and International Treaties

The AP Environmental Exam may include multiple-choice questions regarding environmental laws or international treaties. You may also be asked to provide an appropriate environmental law on a free-response question. On the free-response question, be sure you include a law that is applicable to the environmental issue at hand. Don't just select any environmental legislation assuming that it is appropriate for the question you are answering. It is important to remember some international environmental treaties have been ratified by many countries but **not** by the United States. The AP exam will expect you to know which treaties the United States is an active participant in. Below are the main environmental laws or international treaties arranged in the categories similar to the units you have studied in this review book.

Introduction to Environmental Science

National Environmental Policy Act (NEPA): requires federal agencies to integrate environmental values into their decision-making processes by considering the environmental impacts of their proposed actions; requires agencies to prepare an Environmental Impact Statement detailing impact to the surrounding environment.

Conservation of Biodiversity

Endangered Species Act: identifies threatened and endangered species in the United States, and puts their protection ahead of economic considerations.

Convention on International Trade in Endangered Species CITES (international treaty): lists species that cannot be commercially traded as live specimens or wildlife products.

Marine Mammal Protection Act: protects all marine mammals by prohibiting, with certain exceptions, the taking of marine mammals in U.S. waters and by U.S. citizens on the high seas, and the importation of marine mammals and marine mammal products into the United States.

Lacey Act: prohibits interstate transport of wild animals—dead or alive—without federal permit.

[handwritten margin note: Know at least 1 law in each category]

AGRICULTURE AND PESTICIDE USE

Federal Insecticide, Fungicide, Rodenticide Act: regulates the effectiveness of pesticides.

Food Quality Protection Act: sets pesticide limits in food, and all active and inactive ingredients must be screened for estrogenic/endocrine effects.

Persistent Organic Pollutants (POPs) Treaty (international treaty not ratified by the United States as of 2009): this treaty originated at the Stockholm convention. It is an international agreement to phase out 12 organic persistent pollutants, also known as the "dirty dozen," such as DDT and PCBs.

Pick 1 to Know

ENERGY AND MINING PRACTICES

Surface Mining Control and Reclamation Act: regulates coal mining activities in the United States and requires reclaiming of land after use.

Federal Mine Safety and Health Act: sets forth federal health and safety regulations for all coal and non-coal mining operations in the United States.

Energy Policy Act: this U.S. law provides incentives, typically in the form of government subsidies, for various energy resources including fossil fuels, and nuclear and alternative energy sources.

know 1

WATER RESOURCES AND POLLUTION

Safe Drinking Water Act: sets maximum contaminant levels for pollutants that may have adverse effects on human health.

Clean Water Act: sets maximum permissible amounts of water pollutants that can be discharged into waterways. Main goals are to reduce surface water pollution into lakes, rivers, and streams.

Water Quality Act: amended the Clean Water Act by addressing storm water pollution issues – requires industrial storm water discharges and municipal sewage discharge facilities to acquire permits.

Ocean Dumping Ban Act: bans dumping of sewage sludge and industrial waste in the ocean.

know 1

AIR POLLUTION

Clean Air Act: sets emission standards for cars, addresses requirements for reducing ozone depletion and acid deposition.

Kyoto Protocol (international agreement not signed by the United States as of early 2010): controls global warming by setting greenhouse gas emissions targets for developed countries.

Montreal Protocol (international agreement signed by the United States): phase-out of ozone-deleting substances such as chlorofluorocarbons (CFCs) and hydrochlorofluorocarbons (HCFCs).

WASTE DISPOSAL

Resource Conservation and Recovery Act: controls hazardous waste with cradle-to-grave system requirements.

Comprehensive Environmental Response, Compensation and Liability Act: identifies superfund sites – designed to identify and clean up abandoned hazardous waste dump sites (CERCLA).

Nuclear Waste Policy Act: encourages development of a U.S. high-level nuclear waste repository site by 2015 (original proposed site was Yucca Mountain, Nevada).

Low-Level Radioactive Policy Act: requires all states to have facilities to handle low-level radioactive wastes.

Basel Convention (international treaty not signed by the United States): treaty drafted as a result of hazardous waste from developed nations being shipped overseas to developing countries. It requires that developing countries must give full permission to accept the hazardous waste. As of early 2010, this treaty has been signed by 172 countries.

Part IV

Practice Tests

PRACTICE TEST 1

ENVIRONMENTAL SCIENCE
Section I: Multiple-Choice Questions
Time: 1 hour and 30 minutes
Number of Questions: 100

Part A

Directions: Each set of choices below, labeled A through E, will refer to a question or statement directly following the lettered choices. The questions or statements may also refer to a diagram or graph. Each lettered answer may be used more than once, only once, or not at all. Choose the one lettered choice you feel best answers the question or statement above.

Questions 1–4 refer to the map below.

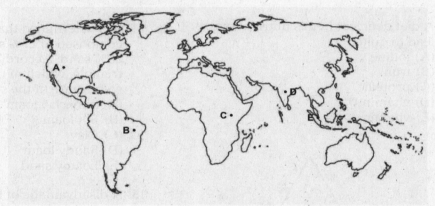

1. This country has the second largest population on earth.

2. Orangutans are endangered here due to the destruction of their habitat.

3. This country has undergone the most complete demographic transition.

4. The first national park system was established in this country.

Questions 5–8 refer to the numbers listed below.

(A) 1
(B) 10
(C) 100
(D) 1,000
(E) 1,000,000

5. The minimum number of half-lives that must pass before radioactive waste is reduced by a factor of 1000.

6. The concentration in ppb of a 1 ppm solution.

7. The approximate number of Fahrenheit degrees the earth has warmed in the past one hundred years.

8. The factor by which rainfall with a pH of 4.6 is more acidic than rainfall with a pH of 5.6.

Questions 9–12 refer to the national parks listed below.

(A) Everglades National Park
(B) Yellowstone National Park
(C) Grand Canyon National Park
(D) Yosemite National Park
(E) Great Smoky Mountains National Park

9. The most visited U.S. National Park, also known for the Appalachian Trail and the mist that hangs over its mountains and valleys.

10. Burmese pythons are an invasive species whose population is growing rapidly in this park.

11. The proposed site of a dam that was famously blocked by the Sierra Club in the 1960s.

12. Gray wolves were reintroduced to this park in 1995.

Part B

Directions: Five answer choices, lettered A through E, will follow each one of the following questions or incomplete statements below. The questions or statements may refer to a graph, diagram, or table. Choose the one answer that best fits each question or completes the statement.

13. A diet deficient in this nutrient may lead to goiter.
(A) iodine
(B) iron
(C) protein
(D) vitamin D
(E) vitamin A

14. It is determined that a soil sample is composed of 27% silt, 45% clay, and 28% sand. According to the soil triangle, which of the following is the soil texture of the soil?
(A) Silty clay loam
(B) Silt loam
(C) Clay
(D) Sandy loam
(E) Loamy sand

15. A disadvantage of liquefied natural gas is that it
(A) must be stored and transported at high temperatures
(B) produces more carbon dioxide than most other fossil fuels
(C) cannot be used in conventional power plants
(D) must be stored and transported at high pressure
(E) is less efficient than most other fossil fuels

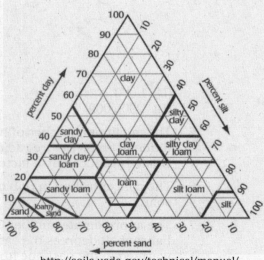

http://soils.usda.gov/technical/manual/print_version/chapter3.html

16. Which of the following has the lowest average net primary productivity?
(A) Swamps
(B) Savanna
(C) Tropical forest
(D) Tundra
(E) Coniferous forest

17. Ranges of active volcanoes are often abundant near
(A) convergent plate boundaries
(B) coastal estuaries
(C) divergent plate boundaries
(D) sub-bituminous coal deposits
(E) transform faults

18. The largest proven reserves of oil are located in
(A) the North Sea
(B) the Gulf of Mexico
(C) South America
(D) the Middle East
(E) Alaska

19. The pH of precipitation in the United States is highest in the
(A) southwest and lowest in the northwest
(B) southeast and lowest in the northeast
(C) southeast and lowest in the northwest
(D) southwest and lowest in the northeast
(E) northeast and lowest in the southwest

20. The active ingredient in most solar cells is
(A) iron
(B) silicon
(C) aluminum
(D) platinum
(E) oxygen

21. To most effectively capture solar energy in the United States, solar panels should be placed so that they face
(A) northwest
(B) north
(C) northeast
(D) west
(E) south

22. Bycatch refers to which of the following?
(A) a filtering method for removing particulates from coal smoke
(B) near-shore trawling for shellfish
(C) organisms that are unintentionally caught while fishing
(D) the harvesting of fish in arctic seas
(E) the harvesting of fish in tropical seas

23. Which of the following is least vulnerable to biomagnification?
(A) Bald eagle
(B) Human
(C) Bottlenose dolphin
(D) Moose
(E) Bluefin tuna

24. The population of a country is 6 million in 2010 and growing at a rate of 1.4% each year. If the rate of population growth remains constant, the population will reach 24 million in
(A) 2045
(B) 2050
(C) 2060
(D) 2080
(E) 3010

25. Of the following, the factor that is most directly responsible for the growth of the human population in the past one hundred years is
(A) increased numbers of women working outside the home
(B) improved birth control methods
(C) improved medical care and sanitation
(D) increased urbanization
(E) increased immigration

26. In the troposphere, oxygen is found primarily as ____, while nitrogen is found primarily as ____.
(A) O_3; N_2
(B) O_2; NO_2
(C) O; NO_2
(D) O_2; NH_3
(E) O_2; N_2

GO ON TO NEXT PAGE

27. Which of the following is used to determine soil texture?
    (A) The water content
    (B) The decomposition rate of organic material
    (C) The relative proportions of different particle sizes
    (D) The mineral composition
    (E) The dominant type of humus

28. Which of the following is true of oligotrophic lakes?
    (A) They have high nutrient levels and low productivity.
    (B) They have low nutrient levels and low productivity.
    (C) They have high nutrient levels and high productivity.
    (D) They have low nutrient levels and high productivity.
    (E) They have unpredictable nutrient levels and productivity.

29. Which of the following is true of estuaries?
    (A) The temperature and salinity change little during the day.
    (B) The temperature remains fairly constant during the day, but the salinity varies.
    (C) The temperature varies during the day, but the salinity remains fairly constant.
    (D) The temperature and salinity vary during the day.
    (E) The temperature remains fairly constant and they have no measurable salinity.

30. Which of the following is true of modern intensive farming practices?
    (A) They result in little or no change in species diversity.
    (B) They result in a sharp increase followed by a slow, steady decrease in species diversity.
    (C) They result in an increase in species diversity.
    (D) They result in a decrease in species diversity.
    (E) They result in unpredictable changes in species diversity.

31. Consider the following food chain:

    Switch grass → Grasshopper → Western fence lizard → Red-tailed hawk

    If each species feeds exclusively on this food chain, which of the following is most likely required to support a 1-kg hawk?
    (A) 10,000 kg of grass
    (B) 100 kg of grasshoppers
    (C) 1 kg of lizards
    (D) 1,000 kg of lizards
    (E) 100 kg of grass

32. Which of the following is a density-independent population control factor?
    (A) Predation
    (B) Disease
    (C) Habitat destruction
    (D) Parasitism
    (E) Competition

33. Primary succession occurs before secondary succession to
    (A) establish soil in the area
    (B) introduce early successional plants and animals
    (C) decompose fire-damaged vegetation
    (D) increase nutrient levels in the soil
    (E) provide moisture for the soil

34. Which of the following practices is most damaging to species of coral?
    (A) Pelagic whaling
    (B) Long-line fishing
    (C) Purse-seine fishing
    (D) Deep-sea aquaculture cages
    (E) Bottom trawling

35. Which of the following possesses the highest energy content?
    (A) Anthracite coal
    (B) Lignite
    (C) Bituminous coal
    (D) Biomass
    (E) Peat

36. The treaty that cut emissions of ozone-depleting compounds was signed in
    (A) Kyoto, Japan
    (B) Stockholm, Sweden
    (C) Montreal, Canada
    (D) Kona, Hawaii
    (E) Rio de Janeiro, Brazil

37. Which of the following is true about the Antarctic ozone "hole"?
    (A) It is about the same area all year and it rotates clockwise around the South Pole.
    (B) It is about the same area all year and it rotates counterclockwise around the South Pole.
    (C) It appears and disappears without warning and with no discernible pattern.
    (D) It is at its peak area during the Antarctic spring.
    (E) It is at its peak area during the Antarctic winter.

38. Of the following, the factors that best explain why the earth has seasons are
    (A) the tilt of the earth's axis and the rotation of the earth around its axis
    (B) the distance of the earth from the sun and the rotation of the earth around its axis
    (C) the tilt of the earth's axis and the distance of the earth from the sun
    (D) the orbit of the earth around the sun and the rotation of the earth around its axis
    (E) the tilt of the earth's axis and the orbit of the earth around the sun

39. The thawing of permafrost will most likely result in
    (A) additional water vapor in the atmosphere
    (B) less water vapor in the atmosphere
    (C) additional nitrogen oxides in the atmosphere
    (D) additional sulfur oxides in the atmosphere
    (E) additional methane in the atmosphere

40. Which of the following is a significant indoor air pollutant?
    (A) Sulfur dioxide
    (B) Formaldehyde
    (C) Dieldrin
    (D) Malathion
    (E) Dioxin

41. Which of the following is NOT identified by the EPA as one of its six criteria air pollutants?
    (A) Particulate matter
    (B) PANs
    (C) Lead
    (D) Ozone
    (E) Carbon monoxide

42. The air temperature increases with altitude, due to the destruction of ozone by ultraviolet light in the
    (A) stratosphere
    (B) lithosphere
    (C) aethenosphere
    (D) troposphere
    (E) mesosphere

43. Which of the following is the most likely to lead to acid rain?
    (A) The release of carbon dioxide from a coal-fired power plant
    (B) The release of carbon monoxide from automobiles
    (C) The release of sulfur dioxide from a coal-fired power plant
    (D) The release of methane from a cattle feedlot
    (E) The release of particulates from a coal-fired power plant

44. A company pollutes a river, rationalizing that they will release a small quantity of pollutants that will quickly be diluted and have little effect on the water quality of the river. This best illustrates a
    (A) synergistic interaction
    (B) negative feedback
    (C) positive feedback
    (D) tragedy of the commons
    (E) carcinogenic effect

GO ON TO NEXT PAGE

45. Which of the following is NOT a mechanism that is employed by plants to defend themselves against predators?
(A) Foul-smelling chemicals
(B) Clumping
(C) Thorns
(D) Toxic chemicals
(E) Thick bark

46. This law enables corporations to acquire large tracts of public land at far below market prices.
(A) the Endangered Species Act
(B) the General Mining Law
(C) the Lacey Act
(D) the Clean Air Act
(E) the Surface Mining Control and Reclamation Act

47. Which of the following is the natural source of ozone in the stratosphere?
(A) Photochemical reactions
(B) Combustion of fossil fuels
(C) Volcanic eruptions
(D) The spontaneous decay of diatomic oxygen
(E) Solar winds

48. The phosphorus and nitrogen concentration found in groundwater most likely would be greatest beneath
(A) undisturbed forest land
(B) an animal feedlot
(C) a coal-fired power plant
(D) an automobile salvage facility
(E) a petroleum refinery

49. Mountaintop removal is associated with which of the following?
(A) Geothermal energy
(B) Rice cultivation
(C) Coal mining
(D) Irrigation
(E) Hog farming

50. The _____ is an endangered species; the _____ is an invasive species; and the _____ is an extinct species.
(A) passenger pigeon; American alligator; dodo
(B) giant panda; Zebra mussel; California condor
(C) whooping crane; Africanized honeybee; passenger pigeon
(D) African black rhinoceros; dodo; Africanized honeybee
(E) giraffe; gypsy moth; blue whale

51. Catalytic converters remove which of the following from automobile exhaust?
I. Carbon monoxide
II. Carbon dioxide
III. Nitrogen dioxide

(A) I only
(B) II only
(C) III only
(D) I and II only
(E) I and III only

52. A 2000-watt electric space heater was used for 3 hours and 30 minutes. How much energy did the heater use?
(A) 2000 W
(B) 7000 kWh
(C) 7 kWh
(D) 2 kW
(E) 6500 kWh

53. A Dobson unit measures the concentration of which of the following substances?
(A) CFCs
(B) Phosphorus
(C) UV-B radiation
(D) O-zone
(E) Carbon dioxide

54. Which of the following species is the best suited to be a successful invasive species?
(A) Giant panda
(B) Clownfish
(C) Emperor penguin
(D) American cockroach
(E) Adonis blue butterfly

Questions 55–57 refer to total and per capita U.S. production of municipal solid waste as shown in the graph below.

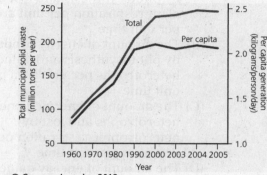

© Cengage Learning 2012

55. Use the graph to determine the total quantity of solid waste the average person in the United States generated during the 2005 calendar year. The amount is nearest
   (A) 2 kg
   (B) 200 kg
   (C) 350 kg
   (D) 750 kg
   (E) 2000 kg

56. The percent changes in total solid waste during the time periods from 1980–1990 and 2000–2005 is nearest
   (A) 1000% and 0%
   (B) 3 % and 25%
   (C) 50% and 5%
   (D) 30% and 2%
   (E) 100% and 0%

57. Which of the following best explains the trend in solid waste production between 1980 and 2005?
   (A) Additional consumption leading to more waste production
   (B) Increased awareness of air pollution problems associated with incineration that led to more waste being diverted to landfills
   (C) Increased recycling including curbside pickup of mixed recyclables
   (D) Additional export of solid waste to developing countries
   (E) Decreased consumption resulting in less production of consumables

58. Which of the following occurs during an ENSO event?
   (A) The north to south Arctic winds reverse directions.
   (B) Upwelling of warm nutrient-rich water in the South Pacific.
   (C) The east to west Pacific trade winds strengthen.
   (D) The east to west Pacific trade winds reverse directions.
   (E) Upwelling of cold nutrient-rich water off the west coast of South America.

59. As glacial ice melts, it exposes soil that absorbs more energy than ice, which causes it to get warmer, which melts more ice, exposing more soil, and so on. This is an example of
   (A) a tragedy of the commons
   (B) a point source of pollution
   (C) a negative feedback loop
   (D) a positive feedback loop
   (E) secondary succession

60. Well water is often contaminated with which naturally occurring element?
   (A) Mercury
   (B) MTBE
   (C) Lead
   (D) Arsenic
   (E) DDT

GO ON TO NEXT PAGE

61. Which of the following is true of the production of ammonium nitrate fertilizer?
   (A) It artificially completes the assimilation step of the nitrogen cycle and requires large inputs of fossil fuels.
   (B) It artificially completes the denitrification step of the nitrogen cycle and requires large input of fossil fuels.
   (C) It artificially completes the denitrification step of the nitrogen cycle and requires small inputs of fossil fuels.
   (D) It artificially completes the fixation step of the nitrogen cycle and requires small inputs of fossil fuels.
   (E) It artificially completes the fixation step of the nitrogen cycle and requires large inputs of fossil fuels.

62. Which of the following is an example of a brownfield?
   (A) The silted floodplains following a flood
   (B) An abandoned oil refinery
   (C) Abandoned farmland
   (D) The remains after a devastating forest fire
   (E) Recently harvested farmland

63. Which of the following is most likely to increase mutations in oceanic phytoplankton populations?
   (A) An increase in stratospheric ozone concentrations
   (B) A decrease in stratospheric ozone concentrations
   (C) An increase in tropospheric ozone concentrations
   (D) A decrease in tropospheric ozone concentrations
   (E) Atmospheric ozone concentrations do not affect oceanic phytoplankton populations

64. Which of the following is necessary to calculate the net primary productivity of an ecosystem?
   (A) The amount of energy produced by photosynthesis and lost by plant respiration per unit area per unit time
   (B) The amount of energy produced by photosynthesis and gained by heterotrophs per unit area per unit time
   (C) The amount of energy gained by heterotrophs and lost by heterotrophic respiration per unit area per unit time
   (D) The amount of energy gained by heterotrophs and lost by plant respiration per unit area per unit time
   (E) The amount of energy lost by plant respiration and lost by heterotrophic respiration per unit area per unit time

65. Consider the following population data, and determine the values of X, Y, and Z.

Country	Crude Birth Rate	Crude Death Rate	Population Growth Rate
Country A	45	26	X%
Country B	12	Y	0.3%
Country C	Z	11	1.1%

   (A) X = 19; Y = 11.7; Z = 12.1
   (B) X = 19; Y = 9; Z = 22
   (C) X = 9.5; Y = 5.85; Z = 6.05
   (D) X = 1.9; Y = 9; Z = 22
   (E) X = 1.9; Y = 12.3; Z = 12.1

66. Which of the following removes nitrogen from the atmosphere?
   (A) Fertilizer production
   (B) Decomposition
   (C) Forest fires
   (D) Denitrification
   (E) Burning coal

67. Which of the following areas would most likely have the highest biodiversity?
(A) A low altitude area near the equator
(B) A low altitude area at a polar latitude
(C) A high altitude area at a temperate latitude
(D) A high altitude area near the equator
(E) A high altitude area at a polar latitude

68. The size and isolation of an island will have the greatest effect on its
(A) elevation
(B) average temperature
(C) climate
(D) species diversity
(E) albedo

69. Consider the following: a red-billed oxpecker picks ticks off a black rhinoceros. The relationships between i) the oxpecker and the ticks; ii) the oxpecker and the rhinoceros; and iii) the ticks and the rhinoceros are best described as
(A) i) parasitism; ii) competition; and iii) commensalism
(B) i) predation; ii) mutualism; and iii) commensalism
(C) i) predation; ii) mutualism; and iii) parasitism
(D) i) commensalism; ii) parasitism; and iii) parasitism
(E) i) competition; ii) commensalism; and iii) parasitism

70. Which of the following would lead to a species' adapting quickly to environmental change?
(A) A role as a keystone species
(B) Short generational time periods
(C) A long life expectancy
(D) Bearing few offspring
(E) Reproducing late in life

71. Which of the following infectious diseases is not directly transmitted from human to human?
(A) Influenza
(B) Tuberculosis
(C) Measles
(D) Malaria
(E) HIV/AIDS

72. Which of the following is true of a 60-watt incandescent light bulb with an efficiency of 5%?
(A) It produces about 5 joules of light and 55 joules of heat per hour.
(B) It produces about 3 joules of light and 57 joules of heat per hour.
(C) It produces about 3 joules of light and 57 joules of heat per second.
(D) It produces about 5 joules of light and 55 joules of heat per minute.
(E) It produces about 3 joules of light and 57 joules of heat minute.

73. To feed the world's population an adequate diet, the total number of calories needed per day is nearest
(A) 7 billion
(B) 21 billion
(C) 700 billion
(D) 14 trillion
(E) 70 trillion

74. In a river, which of the following will most likely occur downstream as a result of the effluent discharge of a primary sewage treatment facility?
(A) An increase in the dissolved oxygen concentration of the river's water
(B) An increase in the biological oxygen demand of the river's water
(C) A decrease in the turbidity of the river's water
(D) A decrease in the pH of the river's water
(E) No change in the quality of the river's water

GO ON TO NEXT PAGE

75. If the relative humidity is 30%, the air temperature is 60°F, and the air temperature rises to 90°F without any additional moisture entering the atmosphere, which of the following is most likely?
    (A) The relative humidity will remain at 30%.
    (B) The relative humidity will increase and rain is unlikely.
    (C) The relative humidity will decrease and rain is unlikely.
    (D) The relative humidity will increase and it may rain.
    (E) The relative humidity will decrease and it may rain.

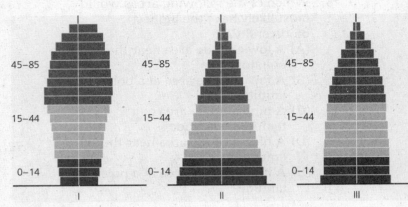

© Cengage Learning 2012

76. Replacement-level fertility in a developed nation is likely to be nearest
    (A) 1.4
    (B) 2.1
    (C) 2.5
    (D) 2.9
    (E) 3.5

77. Which of the following is removed by scrubbers installed in smokestacks?
    (A) Sulfur dioxide
    (B) Carbon dioxide
    (C) Lead
    (D) Carbon monoxide
    (E) Mercury

78. Which of the following is NOT an ecosystem service?
    (A) Pollination
    (B) Ozone depletion
    (C) Water purification
    (D) Nitrogen fixation
    (E) Soil formation

79. The LD-50s of five chemicals are listed below. Which is the most toxic?
    (A) 5 mg/kg body weight
    (B) 500 mg/kg body weight
    (C) 5 g/kg body weight
    (D) 50 g/kg body weight
    (E) 500 g/kg body weight

80. Arrange in order from fastest to slowest the population growth rate of the countries represented by the age structure diagrams above.
    (A) I, II, III
    (B) I, III, II
    (C) II, I, III
    (D) II, III, I
    (E) III, II, I

Questions 81–83 refer to the situation described below.

The citizens of Fremont notice that one area of Lake Fremont has fewer fish than other areas. The decreased fish population is near a power plant where lake water at 65°F is pumped out of the lake to cool equipment, and returned at 75°F. An experiment was conducted in which water from the lake was collected along with fish and divided equally into several large experimental aquariums. Each aquarium was maintained at a different temperature between 67°F and 76°F. The mortality rate of the fish population in each aquarium was monitored for several weeks. The fish were found to survive at the highest rate in the aquarium with 67°F water and at the lowest rate in the 76°F water.

81. The dependent variable in the experiment was
(A) the water temperature
(B) the species of fish
(C) the mortality rate of the fish
(D) the lake water
(E) the latitude of Lake Fremont

82. The independent variable in the experiment was
(A) the water temperature
(B) the species of fish
(C) the mortality rate of the fish
(D) the lake water
(E) the latitude of Lake Fremont

83. Of those listed below, the most plausible explanation for the experimental results is
(A) the biological oxygen demand in the water
(B) the dissolved oxygen concentration in the water
(C) pollutants washed off from the power plant equipment
(D) air pollutants mixing with lake water
(E) the pH of the water

84. A city with a population of 300,000 uses 8 million Btu of energy each day. The yearly per capita energy consumption in the city is nearest
(A) 10 thousand Btu
(B) 1 million Btu
(C) 10 million Btu
(D) 1 billion Btu
(E) 10 billion Btu

85. Which of the following has the greatest permeability?
(A) Silt
(B) Sand
(C) Humus
(D) Loam
(E) Clay

86. Which of the following is a major cause of cultural eutrophication?
(A) Global warming
(B) Pesticide runoff
(C) Organic waste
(D) Burning coal
(E) Fertilizer runoff

87. In general, what percentage of energy is transferred from one trophic level to the next?
(A) 0.1%
(B) 1%
(C) 3%
(D) 5%
(E) 10%

88. The worst nuclear accident in history occurred in which of the following locations?
(A) Love Canal, New York
(B) Valdez, Alaska
(C) Minamata, Japan
(D) Three Mile Island, Pennsylvania
(E) Chernobyl, Ukraine

89. Which of the following is most similar to overfishing?
(A) Mountaintop removal
(B) Malnutrition
(C) Slash and burn agriculture
(D) Overgrazing on public lands
(E) Water diversion

90. Which of the following species is extinct because of overhunting?
(A) Bald eagle
(B) Blue whale
(C) Passenger pigeon
(D) Whooping crane
(E) Orangutan

91. The most common form of renewable energy used by citizens of developing countries is
(A) solar
(B) coal
(C) wind
(D) biomass
(E) geothermal

92. Which of the following biomes is best suited for modern intensive agriculture?
(A) Chaparral
(B) Temperate grassland
(C) Deciduous forest
(D) Tundra
(E) Coniferous forest

GO ON TO NEXT PAGE

93. Which of the following occurs at an oil refinery?
    (A) Crude oil is separated into its components using their densities.
    (B) Crude oil is filtered to remove impurities and the filtrate is converted to gasoline.
    (C) Crude oil is burned to produce gasoline.
    (D) Crude oil is separated into its components using their boiling points.
    (E) Crude oil is separated into its components using their water solubility.

94. Which of the following decreases the amount of carbon dioxide in the troposphere?
    (A) Combustion
    (B) Decomposition
    (C) Respiration
    (D) Photosynthesis
    (E) Volcanic eruptions

95. Which of the following countries relies on geothermal energy to provide a large portion of its energy?
    (A) Iceland
    (B) India
    (C) Canada
    (D) Spain
    (E) Ireland

96. Rachel Carson is to DDT as
    (A) Leopold and Muir are to carbon dioxide
    (B) Pinchot is to water
    (C) Roland and Molina are to CFCs
    (D) Hardin is to fisheries
    (E) Carter is to OPEC

97. Which of the following is/are used to disinfect municipal water supplies?
    I.   Fluorine
    II. Ozone
    III. Chlorine

    (A) I only
    (B) II only
    (C) III only
    (D) I and III only
    (E) II and III only

98. If the population of the United States grows by 1% next year, the number of people who will be added to the population is nearest
    (A) 500 thousand
    (B) 1 million
    (C) 2 million
    (D) 3 million
    (E) 5 million

99. Which of the following is a feature of no-till agriculture?
    (A) Pesticides are allowed to naturally degrade after being applied.
    (B) No crop rotation takes place.
    (C) No artificial pesticides are used.
    (D) Trees are planted around fields to reduce wind erosion.
    (E) The land is not plowed.

100. The diversion of water from rivers that flow into a lake that has no outlet to the sea will increase the
    (A) volume of water in the lake
    (B) available bird habitat around the lake
    (C) recreational value of the lake
    (D) water quality of the lake
    (E) salinity of the lake

Section II: Free-Response Questions
Time: 1 Hour and 30 Minutes
Number of Questions: 4

Section II of the AP Environmental Science Exam counts for 40% of the total test grade. You will have four essay questions, each involving several parts. Calculators may not be used on the free-response section.

1) Read the following excerpt from a press release from the U.S. Environmental Protection Agency, and answer the questions that follow.

U.S. EPA PROPOSES PLAN TO ADDRESS CONTAMINATED FISH

SAN FRANCISCO – The U.S. Environmental Protection Agency today proposed a three-prong strategy to prevent people from consuming fish containing high levels of DDT and PCBs found in contaminated ocean sediments off the Palos Verdes peninsula.

"This is the largest DDT contamination site in the country," said EPA's regional Superfund division director. "The first step to protect public health is to make sure people aren't eating white croaker contaminated with dangerous levels of DDT."

The EPA plan recommends three short-term actions: increasing enforcement of the commercial fishing ban and recreational catch limit for white croaker along the Palos Verdes coast, educating people about fish consumption advisories, and monitoring contaminant levels in commercially sold fish to evaluate the effectiveness of enforcement measures.

For the past several years, the EPA has been investigating the 100 tons of DDT and 10 tons of PCBs that remain in ocean sediments on the Palos Verdes shelf. In ocean waters there, DDT concentrations have been recently measured at levels nearly 100 times greater than the California Ocean Plan objectives for the protection of human health.

In addition to the proposed plan released today, the EPA is continuing to evaluate capping a portion of the ocean floor with a layer of clean sediment. The cap would isolate the contaminants, reducing the amount of DDT and PCBs that flow from the deposit into ocean waters. The EPA will conduct a pilot-capping project later this year to help the agency refine cost estimates and determine the most effective cap placement methods.

---

http://osemite.epa.gov/opa/admpress.nsf/905a0f1800315fd385257359003d4808/b1cb7c1dd65de2fd852570d80 05e13a6!OpenDocument

a) Identify ONE use for DDT and ONE use for PCBs.
b) Identify a specific species that is not identified in the press release that has been affected by the use of DDT and discuss how DDT affected the population of that species.
c) The solution to the DDT/PCB problem off the Palos Verdes Peninsula has been to wait for the chemicals to break down into less harmful chemical by-products. Write an argument in support of this solution and write an argument opposed to this solution.

Another problem off the Palos Verdes Peninsula is elevated mercury levels in fish.

d) Explain why mercury levels are higher in bigger, older fish than they are in smaller, younger fish or fish lower on the food chain.

GO ON TO NEXT PAGE

2) The population of Fremont is 150,000 and the average daily per capita production of wastewater is 50 gallons. The city is planning to build a new wastewater treatment facility that incorporates primary, secondary, and tertiary treatment. During rainstorms, the peak inflow from runoff increases the volume of water that will flow into the plant by a factor of four.

  a) Calculate the total volume of wastewater that is generated daily by the citizens of Fremont.

  b) Calculate the minimum volume of wastewater that the new treatment facility must be capable of processing daily if it is built to handle all of the influent during peak periods.

  c) Explain how the city could treat all of the wastewater with a wastewater treatment plant less than half the size calculated above.

  d) Identify two pollutants that are removed during tertiary treatment, and discuss the environmental consequences of not removing one of those two pollutants.

  e) Currently, the wastewater treatment plant in Fremont only performs primary treatment, and it does so with insufficient capacity to treat inflows at peak volumes. Identify TWO infectious diseases that spread as a result of insufficient sewage treatment.

3) Although coral reefs occupy less than one-quarter of one percent of the world's oceans, they provide numerous ecosystem services. Currently, human activities are resulting in the destruction of coral reefs at an alarming rate. Some scientists believe that because of their extreme sensitivity to environmental change, coral reefs may serve as an early warning of more future damage to the life zones of the world's oceans.

  a) Describe the climatic and water conditions that are best suited for coral reef formation and identify a specific geographic region of the world's oceans where coral reefs can be found.

  b) Identify and describe THREE ecosystem services that coral reefs provide.

  c) Describe TWO human activities that contribute to the degradation and destruction of coral reefs, and explain how each activity contributes to the loss of coral reefs.

  d) Discuss ONE action that could be taken to reduce the destruction of coral reefs.

4) Once out of favor, nuclear energy is now being touted as a replacement for coal and a way of slowing global warming. As a result, for the first time in many years, the construction of new nuclear power plants is being proposed in the United States.

  a) Nuclear power fell out of public favor following two incidents at nuclear power plants. Identify the location of both of those incidents and for one of the incidents, briefly describe what happened.

  b) Describe the negative effects that the cooling of nuclear power plants has on the environment.

  c) New, advanced nuclear reactors are touted as safer than older reactors. Identify and describe ONE of the technological advances employed in these second-generation nuclear reactors.

  d) Discuss the assertion that nuclear energy is a feasible way of slowing global warming.

  e) Describe ONE currently used disposal method for nuclear fuel in the United States.

ANSWERS FOR MULTIPLE-CHOICE QUESTIONS

Using the table below, score your test. You will find explanations of the answers on the following pages.

1. D	21. E	41. B	61. E	81. C
2. E	22. A	42. A	62. B	82. A
3. A	23. D	43. C	63. B	83. B
4. A	24. E	44. D	64. A	84. A
5. B	25. C	45. B	65. D	85. B
6. D	26. E	46. B	66. A	86. E
7. A	27. C	47. A	67. A	87. E
8. B	28. B	48. B	68. D	88. E
9. E	29. D	49. C	69. C	89. D
10. A	30. D	50. C	70. B	90. C
11. C	31. B	51. D	71. D	91. D
12. B	32. C	52. C	72. C	92. B
13. A	33. A	53. D	73. D	93. D
14. C	34. E	54. D	74. B	94. D
15. D	35. A	55. D	75. C	95. A
16. D	36. C	56. D	76. B	96. C
17. A	37. D	57. C	77. A	97. E
18. D	38. E	58. D	78. B	98. D
19. D	39. E	59. D	79. A	99. E
20. B	40. B	60. D	80. D	100. E

1. **ANSWER: D.** India has the second largest population in the world with over 1.1 billion people. The population of India is growing at a faster rate than that of China with the world's largest population at 1.3 billion. By 2025, India will be close to overtaking China with the world's largest population (*Living in the Environment,* 16th ed., page 126 / 17th ed., page 127).

2. **ANSWER: E.** Orangutans are native in Indonesia where they are endangered due to habitat loss, which is largely the result of deforestation to clear land for palm oil plantations (*Living in the Environment*, 16th ed., page 189 / 17th ed., page 195).

3. **ANSWER: A.** The United States is the most developed country that is marked on the map. As the most developed country, the United States would have undergone the most complete demographic transition (*Living in the Environment*, 16th ed., pages 133–134 / 17th ed., pages 139–141).

4. **ANSWER: A.** The National Park System in the United States was the first such system in the world (*Living in the Environment*, 16th ed., pages 234–235 / 17th ed., page 236).

5. **ANSWER: B.** The half-life of a radioactive substance is the time it takes to reduce the amount of the substance by one half; after 10 half-lives, the amount of the radioactive substance is reduced by a factor of 1028 (2, 4, 8, 16, 32, 64, 128, 256, 512, 1028) (*Living in the Environment*, 16th ed., not included / 17th ed., not included).

6. **ANSWER: D.** 1ppm (part per million) is equivalent to 1,000ppb (parts per billion) (*Living in the Environment*, 16th ed., page G12 / 17th ed., page G11).

7. **ANSWER: A.** The average global surface temperature increased by about 1.3°F (0.74°C) between 1906 and 2005 (*Living in the Environment*, 16th ed., page 501 / 17th ed., page 497).

8. **ANSWER: B.** pH is a logarithmic scale, and a pH difference of one corresponds to a hydrogen ion concentration change of 10 to the first power (10^1) or 10. A pH difference of two would be a 100-fold change in acidity (10^2) (*Living in the Environment*, 16th ed., page S41 / 17th ed., page S13).

9. **ANSWER: E.** Great Smoky Mountains National Park is the most visited U.S. National Park. The Great Smoky Mountains were named for the blue mist that sits over the mountains and valleys like smoke. The Appalachian Trail passes through Great Smoky Mountains National Park (*Living in the Environment*, 16th ed., pages 234–235 / 17th ed., page 236).

10. **ANSWER: A.** Everglades National Park became a popular location for releasing unwanted pets, including Burmese pythons (*Living in the Environment*, 16th ed., page 200 / 17th ed., page 202).

11. **ANSWER: C.** Grand Canyon National Park was the proposed site of a dam that was successfully blocked by the Sierra Club, in part by employing the controversial advertisement in the *New York Times* entitled, "Would You Flood the Sistine Chapel so Tourists Could Get Closer to the Ceiling?" (*Living in the Environment*, 16th ed., not included / 17th ed., not included).

12. **ANSWER: B.** Gray wolves were reintroduced into Yellowstone National Park (*Living in the Environment*, 16th ed., page 214 / 17th ed., page 238).

13. **ANSWER: A.** Goiter is a malady that results from a deficiency of iodine in one's diet. The iodization of salt is done to prevent iodine deficiency (*Living in the Environment* 16th ed., page 272 / 17th ed., page 280).

14. **ANSWER: C.** Begin by extending the clay line horizontally to the right from 45% to meet the silt line coming down from 27% and the sand line coming up from 28%. They meet in the bottom of the clay region of the triangle (*Living in the*

Environment 16th ed., not included / 17th ed., not included).

15. **ANSWER: D.** Liquefied natural gas must be kept at low temperature and high pressure while it is transported. This requires much energy, which reduces the net energy yield for liquefied natural gas (*Living in the Environment*, 16th ed., page 381 / 17th ed., page 380).

16. **ANSWER: D.** Tundra has the lowest net primary productivity of the options listed. Only desert biomes have a lower net primary productivity than tundra (*Living in the Environment,* 16th ed., page 64 / 17th ed., page 66).

17. **ANSWER: A.** Most volcanoes form on continental plates at convergent plate boundaries where oceanic plates collide and move under continental plates (*Living in the Environment*, 16th ed., pages 347–348 / 17th ed., pages 348–349).

18. **ANSWER: D.** The largest proven reserves of crude oil are in the Middle East (*Living in the Environment,* 16th ed., page 376 / 17th ed., page 375).

19. **ANSWER: D.** The pH of precipitation in the United States is highest (least acidic) in the west and lowest (most acidic) in the east. The pH does not change significantly from north to south (*Living in the Environment*, 16th ed., page S9 / 17th ed., pages 477–478).

20. **ANSWER: B.** Silicon is the semiconducting element whose properties allow an electric current to result from its absorption of light energy (*Living in the Environment*, 16th ed., page 415 / 17th ed., pages 412–413).

21. **ANSWER: E.** In the northern hemisphere, the sun passes through the southern sky all year, making the southern side of a building the sunny side all year (*Living in the Environment*, 16th ed., page 411 / 17th ed., page 409).

22. **ANSWER: C.** Species that are caught inadvertently during fishing are referred to as bycatch. These species are often killed in the process of being caught and may include protected species such as turtles and dolphins (*Living in the Environment,* 16th ed., page 255 / 17th ed., page 259).

23. **ANSWER: D.** Biomagnification most severely affects species that occupy high trophic levels, like apex predators. Moose are herbivores that occupy the second trophic level. All of the other species listed are carnivores (*Living in the Environment*, 16th ed., page 202 / 17th ed., page 203).

24. **ANSWER: E.** Using the rule of 70, the doubling time of the population is 70/1.4 = 50 years. It will double twice to reach 24 million from 6 million; therefore, the year will be 2010 + (50 x 2) = 3010 (*Living in the Environment*, 16th ed., page G15 / 17th ed., page G14).

25. **ANSWER: C.** Improved medical care and sanitation have allowed the life expectancy of the world's population to rise, resulting in an increase in population even as birthrates fall. The other options either work to decrease population size or have little effect on population size (*Living in the Environment*, 16th ed., pages 128–129 / 17th ed., pages 126–127).

26. **ANSWER: E.** Both oxygen and nitrogen are found in the troposphere primarily as diatomic molecules (*Living in the Environment*, 16th ed., pages 59, 68 / 17th ed., pages 59, 71).

27. **ANSWER: C.** Soil texture is determined based on the relative proportions by weight of sand, silt, and clay (*Living in the Environment*, 16th ed., not included / 17th ed., not included).

28. **ANSWER: B.**   Oligotrophic lakes are characterized by low nutrient levels and low productivity. They typically have little plant or algae growth and high dissolved oxygen levels (*Living in the Environment*, 16th ed., page 174 / 17th ed., page 181).

29. **ANSWER: D.**   An estuary is a coastal wetland at the mouth of a river where freshwater mixes with saltwater. It is characterized by daily changes in water temperature and salinity that cycles with the tides (*Living in the Environment*, 16th ed., pages 166–168 / 17th ed., pages 173–175).

30. **ANSWER: D.**   Modern farming practices employ monocultures, which reduce the species diversity of the area. They also require large inputs of artificial fertilizers, pesticides, irrigation water, and fossil fuels (*Living in the Environment*, 16th ed., page 286 / 17th ed., page 281).

31. **ANSWER: B.**   In a typical food web 10% of the energy that is transferred to each successive trophic level is converted to body mass. The remaining energy is converted to waste heat. In this example, the 1-kg hawk would require 10 kg of lizards, 100 kg of grasshoppers, and 1,000 kg of grass (*Living in the Environment*, 16th ed., pages 62–63 / 17th ed., pages 64–65).

32. **ANSWER: C.**   Habitat destruction, whether by humans or a flood, volcano, tsunami, or other natural events, will affect population growth regardless of population density. The effectiveness of the other factors to control population size is dependent on the density of the population (*Living in the Environment*, 16th ed., page 113 / 17th ed., page 117).

33. **ANSWER: A.**   Primary succession establishes soil in an area prior to secondary succession, which will establish an ecological community in the area (*Living in the Environment*, 16th ed., page 116 / 17th ed., page 119).

34. **ANSWER: E.**   Bottom trawlers drag chainmail nets over the seafloor to collect bottom-dwelling shellfish, crustaceans, and mollusks. When dragged over coral reefs, trawler nets will severely damage or destroy the reef (*Living in the Environment*, 16th ed., page 251 / 17th ed., page 252).

35. **ANSWER: A.**   Anthracite coal is the oldest of the ranks of coal and the most dense, both by weight and energy content (*Living in the Environment*, 16th ed., page 383 / 17th ed., page 382).

36. **ANSWER: C.**   The Montreal Protocol was signed in Montreal, Canada. The treaty restricts the production and use of ozone depleting chemicals such as CFCs, halons, and methyl bromide (*Living in the Environment*, 16th ed., page 527 / 17th ed., page 523).

37. **ANSWER: D.**   The Antarctic ozone hole varies in size throughout the year, making its first appearance and reaching its largest area during the spring (October) in Antarctica. It rotates counterclockwise around the South Pole, but it varies in area (*Living in the Environment*, 16th ed., page 523 / 17th ed., page 521).

38. **ANSWER: E.**   The tilt of the earth and its rotation around the sun are the two factors that determine the earth's seasons (*Living in the Environment*, 16th ed., page 141 / 17th ed., pages 148–150).

39. **ANSWER: E.** The thawing of permafrost will release methane and carbon dioxide into the troposphere. This could lead to additional heating, which would melt more permafrost and release more methane, which would increase

warming, and so on. This is an example of positive feedback (*Living in the Environment*, 16th ed., page 510 / 17th ed., page 497).

40. ANSWER: **B.**   Formaldehyde is a common chemical found in building materials and products used indoors (*Living in the Environment*, 16th ed., pages 484–485 / 17th ed., pages 482–483).

41. ANSWER: **B.**   The six criteria air pollutants are ozone, lead, nitrogen dioxide, particulate matter, sulfur dioxide, and carbon monoxide (*Living in the Environment*, 16th ed., page 488 / 17th ed., page 485).

42. ANSWER: **A.**   The reaction between ozone and ultraviolet light occurs in the stratosphere and generates heat; as a result, the temperature in the stratosphere increases with increasing altitude (*Living in the Environment*, 16th ed., page 470 / 17th ed., page 467).

43. ANSWER: **C.**   Sulfur dioxide, along with nitrogen oxides, is the precursor to acid rain (*Living in the Environment*, 16th ed., page 479 / 17th ed., page 470).

44. ANSWER: **D.**   This is an example of a tragedy of the commons. In this case the commons is the river. The company's perceived small impact on a large resource, like the proverbial herdsman placing additional animals onto a publicly-owned pasture, is the tragedy (*Living in the Environment*, 16th ed., page 13 / 17th ed., page 15).

45. ANSWER: **B.**   Clumping will likely have the opposite effect of making the plant more vulnerable to predators. All of the other options are adaptations that make plants less vulnerable to predators (*Living in the Environment*, 16th ed., pages 102–103 / 17th ed., pages 107–108).

46. ANSWER: **B.**   The General Mining Law of 1872 still allows corporations to acquire land at prices that are far below market value (*Living in the Environment*, 16th ed., pages 363–364 / 17th ed., pages 362–363).

47. ANSWER: **A.**   Ozone forms in the stratosphere during photochemical reactions when ultraviolet light breaks the bonds between the atoms of a diatomic oxygen molecule and the oxygen atoms react with another oxygen molecule, forming ozone (*Living in the Environment*, 16th ed., page 470 / 17th ed., pages 467–468).

48. ANSWER: **B.**   Phosphorus and nitrogen run off in large quantities of animal wastes from feedlots, after which they can enter groundwater (*Living in the Environment*, 16th ed., page 539 / 17th ed., pages 536–537).

49. ANSWER: **C.**   Mountaintop removal is a type of surface (strip) mining in which heavy equipment removes mountaintops to expose coal seams for removal by more equipment (*Living in the Environment*, 16th ed., page 358 / 17th ed., page 357).

50. ANSWER: **C.**   The whooping crane is an endangered species, the Africanized honeybee is an invasive species, and the passenger pigeon is an extinct species (*Living in the Environment*, 16th ed., pages 185, 187, 199 / 17th ed., pages 193, 194, 200).

51. ANSWER: **D.**   Catalytic converters remove carbon monoxide from exhaust by oxidizing it to carbon dioxide, and nitrogen oxides by reducing them to nitrogen and oxygen (*Living in the Environment*, 16th ed., not included / 17th ed., not included).

52. ANSWER: **C.**   Power is defined as energy use per unit time. To calculate the

energy used, multiply power and time to get: 2 kW x 3.5 hours = 7 kWh (*Living in the Environment*, 16th ed., not included / 17th ed., not included).

53. **ANSWER: D.** A Dobson unit (DU) is the unit used for the measurement of ozone concentration. One DU is equivalent to a column of ozone 0.01 mm thick at a temperature of 0°C and 1 atmosphere pressure (*Living in the Environment*, 16th ed., page 523 / 17th ed., not included).

54. **ANSWER: D.** Successful invasive species are generalists with a wide range of tolerance limits. In this case the American cockroach is an outstanding candidate (*Living in the Environment*, 16th ed., page 201 / 17th ed., page 193).

55. **ANSWER: D.** The per capita generation according to the graph is slightly greater than 2.0 kg/person/day; therefore in one year, a person generates slightly more than approximately 2.0 kg/person/day × 365 days/year = 730 kg/person/year. The nearest answer is 750 kg (*Living in the Environment*, 16th ed., not included / 17th ed., not included).

56. **ANSWER: D.** The change from 1980 to 1990 is from approximately 150 million to 200 million tons; the percent change is (200 − 150)/150 × 100 = 33%. From 2000 to 2005 the change is from approximately 230 million to 235 million tons (you may get something slightly different, but you should recognize a slight increase between 2000 and 2005); the percent change is (235 − 230)/230 = 2%. The nearest answer is 30% and 2% (*Living in the Environment*, 16th ed., not included / 17th ed., not included).

57. **ANSWER: C.** The trend is a decrease in the amount of solid waste produced per capita. A corresponding increase in recycling has also occurred during that time (*Living in the Environment*, 16th ed., page 563 / 17th ed., page 561).

58. **ANSWER: D.** During an El Niño Southern Oscillation, the east to west Pacific trade winds reverse directions (*Living in the Environment*, 16th ed., page S48 / 17th ed., pages S26–S28).

59. **ANSWER: D.** In the system described, the original disturbance, melting glacial ice, results in a series of changes to the system that eventually results in additional melting of ice. This is an example of positive feedback (*Living in the Environment*, 16th ed., page 45 / 17th ed., page 49).

60. **ANSWER: D.** Arsenic is commonly found in groundwater due to naturally occurring arsenic deposits in soils and rocks (*Living in the Environment*, 16th ed., page 544 / 17th ed., pages 540–541).

61. **ANSWER: E.** Ammonium nitrate is an inorganic fertilizer that is produced by taking atmospheric nitrogen and fixing it by inputting large quantities of fossil fuels (*Living in the Environment*, 16th ed., page 69 / 17th ed., page 72).

62. **ANSWER: B.** A brownfield is an abandoned industrial site such as a factory, gas station, power plant, steel mill, etc. (*Living in the Environment*, 16th ed., page 583 / 17th ed., page 579).

63. **ANSWER: B.** A decrease in stratospheric ozone concentrations will lead to an increase in UV radiation capable of ionizing cellular DNA in oceanic phytoplankton, leading to mutations (*Living in the Environment*, 16th ed., pages 524–525 / 17th ed., page 523).

64. **ANSWER: A.** The net primary productivity of an ecosystem is a measure of the amount of energy converted to biomass that is produced less the amount of

energy lost by respiration per unit area per unit time in the ecosystem (*Living in the Environment*, 16th ed., page 64 / 17th ed., page 65).

65. **ANSWER: D.** The percentage growth rate of a population in the table is the difference between the birth rates and the death rates. To determine the growth rates as a percentage (per 100) from the crude rates (per 1000) divide by 10, or move the decimal one place to the left (*Living in the Environment*, 16th ed., page 126 / 17th ed., page 130).

66. **ANSWER: A.** Fertilizer production removes nitrogen from the atmosphere and artificially fixes it to produce nitrogen-based fertilizers. All of the other options add nitrogen or have no effect on the amount of nitrogen in the atmosphere (*Living in the Environment*, 16th ed., page 69 / 17th ed., page 72).

67. **ANSWER: A.** The highest biodiversity on earth can be found near the equator (at low latitudes) and at low elevations (*Living in the Environment*, 16th ed., page 90 / 17th ed., page 94).

68. **ANSWER: D.** The theory of island biogeography predicts that small, isolated islands will have the lowest species diversity as well as the highest extinction rates and lowest immigration rates, and that large nearby islands will have the highest species diversity as well as the lowest extinction rates and highest immigration rates (*Living in the Environment*, 16th ed., page 90 / 17th ed., page 94).

69. **ANSWER: C.** The oxpecker preys on the ticks. The oxpecker and the rhinoceros both benefit from each other. The ticks are parasites on the rhinoceros (*Living in the Environment*, 16th ed., pages 105–106 / 17th ed., pages 110–111).

70. **ANSWER: B.** Species that adapt quickly to environmental change are those with characteristics typical of r-strategists, including short generational time periods (*Living in the Environment*, 16th ed., page 112 / 17th ed., page 117).

71. **ANSWER: D.** Malaria is a tropical disease caused by a parasite that is spread by the bite of the female *Anopheles* mosquito (*Living in the Environment*, 16th ed., pages 444–447 / 17th ed., pages 443–445).

72. **ANSWER: C.** The efficiency of five percent means that five percent of sixty watts, or three watts, of light will be created—the remaining 57 watts will be waste heat. A watt is a joule per second; therefore the bulb produces about 3 joules of light and 57 joules of heat per second (*Living in the Environment*, 16th ed., pages 401–402 / 17th ed., pages 398–399).

73. **ANSWER: D.** To live an active, healthy life, people need on average about 2200 calories each day. With nearly 7 billion people needing 2200 calories, approximately 14 trillion calories are needed (*Living in the Environment*, 16th ed., not included / 17th ed., not included).

74. **ANSWER: B.** The discharge from primary sewage treatment is classified as organic waste, and its decomposition will result in a decrease in the dissolved oxygen concentration and an increase in the biological oxygen demand in the river downstream from the discharge (*Living in the Environment*, 16th ed., pages 535–536 / 17th ed., pages 533–534).

75. **ANSWER: C.** The relative humidity is the percentage of water content in the air, where 100% humidity is the condition when the air is saturated with moisture. The amount of water that can be present in the atmosphere increases as the temperature increases; therefore, as the temperature rises the relative humidity

will decrease when the amount of water in the atmosphere remains constant. The chance of rain increases as the relative humidity approaches 100% (*Living in the Environment,* 16th ed., not included / 17th ed., not included).

76. **ANSWER: B.** The replacement-level fertility is the average number of children a couple must bear to replace themselves in the population. In most developed countries the replacement-level fertility is slightly higher than 2.0 (*Living in the Environment,* 16th ed., page 126 / 17th ed., page 130).

77. **ANSWER: A.** Scrubbers spray mists of calcium carbonate or calcium oxide solutions into the smoke created by burning coal to remove sulfur dioxide (*Living in the Environment,* 16th ed., not included / 17th ed., not included).

78. **ANSWER: B.** Ozone depletion is an environmental problem. All of the other options are ecosystem services (*Living in the Environment,* 16th ed., page 523 / 17th ed., page 521).

79. **ANSWER: A.** The LD-50 with the smallest dose per unit of body weight is the most toxic (*Living in the Environment,* 16th ed., pages 455–456 / 17th ed., page 453).

80. **ANSWER: D.** The fastest growing population is II (the broadest base) followed by III, and then I (the narrowest base) (*Living in the Environment,* 16th ed., page 131 / 17th ed., pages 135–136).

81. **ANSWER: C.** The dependent variable is the variable that is measured during the experiment. In this case the dependent variable is the mortality rate of the fish (*Living in the Environment,* 16th ed., not included / 17th ed., not included).

82. **ANSWER: A.** The independent variable is the variable that is manipulated by the experimenter. In this case, the independent variable is the water temperature (*Living in the Environment,* 16th ed., not included / 17th ed., not included).

83. **ANSWER: B.** The dissolved oxygen levels in water decrease as the water temperature increases, and fish are very sensitive to dissolved oxygen levels (*Living in the Environment,* 16th ed., not included / 17th ed., not included).

84. **ANSWER: A.** Per capita means per person; therefore: (8×10^6 Btu/day x 3.65×10^2 days/year)/3×10^5 people = 9733 Btu/person, which is closest to 10 thousand Btu (*Living in the Environment,* 16th ed., not included / 17th ed., not included).

85. **ANSWER: B.** Sand, the largest particle size listed, has the greatest permeability (*Living in the Environment,* 16th ed., not included / 17th ed., not included).

86. **ANSWER: E.** Cultural eutrophication is caused by the nitrogen and phosphorus fertilizers in agricultural runoff (*Living in the Environment,* 16th ed., pages 539–540 / 17th ed., pages 536–537).

87. **ANSWER: E.** Approximately ten percent of the energy at one trophic level is transferred to the next with the remaining ninety percent lost as waste heat (*Living in the Environment,* 16th ed., pages 62–63 / 17th ed., pages 63–64).

88. **ANSWER: E.** The worst nuclear accident in history occurred in Chernobyl, Ukraine, in the former Soviet Union (*Living in the Environment,* 16th ed., page 390 / 17th ed., page 389).

89. **ANSWER: D.** Overfishing and overgrazing on public lands are both examples of tragedies of the commons (*Living in the Environment,* 16th ed., page 13 / 17th ed., page 15).

90. **ANSWER: C.** The passenger pigeon became extinct when it was hunted for food in the 19th century (*Living in the Environment*, 16th ed., page 183 / 17th ed., pages 194–195).

91. **ANSWER: D.** Biomass is the most commonly used form of renewable energy in developing countries (*Living in the Environment*, 16th ed., page 422 / 17th ed., page 419).

92. **ANSWER: B.** Temperate grasslands have deep, fertile soils that are well suited for growing crops. Unfortunately, when the native grasses are removed along with their tangled root network, the topsoil becomes vulnerable to severe wind erosion (*Living in the Environment*, 16th ed., page 150 / 17th ed., pages 157–158).

93. **ANSWER: D.** Oil refineries make use of a process called fractional distillation to separate crude oil into its components based on their boiling points (*Living in the Environment*, 16th ed., page 375 / 17th ed., page 375).

94. **ANSWER: D.** Photosynthesis converts carbon dioxide and water into sugar and oxygen. All the other options increase the amount of carbon dioxide in the atmosphere (*Living in the Environment*, 16th ed., page 59 / 17th ed., page 59).

95. **ANSWER: A.** Iceland lies on the mid-Atlantic Ridge, an area that is ideally situated to tap heat that lies near the surface of the earth (*Living in the Environment*, 16th ed., page 399 / 17th ed., page 425).

96. **ANSWER: C.** Rachel Carson's book, *Silent Spring*, raised public awareness about the environmental hazards of the pesticide DDT in much the same way as the publication of the research of F. Sherwood Rowland and Mario Molina raised public awareness about the role CFCs play in the depletion of stratospheric ozone (*Living in the Environment*, 16th ed., pages 295, 524 / 17th ed., pages 298, 522).

97. **ANSWER: E.** Ozone and chlorine are used to disinfect water supplies (*Living in the Environment*, 16th ed., page 554 / 17th ed., page 551).

98. **ANSWER: D.** The U.S. population is slightly more than 300 million people. One percent of 300 million is 3 million (*Living in the Environment*, 16th ed., page 126 / 17th ed., page 127).

99. **ANSWER: E.** Tilling refers to plowing the soil; no-till refers to not plowing the soil (*Living in the Environment*, 16th ed., page 303 / 17th ed., page 306).

100. **ANSWER: E.** The diversion of water from lakes or inland seas with no outlet to the sea will result in an increase in salinity of the lake's water. Examples include the Aral Sea in the former Soviet Union and Mono Lake in California (*Living in the Environment*, 16th ed., pages 330–331 / 17th ed., pages 332–333).

SCORING GUIDELINES FOR FREE-RESPONSE QUESTIONS

1. (a) Identify ONE use for DDT and ONE use for PCBs.

    2 points can be earned—1 point for a correct use for DDT and 1 point for a correct use for PCBs
    DDT – Used as pesticide, especially in developing countries, for control of the *Anopheles* mosquito, carrier of the microbe that causes malaria.

PCBs – used as electrical insulators, lubricants, hydraulic fluid, and as an ingredient in paints, fire retardants, adhesives, preservatives, and pesticides.

(b) Identify a specific species that is not identified in the press release that has been affected by the use of DDT and discuss how DDT affected the population of that species.

3 points can be earned—1 point for correctly identifying a species and 2 points for the discussion (1 point for correctly describing how biomagnification concentrates DDT and PCBs in higher trophic levels and 1 point for the effect that led to the demise)
Species – bald eagle, brown pelican, cormorant, peregrine falcon, osprey, songbirds (must identify a specific species for example, a robin, jay, wren or dove).
Biomagnification – DDT is not easily broken down so it persists in the environment. Moreover, it is fat soluble so it accumulates in the liver and other fatty tissues of prey species. This leads to increased concentrations in higher trophic levels.
Effects – Decreased fecundity or reproductive success as a result of the fragility of eggshells; low sperm counts; crossed or otherwise deformed beaks; feminization of males; small penises; or the presence of both male and female sex organs in individuals.

(c) The solution to the DDT/PCB problem off the Palos Verdes Peninsula has been to wait for the chemicals to break down into less harmful chemical by-products. Write an argument in support of this solution and write an argument opposed to this solution.

4 points can be earned—2 points for each argument

In support of waiting for the chemicals to break down:

1 point for each correct supporting statement—2 points maximum
Trying to remove the deposit will disturb the chemicals, re-releasing them into the water.
It is not possible to clean up the entire deposit.
Disturbing the sea floor will damage ecosystems.
Cleanup is expensive and money should be used elsewhere.

In opposition to waiting for the chemicals to break down:

1 point for each correct supporting statement—2 points maximum
The chemicals will continue to enter food chains for hundreds of years.
Humans have a moral responsibility to cleanup hazardous materials.
People will continue to get sick or die from seafood contamination.

(d) Explain why mercury levels are higher in bigger, older fish than they are in smaller, younger fish or fish lower in the food chain.

2 points can be earned—1 point explaining how biomagnification leads to high concentrations in large fish and 1 point for explaining how bioaccumulation leads to higher concentrations in older fish

Mercury biomagnifies and its concentration is highest in the highest trophic levels. The fish that occupy the highest trophic levels are large fish.

Mercury bioaccumulates and its concentration increases as an organism ages. The oldest fish will have the highest mercury concentrations.

2. (a) Calculate the total volume of wastewater that is generated daily by the citizens of Fremont.

2 points can be earned—1 point for a correct setup and 1 point for the correct answer with units

$$5 \times 10^1 \frac{\text{gallons}}{\text{person-day}} \times 1.5 \times 10^5 \text{ people} = 7.5 \times 10^6 \frac{\text{gallons}}{\text{day}}$$

(The unit for time – day – is not required since the question asked for the daily volume.)

(b) Calculate the minimum volume of wastewater that the new treatment facility must be capable of processing daily if it is built to handle all of the influent during peak periods.

1 point can be earned for the correct answer with units

$$7.5 \times 10^6 \frac{\text{gallons}}{\text{day}} \times 4 = 3 \times 10^7 \frac{\text{gallons}}{\text{day}}$$

(The unit for time – day – is not required since the question asked for the daily volume.)

(c) Explain how the city could treat all of the wastewater with a wastewater treatment plant less than half the size calculated above.

1 point can be earned for a correct explanation
Install a separate system for the runoff to allow it to be diverted past the treatment plant.
(Reducing residential output alone is not acceptable since even if all residential sewage is stopped, the peak volume will still be 75% of the current amount)

(d) Identify two pollutants that are removed during tertiary treatment, and discuss the environmental consequences of not removing one of those two pollutants.

4 points can be earned—1 point for each correctly identified pollutant
Pollutants removed by tertiary treatment: nitrogen or phosphorus

Consequence	Environmental effect
Increased algal blooms	Increased fish mortality
Increased plant growth	Disruption of food chains
Eutrophication	Inability of native species to compete in hypoxic conditions
Decreased dissolved oxygen	Reduced biodiversity and poorer health of aquatic life

(e) Currently, the wastewater treatment plant in Fremont only performs primary treatment, and it does so with insufficient capacity to treat inflows at peak volumes. Identify TWO infectious diseases that spread as a result of insufficient sewage treatment.

2 points can be earned—1 point for each correct infectious disease
Infectious diseases – Cholera; giardiasis; hepatitis; typhoid; cryptosporidiosis

3. (a) Describe the climatic and water conditions that are best suited for coral reef formation and identify a specific geographic region of the world's oceans in where coral reefs can be found.

3 points can be earned—1 point for a correct description of climatic conditions, 1 point for a correct description of water conditions, and 1 point for a correct geographic region
Climatic conditions – warm; hot; reliable sunlight; intense sunlight
Water conditions – warm; clear; nutrient-rich; shallow
Geographic regions – shallow tropical and sub-tropical seas – e.g., Florida Keys, Mexico and Central American Coasts, Hawaii, Australia

(b) Identify and describe THREE ecosystem services that coral reefs provide.

3 points can be earned—1 point for each correct description of an ecosystem service

Ecosystem Service	Description
Food production	Maintain habitats and nurseries for fisheries that provide food
Protection	Shelter the coastline from the direct impact of severe storms
Carbon storage	Remove carbon from the atmosphere and provide long-term storage on the seafloor
Pharmaceuticals	Natural products extracted from marine organisms are used in pharmaceuticals that improve human health
Recreation	Resorts attract tourists who participate in snorkeling, scuba diving, and other activities associated with coral reefs that improve the local economy
Climate regulation	Removal of carbon dioxide from the atmosphere decreases greenhouse gases, which reduces the effects of global climate change
Job creation	Fishing and recreation provide jobs, reducing poverty and the associated environmental impact

(c) Describe TWO human activities that contribute to the degradation and destruction of coral reefs, and explain how each activity contributes to the loss of coral reefs.

2 points can be earned—1 point for each correct human activity

Human Activity	Contribution to Coral Loss
Bottom Trawling	Destruction of coral reef habitat by dragging trawling net across the sea floor
Overfishing	Loss of species diversity, disruption of food chains (elimination of predator/prey species)
Construction, development, or deforestation along the coast	Sediment pollution from runoff, reducing visibility; sunlight penetration, killing plant life below the surface and bleaching coral
Agriculture along the coast	Sediment pollution from runoff, reducing visibility; sunlight penetration, killing plant life below the surface and bleaching coral
Fertilizer/nutrient runoff	Algae blooms that block sunlight, reducing visibility and killing plant life below the surface
Pesticide runoff	The poisoning of sea life
Introduction of invasive species (for example, from the ballast tanks, bilge pumps, and bait tanks of vessels from distant ports)	Introduced species out-compete native species for resources, causing extinction
Burning of fossil fuels	Global warming resulting in warmer seas, causing coral bleaching Increase in CO_2 concentrations acidify ocean water which can cause corals to dissolve

(d) Discuss ONE action that could be taken to reduce the destruction of coral reefs.

2 points can be earned—1 point for a correct action that can be taken and 1 point for discussing how the action would reduce the destruction of coral reefs

Action	Means of Reduction
Stop eating seafood caught using fishing methods that damage reefs	Less demand for fish leading to less destructive fishing practices

Action	Means of Reduction
Stop buying products made from raw materials harvested from coral reefs	Less demand for products leading to less harvesting of resources from coral reefs
Stop supporting businesses that encourage activities that result in sediment pollution in areas that have coral reefs	Pressure on businesses will lead to less sediment production and pollution
Visit areas with coral reefs and participate in the associated recreational activities that support the local economy	Provides capital and incentive to maintain healthy coral reefs
Reduce fossil fuel use	Reduces CO_2 concentrations in the oceans reducing the threat of acidic waters dissolving coral or warming oceans bleaching coral

4. (a) Nuclear power fell out of public favor following two incidents at nuclear power plants. Identify the location of both of those incidents and for one of the incidents, briefly describe what happened.

3 points can be earned—1 point for each correct incident and 1 point for a correct description of one of the incidents

Chernobyl – Meltdown of a nuclear reactor that occurred in Ukraine in 1987. Released massive quantity of radioactive gas that will increase cancer rates for millions of Europeans.

Three Mile Island – Loss of coolant accident that led to the release of radioactive gas in a nuclear power plant in Pennsylvania in 1979. A more serious accident was narrowly avoided.

(b) Describe the negative effects that the cooling of nuclear power plants has on the environment.

2 points can be earned—1 point for describing thermal pollution and 1 point for making the connection to lower levels of dissolved oxygen

The cooling of nuclear power plants leads to thermal pollution.

When cooling water is drawn out of rivers, lakes and oceans, and returned at elevated temperatures, the dissolved oxygen levels can fall outside the tolerance limits of some aquatic species. This can lead to a loss of species diversity.

(c) New, advanced nuclear reactors are touted as safer than older reactors. Identify and describe ONE of the technological advances employed in these second-generation nuclear reactors.

2 points can be earned—1 point for a correct new reactor and 1 point for a correct description

Advanced light water reactors or high-temperature, gas-cooled reactors – cooled by gas rather than water, increasing safety.

Pebble bed modular reactor – uses fuel pellets that are more manageable rather than rods. Also, cooled by gas rather than water, increasing safety.

Modular designs lead to smaller reactors that are inherently safer.

(d) Discuss the assertion that nuclear energy is a feasible way of slowing global warming.

2 points can be earned—1 point for each correct statement in the discussion

The production of nuclear power emits less carbon dioxide than burning coal.

The production of nuclear power still emits some carbon dioxide during mining, processing, transportation and disposal of the fuel.

Nuclear power is a nonrenewable resource and will need to be replaced in the future.

There is no long-term storage facility for spent nuclear fuel and onsite storage may prove more hazardous than global warming.

A nuclear meltdown may be more hazardous than the threat of global warming.

(e) Describe ONE currently used disposal method for spent nuclear fuel in the United States.

1 point can be earned for a correct description of current practice for the storage of spent nuclear fuel
It is stored on the site of the nuclear power plant in water-filled pools and dry casks above and below ground outside the containment shell of the reactor.

CALCULATING YOUR SCORE

This scoring worksheet is based on the 2008 AP Environmental Science released exam. While the AP grade conversion chart is NOT the same for each testing year, it gives you an approximate breakdown.

SECTION 1: MULTIPLE CHOICE

$$\underline{\hspace{4cm}} \times 0.90 = \underline{\hspace{4cm}}$$

Number Correct (out of 100)   Weighted Section I Score

SECTION II: FREE RESPONSE

Document-Based Question $\dfrac{\underline{\hspace{2cm}}}{\text{Score}} \times 1.50 = \dfrac{\underline{\hspace{2cm}}}{(Do\ not\ round)}$
(out of 10)

Data-Set Question $\dfrac{\underline{\hspace{2cm}}}{\text{Score}} \times 1.50 = \dfrac{\underline{\hspace{2cm}}}{(Do\ not\ round)}$
(out of 10)

Synthesis & Evaluation Question $\dfrac{\underline{\hspace{2cm}}}{\text{Score}} \times 1.50 = \dfrac{\underline{\hspace{2cm}}}{(Do\ not\ round)}$
(out of 10)

Synthesis & Evaluation Question $\dfrac{\underline{\hspace{2cm}}}{\text{Score}} \times 1.50 = \dfrac{\underline{\hspace{2cm}}}{(Do\ not\ round)}$
(out of 10)

$$\textbf{Sum} = \dfrac{\underline{\hspace{2cm}}}{\substack{\text{Weighted} \\ \text{Section II} \\ \text{Score}}}$$

COMPOSITE SCORE

$$\dfrac{\underline{\hspace{2cm}}}{\substack{\text{Weighted} \\ \text{Section I} \\ \text{Score}}} + \dfrac{\underline{\hspace{2cm}}}{\substack{\text{Weighted} \\ \text{Section II} \\ \text{Score}}} = \dfrac{\underline{\hspace{2cm}}}{\substack{\text{Composite} \\ \text{Score}}}$$

AP GRADE CONVERSION CHART

Composite Score Range	AP Grade
107–150	5
87–106	4
75–86	3
62–74	2
0–61	1

PRACTICE TEST 2

ENVIRONMENTAL SCIENCE
Section I: Multiple-Choice Questions
Time: 1 hour and 30 minutes
Number of Questions: 100

Part A

Directions: Each set of choices below, labeled A through E, will refer to a question or statement directly following the lettered choices. The questions or statements may also refer to a diagram or graph. Each lettered answer may be used more than once, only once, or not at all. Choose the one lettered choice you feel best answers the question or statement above.

Questions 1–5 refer to the map below.

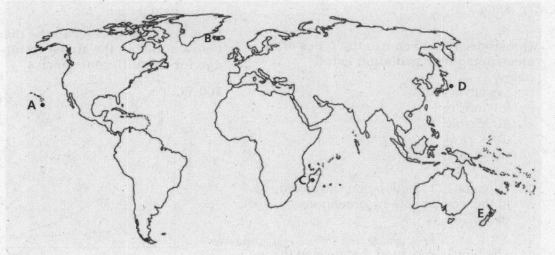

1. The residents of this island have been exposed to high levels of UV radiation due to human activities.

2. This island produces most of its energy from geothermal and hydroelectric sources.

3. This island has the highest population density.

4. This island sits atop a geologic hot spot far from any plate boundaries.

5. This island is part of a developing nation.

GO ON TO NEXT PAGE 313

Questions 6–9 refer to the U.S. states listed below.
(A) Ohio
(B) Louisiana
(C) California
(D) Washington
(E) Massachusetts

6. Overfishing off the coast of this state has devastated cod fisheries.

7. Human activities along its coastline are responsible for increasing the damage by one of the most destructive hurricanes in history.

8. The photochemical smog in its largest city is intensified by frequent inversion layers due to the mountains that surround it on three sides.

9. The largest watershed in North America drains into the sea in this state.

Questions 10–13 refer to the types of electromagnetic radiation listed below.
(A) ultraviolet
(B) infrared
(C) visible
(D) x-rays
(E) microwaves

10. The type of radiation that is trapped in the troposphere by greenhouse gases.

11. The type of radiation that formed the ozone layer.

12. The type of radiation with the most energy.

13. The type of radiation with the least energy.

Questions 14–17 refer to the following acronyms.
(A) ENSO
(B) CERCLA
(C) RCRA
(D) IPM
(E) CITES

14. The international treaty that restricts trade in products manufactured from endangered species.

15. Used to decrease dependence on large inputs of broad-spectrum pesticides.

16. Results in fishery deterioration off the coast of South America.

17. Resulted in a process by which the U.S. government will intervene in the event of massive environmental contamination.

Questions 18–19 refer to the diagram below showing the survivorship and age for five different species.

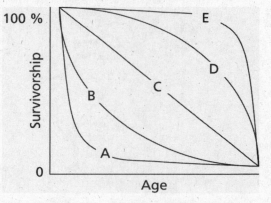

18. Which of the species would be the slowest to recover from a significant change to its environment?

19. Which of the species most likely bears the fewest offspring per generation?

Questions 20–23 refer to the following tests of water quality.
(A) BOD
(B) turbidity
(C) hardness
(D) pH
(E) dissolved oxygen

20. Sediment pollution will result in an immediate change in this measurement.

21. Changes in inverse proportion to water temperature.

22. Higher for waters that flow through regions rich in calcium.

23. Decreases in areas with highly active decomposers.

Questions 24–28 refer to the following agricultural products:
(A) alfalfa
(B) potato
(C) palm
(D) rice
(E) corn

24. Its use as biodiesel fuel has resulted in the destruction of large areas of tropical rain forest.

25. It can be grown in crop rotation to restore soil nitrogen.

26. Traditionally a food crop, it is now also considered as a source of fuel.

27. Sweeteners made from this crop have been widely blamed for obesity in the developed world.

28. Genetically modified strains have been created that reduce occurrences of childhood blindness.

Part B

Directions: Five answer choices, lettered A through E, will follow each one of the following questions or incomplete statements below. The questions or statements may refer to a graph, diagram, or table. Choose the one answer that best fits each question or completes the statement.

29. DDT is hazardous to animals because
(A) it has a high LD-50
(B) it has a similar chemical structure to sex hormones
(C) it kills nerve cells
(D) it is substituted into the shells of eggs, which creates frail shells
(E) it is absorbed into spinal fluid

30. Which of the following best explains why rising warm moist air masses result in precipitation?
(A) As an inversion layer forms, the moisture is forced out of the air mass.
(B) The relative humidity of the air mass decreases as it rises, producing rain.
(C) The air mass cools and is capable of holding less moisture as it rises.
(D) The moisture condenses as the air warms up as it rises.

(E) The gravitational pull of the earth decreases with altitude, which causes the water to fall out of the air mass.

31. It is likely that in the next 10 to 30 years there will be an increase in cancer in northern Europe due to the events that occurred in
(A) Chernobyl, Ukraine
(B) Valdez, Alaska
(C) Yucca Mountain, Nevada
(D) Stockholm, Sweden
(E) Bhopal, India

GO ON TO NEXT PAGE

32. An incandescent light bulb has an efficiency of 5% and a compact fluorescent bulb has an efficiency of 25%. In order to replace a 100-watt incandescent bulb and still provide approximately the same amount of light energy, a compact fluorescent bulb must have a power rating of
    (A) 5 watts
    (B) 10 watts
    (C) 20 watts
    (D) 25 watts
    (E) 50 watts

33. Of the following, the ozone layer is vital to protect life from
    I.   UV-A
    II. UV-B
    III. UV-C

    (A) I only
    (B) II only
    (C) III only
    (D) I and III only
    (E) II and III only

34. Which of the following invasive species was not intentionally introduced?
    (A) The cane toad in Australia
    (B) The gypsy moth in the northeastern United States
    (C) The Indian mongoose in Hawaii
    (D) The Zebra mussel in the Great Lakes
    (E) The Kudzu vine in the southeastern United States

35. Complete the following series of reactions:
    $$Cl + O_A \rightarrow ClO + O_B$$
    $$ClO + O \rightarrow Cl + O_C$$
    (A) A = 2; B = 2; C = 2
    (B) A = 3; B = 2; C = 2
    (C) A = 3; B = 2; C = 3
    (D) A = 2; B = 3; C = 3
    (E) A = 2; B = 2; C = 3

36. Methemoglobiemia or blue baby syndrome is caused by
    (A) excessive nitrites in drinking water
    (B) excessive phosphates in drinking water
    (C) drinking water that lacks sufficient dissolved oxygen
    (D) excessive nitrates in drinking water
    (E) drinking water that lacks sufficient nitrites

37. If the emissions that contribute to acid rain were completely eliminated, acid rain would stop falling in approximately
    (A) 1–2 days
    (B) 2–3 weeks
    (C) 4–6 months
    (D) 1–2 years
    (E) 10–20 years

38. Acid rain with a pH of 4.6 is more acidic than normal rainfall by a factor of
    (A) 10
    (B) 100
    (C) 1,000
    (D) 10,000
    (E) 1,000,000

39. Which of the following regulates the flow of nitrogen into and out of its largest reservoir?
    (A) Green plants
    (B) Water
    (C) Animals
    (D) Permafrost
    (E) Bacteria

40. Which of the following is the smallest reservoir of the global hydrologic cycle?
    (A) Groundwater
    (B) Lakes
    (C) Rivers
    (D) The atmosphere
    (E) Polar ice and glaciers

41. Plants that are bioengineered to kill their own seeds are
    (A) banned worldwide by an international treaty
    (B) produced to prevent the escape of genetically modified plants
    (C) produced to force farmers to buy new seeds every year
    (D) impossible to create because a living organism cannot be made to eliminate itself through natural selection
    (E) thought to be possible to produce in the next 10–20 years

42. When cattle overgraze rangeland they leave the soil vulnerable to erosion by wind and water. Erosion makes it difficult for grass to grow and more likely for the remaining grass to be eaten even faster. This leaves the soil bare and vulnerable to erosion making it even harder to grow grass. This is an example of
    (A) a tragedy of the commons
    (B) a marginal cost
    (C) an external cost
    (D) a negative feedback loop
    (E) a positive feedback loop

43. Which of the following is not considered a method for slowing global warming?
    (A) Switch from burning coal to natural gas
    (B) Reduce fossil fuel use
    (C) Reduce energy efficiency
    (D) Reduce urban sprawl
    (E) Reduce deforestation

44. Car A gets 40 miles per gallon, and Car B gets 15 miles per gallon. If both cars are driven 12,000 miles per year and use gasoline that emits 20 pounds of carbon dioxide per gallon, after 10 years the additional CO_2 that Car B will have emitted will be nearest
    (A) 10,000 lbs
    (B) 20,000 lbs
    (C) 30,000 lbs
    (D) 50,000 lbs
    (E) 100,000 lbs

45. If the average gas price during the 10 years covered by the previous problem is $3 per gallon, the additional cost of gas for the owner of Car B will be nearest
    (A) $1,000
    (B) $3,000
    (C) $7,000
    (D) $9,000
    (E) $13,000

46. While flying high above the ground far from any large cities, a migrating bird sees a series of large circular green patches on the ground. If the bird lands it will likely find itself in
    (A) a series of ponds used for tertiary sewage treatment
    (B) danger from a wind farm that is also being used for agriculture with a drip irrigation system
    (C) a large solar array that is part of a solar power tower
    (D) agricultural land that is using center-pivot irrigation
    (E) a factory farm that is raising hogs

47. Nitrogen fixation will take place in fields that are planted with
    (A) soy
    (B) corn
    (C) rice
    (D) potatoes
    (E) wheat

48. The extinction of which of the following would be most devastating to life on earth?
    (A) Giant panda
    (B) Honeybee
    (C) African black rhinoceros
    (D) Minke whale
    (E) Bald eagle

49. In addition to chlorine, which of the following elements is also linked to stratospheric ozone depletion?
    (A) Oxygen
    (B) Bromine
    (C) Sulfur
    (D) Mercury
    (E) Helium

GO ON TO NEXT PAGE

50. The seasonal turnover of lakes in temperate climates serves to carry
    (A) oxygen and nutrients to the surface of the lake
    (B) oxygen and nutrients to the bottom of the lake
    (C) oxygen to the bottom and nutrients to the surface of the lake
    (D) oxygen to the surface and nutrients to the bottom of the lake
    (E) oxygen to the surface of the lake

51. Species diversity can be quantified by using which of the following sets of data about an ecosystem?
    (A) The number of species and the area
    (B) The number of individuals of each species and the net primary productivity
    (C) The number of species and the number of individuals of each species
    (D) The area and the net primary productivity
    (E) The number of individuals of each species and the area

52. Which of the following explains why more than 99% of the water on earth is not readily available for use as freshwater?
    I.   It is located too deep underground.
    II. It is stored behind dams.
    III. It is frozen or too salty.

    (A) I only
    (B) II only
    (C) I and II only
    (D) I and III only
    (E) II and III only

53. The goals of the Resource Conservation and Recovery Act include which of the following?
    (A) To prevent the unsafe disposal of high-level radioactive wastes at sea
    (B) To prevent the illegal disposal of hospital waste contaminated with infectious agents
    (C) To require the cradle-to-grave monitoring of low-level radioactive wastes
    (D) To prevent the unsafe disposal of hazardous wastes on land
    (E) To clean up abandoned hazardous waste sites

54. A scientist wishes to test the effects of different amounts of water and fertilizer on yields of corn. In a series of experimental fields, she varies the supply of water and the amount of fertilizer applied to a given strain of corn and measures the yield of the crop that results. In this experiment, which is/are the dependent variable(s)?
    (A) Corn yield and the variety of corn
    (B) Water supply and amount of fertilizer
    (C) Corn yield
    (D) Water supply
    (E) Amount of fertilizer and variety of corn strain

55. A fig tree that provides shelter and fruit that are essential to the survival of numerous other species is an example of
    (A) a keystone species
    (B) an exotic species
    (C) a ubiquitous species
    (D) an endemic species
    (E) an indicator species

56. Most photosynthesis in the open sea occurs in the
    (A) euphotic zone
    (B) benthic zone
    (C) littoral zone
    (D) profundal zone
    (E) abyssal zone

57. 3 ppm is equivalent to which of the following?
    (A) 3,000 ppb
    (B) 30,000 ppb
    (C) 300,000 ppb
    (D) 3,000,000 ppb
    (E) 30,000,000 ppb

58. Which of the following would decrease one's ecological footprint?
    (A) Traveling by airplane rather than driving
    (B) Eating more meat
    (C) Walking to school rather than driving
    (D) Purchasing a larger home
    (E) Eating more processed and packaged food

59. Fishing licenses are a legislative attempt to avoid which of the following?
    (A) Island biogeography
    (B) A cost-benefit analysis
    (C) A negative feedback loop
    (D) A tragedy of the commons
    (E) The enforcement of the Endangered Species Act

60. Which of the following is a correct sequence of transformations in the nitrogen cycle?
    (A) Transpiration – nitrification – assimilation – ammonification – respiration
    (B) Fixation – ammonification – nitrification – assimilation – denitrification
    (C) Ammonification – respiration – nitrification – denitrification
    (D) Fixation – nitrification – assimilation – ammonification
    (E) Ammonification – transpiration – nitrification – assimilation

61. Which of the following does NOT emit greenhouse gases?
    (A) The decomposition of animal waste
    (B) The thawing of permafrost
    (C) The photosynthesis of oceanic phytoplankton
    (D) The crushing of old refrigerators
    (E) The burning of biomass

62. The major reason that many of the world's desalination plants are located in the Middle East is
    (A) the innovations that companies operating in the region have made in desalination technology
    (B) the availability of the large amount of reliable, intense sunlight necessary for desalination
    (C) the availability of the large amount of fossil fuels required for desalination
    (D) the availability of the large number of low-wage workers necessary to operate a desalination plant
    (E) the wars and tribal conflicts that make it nearly impossible to relocate water resources within the region

63. Legislation has most effectively reduced which of the following air pollutants?
    (A) Sulfur dioxide
    (B) Carbon dioxide
    (C) Mercury
    (D) Lead
    (E) Nitrogen dioxide

64. Which of the following will likely lead to individuals underestimating the amount of risk associated with an activity?
    I.   Extensive media coverage of the risk associated with the activity
    II. A large degree of control during the activity
    III. A political campaign centered around opposing views over the activity

    (A) I only
    (B) II only
    (C) III only
    (D) I and III only
    (E) II and III only

65. Which of the following is most likely to indicate a rapidly growing population?
    (A) A high percentage of males in the population
    (B) A high percentage of girls with less than a fifth-grade education
    (C) A lack of access to freshwater
    (D) A lack of adequate calories to feed the population
    (E) A low infant mortality rate

GO ON TO NEXT PAGE

66. Which of the following is NOT an infectious disease that is transmitted through water?
(A) Cholera
(B) Tuberculosis
(C) Typhoid fever
(D) Cryptosporidiosis
(E) Giardiasis

67. It is determined that a soil sample is composed of 42% sand, 15% clay, and 43% silt. According to the soil triangle, which of the following is the soil texture of the soil?

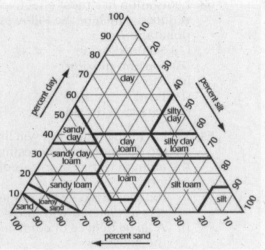

http://soils.usda.gov/technical/manual/print_version/chapter3.html

(A) Loam
(B) Silt loam
(C) Clay
(D) Sandy loam
(E) Loamy sand

68. The Ogallala Aquifer supplies water to much of
(A) the High Plains area of the United States
(B) Western Europe
(C) the Amazon rain forest
(D) California
(E) Eastern China

69. Which of the following justifications do Japan and Iceland use to defend the continuation of their whaling?
(A) Job losses in the whaling industry
(B) Cultural traditions that include whaling
(C) Necessary to provide sufficient food for their citizens
(D) Whales are needed to conduct scientific research
(E) Whale populations are too high and must be culled to ensure healthy populations

70. Which of the following is/are a unit(s) of energy?
I. kilowatt-hour
II. megawatt
III. kilocalorie

(A) I only
(B) II only
(C) III only
(D) I and II only
(E) I and III only

71. Of the following, the largest storage reservoir of the world's freshwater is
(A) the atmosphere
(B) groundwater
(C) lakes
(D) living organisms
(E) rivers

72. Which of the following causes sick-building syndrome?
(A) Building within 100 feet of an operating hazardous waste facility
(B) Building within 100 feet of a hazardous waste facility that was shut down prior to 1980
(C) Building on top of reclaimed mining land
(D) Acid rain
(E) Indoor air pollution

73. In lakes, the nutrient-rich water near the shore is part of the
(A) bathyal zone
(B) euphotic zone
(C) littoral zone
(D) limnetic zone
(E) profundal zone

74. The acronym that residents may employ in trying to prevent a new landfill from being placed in their community is
(A) NIMBY
(B) PEMBT
(C) NOPE
(D) DONT
(E) GOAWAY

75. The U.S. law that requires developers to study the environmental impact of projects funded by the federal government is
(A) CERCLA
(B) CITES
(C) ENSO
(D) NEPA
(E) RCRA

76. Which of the following ways of managing e-waste has the fewest negative environmental and social consequences?
(A) Disposal in sanitary landfills or hazardous waste facilities
(B) E-waste collection and local recycling
(C) E-waste collection and shipment to developing countries for recycling
(D) Incineration
(E) E-waste collection by manufacturers required to take back their products for recycling

77. Radioactive I-131 has a half-life of 8 days. How much time is required for a l-millicurie sample of I-131 to decay to an activity of 1 microcurie?
(A) 8 days
(B) 16 days
(C) About 1 month
(D) About 3 months
(E) About 1 year

78. Which of the following is true about peat?
(A) It does not burn.
(B) It is a more efficient fuel than lignite.
(C) It was formed in arid regions of the world.
(D) It produces more hazardous air pollution per gram of fuel than coal.
(E) It produces no carbon dioxide when burned.

79. Which of the following is a commonly cultivated aquaculture crop?
(A) Tuna
(B) Swordfish
(C) Shark
(D) Oyster
(E) Duck

Questions 80–82 refer to the diagrams of population data from 2005 below.

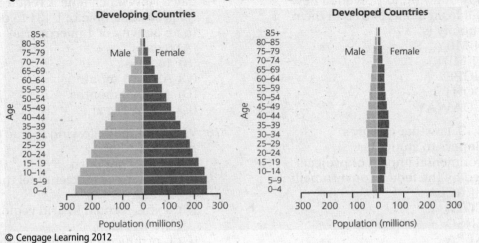

© Cengage Learning 2012

80. In 2005, the number of males in developing countries ages 0–19 was nearest
    (A) 25 million
    (B) 100 million
    (C) 250 million
    (D) 1 billion
    (E) 2.5 billion

81. In 2005, the number of females in developing countries ages 15–49 was nearest
    (A) 60 million
    (B) 150 million
    (C) 700 million
    (D) 1.3 billion
    (E) 3 billion

82. Which of the following CANNOT be determined from the diagrams?
    (A) The population of the world
    (B) The number of men living in developing countries
    (C) The growth rate of the population in developed countries
    (D) The population momentum of developing countries
    (E) The number of pre-reproductive aged females in developed countries

83. Which of the following is NOT an ecosystem service provided by forests?
    (A) Carbon sequestration
    (B) Water purification
    (C) Lumber production
    (D) Food production
    (E) Road construction

84. In an experiment, a researcher fills three aquariums labeled A, B, and C with seawater collected from a local estuary. To aquarium A, nitrate and phosphate are added. To aquarium B only nitrate is added. To aquarium C only phosphate is added. The results show that algae growth accelerated in aquariums A and B, but not in aquarium C. One conclusion that may be drawn from these results is that
    (A) phosphate is not required for algae growth in seawater
    (B) for algae in seawater, nitrate is a more essential nutrient than phosphate
    (C) phosphate is a limiting agent for algae growth in seawater
    (D) nitrate is a limiting agent for algae growth in seawater
    (E) nitrate is not required for algae growth in seawater

85. This layer of soil is also known as the topsoil; it contains much humus.
    (A) A horizon
    (B) B horizon
    (C) C horizon
    (D) H horizon
    (E) O horizon

86. In general, far less than 100% of the energy from one trophic level is converted to energy at the next trophic level. This is best explained by
    (A) the competitive exclusion principle
    (B) the theory of island biogeography
    (C) the first law of thermodynamics
    (D) the second law of thermodynamics
    (E) resource partitioning

87. Which of the following allows polluters to buy and sell the right to pollute?
    (A) Cap and trade programs
    (B) Marginal costs
    (C) The Troubled Asset Relief Program
    (D) CAFE standards
    (E) The Montreal Protocol

88. The surface mining technique known as mountaintop removal is associated with the extraction of
    (A) oil
    (B) gold
    (C) silver
    (D) coal
    (E) aluminum

89. During the refining of crude oil, which of the following will boil away first?
    (A) Propane
    (B) Diesel fuel
    (C) Asphalt
    (D) Aviation (jet) fuel
    (E) Gasoline

90. If oil sands become a cost effective resource, its extraction may lead to significant environmental damage in
    (A) China
    (B) Venezuela
    (C) Canada
    (D) Alaska
    (E) Argentina

91. Select the locations of the environmental disasters associated with (I) mercury, (II) crude oil, and (III) methyl isocyanate.
    (A) (I) Minamata, (II) Valdez, and (III) Love Canal
    (B) (I) Bhopal, (II) Valdez, and (III) Love Canal
    (C) (I) Minamata, (II) Valdez, and (III) Bhopal
    (D) (I) Bhopal, (II) Love Canal, and (III) Bhopal
    (E) (I) Love Canal, (II) Bhopal, and (III) Minamata

92. Which of the following is the best example of mitigation?
    (A) A developer wants to fill in a marsh. He locates similar land nearby that was previously filled and restores that marsh to compensate for the new development.
    (B) A company uses plants to take up contaminants on land that they own. The plants are then disposed of in a landfill.
    (C) The federal government cleans up a former hazardous waste site that was abandoned by a bankrupt company.
    (D) A mining company re-contours and restores the vegetation on land that it formerly mined for coal.
    (E) A landowner sells property to a non-governmental organization for use as wilderness preserve.

GO ON TO NEXT PAGE

93. Of those listed below, the earliest stage of the succession of a lake will most likely result in
    (A) a mature forest community
    (B) a young pine forest
    (C) a meadow
    (D) rocks covered with mosses and lichens
    (E) a series of hills covered with grasses

94. A forest ecosystem in which forest fires have been suppressed for many decades may benefit from which of the following?
    (A) Thinning by removing medium-sized trees
    (B) Thinning by removing the largest trees
    (C) Building roads to provide for recreation
    (D) Setting small contained surface fires
    (E) Clear-cutting the forest to initiate secondary succession

95. Which of the following is a pollutant that is NOT usually associated with the use of modern sanitary landfills?
    (A) Mercury vapor
    (B) Methane
    (C) Particulate matter
    (D) Noise
    (E) Nitrogen oxides

96. Which of the following has been proposed as a method for sequestering carbon dioxide?
    I.   Using a catalyst, reduce CO2 emissions to methane.
    II. Transport CO2 generated on land to offshore oil rigs where it can be pumped into the deep ocean.
    III. Plant fast-growing perennial plants to remove CO2 from the air and store it in soil.

    (A) I only
    (B) II only
    (C) I and III only
    (D) I and II only
    (E) II and III only

Questions 97–99 refer to the diagram below showing the dissolved oxygen (DO) and biological oxygen demand (BOD) levels of a river.

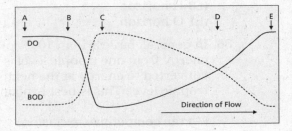

97. This diagram is a depiction of what typically happens in a river when
    (A) a river flows past a point source of pesticide pollution
    (B) a river flows past a non-point source of nutrient pollution
    (C) a river flows past agricultural land
    (D) a river flows past a point source of organic waste
    (E) a river flows past a golf course

98. Which of the following is most likely true of human activity along the river?
    (A) The river is being polluted at the point labeled "A."
    (B) The river is being polluted at the point labeled "B."
    (C) The river is being polluted at the points labeled "B" and "D."
    (D) The river is being polluted at the points labeled "B", "D," and "E."
    (E) The river is being polluted at all of the labeled points.

99. The healthiest aquatic ecosystem can most likely be found at
    (A) the point labeled "C."
    (B) the point labeled "D."
    (C) the points labeled "B" and "D."
    (D) the points labeled "C" and "D."
    (E) the points labeled "A" and "E."

100. Which of the following best explains why the Antarctic ozone "hole" largely disappears a few months after its first appearance each year?
  (A) Warmer temperatures increase the evaporation of water that blocks UV-B radiation.
  (B) Warmer temperatures increase the photochemical production of ozone.
  (C) The sun heats up the air over Antarctica breaking up the polar stratospheric clouds.
  (D) The input of UV-C radiation is reduced.
  (E) Anthropogenic emissions of ozone slowly make their way into the stratosphere to replace the depleted ozone.

Section II: Free-Response Questions
Time: 1 Hour and 30 Minutes
Number of Questions: 4

Section II of the AP Environmental Science Exam counts for 40% of the total test grade. You will have four essay questions, each involving several parts. Calculators may not be used on the free-response section.

1. Read the advertisement that appeared in the *Fremont Post* below and answer the questions that follow.

FREMONT ECOTRAVEL

SO, YOU WAITED TO SEE THE GOLDEN TOADS OF MONTEVERDE?
WELL, YOU SNOOZE: YOU LOSE!

DON'T MAKE THAT MISTAKE AGAIN!

VISIT THE BLUE-SIDED TREE FROGS OF COSTA RICA!
THE MOUNTAIN GORILLAS OF RWANDA!
AND THE ORANGUTANS OF BORNEO!

BEFORE IT'S TOO LATE!

FREMONT ECOTRAVEL WILL TAKE YOU THERE!

ALL EXPEDITION VEHICLES USE 100% BIODIESEL MADE FROM PALM OIL!

CALL 555-APES

(a) The ad makes reference to the golden toads of Monteverde. Explain why this reference is made.
(b) A large share of the world's ecotourism takes place in developing countries. Describe TWO ways in which ecotourism can help reduce poverty in these countries.
(c) Discuss the conflict between people living in poverty and efforts to conserve biodiversity.

GO ON TO NEXT PAGE

(d) Other than those listed above, identify a specific endangered species that people might be willing to pay to visit and the location of the species' native habitat.

(e) The ad touts the use of biodiesel fuel made from palm oil. Explain why this advertising tactic might have been a mistake.

(f) Roundtrip airline travel from the central United States to central Africa will generate about 3 metric tons (3000 kg) of carbon dioxide, and a trip to Southeast Asia will generate about 4 metric tons (4000 kg). Discuss the conflict that this brings about with the ideals of ecotourism.

2. Dr. Beverly, a wildlife biologist, is placed in charge of managing the white-tailed deer population in a 500-hectare state park that is completely surrounded by agriculture and urban sprawl. The carrying capacity of the park was previously determined to be 800 deer. Dr. Beverly's first task is to estimate the current population of deer in order to determine if the deer have exceeded their carrying capacity. She decides to estimate the number of deer in the park by determining the average number of droppings left behind by deer in a given area, and the length of time deer droppings persist in the park.

After surveying hundreds of 10 x 10 meter quadrats (squares), Dr. Beverly determines that the average number of droppings per quadrat is 24. She also determines that the average deer leaves 30 droppings each day and that after 40 days the droppings have completely assimilated back into the soil and can no longer be seen (1 ha = 1×10^4 m^2).

(a) Determine the total number of observable droppings in the park for each deer at any time.

(b) Determine the number of deer in the park per hectare.

(c) Determine the total number of deer in the park.

(d) Dr. Beverly's report on the deer population prompts the state park service to issue hunting licenses. Determine the number of hunting licenses that should be issued and explain the rationale for issuing that number of licenses.

(e) Describe another way to control the deer population.

(f) Identify and describe another way to estimate the population size of the deer.

3. Hydroelectric power plants supply approximately 20% of the world's electrical energy, and once they are built, these facilities provide energy that is virtually free. However, hydropower requires the construction of dams and water storage reservoirs that are expensive and dangerous to build.

(a) Identify and describe the series of energy transformations (conversions) that are used to generate electricity in a hydroelectric power plant.

(b) Explain why the energy provided by existing hydropower dams is virtually free.

(c) Identify ONE species whose numbers have diminished as the result of a hydropower project and describe how the project led to the decline in their population.

(d) Identify ONE infectious disease that could spread more rapidly among people as a result of a hydropower project and explain how the project could lead to an increase in the spread of the disease.

(e) Hydroelectric dams have a limited lifetime. Describe two natural processes that could lead to the end of the effective lifetime of a hydroelectric dam.

4. The decline of the world's fisheries is of great concern and has been the subject of international conflict. Humans get much of their food supply from the oceans. Some of the fish used for food are caught wild by commercial fishing fleets and others are farmed.

   (a) Unsustainable commercial fishing practices for wild species receive much of the blame for the depletion of the world's fisheries. Identify and describe ONE commercial fishing practice that is used to catch wild species and ONE negative environmental consequence of that practice.

   (b) Identify and describe TWO negative environmental consequences of fish farming.

   (c) Discuss the effect that an El Niño-Southern Oscillation event can have on fisheries.

   (d) Some of the world's fish have high concentrations of mercury in their flesh.

       (i) Identify a major source of the mercury.

       (ii) Explain why the concentration of mercury differs from species to species.

ANSWERS FOR MULTIPLE-CHOICE QUESTIONS

Using the table below, score your test. You will find explanations of the answers on the following pages.

1. E	21. E	41. C	61. C	81. D
2. B	22. C	42. E	62. C	82. C
3. D	23. E	43. C	63. D	83. E
4. A	24. C	44. E	64. B	84. D
5. C	25. A	45. E	65. B	85. A
6. E	26. E	46. D	66. B	86. D
7. B	27. E	47. A	67. A	87. A
8. C	28. D	48. B	68. A	88. D
9. B	29. B	49. B	69. D	89. A
10. B	30. C	50. C	70. E	90. C
11. A	31. A	51. C	71. B	91. C
12. D	32. C	52. D	72. E	92. A
13. E	33. B	53. D	73. C	93. C
14. E	34. D	54. C	74. A	94. D
15. D	35. B	55. A	75. D	95. A
16. A	36. D	56. A	76. E	96. E
17. B	37. B	57. A	77. D	97. D
18. E	38. A	58. C	78. D	98. B
19. E	39. E	59. D	79. D	99. E
20. B	40. D	60. D	80. B	100. C

1. **ANSWER: E.**   New Zealand has regularly been under masses of ozone-depleted air that float northward from over Antarctica. The masses may linger for weeks and they expose all life to damaging levels of UV-B radiation (*Living in the Environment*, 16th ed., page 523 / 17th ed., page 521).

2. **ANSWER: B.**   Iceland is above the mid-Atlantic trench and gets about 75% of its energy and 95% of its electricity from geothermal sources (*Living in the Environment*, 16th ed., page 399 / 17th ed., page 425).

3. **ANSWER: D.**   Japan has the world's tenth-largest population with about 128 million people—far more than any of the other islands labeled (*Living in the Environment*, 16th ed., page 126 / 17th ed., page 138).

4. **ANSWER: A.** Hawaii was formed by a geologic hot spot in the center of the Pacific plate, thousands of miles from any plate boundaries (*Living in the Environment*, 16th ed., not included / 17th ed., not included).

5. **ANSWER: C.** Madagascar is the only developing nation that is labeled (*Living in the Environment*, 16th ed., pages 10–11 / 17th ed., page 12).

6. **ANSWER: E.** Overfishing has severely depleted the North Atlantic cod fishery. In fact, a moratorium has been placed on cod fishing off the northeast coast of North America (*Living in the Environment*, 16th ed., page 254 / 17th ed., page 257).

7. **ANSWER: B.** Some of the natural features that would have weakened Hurricane Katrina were eliminated by the development of wetlands along the Louisiana coast (*Living in the Environment*, 16th ed., pages 177–178 / 17th ed., pages 184–186).

8. **ANSWER: C.** Los Angeles is surrounded on three sides by mountains and the Pacific Ocean on the fourth side. This provides ideal conditions for the formation of an inversion layer that traps photochemical smog over the city (*Living in the Environment*, 16th ed., page 478 / 17th ed., page 476).

9. **ANSWER: B.** The Mississippi River watershed drains nearly two-thirds of the continental U.S. land area into the Gulf of Mexico through the Mississippi River Delta in Louisiana (*Living in the Environment*, 16th ed., page 550 / 17th ed., page 546).

10. **ANSWER: B.** The earth emits infrared radiation, which is trapped in the troposphere by greenhouse gases (*Living in the Environment*, 16th ed., pages 56–57 / 17th ed., page 57).

11. **ANSWER: A.** The stratospheric ozone layer was formed by the reaction between oxygen and ultraviolet radiation (*Living in the Environment*, 16th ed., page 470 / 17th ed., pages 467–468).

12. **ANSWER: D.** X-rays have the highest energy of those listed (*Living in the Environment*, 16th ed., page 42 / 17th ed. pages 44–45).

13. **ANSWER: E.** Microwaves have the lowest energy of those listed (*Living in the Environment*, 16th ed., page 42 / 17th ed. pages 44–45).

14. **ANSWER: E.** The Convention on International Trade of Endangered Species of Flora and Fauna (CITES) treaty restricts trade in products that are manufactured from endangered species (*Living in the Environment*, 16th ed., pages 206–207 / 17th ed., page 209).

15. **ANSWER: D.** Integrated Pest Management (IPM) makes use of a combination of strategies including biological control, crop rotation, and narrow spectrum pesticides to manage pest populations at acceptable levels without using more hazardous broad spectrum pesticides (*Living in the Environment*, 16th ed., page 300 / 17th ed., pages 302–303).

16. **ANSWER: A.** An El Niño Southern Oscillation (ENSO) is a climatic event that occurs every few years and results in, among other things, a decline in the populations of fisheries off the coast of South America (*Living in the Environment*, 16th ed., pages S48–S49 / 17th ed., pages S26–S28).

17. **ANSWER: B.** The Comprehensive Environmental Response, Compensation, and Liability Act (CERCLA), also known as the Superfund Act, created a process by which the U.S. government identifies sites where hazardous materials have contaminated the environment and cleans them up (*Living in the Environment*, 16th ed., pages S48–S49 / 17th ed., page S8).

18. **ANSWER: E.**   Species that are slow to recover from environmental change are typically K-strategists and follow a late-loss survivorship curve, which is exemplified by the line labeled "E" above (*Living in the Environment*, 16th ed., not included / 17th ed., not included).

19. **ANSWER: E.**   Species that bear few offspring per generation are typically K-strategists and follow a late-loss survivorship curve, which is exemplified by the line labeled "E" above (*Living in the Environment*, 16th ed., not included / 17th ed., not included).

20. **ANSWER: B.**   The turbidity of water measures the amount of light that passes through the water. When sediments pollute water the turbidity will immediately change (*Living in the Environment*, 16th ed., page 535 / 17th ed., page 533).

21. **ANSWER: E.**   Dissolved oxygen levels decrease as water temperature increases and increase as water temperature decreases. Therefore, water temperature and the dissolved oxygen concentration are inversely proportional (*Living in the Environment*, 16th ed., not included / 17th ed., not included).

22. **ANSWER: C.**   Water hardness is a measurement of the concentration of magnesium and calcium in water. As water flows through areas rich in calcium, magnesium or both, the hardness increases (*Living in the Environment*, 16th ed., not included / 17th ed., not included).

23. **ANSWER: E.**   Decomposers consume dissolved oxygen, making it difficult for fish and other aquatic species to survive in the same area that decomposition is occurring (*Living in the Environment*, 16th ed., page 536 / 17th ed., page 534).

24. **ANSWER: C.**   Palm oil is a commonly used crop to produce biodiesel fuel, and the recent increase in fuel prices has resulted in large areas of tropical rain forest destruction, especially in Southeast Asia (*Living in the Environment*, 16th ed., page 423 / 17th ed., page 421).

25. **ANSWER: A.**   Alfalfa is a legume that has nitrogen-fixing *Rhizobium* bacteria living in nodules on its roots. Growing legumes like alfalfa (also, soybeans, peanuts, peas, and clover) in rotation with other crops can restore soil nitrogen without adding inorganic fertilizers (*Living in the Environment*, 16th ed., not included / 17th ed., not included).

26. **ANSWER: E.**   Corn is being used to produce ethanol and as a result the price of corn has risen along with energy prices in recent years (*Living in the Environment*, 16th ed., page 425 / 17th ed., pages 419–421).

27. **ANSWER: E.**   High-fructose corn syrup is a ubiquitous sweetener that has played a role in the high caloric intake that in turn has led to the obesity epidemic in developed countries (*Living in the Environment*, 16th ed., not included / 17th ed., not included).

28. **ANSWER: D.**   Golden rice is genetically modified to produce vitamin A, an essential vitamin to fight off infectious diseases and maintain good eyesight. Children with vitamin A deficiencies are more vulnerable to infectious diseases and can become blind (*Living in the Environment*, 16th ed., page 275 / 17th ed., page 294).

29. **ANSWER: B.**   DDT is an endocrine disrupter that is linked to feminization of males, inadequate eggshell production, and several other problems associated with sex hormones. Endocrine disrupters have similar chemical structures to sex hormones (often estrogen), which allow them to mimic hormones in the body and confuse the endocrine system (*Living in the Environment*, 16th ed., page 452 / 17th ed., pages 449–450).

30. **ANSWER: C.**   Cool air can hold less moisture than warm air. As an air mass rises in the troposphere it cools, and as a result, water condenses out of the cooler air mass and falls back to earth (*Living in the Environment*, 16th ed., page 143 / 17th ed., page 150).

31. **ANSWER: A.**   The release of radioactive gas during the meltdown of the nuclear power plant in Chernobyl, Ukraine, exposed much of the population of northern Europe to enough radiation to result in an increased risk of cancer (*Living in the Environment*, 16th ed., page 390 / 17th ed., page 389).

32. **ANSWER: C.**   The bulb's efficiency is a measure of how much of the energy input to the bulb is converted to light energy (the rest is converted to waste heat). Since power is the rate at which the bulb consumes energy, a bulb that is five times more efficient will need five times less energy input to produce the same amount of light and 100 watts / 5 = 20 watts (*Living in the Environment*, 16th ed., page 402 / 17th ed., page 407).

33. **ANSWER: B.**   UV-A has the least energy, low potential to harm life, and is not absorbed by the ozone layer. UV-C has the most energy and the most potential to harm life. UV-C has sufficient energy to break down oxygen molecules, and as a result, even with no ozone layer it would still be absorbed by oxygen in the atmosphere. UV-B can do considerable harm to life, and it is strongly absorbed by the ozone layer, and as a result the ozone layer is vital to protect life from UV-B radiation (*Living in the Environment*, 16th ed., pages 525–526 / 17th ed., page 523).

34. **ANSWER: D.**   The Zebra mussel was unintentionally introduced to the Great Lakes, probably in the ballast water of a ship (Gypsy moths were intentionally introduced in a failed attempt to improve the U.S. silk industry) (*Living in the Environment*, 16th ed., page 199 / 17th ed., page 200).

35. **ANSWER: B.**   The only set of numbers that will balance the equation. You should recognize these reactions as the chain reaction that destroys ozone in the stratosphere (*Living in the Environment*, 16th ed., page 525 / 17th ed., not included).

36. **ANSWER: D.**   Methemoglobiemia, or blue baby syndrome, is caused when drinking water is contaminated with excessive nitrates (*Living in the Environment*, 16th ed., page 544 / 17th ed., page 540).

37. **ANSWER: B.**   Acid rain falls within 1–2 weeks of the release of the pollutants (SO_2 and NO_x) that cause it (*Living in the Environment*, 16th ed., page 479 / 17th ed., pages 476–477).

38. **ANSWER: A.**   A pH difference of 1 unit corresponds to a factor of 10 of the logarithmic pH scale. Normal rain has a pH of about 5.6; therefore the difference is closest to 1 pH unit, which corresponds to a factor of 10 (*Living in the Environment*, 16th ed., pages 479, S41 / 17th ed., pages 477, S13).

39. **ANSWER: E.**   Bacteria remove nitrogen from its largest reservoir, the atmosphere, during nitrogen fixation and denitrifying bacteria return nitrogen to the atmosphere (*Living in the Environment*, 16th ed., pages 68–69 / 17th ed., page 71).

40. **ANSWER: D.**   The atmosphere is the smallest of the listed reservoirs in the global hydrologic (water) cycle. The water in the atmosphere also has the shortest residence time (1–2 weeks) of the reservoirs in the global hydrologic (water) cycle that are listed (*Living in the Environment*, 16th ed., not included / 17th ed., not included).

41. ANSWER: C. Called terminator seeds, these plants are produced to force farmers to buy new seeds every year (*Living in the Environment*, 16th ed., not included / 17th ed., not included).

42. ANSWER: E. This is an example of positive feedback. The initial change to the system is overgrazing and the system reacts to further the change in the same direction (*Living in the Environment*, 16th ed., page 45 / 17th ed., page 49).

43. ANSWER: C. Reducing energy efficiency will result in more fuel being burned rather than less and will not reduce global warming (*Living in the Environment*, 16th ed., page 515 / 17th ed., page 513).

44. ANSWER: E. Car A uses 12,000/40 = 300 gal/year x 20 lbs CO_2/gal = 6,000 lbs/year x 10 years = 60,000 lbs. Car B uses 12,000/15 = 800 gal/year x 20 lbs CO_2/gal = 16,000 lbs/year x 10 years = 160,000 lbs. Car B uses 100,000 pounds or 50 tons of additional CO_2 during the 10 years (*Living in the Environment*, 16th ed., not included / 17th ed., not included).

45. ANSWER: E. Car A uses 12,000/40 = 300 gal/year x 10 years = 3,000 gallons x $3/gal = $9,000. Car B uses 12,000/15 = 800 gal/year x 10 years = 8,000 gallons x $3/gal = $24,000. The fuel for Car B costs an additional $13,000 during the 10 years (*Living in the Environment*, 16th ed., not included / 17th ed., not included).

46. ANSWER: D. Center-pivot irrigation is an irrigation method used in industrialized agriculture in which large pipes on wheels with sprinklers attached are rotated around a central pivot point, creating large circular fields of crops (*Living in the Environment*, 16th ed., pages 334–335 / 17th ed., page 335).

47. ANSWER: A. Soy or soybeans, like other legumes, have a symbiotic relationship with specialized bacteria attached to their roots that fix nitrogen (*Living in the Environment*, 16th ed., page 305 / 17th ed., page 307).

48. ANSWER: B. Honeybees have coevolved with numerous species of flowering plants. Without them pollination would not happen in many of the plant species, which would decimate food supplies (*Living in the Environment*, 16th ed., pages 202–203 / 17th ed., page 204).

49. ANSWER: B. Bromine in halons and methyl bromide depletes stratospheric ozone (*Living in the Environment*, 16th ed., page 525 / 17th ed., page 522).

50. ANSWER: C. In the fall and spring lakes in temperate climates mix, carrying dissolved oxygen from the surface to the bottom of the lake and nutrients from the bottom to the surface of the lake (*Living in the Environment*, 16th ed., not included / 17th ed., not included).

51. ANSWER: C. The calculation of a species diversity index of an ecosystem requires the total number of species and the number of individuals of each species. These data are then manipulated in a statistical formula to determine a diversity index (*Living in the Environment*, 16th ed., not included / 17th ed., not included).

52. ANSWER: D. Only about 0.024% of the water on earth is readily available; the rest is too salty, frozen, or too far underground to reach (*Living in the Environment*, 16th ed., page 315 / 17th ed., page 319).

53. ANSWER: D. The goals of the Resource Conservation and Recovery Act (RCRA) include preventing the unsafe disposal of hazardous wastes on land. The act requires the cradle-to-grave monitoring of hazardous materials, and does not regulate

radioactive materials (*Living in the Environment,* 16th ed., page 582 / 17th ed., page 578).

54. **ANSWER: C.** The dependent variable is the variable that is measured during the experiment. In this case the dependent variable is the corn yield (*Living in the Environment,* 16th ed., not included / 17th ed., not included).

55. **ANSWER: A.** In this situation the loss of the fig trees will lead to the population crash or extinction of numerous species, which defines it as a keystone species (*Living in the Environment,* 16th ed., pages 95–96 / 17th ed., page 99).

56. **ANSWER: A.** The euphotic zone is the upper layer of an aquatic ecosystem through which sunlight can penetrate and where photosynthesis takes place (*Living in the Environment,* 16th ed., page 170 / 17th ed., page 172).

57. **ANSWER: A.** 3 ppm is equivalent to 3,000 ppb (1 ppm = 1,000 ppb = 1,000,000 ppt) (*Living in the Environment,* 16th ed., page G12 / 17th ed., page G11).

58. **ANSWER: C.** Walking to school rather than driving will decrease the use of fossil fuel energy and lower one's ecological footprint (*Living in the Environment,* 16th ed., page 14 / 17th ed., pages 15–16).

59. **ANSWER: D.** Issuing fishing licenses is a way of limiting access to a shared resource, or commons, in an attempt to limit the annual harvest of fish and maintain a sustainable population (*Living in the Environment,* 16th ed., page 13 / 17th ed., page 15).

60. **ANSWER: D.** The sequence fixation, nitrification, assimilation, and ammonification is a feasible sequence. Denitrification does not immediately follow assimilation, and transpiration and respiration are not steps in the nitrogen cycle (*Living in the Environment,* 16th ed., page 69 / 17th ed., pages 71–72).

61. **ANSWER: C.** Photosynthesis emits oxygen, which is not a greenhouse gas; all of the other options release greenhouse gases (*Living in the Environment,* 16th ed., page 59 / 17th ed., page 59).

62. **ANSWER: C.** A large amount of energy is required to desalinate water. The countries in the Middle East have the largest reserves of fossil fuels in the world, and are equipped to essentially trade oil for water by building and operating desalination plants (*Living in the Environment,* 16th ed., pages 332–333 / 17th ed., page 333).

63. **ANSWER: D.** Lead concentration in air has fallen dramatically since lead additives were completely banned from gasoline in 1986. The 1990 Clean Air Act reduced the release of SO_2 and NO_2 but neither has been reduced as effectively as lead (*Living in the Environment,* 16th ed., page 474 / 17th ed., page 472).

64. **ANSWER: B.** Individuals tend to underestimate risk when they feel that they have a large degree of control during the activity; for example, driving an automobile is a high-risk activity (40,000 deaths annually in the United States) that most people think is relatively safe. On the other hand, most people tend to overestimate risk when it gets a large amount of publicity as it does during extensive media coverage or during a political campaign. For example, flying commercial airlines may be perceived as a high-risk activity soon after an accident when it receives extensive media coverage, and the health risk of drinking tap water might be overestimated by individuals during a political campaign in which the candidates disagree on the water quality of the city's water supply (*Living in the Environment,* 16th ed., page 464 / 17th ed., page 461).

65. **ANSWER: B.** A lack of educational opportunities for women is a strong indicator for rapid population growth (*Living in the Environment*, 16th ed., page 135 / 17th ed., page 132).

66. **ANSWER: B.** Tuberculosis is transmitted through the air. All the other options are transmitted through untreated water supplies (*Living in the Environment*, 16th ed., page 442 / 17th ed., pages 439–441).

67. **ANSWER: A.** Begin by extending the clay line horizontally to the right from 15% to meet the silt line coming down from 43% and the sand line coming up from 42%. They meet in the center of the loam region of the triangle (*Living in the Environment*, 16th ed., not included / 17th ed., not included).

68. **ANSWER: A.** The Ogallala Aquifer is the world's largest aquifer. It lies beneath parts of the U.S. states of South Dakota, Wyoming, Colorado, Nebraska, Kansas, Oklahoma, New Mexico, and Texas (*Living in the Environment*, 16th ed., page 323 / 17th ed., page 326).

69. **ANSWER: D.** Japan, Iceland, and Norway kill about 1,000 whales each year for scientific purposes, a rationale that critics believe is simply a commercial whaling operation (*Living in the Environment*, 16th ed., page 258 / 17th ed., pages 250, 261).

70. **ANSWER: E.** Kilowatt-hours and kilocalories are units of energy while the megawatt is a unit of power (*Living in the Environment*, 16th ed., page S2 / 17th ed., page S2).

71. **ANSWER: B.** Most of the world's freshwater is frozen, but the second largest storage reservoir, and by far the largest on the list, is groundwater (*Living in the Environment*, 16th ed., not included / 17th ed., page 320).

72. **ANSWER: E.** Sick-building syndrome occurs when living organisms (bacteria, viruses, pollen, dust mites, mildew, mold, and yeast) circulate through a building in the heating, ventilation, and air conditioning systems, making the occupants sick (*Living in the Environment*, 16th ed., pages 484–485 / 17th ed., pages 482–483).

73. **ANSWER: C.** The littoral zone is the area of a freshwater lake near the shore where most of the plant life grows. There are also high nutrient levels because of runoff from the adjacent land areas (*Living in the Environment*, 16th ed., page 174 / 17th ed., page 181).

74. **ANSWER: A.** NIMBY (Not In My Back Yard) is a commonly used rallying cry in communities trying to dissuade developers from building near their homes (*Living in the Environment*, 16th ed., page 583 / 17th ed., page 579).

75. **ANSWER: D.** The National Environmental Policy Act was passed by Congress in 1969 and enacted in 1970. It requires developers to study the environmental impact of projects funded by the federal government and to produce an environmental impact report that describes the results (*Living in the Environment*, 16th ed., pages 646–647 / 17th ed., page 650).

76. **ANSWER: E.** Requiring electronics manufacturers to take back their products for recycling will build the costs of recycling into the price of a product (also known as a cradle-to-grave approach) (*Living in the Environment*, 16th ed., page 560 / 17th ed., page 557).

77. **ANSWER: D.** The activity of a radioisotope decays by a factor of 1/2 after one half-life. In order to reduce the activity of a sample from 1 mCi to 1μCi (a factor of 1/1000), one must wait for about ten half-lives ($2^{10} = 1024$). Thus, 80 days or almost 3 months is required (*Living in the Environment*, 16th ed., not included / 17th ed., not included).

78. **ANSWER: D.** Peat is a highly polluting energy source that produces higher quantities of air pollutants per unit of fuel than the coal that it would eventually form if heated under pressure in the earth's crust for millions of years. It is formed in bogs where, despite its hazardous air pollution, it is still used as fuel, often illegally (*Living in the Environment*, 16th ed., page 383 / 17th ed., page 382).

79. **ANSWER: D.** Many types of shellfish including oysters are commonly cultivated in aquaculture (the fish species listed are all large predatory fish that are not farmed) (*Living in the Environment*, 16th ed., page 285 / 17th ed., pages 287–288).

80. **ANSWER: B.** Estimating the extent to the left (the male side) of the right-hand age-structure diagram (developed countries) for the first four age groups, it appears that added together they would extend to approximately the 100-million mark (*Living in the Environment*, 16th ed., pages 130–131 / 17th ed., pages 135–136).

81. **ANSWER: D.** Estimating the extent to the right (the female side) of the left-hand age-structure diagram (developing countries) for the seven age groups, it appears that they average slightly less than 200 million (3 7), which makes the total population estimate approximately 1300 million, or 1.3 billion (*Living in the Environment*, 16th ed., pages 130–131 / 17th ed., pages 135–136).

82. **ANSWER: C.** The growth rate of populations cannot be determined using an age structure diagram. It can only be inferred (fast growth, slow growth, negative growth, etc.) (*Living in the Environment*, 16th ed., pages 130–131 / 17th ed., pages 135–136).

83. **ANSWER: E.** Forests do not construct roads; all of the other options are ecosystem services provided by forests (*Living in the Environment*, 16th ed., pages 217–218 / 17th ed., pages 220–221).

84. **ANSWER: D.** The results show that when nitrate is added to the seawater, algae growth accelerates (A and B), and when phosphate is added (A and C) it accelerates in one case (A) and does not change in one case (C). The conclusion supported by this data is that nitrate is a limiting agent for algae growth in seawater (*Living in the Environment*, 16th ed., not included / 17th ed., not included).

85. **ANSWER: A.** The A horizon is also known as topsoil. It is composed of mineral-containing weathered parent material and humus (*Living in the Environment*, 16th ed., page 281 / 17th ed., page 284).

86. **ANSWER: D.** Energy transfer through food chains typically has an efficiency of only about 10% because of energy that is converted to waste heat, a consequence of the second law of thermodynamics (*Living in the Environment*, 16th ed., page 62 / 17th ed., pages 64–65).

87. **ANSWER: A.** Cap and trade programs place a cap or limit on the total amount of a pollutant that may be emitted. Polluters are then either given or allowed to purchase credits that allow them to emit a given quantity of the pollutant. If a polluter does not need all of its credits, it may trade (sell) them to another polluter who has come up short. By lowering the cap each year, governments can decrease the total amount of the pollutant that is emitted (*Living in the Environment*, 16th ed., page 490 / 17th ed., pages 516–517).

88. **ANSWER: D.** Coal mining by mountaintop removal is practiced in West Virginia, Virginia, Tennessee, Kentucky, and Pennsylvania (*Living in the Environment*, 16th ed., page 358 / 17th ed., page 357).

89. **ANSWER: A.** During the refining of crude oil, heat is applied and the components of the oil are distilled off one by one. The first components to distill off are those with the lowest boiling points. Compounds like propane that are gases at room temperature are the first to boil away (*Living in the Environment*, 16th ed., page 375 / 17th ed., pages 374–375).

90. **ANSWER: C.** Canada has 75% of the world's oil sand resources in northeastern Alberta. The mining of oil sands requires a surface mining operation and results in corresponding environmental damage (*Living in the Environment*, 16th ed., page 379 / 17th ed., page 378).

91. **ANSWER: C.** Mercury pollution that was converted to methylmercury caused a large number of birth defects in the population of Minamata, Japan. The crude oil spill of the tanker Exxon Valdez into Prince William Sound off the coast of Valdez, Alaska, devastated an ecosystem. The leak of methyl isocyanate from a Union Carbide pesticide plant in Bhopal, India, killed thousands of people and injured tens of thousands overnight (*Living in the Environment*, 16th ed., page S37 / 17th ed., not included).

92. **ANSWER: A.** Mitigation allows the destruction of a wetland if an equal area of the same type of wetland is created (*Living in the Environment*, 16th ed., page 266 / 17th ed., page 268).

93. **ANSWER: C.** The succession of a lake will result in a flat meadow, usually with a slow-moving stream meandering through it (*Living in the Environment*, 16th ed., not included / 17th ed., not included).

94. **ANSWER: D.** Setting small contained surface fires, also called prescribed burns, can help to clear away accumulated underbrush and small trees in an attempt to avoid fueling a devastating crown fire (*Living in the Environment*, 16th ed., page 228 / 17th ed., page 231).

95. **ANSWER: A.** Mercury vapor is the result of burning fuel containing mercury. The only burning that may occur at a sanitary landfill is that of methane, produced during anaerobic respiration, for electricity production (*Living in the Environment*, 16th ed., pages 575–576 / 17th ed., pages 570–572).

96. **ANSWER: E.** Both methods have been proposed to sequester carbon along with pumping into underground caverns and abandoned mines (*Living in the Environment*, 16th ed., page 516 / 17th ed., pages 513–514).

97. **ANSWER: D.** This is a depiction of the oxygen-sag curve that typically results when a river flows past a point source of organic waste (*Living in the Environment*, 16th ed., page 536 / 17th ed., page 534).

98. **ANSWER: B.** The source of the organic waste is point "B" along the river. Following the addition of the organic waste, the dissolved oxygen levels fall dramatically and the biological oxygen demand rises rapidly (*Living in the Environment*, 16th ed., page 536 / 17th ed., page 534).

99. **ANSWER: E.** The points labeled "A" and "E" are in areas referred to as the clean zone, where normal levels of dissolved oxygen allow the native aquatic ecosystem to exist (*Living in the Environment*, 16th ed., page 536 / 17th ed., page 534).

100. **ANSWER: C.** The ozone thinning that is sometimes called a "hole" is worsened following the Antarctic winter when polar stratospheric clouds form and allow the ozone-destroying chain reactions to proceed virtually unchecked. Once the sun sufficiently warms the air above Antarctica, the polar stratospheric clouds break up

and ozone depletion slows down to its normal pace (*Living in the Environment*, 16th ed., page 523 / 17th ed., page 521).

SCORING GUIDELINES FOR FREE-RESPONSE QUESTIONS

1.

(a) The ad makes reference to the golden toads of Monteverde. Explain why this reference is made.

1 point can be earned—Golden toads are extinct

(b) A large share of the world's ecotourism takes place in developing countries. Describe TWO ways in which ecotourism can help reduce poverty in these countries.

2 points can be earned—1 point for each poverty reduction method with a description

Method	Description
Job creation	Construction jobs building infrastructure Jobs as guides Service industry jobs
Income to provide children with a nutritious diet	Money from jobs can provide a nutritious diet for families.
Income to provide adequate shelter for children	Money from jobs can provide shelter for families.
Revenue to provide clean water	Clean water needed to attract tourists is made available to locals.
Improved health care	Adequate health care needed to treat tourists in emergencies is made available to locals.
Revenue to build schools	State tourism tax revenue can be used to build schools.

(c) Discuss the conflict between people living in poverty and efforts to conserve biodiversity.

2 points can be earned—1 point for each item discussed

- Bushmeat is harvested for food.
- Habitat is slashed and burned for subsistence agriculture.
- Fuelwood may be gathered unsustainably.
- Illegal hunting (poaching) is practiced to earn money.
- Marginal land is used as pasture or placed under cultivation increasing desertification.

(d) Other than those listed above, identify a specific endangered species that people might be willing to pay to visit and the location of the species' native habitat.

2 points can be earned—1 point for identifying a species and 1 point for the location of its habitat

For example:

- African lion in Kenya
- Nene in Hawaii

Many other possibilities – *must be on an endangered species list*

(e) The ad touts the use of biodiesel fuel made from palm oil. Explain why this advertising tactic might have been a mistake.

2 points can be earned—1 point for each item in the explanation

- Palm oil is grown unsustainably.
- Palm oil is grown on plantations in tropical rain forests.
- Tropical forests are cleared to create palm oil plantations.
- Loss of tropical rain forest eliminates it as a carbon storage reservoir.
- Loss of tropical rain forest eliminates habitat and results in a loss of biodiversity.

(f) Roundtrip airline travel from the central United States to central Africa will generate about 3 metric tons (3000 kg) of carbon dioxide, and a trip to Southeast Asia will generate about 4 metric tons (4000 kg). Discuss the conflict that this brings about with the ideals of ecotourism.

2 points can be earned—1 point for an item on each side of the conflict

Ideal	Conflict
Ecotourists value biodiversity	CO_2 causes global warming/climate change which destroys habitat which causes extinction
Ecotourists value nature for aesthetic reasons	CO_2 causes global warming/climate change which destroys habitat which causes extinction
Ecotourists choose to support the local people	Without air travel, ecotourists cannot visit, and poverty may return

2. (a) Determine the total number of observable droppings in the park for each deer at any time.

1 point can be earned for a correct setup with the correct answer

$$\frac{30 \text{ droppings}}{\text{deer per } \cancel{\text{day}}} \times 40 \; \cancel{\text{days}} = 1200 \; \frac{\text{droppings}}{\text{deer}}$$

Units are not required because they are implicit in the prompt.

(b) Determine the number of deer in the park per hectare.

2 points can be earned—1 point for a correct set up that includes units and 1 point for the correct answer

Area of each quadrat 5 10 m 3 10 m 5 100 m²

$$\frac{24 \; \cancel{\text{droppings}}}{1 \; \cancel{\text{quadrar}}} \times \frac{1 \; \cancel{\text{quadrar}}}{100 \; \cancel{m^2}} \times \frac{1 \times 10^4 \; \cancel{m^2}}{1 \text{ha}} \times \frac{1 \text{ deer}}{1200 \; \cancel{\text{droppings}}} = 2 \; \frac{\text{deer}}{\text{ha}}$$

Units are not required on the final answer because they are implicit in the prompt.

(c) Determine the total number of deer in the park.

1 point can be earned for a correct setup with the correct answer

$$\frac{2 \text{ deer}}{\cancel{\text{ha}}} \times \frac{500 \cancel{\text{ha}}}{\text{park}} = 1000 \frac{\text{deer}}{\text{park}}$$

(d) Dr. Beverly's report on the deer population prompts the state park service to issue hunting licenses. Determine the number of hunting licenses that should be issued and explain the rationale for issuing that number of licenses.

3 points can be earned—1 point for a value between 200 and 600, 1 point for calculating the maximum sustainable yield (MSY), and 1 point for an acceptable rationale)

$$MSY = \frac{\text{Carrying Capacity}}{2} = \frac{800}{2} = 400 \text{ (1 point)}$$

RATIONALE

- With a current population of 1000, issuing 600 licenses will reduce the population to the MSY of 400.
- A number less than 600 but greater than 200 is acceptable, with acknowledgment of the MSY, and a rationale that the carrying capacity may be overestimated.
- Issuing a number of licenses that will bring the deer population below 800 will allow the population to remain healthy.

(e) Describe another way to control the deer population.

1 point can be earned for a description

- Introduce a predator.
- Trap and relocate deer.
- Allow the deer to continue on their natural boom and bust population cycle.

(f) Identify and describe another method to estimate the population size of the deer.

2 points can be earned—1 point for a correct method and 1 point for a correct description

Method	Description
Tag, release, and recapture	Capture, tag, release, and recapture individuals. Estimate the population size based of the rate at which tagged individuals are recaptured.
Sampling	Count the number of individuals in a given area and extrapolate to the entire area. Aerial photography could be used.
Use a different field sign (tracks, feeding signs, remains, etc.)	Use the quadrat sampling method with a different field sign.
Transect Survey	Walk a transect line and count all the individuals seen; extrapolate out to the entire area.

3. (a) Identify and describe the series of energy transformations (conversions) that are used to generate electricity in a hydroelectric power plant.

4 points can be earned—1 point for each correct energy transformation with a correct description

Energy Transformation	Description
Potential energy to kinetic energy	Water flows out of an elevated reservoir (downhill), converting potential energy to kinetic energy.
Kinetic energy of water to kinetic energy of a turbine	The kinetic energy of the water is used to push a turbine, transferring kinetic energy from the water to the turbine.
Kinetic energy to electrical energy	The kinetic energy of the turbine (water is acceptable if the previous transformation was missed) is converted to electricity through a generator connected to the rotating shaft of the turbine (electric potential energy).
Potential and/or kinetic energy to heat	Potential energy and kinetic energy are both converted to heat (waste heat) at each step.

(b) Explain why the energy provided by existing hydropower dams is virtually free.

1 point can be earned for a correct explanation

- The global water cycle returns water to the elevated reservoir (returns its potential energy) at no cost.
- The ecosystem service is provided by the sun that evaporates the water and returns it to the reservoir.
- No fuel purchases are required.

(Similar explanations are acceptable, but they must include the free return of water to the reservoir by nature.)

(c) Identify ONE species whose numbers have diminished as the result of a hydropower project and describe how the project led to the decline in their population.

2 points can be earned—1 point for a the identification of a correct species and 1 point for a correct description

Species	Description
Salmon	Migration route is blocked by dams.
Baiai (River) Dolphin	Habitat fragmentation limits food supply.
River Sturgeon	Changes in water temperature, habitat fragmentation.
Steelhead	Migration route blocked by the dam.